M000011965

73-99
47 /5
GA

COUNTRY
EYE

COUNTRY EYE

A WALKER'S GUIDE TO BRITAIN'S TRADITIONAL COUNTRYSIDE

GEOFFREY YOUNG

Illustrations by
MARK ILEY

GEORGE
PHILIP

Acknowledgements

Photographs were supplied by the photographers and agencies listed below:

p.2 VisionBank; 6 Mike Williams; 9 Swift Picture Library; 10 Geoffrey Young; 11 AA Picture Library; 13 Derek Forss; 16 Swift Picture Library; 17 Derek Forss; 20–21 Swift Picture Library; 28 Gillian Beckett; 29 John Mason; 30–31 Anne Sullivan; 34–35 Susan Griggs Agency; 38–39 Julian Lightfoot; 41 Wildscape; 44 Landscape Only; 46–47 Aerofilms; 50–51 Jeffrey Beazley; 54–55 English Heritage; 59 Mike Williams; 60–61 VisionBank; 62–63 John Bethell; 64, 66 Swift Picture Library; 69 Derek Forss; 70–71 Derek St Romaine; 76 Swift Picture Library; 77 Julian Lightfoot; 78–79 West Sussex County Record Office (the Garland Collection); 80–81 John Mason; 82–83, 86–87, 90–91 Institute of Agricultural History, University of Reading; 92 Derek Forss; 93 VisionBank; 94–95, 98–99, 102–103 Institute of Agricultural History, University of Reading; 106, 107 Simon Warner; 110–111 Institute of Agricultural History, University of Reading; 112 VisionBank; 113 Gillian Beckett; 115 Institute of Agricultural History, University of Reading; 116–117 Anne Sullivan; 119 Derek St Romaine; 122–123 Institute of Agricultural History, University of Reading; 124, 125; 128 Gillian Beckett; 129 Swift Picture Library; 130–131, 132 Simon Warner; 133 VisionBank; 138–139 Institute of Agricultural History, University of Reading; 140 Swift Picture Library; 141 John Mason; 142 Derek St Romaine; 145 Landscape Only; 147 Ernest Cressey; 150–151 Jeffrey Beazley; 152 John Mason; 153 Simon Warner; 155 Institute of Agricultural History, University of Reading; 156 Swift Picture Library; 157 AA Picture Library; 161 Planet Earth Pictures

First published in 1991 by George Philip Limited, 59 Grosvenor Street, London W1X 9DA

Text © Geoffrey Young 1991
Illustrations © George Philip 1991

All rights reserved. Apart from any fair dealing for the purpose of private study, research, criticism or review, as permitted under the Copyright Designs and Patents Act, 1988, no part of this publication may be reproduced, stored in a retrieval system, or transmitted in any form or by any means, electronic, electrical, chemical, mechanical, optical, photocopying, recording, or otherwise, without prior written permission. All enquiries should be addressed to the Publishers.

British Library Cataloguing-in-Publication Data

Young, Geoffrey, 1936–
  Country eye: a walker's guide to Britain's
  traditional countryside.
  I. Title
  796.510941

ISBN 0–540–01247–5

Designer Derek St Romaine
Editor Richard Dawes
Printed in Hong Kong

Contents

This book is for anyone who wants to find out more about the British countryside. The landscape of England, Scotland and Wales is one of the most varied in the world. Scenically it can be exciting. Historically it is packed with souvenirs of the past.

The variety of views within a short compass is largely the legacy of an intricate geology. The old rocks have been sculptured by more recent erosion. The glaciers and ice sheets that spread widely during the Ice Age have been a major force here, but the softer chisel of water has been just as dramatic in some areas.

Man too has sculptured the landscape and the look of many places now owes more to human activity than to nature. This historic face of the countryside is of considerable age, however. The oldest surviving man-made marks on the landscape date back more than 6000 years, to Neolithic (New Stone Age) times. But since then man has almost entirely reclothed the land, filling it with inventions of his own. He has created the patchwork fields, farmsteads and villages which enliven the coloured counties.

From this long past come features which are both picturesque and interesting. They range from holloways to gold mines, from stone circles to farmyard barns, from hammer ponds to traditional field gates.

This book describes these interesting features. They can be expected on any walk and indeed also on any drive, for much of interest can be seen from our roads, many of which have ancient origins. This book also deciphers, interprets and explains what you see in the landscape and sets it in its place in the story of the countryside. In many cases the true interest of a feature cannot be guessed at without a nudge in the right direction, and this book hopes to provide just that. Accurate identification, interpretation and dating of landscape features are often assumed to require specialized knowledge, but this book short-cuts this need. It is a book for those who are not experts in geology or archaeology or folklore or farming or the history of land use, although it should also be of interest to those who are.

HOW TO USE THIS BOOK

There are seven chapters, each covering a main aspect of the countryside story:

Chapter 1 **Geology and Landscape**

Chapter 2 **The Imprint of Man**

Chapter 3 **Farms and Farmland**

Chapter 4 **Village and Market**

Chapter 5 **Roads, Lanes and Paths**

Chapter 6 **Waterways and Wetlands**

Chapter 7 **Wild Britain**

Within the chapters, the information is for convenience organized in spreads—that is, in pairs of facing pages. The titles of these spreads will enable you to locate the information you need.

However, it is the intention of this book to delve into the origins and evolution of many landscape features that we take for granted, and so any spread—and hopefully many spreads—can contain information which may surprise and entertain you. To take just one example, pp. 132–133 relate the geological explanation of *springs*. Freshwater springs always seem rather miraculous. Indeed in earlier times before geology became a science and rock formations were understood, many and varied were the theories devised to explain how it was that pure water fell as rain and welled up in springs and streams, while the oceans were distinctly salty. More than a few medieval, and later, philosophers were convinced that there dwelt deep in the earth a race of gnomes, the 'alembics', who distilled sea water and issued it as clear, freshwater springs. So, as well as giving the scientific explanation of springs, those pages also explain such things as how wishing wells evolved from a belief in magic and also in astrology.

Although many of the spreads relate to others preceding and following, each is essentially self-contained, and they are all written to provide an overview which will allow you to both investigate and understand what you see. Many spreads also contain cross-references to others that are of direct relevance. In each spread the information is arranged under eight self-explanatory headings.

As noted above, many spreads relate to others preceding and following. This is particularly true in Chapter 2, where pp. 34–53—from 'Man's first marks on the landscape' to 'Dark Ages ditches and parishes'—have been devised to provide a concise description of the kinds of development and change which took place from prehistoric through Roman to medieval times.

An alternative way of locating information is to use the comprehensive index on pp. 196–199.

Many countryside features referred to in the book are indicated on 1:50000 and 1:25000 Ordnance Survey maps.

On pp. 164–195 is a gazetteer that includes eight maps showing the location of a wide variety of places of interest throughout Britain. These are identified by italic type in the main part of the book and further information is given in the gazetteer.

The locations have been chosen to offer the reader a wide choice of visits within the scope of a Sunday afternoon. And as far as possible, the selection has been taken from throughout the main subject areas of the book. So whatever your own particular interests, the gazetteer should always be able to suggest an afternoon or day out.

However, the book can be used as a resource on its own without reference to the gazetteer. Indeed its purpose is to act as a handy encyclopedia of reliable facts to enable you to make your own discoveries and to help you to understand the history and significance of numerous features of Britain's countryside, both natural and man-made.

The hand of man

The story of the landscape is rooted in a past so distant that the human imagination can barely comprehend it. Rocks hold the story of these vast periods, but the face of the landscape that is familiar today was in the main sculptured fairly recently in comparison—during the last couple of million years. Ice played a major role. There were in fact several advances and retreats of the ice sheets, but it is quite usual to refer to the period as a whole as one single 'Ice Age'.

When the Ice Age drew to a close and the climate improved, quite numerous hunting tribes wandered the wildwood, which could now grow and would in time clothe much of the land, but nothing obvious remains of their activities. The clues to their way of life are usually buried, and revealed only by accident or by excavation.

However, the earliest mauls or marks on the landscape that remain visible today are of appreciable age. They date back some 6000 years, to Neolithic (New Stone Age) times, when Britain had recently been separated from Europe by the rise in the sea level following the melting of the ice. It was then that farming, which is basically the sowing of crops and the domestication and pasturage of animals, was becoming widespread. And since then the story of the land has been essentially that of the evolution and entrenchment of farming and its communities. These consumed the landscape, filling the map with farms and fields, roads and villages and market towns. The features we see today are very different from those that first appeared, but such is the long history of the countryside that many have been in place for thousands of years.

It was only in recent centuries that another economic force, that of industrialization, grew to rival farming. Although concentrated in towns, it too changed the countryside, altering its very shape in some areas. Some industrial landscapes, such as the lunar landscapes of mining and the china-clay diggings of Cornwall, are tremendous sculptures.

It is not surprising, therefore, that

	TIME CHART
	The dates given below are broadly accurate, but there is still uncertainty about those preceding the Bronze Age.

4700–4300 BC	Neolithic (New Stone Age) pioneering phase
4300–2000 BC	Main Neolithic
around 2000 BC	Arrival of Beaker people with copper knives; the start of the Bronze Age
2000–1000 BC	Bronze Age
1000–700 BC	Late Bronze Age
700–500 BC	Early Iron Age
500–100 BC	Middle Iron Age
100 BC–AD 43	Late Iron Age
43–425	Britain is a Roman province
425–1066	The Dark Ages and the establishment of great warrior kingdoms
1066–1400	The Middle Ages. Some would extend this period to 1485, the end of the Wars of the Roses and the accession of the first Tudor
1485–1603	The Tudors
1603–1689	The Stuarts
1689–1830	William and Mary, Anne, Georges I–IV. In the Georgian period occurred most of the field enclosures we see today
1837–1900	The Victorian era
1900–1914	The dying years of the old countryside
1914–1945	World War I (1914–18) was followed by vast changes in rural life and the countryside, including the first plantings of extensive conifer forests
1945–	'The New Agricultural Revolution'—the intensive use of agrochemicals and machinery, altering substantially the face of the farmed countryside

very little of the countryside is 'natural' in the sense of escaping the hand of man.

The Ordnance Survey maps are generously sprinkled with archaeological features, marked and named. This detailed mapping in part reflects our nostalgia for ruins and things old. Some antiquities, such as Stonehenge, are dramatic. Others, such as the terracing of downland slopes into lynchets, are more modest. Once considered to be prehistoric, this lynchet terracing is now thought to be largely medieval. If so, it does turn on its head an enduring idea about medieval times: that the countryside was relatively unpopulated. In fact there must have been an immense hunger for land to force the laborious creation of these terraces.

And this one example underlines an important point. This book's exploration of the countryside is not simply an investigation of dry-as-dust souvenirs of the past. It is really about

people—both as individuals and as communities. Even the 'ridge and furrow' which still corrugates many pasture fields is a memorial to medieval ploughmen and their oxen, who century after century doggedly trod these narrow strips. But a lot remains unknown and many dramatic puzzles remain unsolved. Britain's 1000 stone circles remain mysterious; we have no real idea how they were used by the people who built them. Although we can explore prehistoric burial mounds, we have no idea what language their builders spoke, what they believed in, or what jokes they made.

Nevertheless, discoveries are being made all the time. Some rely on expert archaeological excavation and related techniques. Others rely on the observant amateur—the reader of this book maybe—who happens to be at that place at that time when the setting sun for a brief few minutes casts long shadows, revealing the traces of a forgotten prehistoric community.

An eye for a map

A landscape painting makes use of visual tricks to suggest perspective and distance. We take these for granted. In a way a map is just another picture of a view and we similarly take for granted its codes, for example the lines and symbols that show the position of roads and settlements. But maps like this had to evolve.

Although there had been early plans showing estate boundaries and the like, the first larger-area maps were drawn in the 16th century. Reflecting the needs of travellers of the time, they named settlements, which they sometimes symbolized by a church or a row of houses. Roads between these settlements were usually shown and also rivers and bridges—vital information for travellers. Hills, however, were childishly drawn hummocks, giving little clue to their form or height. There was no need, for no traveller of the day would go out of his way to climb them.

In time new codes were adopted, such as suggesting slopes by means of shading, but a major step was the publication in the mid 19th century of the first Ordnance Survey maps. These were commissioned, as their name suggests, for military as much as public use. OS maps use a wide range of symbols and name many historic features. Very often the name of a feature is a good clue to its character.

The relief or land-form on these maps is shown by contours. These too can be 'read' conveniently to give an overall impression of the shape of the land in a particular place. Contours running close together, for example, represent a steep slope, and so a steep-sided stream valley can be deduced from such contours. The areas occupied by features such as woods are shown and also, on the larger-scale (1:25000) OS maps, the hedges, although the exact appearance of the woods or hedges can be discovered only at the spot.

Most of the maps we use have been simplified from detailed Ordnance Survey maps, but they can still be rewarding. A place or site picked out by name is usually well worth a detour. Old Sarum, two miles north of Salisbury, for example, has a long history. The name means 'Old Salisbury'.

Old Sarum was originally built as an Iron Age stronghold, but we can deduce that it remained important in Roman times since the two roads leading to it from the east are Roman roads. The OS maps trace their route across country.

Old Sarum, magnificently sited on the chalk heights to the north of Salisbury, has always controlled a network of important routes.

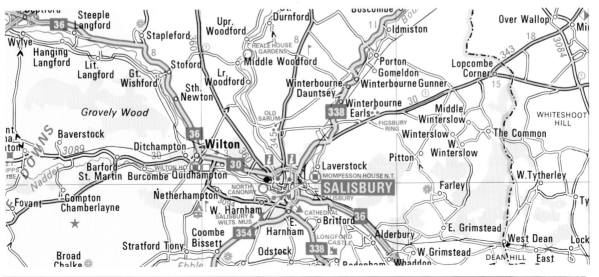

A country eye

We see the countryside very much from the standpoint of our own time. The modern age was really under way by the middle of the last century, by mid-Victorian times, when the first Ordnance Survey maps appeared. By then railways had not only thrown a web across Britain, but were also changing its very nature. They both served and united the towns, making travel easier than ever before.

But these were no longer the market towns of yore, full of farmers, rich from dealing in corn or cattle. In this book we trace some of the changes that took place in towns in that era. Productive industrial towns were for the first time becoming more important to the economic health of the nation than the harvests of corn and wool of the open countryside and its farms. At the same time the new centres of wealth, together with the railways, created a new kind of citizen, who thought nothing of travelling, even if it was simply for entertainment — to view as an outsider what the countryside had to offer.

In fact, travel for its own sake, which we take for granted today, was already well established by the end of the 18th century. As often happens, a handful of individuals led the way, popularizing the idea by writing accounts of their journeys. One was Daniel Defoe, better known as the author of *Robinson Crusoe* than for his *Tour through the Whole Island of Great Britain*, published 1724–7. Another was the poet Thomas Gray, who wrote *Elegy in a Country Churchyard*; on his tour of the Lake District in 1769 he records drawing the curtains of his coach to shut out the sight of the 'awesome' crags.

As much as anything else, these early tourists travelled to lubricate emotions. Today we do exactly the same — we like a 'nice day out'. However, their reactions were usually somewhat different from ours. They often derided what we would call 'quaint' and 'traditional', preferring productivity and profit. Defoe, for example, discounted the hills of the Lake District, which give us so much pleasure today. He wrote: 'nor were those hills high and formidable only, but they had a kind of inhospitable terror in them. Here were no rich pleasant valleys, no lead mines and veins of rich ore, no coal pits ... but all barren and wild, of no use or advantage either to man or beast....'

Yet feelings were evolving which resemble ours today. Take that most pleasant of views, a village set with trees, with glimpses of cottages, perhaps smoke lazily rising from a chimney. Someone had first to recognize this as a pleasant scene. The man who put the words down was James Thomson, a poet who died in 1748, and whose *The Seasons* was one of the very first poems to be entirely dedicated to the countryside and its pleasures. He wrote of 'villages embosom'd soft in trees', and we today like our villages leafy, in part because his poem was so widely read two centuries ago.

Ideas seeded in one generation become accepted in the next. Enthusiasm for the older countryside features, for the ancient past, for stone circles, for ruined castles and abbeys, and all the better if lit by moonlight — in short, 'romantic' things which ap-

Perspectives change: only in recent years would an abandoned brick kiln (below) be counted interesting.

A castle ruin, unlike, for example, a brick kiln, has been seen as 'romantic' for the last couple of centuries.

peal to the imagination—also had its origins in the 18th century. In fact, ruins were thought to be of such benefit to a view that a good many were ordered by the gentry, and numerous hilltops and other knolls are crowned with follies—instant ruins that never had a proper job. Some examples are included in this book.

Undeniably we inherit feelings such as these and as a result we also value the old and ancient. Yet we are part of an evolutionary process which has still some way to run. Thus, although castles and abbey ruins are protected, there is still no protection for fine old farm barns which can match them in age and interest. Scenery in its own

right has little absolute protection, even in the National Parks. The survival of many fine views is a matter of good luck—and many have been spoiled. For example, there is scant protection for countryside trees, and no control as yet over the destruction of hedgerows.

If this book succeeds in showing how interesting the countryside is as a whole—and not just the favourite places—it will have done its job. It is clear that it is impossible to make hard and fast judgements—that this bit is more valuable than that bit. No two fields are alike, let alone two villages. And isn't a wartime pillbox or derelict airfield from which fighters took off in the Battle of Britain as historic as a Roman fort?

Nevertheless, overall judgements do have to be formed, and choices made

between this and that. There is continual pressure on and erosion of the features described in this book—the very features which make the countryside such an interesting and delightful place.

Old lanes are bulldozed wider, ancient hedges grubbed up, prehistoric burial mounds ploughed under. Wilderness areas are despoiled, ponds filled in. Villages become swamped unnecessarily by insensitive road or building development when, with a little care, the graft of new on to old could have been positively pleasing, as it is in some towns.

The countryside needs conservation, but that is impossible without having a country eye—the ability to see what the countryside actually is and understand how its features have developed and relate to each other.

The shaping of the landscape

A distant view is a negative image revealing the effects of erosion. The landscape shows that this has taken place on a massive scale.

ATMOSPHERIC EFFECTS

Blue remembered hills across the plain are among the most emotive memories of a familiar landscape. The tint results from the fact that dust in the atmosphere scatters the blue component of light more than the red and others (we see light divided up into these components in a rainbow). Hence the sky above is blue, and distant hills and other features seen across the lower, dustier part of the atmosphere take on a blue tinge.

Blue is used by artists to indicate distance, often the rather nostalgic distance of a dreamy landscape. This poetic vision became so popular in the 18th century that there was a ready market for 'Claude glasses', named after the noted French painter Claude Lorraine. These were hollow, tinted mirrors which allowed views to be observed not only blued but in miniature, a 'real life' picture in pre-camera days. The optical laws of reflection meant that the viewer had to stand facing away from the view, holding the device up in front—and certainly one Lake District tourist tumbled into a waterfall in the process. But in the study of landscape, blue distance has extra meaning.

THE PERSPECTIVE OF DISTANT VIEWS

There is a superb view from the tower perched on the top of *Broadway Hill* (Hereford & Worcs) at the edge of the Cotswolds. No fewer than twelve patchwork counties can be seen on a clear day. Crags exposed on the way reveal that up here we have our feet on hard limestone rock, and from the foot of the slopes below, the Vale of Evesham, a wide clay plain, stretches away past the River Severn to the blue *Malvern Hills* (Hereford & Worcs), 20 or more miles away.

That great plain fading into blue distance between Broadway Hill and the Malverns represents land which has disappeared. The hump of Bredon Hill not far off provides a clue—it is a stub of rock, showing that the Cotswold limestone once extended out to the west. In the course of time those deep layers of missing rock have been removed. This view provides a vivid insight into the slow but remorseless scale of geological change. It shows that a view is the result of a forceful negative in the landscape.

RIVER GAPS

River corridors can provide a second dramatic example of the scale of landscape sculpturing. From the *Ridgeway* (Oxon) the view stretches north over the great Oxfordshire plain across which snakes the River Thames. On its way to London the Thames pierces the chalk heights at *Goring Gap* (Oxon), running for 6 miles between slopes which reach a good 250 ft on each side. Originally, of course, the Thames must have been level with the *top* of the chalk, but slowly it has cut its deep corridor. The implication of this is startling, for through this narrow doorway, carried as silt in the river water, must have passed the material of a 250-ft layer of the Oxfordshire plain behind.

SUMMITS

The view from the ground below can be misleading. Seen from some places, the *Cairngorms* (Highland) appear to be a row of peaks. An eagle's eye view shows that the range is in fact a deeply scooped plateau.

Individual summits are usually outliers or stubs remaining after vast amounts of material have been eroded on every side. Bredon Hill seen from *Broadway Tower* (above) is one example, and *Ingleborough* (N. Yorks) another. The bulk of Ingleborough has a hard hat of millstone-grit sandstone, which has to some extent protected the limestone rock below. *Suilven* (Highland) is also majestically isolated; it too has a hard summit cap. But few summits are as surprising as *Charnwood Forest* (Leics). The crags that rear up amid the gentle red fields of the Midland plain are the tip of a buried mountain chain that was once engulfed by reddish desert-laid sandstones that were in turn covered by ocean limestones. But these two later rocks have slowly been stripped away, so that the original summits are left exposed.

If rock is exposed at the summit, it may be deeply sculptured. Lines of weakness in the granite have been etched away to create separated blocks and plates of rock which make the characteristic forms of the tors of *Dartmoor* (Devon). Some are rocking- or logan-stones. Frost attacks lines of weakness, and broken pieces fall as a loose scree (called 'clitter' on Dartmoor). This scree is in time broken smaller by chemistry, frost and the tumbling torrents that follow cloudbursts.

EROSION AND WEATHERING

These words describe different aspects of one natural process, namely the removal of land. Erosion is the wearing away of the land surface on a large scale. Weathering usually describes the smaller-scale disintegration of exposed rock faces. These processes occur under the action of wind, water, ice and chemistry.

Landscape is thus in a perpetual state of change or evolution, although the timescale is slow. But if a stream deepens its bed by 0.5 mm a year (the thickness of a sheet of blotting paper), this could represent trenching to 10 ft in the 6000 years since the first Neolithic settlements.

WIND EROSION

Erosion by wind is fiercest in desert conditions, but can play a role in sculpturing exposed rocks. Soft sandstones are vulnerable to wind erosion, which has helped create the odd-shaped masses at *West Hoathly* (W. Sussex) and *Brimham Rocks*, near *Knaresborough* (N. Yorks).

WATER EROSION

Water erodes by abrasion, but also chemically, by dissolving minerals to open lines of weakness. When water freezes it expands, and so frost helps to expand cracks. There are many landscape clues to water erosion (see pp. 14–15).

The view from Ilkley Moor (W. Yorks) reveals erosion on a huge scale.

ICE EROSION

In Britain, the harsh sculpturing of mountain landscapes is largely the work of ice, and it has left recognizable evidence, as can be clearly seen on *Snowdon* (Gwynedd) (see pp. 148–149). The Ice Age was in fact a series of cold epochs in the last two million years, with warmer interglacial periods. As important to the landscape as ice was the power released as flood water when glaciers and frozen ground melted. The 'dry' riverless valleys and dry 'windgaps' in the chalk downs are just two of the results.

One less obvious result is the flour of rock scraped by the creeping of glaciers and ice sheets, and perhaps also carried by floodwater, to be spread as 'boulder clay'. It is often laden with stones (hence its name) and is now a hummocky, compacted layer several feet deep in some lowland areas, forming the bedrock below today's soil.

Water in the landscape

Most rivers bear a direct relationship to the landscape in which they run, but there are some surprising exceptions.

THE EYE OF THE LANDSCAPE

Among the landscape painters and poets of Regency days, water was known as 'the eye of the landscape'. It is an apt description, for the beady gleam of water is everywhere to be seen. Water and landscape are part and parcel of the same picture, and rivers are usually, but not always, related to the landscape around them. The science of landscape—geomorphology—is in one sense that of moving water. It is a recent science, largely based on the work of an American, W. M. Davis, who died in 1934.

THE AGES OF A RIVER

It is helpful to visualize the different 'ages' of a river. This is never an age in years, but is linked with the landscape through which rivers run and which they help to fashion.

The young river (below left) forms sharply interlocking spurs in its steep-sided valley while an old river (below right) meanders.

A good many British rivers run through two very different landscapes. They begin in the uplands as a fast beck cascading over a bed of solid rock, boulders and stones, with waterfalls and with pools where trout lurk. Where the flow eases, gravel settles in 'minnow reaches'.

Then, often where the first ploughed fields are in sight, the river begins to lose its youthful exuberance. Cascades are less common, and mud begins to settle. The river is now settling into middle age in quite wide valleys. Later, in old age, it winds slowly across what may be a vast plain, its curves become snaking meanders. Rather than scouring the land as it did in its turbulent youth, it tends to deposit what it carries.

There may still be some way to run before reaching the sea, and indeed the 'old' winding river may become the tributary of another, younger one. Meanders are not a sign that the breezes carry the tang of salt, although most rivers near the sea do meander.

But every river has its own story. Some in the west of Britain rush directly from mountain slopes to sea, with no true lowland stretch. In the east and south, many rivers are born middle-aged, and rapid upland stretches are largely absent.

CHALK AND CLAY RIVERS

Another difference can be noted in the south. Streams and rivers in clay countryside are partly fed by direct run-off from the fields around and they may flood after heavy rain. A chalk stream, however, feeds largely from its underground reservoirs (see pp. 132–133) and is less likely to flood. Its bridges need only low arches, by contrast with the high-stepped arches of the clay river.

VALLEYS, BANKS AND MEANDERS

The scouring power of moving water increases by the square of the velocity. However, its 'transport' ability increases by the velocity to the power of five. For the non-mathematician this means that if the speed of the river is doubled, it is not only much more erosive but can also move rocks thirty times larger. Moving at 1 ft a second it will carry silt; at 4 ft a second it can move 20-lb rocks.

This has two results we tend to take for granted. First, valleys of fast streams are more sharply cut into the rock, often v-shaped and littered with

the young river runs in a rocky bed

a steep-sided pothole in the rock of the river bed

A waterfall tumbles into its deep plunge pool over a hard lip of rock; in time it cuts itself a gorge. Potholes are common.

WATERFALLS

When a river cuts its valley down through the crumpled sandwich of rocks, the harder rock remains protruding as a lip. On its descent, the water flows over this lip, falling against the rock below. If this is markedly softer, it is cut back and a sheer waterfall quickly develops. This can be seen on small falls, but *High Force* (Durham) is the most dramatic waterfall in Britain. Here peat-stained water from the moors tumbles 70 ft into a foaming and aptly named 'plunge pool'. The hard-rock lip is quite distinct: it is the famous whin sill, a volcanic intrusion (see pp. 16–17). High Force is reached by a delightful wooded gorge. This too is typical of such waterfalls—in time they back up, filing a deep cleft in the rock. *Aberdulais Falls* (W. Glamorgan) are typical. The natural amphitheatre of *Malham Cove* (N. Yorks) was once home to a broad waterfall, clear evidence of the vast, tumbling torrents loosed when the ice melted at the end of the Ice Age.

If there is little difference in hardness between the rock layers, the descent of the stream is by a stepladder of cascades. But each waterfall has its own character. *Grey Mare's Tail* (Borders) is a 200-ft spume. Scwyd-yr-Eira near *Brecon* (Powys) looses a curtain of spray behind which runs a path. *Pistyll Rhaeadr* near Llanhaeadr-ym-Mochnant (Clwyd) is also worth a detour.

POTHOLES

A mountain stream is often a complex muddle of waterfalls and rapids. Potholes are common, drilled by pebbles swirling in the eddies when the stream is in full spate (no movement can be detected in normal weather). They are often found on the floor of a plunge pool, and are part of the process whereby the stream deepens its channel—slowly, to be sure, but inevitably.

stones and boulders. Second, clay rivers, which are liable to flood, run between steep banks, the depth scoured when the water is in spate. Here the 'summer' river flows in the bed of the 'winter' river.

Any natural process chooses the path that wastes least energy. When water flows, meandering wastes less energy than flowing in a straight line, and so bends develop. The water moves faster at the outside of a bend, and scours a bank, while on the inside of the bend gravel and mud settle to form a gentle slope. In the hills, cliffs are cut on the outside of the bend, and the stream swings from one side to another to create interlocking 'spurs' of hillside.

RIVER TERRACES

The meandering lower stretches of some rivers such as the Thames and Trent run between 'steps' or terraces on each side. What has happened here is that a river has become rejuvenated, often because continental movements have raised it in relation to the sea. Its faster flow cuts a deeper path in the old plain.

THE RIVER WYE

The rise and fall of the land and the changes in river power that result have had some bizarre results. The River Wye loops as splendidly as any old river, but it happens to run in steep-sided valleys in hilly countryside. It was once an 'old' river, but a rise in the land forced it to deepen its path. At the same time the River Severn was also eroding its wide plain alongside. At *Symonds Yat*, a few miles north of Monmouth (Gwent), the Wye following its old course now leaves the upland altogether, only to turn back almost immediately—most unusual behaviour! This river is certainly no longer directly related to the landscapes it runs in.

The geological record

Britain's countryside is a rock enthusiast's treasure house. The different types of rock reflect different periods in the history of the land.

ROCKS, MINERALS AND STONES

A mineral is a solid, inanimate material found in the earth's crust. It has a fixed chemical composition and often, when pure, a recognizable structure which shows itself in the shape of its crystals. If conditions are not right for crystals, it may be crystalline, with the crystal faces and angles partly discernible. Whether clearly crystalline or not, a mineral often has a recognizable colour, apart from such things as density and relative hardness (that is, what it scratches and is scratched by). Another test might be the colour of the streak left when it is rubbed on a coarse white surface.

Minerals are found separated out in rocks; but rock itself is composed of minerals—one (chalk is an almost pure form of the mineral, calcite) or many. Rock is not necessarily hard: clay is geologically a rock and so are the sand and shingle deposits of ancient seashores. Stone is the everyday word for hard rock or pieces of it.

The geological history of the earth's crust has created three main kinds of rock. Identification is sometimes easy, but with well over a hundred different rock types in Britain, confusion is also easy. The three main groups are igneous, sedimentary and metamorphic rock.

IGNEOUS ROCKS

Igneous literally means 'fire-formed', and such rock is created from the cooling and crystallization of molten magma from below the earth's crust. Granite has set some way below the surface, and cooled slowly so that its minerals have had time to become quite large crystals. *Dartmoor* (Devon) granite contains white crystals of feldspar, black specks of mica, and glassy quartz, which solidified last, filling the spaces left—it is best to inspect a freshly broken piece.

Basalt is magma which rose to set close to the surface or on it when spewed out as lava. It cooled quickly

and is fine-grained with small crystals, although massive extrusions may set with gigantic honeycomb-like columns, as can be seen in the whin sill at *High Force* (Durham) and at *Fingal's Cave* (Strathclyde). No obvious volcanic vents remain in Britain (although *Brentor* (Devon) may be a stub), but volcanoes also spewed out dust and ash, which have firmed themselves down into very hard rock indeed. In the central Lake District, for example, glaciers have sculptured such rock to create the most dramatic scenery in Britain.

SEDIMENTARY ROCKS

These are rocks usually hardened from material deposited in oceans and freshwater, but also in deserts. Formed by weathering and erosion of existing rocks, they are influenced by changes in climate and other conditions, and so are usually easily recognized by their

The earliest millstones were in many cases carved out from Pennine gritstone — a sandstone with convenient bedding.

clear layering, the 'bedding' being marked by differences in colour or composition. When exposed, the bedding often becomes weathered, cracks being etched between the rock layers.

Erosion tends to separate the minerals of the original rock: the quartz of granite becomes smoothed as grains of sand and the feldspar becomes clay. In a sedimentary rock, the sand grains, for example, may be cemented by other minerals. In the long history of the earth, many detrital sedimentary rocks—those formed from the scourings of the land—have been eroded and redeposited many times. Shales are rocks originating with mud or silt and are often so finely layered that they can resemble the pages of a closed book; and the rock

The famous chalk cliffs of Beachy Head (E. Sussex) display regular seams of dark, almost black, flint.

may still smell of mud when wet. When exposed, shales quickly weather to form steep, sliding slopes, as seen at Mam Tor, the 'shivering mountain' near *Castleton* (Derbyshire). Conglomerate looks what it is, a pudding stone of pebbles and sand or silt.

LIMESTONE

Limestone or carbonate rock is a sedimentary rock composed mainly of carbonate (limy) minerals, such as calcite. It is a tremendous memorial to past life, as these minerals usually owe their origins to living things. Chalk is composed of the limy skeletons of small marine organisms, while corals, shells and other fossils make up the bulk of many limestones. One type found in a belt from Dorset to York-shire, and seen on the Cotswolds at *Broadway Hill* (Hereford & Worcs), is known as oolite. The rock consists of small granules built up chemically in onion-skin layers. Unlike the granules of sandstone, they do not sparkle in sunshine.

METAMORPHIC ROCKS

In some places the folding of the rock layers (see pp. 18–19), and the pressure, heat and chemical changes that follow, have engineered changes in the rock. The heat from nearby bubbles of molten magma can have a similar effect. Marble has been created from limestone in this way (but there is no true marble in Britain). Slate was in origin a shale but its cleavage planes— along which it splits into thin layers— now usually run at an angle to the original bedding. Ornamental 'green slate' is still quarried in the Lake District, and much of Britain's roof slate came from *Blaenau Ffestiniog* (Gwynedd) and nearby quarries. Cousin to slate but without its useful 'cleavage' is glistening mica schist, found in north-west Scotland. Quartzite is pressed sandstone, in a manner of speaking. Igneous rocks could also be affected, and gneiss (pronounced nice) is a granite with its scattered pattern now banded. Britain's oldest rock is the gneiss below *Suilven* (Highland).

THE COLOURS OF ROCK

The colours result from the mineral make-up. Iron compounds colour many rocks: Shap granite from the Lake District is reddish, for example. The sombre green and purple of the villages and cliffs of the *Lizard* (Cornwall) are given by an unusual rock, serpentine, granite-like but with little quartz. Pure limestones are pale yellow, weathering to gold, but often coloured by iron; and even chalk is sometimes tinted red. In fact many of the differences in the 'coloured counties' result from the slightly different tints of the limestone of cottages and churches.

RAGSTONE AND FREESTONES

Limestones are a favourite building stone. Stone from *Portland* (Dorset) was used for London's St Paul's Cathedral, while *Barnack* (Cambs) had famous quarries, the hollows of which remain. Masons distinguish between ragstones, limestones with a coarse texture which break irregularly, usually because of their shelly content, and more evenly grained freestones, which can be neatly cut.

FLINT

Flint is seen in place as seams of nodules in chalk cuttings. Chalk was laid down beneath clear tropical seas from a rain of minute dead organisms. Silica deposited in small quantities with the lime of the chalk has in some mysterious way coalesced to create these nodules. Flint sometimes impregnates a 'cast' fossil, of a sea-urchin case for example. In the south, many field pebbles and much river and seashore shingle consists of flint eroded from its chalk bed.

Reading the rocks

The rock layering exposed in quarries and natural outcrops provides evidence of the complexity of geological formations, which are only occasionally revealed.

ROCK STRATA

William Smith, a Regency canal engineer and founder of the science of stratigraphy, first recognized that the rock below the landscape was largely arranged in layers or 'strata'. 'Strata' Smith, as he soon became known, deduced that these layers lay at a slant, with the lower, older layers surfacing towards the west. That is by and large true, although by the time the *Malvern Hills* (Hereford & Worcs) are reached, massive faults (side slips) often complicate the picture. There are also bosses of older rock, such as create the high ground of *Charnwood Forest* (Leics); and bosses of relatively recent intrusive rock such as the granite of *Dartmoor* (Devon). In some places lava and ash-rock spewed by long-dead volcanoes are also found.

THE BITE OF EROSION

Although they were originally laid down in straight strata with horizontal bedding, most exposures of layered (sedimentary) rock reveal evidence of contortion. This means that they have been warped and buckled in vast if slow movements, and it is in this displaced form that they have been eroded. Erosion attacks weakness on a grand scale; large volumes of rock are removed and landscape features are fashioned.

Erosion by streams and rivers begins as soon as a difference in height allows water to run and reconstructions of past landscapes must always be tentative. The North Downs at *Box Hill* (Surrey) for example, represent an edge of a bowl of chalk domed up above the Weald, with an opposite edge forming the South Downs about 20 miles away. The bowl may never have existed complete, but it is convenient to imagine it. Similarly the curve of the rock layering at the top of *Snowdon* (Gwynedd) shows that it was at the bottom of a syncline, a trough of rock, maybe even an open valley, but there is no proof that valley slopes ever rose above it. This syncline can be traced on some of the summit crags.

THE MOVEMENTS OF THE CONTINENTS

The bending and slanting of the sedimentary rocks are linked with journeys of a surprising kind. The continents can be imagined as rafts of lighter rock material floating on denser matter in the earth's crust. The movements of continental drift are slow and the timescale peppered with noughts, but as with any free-floating raft, the continents ponderously sway, tilting the layers. Some areas of land are again immersed below oceans so that they accumulate new sedimentary rocks above them. Areas of seabed are raised to become land, in time to be eroded.

Continental drift also means that many of the rocks that we see exposed in cliff faces and quarries will have been formed under very different climates. Many British sedimentary rocks were laid down in tropic seas: corals and other fossils they contain are a clue to this (see pp. 26–27).

The movement and collision of these continental masses crumple rock layers like a napkin, throwing up mountains.

MOUNTAIN BUILDING

There have been three main mountain-raising epochs to distort the rock layers we see in Britain. Rocks in the Lake District and Scotland show contortions resulting from one around 400 million years ago (mya). Three hundred mya another spasm raised the Pennines. Another of 30 mya (which threw up the Alps) bent the layers of chalk and other sedimentary rocks in Dorset and elsewhere, and domed up the chalk and other layers of the Weald.

IGNEOUS INTRUSIONS

These disturbances fracture the rock skin, sometimes allowing molten magma to well up from below. If this reaches the surface it spews as lava and ash from volcanoes. But it may cool and harden deep below the surface, to form granite-like rocks. On a smaller scale, lava-flows can force their way up through joints or cracks in the rock, to solidify as thick dykes. The whin sill which forms the lip of *High Force* waterfall (Durham) (see pp. 14–15) is a lava rock which has forced itself along the bedding of sedimentary rocks. This sill can be traced across country: it also forms some of the crags on which *Hadrian's Wall* strides. Heat and pressure can also force thinner spurts of mineral through lines of weakness to form veins.

ROCK SANDWICH

As a result of these processes a cliff or quarry face may display more than one kind of rock. The layering of a sedimentary rock such as limestone can be very clearly seen, reflecting changing conditions in climates and oceans when it was formed. But the same cliff may show this ocean limestone followed by a rock formed in freshwater, say, or on a delta, or even on land. Low cliffs seen at *Conisbrough* (S. Yorks) display ocean limestone interrupted by black coal seams, coal being a 'fossil' of swamp vegetation. At *Hunstanton* (Norfolk) the cliffs are truly a sandwich of creamy white chalk with a brown-red sandstone.

Sometimes an ancient eroded surface is capped by new rock and the line of the 'unconformity' is clear. In Gullet Quarry in the *Malvern Hills* (Hereford & Worcs), the sheer face beyond the deep pool shows a slab of ancient rock, one of the oldest in England, thrust upwards with horizontal layers of younger rock to each side. It is an impressive geological spectacle and well worth a diversion.

EXTRAVAGANT BUCKLING

Some quarries and cliffs show dramatic wrenching of the layers. At *Lulworth Cove* (Dorset) for example, they zigzag in pleats, as they do also at *Hartland Point* (Devon).

Because of the way they have been formed, it is normally the rule with sedimentary rocks that a lower layer is older than the one above. In a few places, however, the layers have been thrust sideways after bending, to form an overlap, and with the edge eroded, to all intents and purposes we see rock faces with the older layers above the younger, to the puzzlement of generations of geologists.

These contortions can help create some dramatic surface clefts. A famous one has been eroded below a sharp anticline (an arch) in Burrington Combe, *Mendips* (Avon/Som). Here an 18th-century divine sought shelter from a storm and then wrote the famous hymn 'Rock of Ages, cleft for me...'.

JOINTS AND FAULTS

Under geological stress, rock frequently cracks in vertical joints. Jointing is also created when the rock minerals crystallize: the honeycomb structure of the whin sill and seen at *Fingal's Cave* (Mull/Strathclyde) is likewise known as jointing.

If the body of the rock slips along this line a fault is created. A giant fault has sheared as a line of weakness that has become eroded to form the *Great Glen* (Highland), with Loch Ness aligned along it.

There may be only slight surface evidence of dykes and faults (top). Rock exposures (bottom) often display complex geological features.

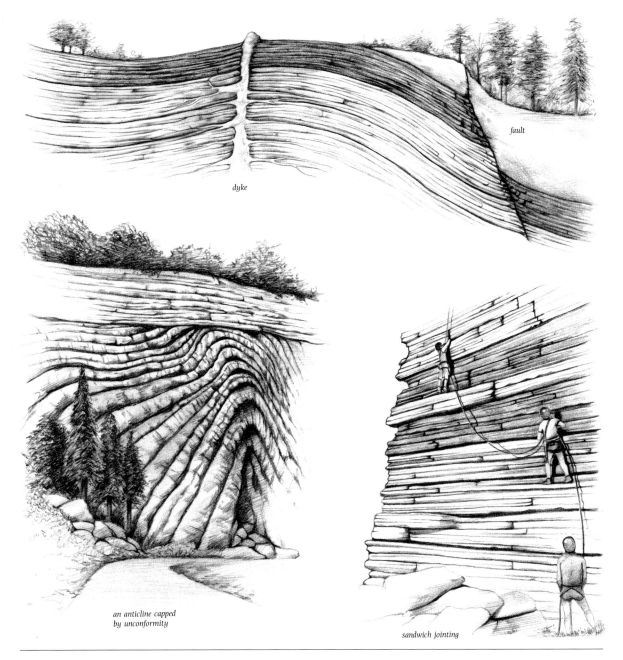

fault

dyke

an anticline capped
by unconformity

sandwich jointing

The treasury of the rocks

Despite many centuries of mining, precious minerals are still easy enough to find. Even pebbles can be of considerable interest when examined closely.

VEINS

Veins of white quartz perhaps patched by metallic glitter are frequently seen striking through granite and other igneous rocks. Here an excess of quartz, the last of the granite constituents to crystallize, has welled into spaces and cracks in the congealing mass around, eventually to cool as the vein. In addition, certain elements did not easily find a niche within the regular crystal frameworks. Sulphur was one of these and it not only tended to remain as a gas but was also liable to attach to other similarly ungainly elements such as copper and lead. This mixture became associated with the fluid vein material, to create veins rich in metal ores, or 'lodes' as they were known to miners of old.

Sometimes crystallization and condensation reduced the mass in the vein to leave a hollow core. With space enough, the quartz may have formed complete crystals of clear 'rock crystal' projecting freely into the open space.

Rather similar events took place when sedimentary rocks came under the pressure and heat induced by folding. In fact in very many hard rock areas, light veins can be seen crossing the dark rock faces of quarries. The white lines which decorate pebbles have the same cause—pebbles are simply pieces of rock worn small.

MINE DUMPS

Most metal mining in Britain involved tunnelling to follow and dig out the metal-rich veins. The ores were crushed at the surface, and the richer pieces kept for smelting. The rest was dumped and these old mine dumps often yield rich pickings of metal ores: tin and copper samples in Cornwall, Wales, the Lake District, lead samples in the Mendips, in the Peak District at *Sheldon* (Derbyshire) and elsewhere, and in the north Pennines.

GOLD

Because of its low melting-point and unreactivity, gold occurs as pure nuggets or smaller grains glinting yellow in veins of quartz in granite. Where the gold-bearing quartz has been eroded, the heavy metal grains have tended to fall to the bottom of the tumbling streams to form 'placer' deposits with the fine gravel of the stream bed. Welsh and Cornish rivers have long

since been searched clean, although specks of this 'alluvial' gold still remain in well-guarded private streams joining the River Helmsdale in Sutherland (Highland) for example.

FOOL'S GOLD

This is in fact pyrite or iron pyrites. Chemically this is iron sulphide, brittle and quick to tarnish. One aid in identifying minerals is the streak they leave when rubbed on coarse white paper or unglazed white pottery. Pyrite has a brown-black streak. It has sometimes impregnated fossils: many of the small ammonites found in the cliffs at *Lyme Regis* (Dorset) glint golden, and square-cornered glinting nuggets of

Pebbles may be seen as geological snapshots, their shape and colour often revealing their origins.

fool's gold can also be found among the shingle on the beaches below.

TIN AND COPPER

Tin and copper are also found in western granite countrysides. Stannite is an ore which combines them together with sulphur (and iron). It is heavy, massive rather than crystalline, brittle and metallic-looking, grey-black in colour but tarnishing blue and with a black streak. Chalcopyrite, which was mined above Coniston in the Lake District, is a brassy-looking ore of copper and iron with a green-black streak.

LEAD AND SILVER

The common lead ore is galena, with dull lead-grey cubic crystals with a metallic lustre and grey streak. Lead first became important in Roman times when it was used for water pipes, coffins and other things. Unlike other ores, galena can be found in large deposits in limestone far from igneous rocks. Waste pieces of ore, or waste slag from it, might be found where ancient lead mines pit the surface of the limestone *Mendips* (Avon/Som) at Priddy. The ore is often contaminated with silver, for which this area was also important. The later centres were in the north, at *Allenheads* (Northumberland) and elsewhere.

SEMIPRECIOUS STONES

Many British semiprecious stones are of the quartz family, and found in the countrysides mentioned above. Purple-tinted amethyst is found in Cornwall and North Wales. Cairngorm is dark smoky brown in colour, and gives its name to the mountain range.

Another largish group are stones which include jasper (coloured deep red with iron) and agate. These are often found in pebble form, transported from further afield; in pebble form their true beauty is only revealed when the bruised surface is stripped off by cutting or polishing.

Two other stones of note, to be found while beachcombing on eastern coasts, are jet and amber. Jet, a hard but lightweight relation of coal, out-

crops near *Whitby* on the Yorkshire coast, but is carried south by longshore drift. It was a popular ornamental stone for jewellery even in prehistoric times, and later for Victorian mourning jewellery. Amber is a yellowish, rather soft substance (it can be pierced with a knife point), the resin of pine trees, and sometimes contains ants, flies and other insects trapped in it when fresh. British finds originate in the Baltic, carried by currents and then down the coast by longshore drift.

PEBBLES

Pebbles are not only snapshots of the geological history of the planet, but are sometimes of semiprecious or mineral content. Some are brightly coloured or intricately patterned. Even the shape of the pebble can be a clue to its original rock formation: the cleavage lines of slate yield flat pebbles while sandstone pebbles are thicker, with evidence of layering (sometimes very fine) on the edges. Many pebbles are crossed by veins. Others (especially flint pebbles) can be fossils (see pp. 26–27).

Pebbles can be found everywhere. The debris of erosion, smoothed and often rounded on their travels, they accumulate in river valleys, where they can form deep beds of gravel and shingle which are now being dug for road and concrete making. These gravel beds are largely the legacy of the flood waters that followed the end of the Ice Age. The sea coast also has its gravel and shingle banks. Along Norfolk's coast near *Cromer*, for example, the shingle can also be viewed as a legacy of the Ice Age—for long periods the North Sea basin was dry land, covered and scoured by ice sheets. Much of the shingle of southeast coasts consists of flint, eroded from the layers of chalk. In the west, most of the shingle which builds up in the coves comes from the rocks behind. Serpentine, found on the *Lizard* (Cornwall), is counted a semiprecious stone. Longshore drift (see pp. 158–159) complicates the picture, however, bringing the beachcomber specimens from far afield.

Mines

Britain's landscape is pitted with mine workings, some of great antiquity. In places the scale of mining has changed the landscape itself.

THE FIRST MINES

The earliest mines were dug for flint in chalk areas in Neolithic times. Their collapsed shafts still pock-mark the ground at *Cissbury* (W. Sussex) and above the *Wilmington Long Man* chalk figure (E. Sussex), and an opened shaft can be visited at *Grimes Graves* (Norfolk). Bronze Age man may have dug for copper and tin (see pp. 54–55) but there is no firm evidence; nor is there for early iron-ore workings. Deeper mining was practised by the Romans

Mining features in the landscape.

and a gold mine with both opencast pits and shafts can be visited at *Dolaucothi* (Dyfed); an iron mine at Clearwell in the *Forest of Dean* (Glos); and evidence has been found of Roman 'hushing' for lead on the Mendips and in the Peak District.

MEDIEVAL AND TUDOR MINING

By Norman times the 'pillar and stall' technique of mining was often practised, in which columns are left to support the roof, allowing more extensive workings. However, it was not until Tudor times that the demand for metal and (from about 1650) the use of gunpowder to blast the rock started to produce the first lunar landscapes that we associate with mining today. In medieval days most coal and metal

was still gained by small-scale opencast working—on *Bodmin Moor* (Cornwall), for example, lead miners have left shallow 'rakes' scarring the ground.

The Weald of Sussex was an early iron-working centre, the ore being found on the surface or in shallow diggings and smelted with charcoal from local woods. The bellows of blast furnaces (in use from Tudor times), forging hammers and other machinery were powered by watermills run from dammed (and hence triangular) 'hammer ponds' still to be seen in the neighbourhood of *Abinger* (Surrey). The secret of smelting with coke, commemorated at *Ironbridge* (Shropshire) took the iron industry north, nearer to the main coalfields. Scotland too has

terraced housing

recent coal mine

engine house

smithy

ruin of manager's house

crushing wheel

its early sites, such as *Bonawe* (Strathclyde).

DIGGING IN THE FIELDS

In some places groups of collapsed bell pits or 'day holes', rather similar to the Neolithic flint mines, can be found, perhaps remaining as damp hollows. They were simple shafts about 7 ft in diameter opening out about 6 ft down, dug for coal and iron ore.

'Dene holes' were frequently dug in the open fields in enclosure times and before. Quite shallow, they were dug to reach chalk, limestone or marl (a limy clay) to spread to counteract the sour flavour of poor soil. Sometimes their memory lingers in 'Marl Pit Lane' and similar names. But a good many single shallow pits are the craters of bombs

tip

adit
(entrance passage)

jettisoned in World War II.

Limekilns, which usually date from the 18th and 19th centuries, are often found out in the fields near an outcrop or quarry of the rock. Built in stone, they are often of elegant shape, with a chimney rising above a chamber where limestone and fuel were burnt for quicklime, used in cement.

CENTRES OF METAL MINING

In time metal-mining centres became established in Cornwall, the Mendips, Shropshire and the Peak District in Derbyshire. There was also much mining in the Lake District, and ruined sheds and chimneys around *Allenheads* (Northumberland) mark Victorian Britain's lead-mining centre; the disused levels stretch 3 miles from the adits, the hillside entrances to the passages. Although much has been demolished, the earliest dour, terraced housing is found in these mining settlements. However, the cottages are now brightly colour-washed at *Wanlockhead* (Dumfries and Galloway) where a museum with old workings is also open. The *Bryn Tail* lead mine (Powys) is also now a museum.

These mining areas were rough and tough, often with customs, courts and laws of their own. Early miners often had privileged 'commons' rights, while the mine owner had rights to part of the produce of the mine. There were always arguments, and the bleak castle of the stannary (tin) town of *Lydford* (Cornwall) recalls the old mining 'justice' where the accused was likely to be hanged before the trial started. One or two small coal mines are still worked by 'freeminers' in the *Forest of Dean* (Glos)—St Briavels was the centre here.

CORNISH MINES

In Cornwall tin mines tended to be in the west, copper in the east and around Camborne. At their peak last century, ten years would see a profit of £900 on £1 invested. Ruined surface sheds with their typical tall chimneys remain, as well as waste heaps. They were deep mines, with the problem of water leaking down through the tunnel roofs. The sheds housed steam

engines endlessly powering pumps, and also machinery for pounding and crushing. At the same time, water was also needed in large quantities for washing the ores, and complex systems of dams and leats were usually dug. The Poldark mine museum near *Helston* (Cornwall) is well worth a visit, offering tours of a classic tin mine.

WELSH MINING

Wales was rich in easily gained gold and lead, copper and also slate. *Parys Mountain* (Anglesey) now stands like a rotted tooth, pillaged of its ore. It was probably mined in Roman times, but it was in 1768 that the world's richest deposit of copper was opened up here. At the edge of Snowdonia are the famous slate mines of *Blaenau Ffestiniog* (Gwynedd). Gloddfa Ganol mine has 42 miles of tunnels, and a railway and explanatory museum. Slate from this area roofed much of Britain in Victorian times.

COAL MINING

Although coal mining is now less extensive, the vast grey 'tips' or spoil heaps of washings and coal waste remain the most familiar mining landmark. The tips are sometimes now green with grass and grazed by sheep. There are many mine museums: one with old 'pillar and stall' workings is at *Beamish* (Durham).

LUNAR LANDSCAPES

Coal mining creates its own lunar landscape, impressive to many. 'Slag heaps have as big a monumentality as any mountain,' said Henry Moore, sculptor extraordinary, and early travellers saw little wrong with industry in the view; but for them, of course, industry meant busy-ness and wealth, not dereliction. The phrase 'lunar landscape' was first coined by George Orwell, who detested the slag heaps.

Britain today offers lunar landscapes aplenty—from the brickfields of Bedfordshire to the giant waste pyramids of white clay at *St Austell* (Cornwall), from the Delabole slate quarry near *Tintagel* (Cornwall)—Britain's largest man-made hole—to the spreading gravel diggings.

Caves

Elaborate cave systems are most frequently a feature of limestone rock, but mines can match them for scale and sometimes for complexity.

CAVING AREAS

Sea caves abound on rocky, western coasts (see pp. 158–159). Caves inland are really a feature of limestone countryside—that is, the areas of the Yorkshire Dales, the Pennine White Peak, South Wales, the Mendips and South Devon. In these areas the layered rock has been buckled to offer numerous cracks both horizontally and in vertical splits or 'joints' through which rainwater percolates. Because it has absorbed carbon dioxide on its way down, this rainwater is slightly acid and slowly attacks the rock. The same process can be seen, much speeded up, if a fragment of limestone is dropped into vinegar, which is a weak acid; it froths furiously and breaks up.

Although chalk is a fine limestone, it is not only softer but more absorbent, so that the water flows which create the cave systems do not occur and any caves that do form tend to slump in. (Unless renewed, chalk cliffs are less long-lived than limestone cliffs.) A few caves are found in lines of weakness in sandstones and other rocks, but never of the complexity and size of limestone caverns.

CLUES TO CAVERNS BELOW

Sometimes there is a saucer-shaped depression or sink-hole which is the entrance to a vertical 'pothole'. There are many of these near *Malham* (N. Yorks): Gaping Ghyll is one, with the deepest shaft, tallest waterfall and largest open chamber in Britain. A disappearing stream or a stream issuing from the hillside at the foot of the cave system are good clues that a cave system exists.

A small stream now issues from the foot of Malham Cove, but its great face was worn by a vast waterfall tumbling from above at the end of the Ice Age. Cave-making was given a boost by the vast amounts of melt water issuing from the retreating ice sheets at the end of the Ice Age. Many 'young' caves

and the more obvious surface clues date from this time.

LIMESTONE GORGES

Many limestone gorges were once part of cave systems, the roof of which has collapsed, leaving any side-caves with convenient entrances. Cheddar Gorge in the *Mendips* (Avon/Som) is one example, and Gordale Scar near *Malham* (N. Yorks) another; here the ground is still littered with the debris of the fallen roof. *Dovedale* (Derbyshire), an open gorge, has many caves along it, set delightfully in trees.

LIMESTONE PAVEMENT

The weathering of limestone is sometimes seen on the surface in the form of 'pavement'. Here rainwater has etched deep gutters or 'grikes' to leave free-standing 'clints', pavement-like blocks which near *Malham Tarn* (N. Yorks) are displayed washed free of soil. They make a natural rock garden, for the shaded grikes are full of wild flowers. Pavement probably exists in many limestone areas, but lies covered with soil, turf and woodland.

STALACTITES AND OTHER FORMATIONS

The geography of limestone caves is always complicated, with narrow passages ballooning out into chambers before constricting again. Rivers, lakes and waterfalls are common, and often a passage becomes a water-filled 'sump' which can only be followed with a breathing mask. These passages are often smoothly lined with calcite, a mineral dissolved from the limestone rock by the water and redeposited where it slides and evaporates over the walls. If the water drips from the cave roof, a stalactite forms, hanging down, the residual salts building a stalagmite up from the floor below. These two may join to form a pillar running from floor to ceiling of the cave.

But caves often become treasure houses of unbelievable form when changes in the water flows and draughts chasing along the passages twist the formation, sometimes even creating cascades and sheets of calcite. Slow evaporation from pools of water

can also create heavy deposits of 'rimstone', and in them rock pearls are sometimes formed by onion-skin accretion if slight currents gently stir the water. The formation of hanging 'straws' of calcite and slender, horizontally branching 'helactites' remains a complete mystery.

Among the most famous 'show caves' with complex formations are those at *Cheddar* (Som), *Dan-yr-Ogof* near Abercraf (Powys) and Treak Cliff, *Castleton* (Derbyshire). Castleton is an ideal village for cave addicts, with its $\frac{1}{2}$-mile-deep Peak Cavern lying below Peveril Castle (its resonance makes it popular for choir exhibitions) and the Blue John caves (see below).

MINES

Some natural caves have been extended by mining, especially for lead ore, which is often found in limestone areas. Treak Cliff Cavern, *Castleton* (Derbyshire) is one interesting example, for here the lead diggings broke into a further natural cavern system which runs from the hillside above, disclosing secret veins of Blue John, one of the rarest of semiprecious stones. This is still mined in two of the local caverns, but there is little left.

DISUSED MINES

Many 'caves', especially those in rock other than limestone, are abandoned mines. Some, such as the vast slate mines at *Blaenau Ffestiniog* (Gwynedd) are busy tourist attractions. Others, such as those which pit the Lake District fellsides, have few visitors, and are usually for safety boarded up. They are found even in chalk: *Chislehurst Caves* (Kent) were dug for chalk during the Napoleonic wars; the elaborate passages acted as air-raid shelters for Londoners in World War II. Also unusual is a 'tar tunnel' dug for bitumen at *Ironbridge* (Shropshire) and the cave at *Royston* (Herts) is a real puzzle.

HABITAT CAVES

Many caves give modern sanctuary to bats, foxes and other wildlife, but many were refuges in the distant eras of the Ice Age. Some caves are famous for the bones of cave bears, hyenas,

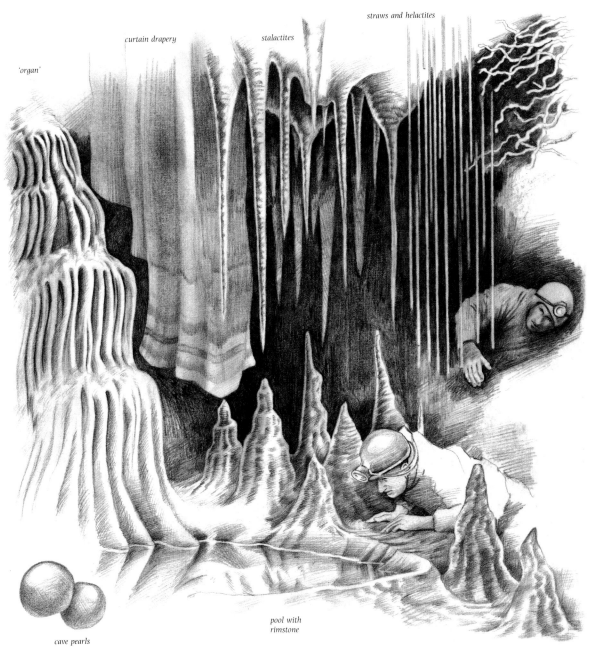

'organ'

curtain drapery

stalactites

straws and helactites

cave pearls

pool with rimstone

sabre-toothed tigers. Some were used by man in very early Stone Age times, and used over very long periods of time. Deposits containing food bones, human bones, flint and other stone-tool flakes are sometimes covered with a layer of calcite as conclusive proof of their age. Wookey Hole in the *Mendips* (Avon/Som), for example, has yielded evidence of early occupation. Gough's Cavern in *Cheddar* (Som) has yielded a skeleton from before 7000 BC (Meso-lithic times) which can be seen in the museum there; occupation continued: Roman spear-heads and coins (arran-ged in piles still undisturbed) were also found.

Many caves were constantly used by squatters until and even after medieval times. Indeed in the Wax Museum in Edinburgh is a tableau depicting the notorious Sawney Beane

Features of a limestone cave.

and his family, who lived in a cave and bred incestuously for 25 years. The entire tribe was arrested and hung for murdering and eating passing travellers—only 200 years ago.

Unusual caves include the folly caves dug by Georgian gentry and weirdly decorated with stones and minerals.

The fossil record

Fossils provide the proof that evolution occurs, but they are also of use in deciphering the complicated story of the rocks lying below the fields.

FOSSIL LOCATIONS

In some areas it is hard not to find fossils. In the grey cliffs and on the foreshore at *Lyme Regis* (Dorset) and *Whitby* (N. Yorks) for example, myriads can be found, many of decorative form. There are many ammonites, of various kinds from 1 in. or less across to 2 ft or more and differing also in the ridging of the shell and the pattern of the sutures between the shell's compartments. Sometimes they

Crinoid or 'sea lily'.

glisten with fool's gold that has impregnated them.

Alongside these, pointed belemnites are scattered, and in some of the strata frequent short lengths of crinoid stem. And there are also shells rather resembling cockles and other bivalves found alive today.

SHAPED STONES

Fossils puzzled the first naturalists, for shellfish could be found even on the heights of Snowdon. Had they been left by the great Flood reported in the Bible? Many thought so. In general lore, the ammonites were called 'snakestones' and believed to cure warts. Belemnites were known as 'thunderstones', for they were thought

Ammonites, called 'snake stones'.

to be bolts of lightning. The earliest field guides, from 300 years ago, showed pictures of these alongside stone axes and natural crystals. They were all lumped together as 'shaped stones' of mysterious origin.

THE STORY OF FOSSILS

We realize today that rather than being cast by lightning a belemnite is the fossil 'backbone' of a squid-like animal. But far from being a mere curiosity, it and thousands of different kinds of fossil have proved not only that life-forms have evolved from each other, but that the land and landscapes also undergo an 'evolution' of

Belemnites.

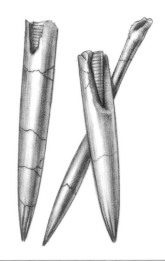

their own. This realization of endless change struck like lightning more than a century ago, leading to disputes between scientists and religious leaders, for it implied that man was no special creation, but himself part of the evolving natural world.

The ammonites and the belemnites found at Lyme Regis, for example, were relatives of the squid. All three are molluscs: animals with a 'head-foot' for movement and feeding, and a protective shell. Today's garden snail is a simple mollusc. In the ammonite the shell became spirally twisted with the head-foot protruding with its tentacles from the end compartment. In today's squid, evolution has had the effect of enclosing the shell within the body, as a cuttlebone. The belemnite was rather similar, except that its 'cuttlebone' was a pointed rod.

READING THE VIEW WITH FOSSILS

By comparing fossils such as these, and following their evolution one from another, the rock layers that hold them can be 'dated' in sequence and tortuous rock layers at opposite ends of Britain matched up. Fossils show that

One of the many fossil corals.

the blue clay at Lyme Regis and Whitby is part of the same formation, which dips down to be hidden below other rocks between the two places.

Fossils forge a direct link with forgotten worlds, a link that is sometimes very easy to comprehend. In parts of the Pennines corals can be found attached like badges to limestone bluffs. These were presumably also cliffs when the corals were alive, but sunken in some long-forgotten ocean where tropical fish lazily swam. When we paddle on the foreshore at Lyme

Regis and feel underfoot a belemnite protruding from the clay which outcrops below the sand, we are pacing the shallows of a 200-million-year-old sea. At times ichthyosaurs (fish lizards) also swam those seas, and the fossils of these early reptiles are also to be found in some of the rock strata here, and are displayed in the shops and museum at Lyme Regis.

THE FORMATION OF FOSSILS

The Lyme Regis fossils had their origin when the animal died and sank to the bottom to be entombed in soft mud. The flesh decayed but the bone or shell matter remained undisturbed. The deposit in time became hardened into rock, whereupon minerals were swapped by complicated chemical seepage between the fossil and the rock around. The Lyme Regis ammonites that glisten with fool's gold (iron pyrites) are one example of this.

Most fossils have had this origin. Although fossils of terrestrial species can be found (and fossils can range from flies trapped in amber to footprints left in wet mud by striding dinosaurs), they are rarer. This is simply because on land the processes of weathering tend to break up and fragment any remains. For this reason, little remains of the abundant plant life.

Some fossils remain as the shell or hard matter with its mineral composition modified. Many are found as a cast—either an inner or outer cast of the hard fragment. In the course of time many fossils have had their shape squashed or distorted. Some may remain only as a stain on a freshly broken rock surface.

BRITAIN'S OLDEST FOSSILS: THE PALAEOZOIC

Among the earlier life-forms that are easy to recognize are graptolites, which look like miniature and often curved fretsaw blades: each creature occupied a 'cup'. They can be found in certain rocks in the Lake District, for example, that date back to 500 million years ago. They were alive in the era known as the 'Palaeozoic', meaning 'old life'. Also in some rocks in this

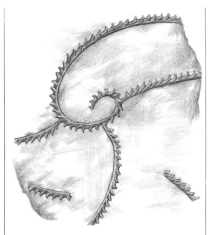

Graptolite, magnified × 3.

period trilobites can be found, which could maybe curl themselves like woodlice. *Builth Wells* (Powys) is one site for them.

THE MESOZOIC

Life-forms diversified and became more varied as they evolved. During

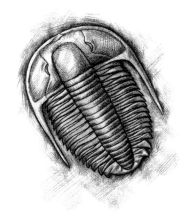

Trilobite.

this era many ocean limestones and hard clays were formed, some, such as the blue lias of Lyme Regis, crammed full of fossils. Limestones usually contain a variety of fossils. Chalk, a fine limestone, was formed in this era. Sea urchins are fairly common chalk fossils, and often found as a flint cast. Sponges are also common chalk-flint fossils, the nodule in many cases hollow. It was in the Mesozoic that the dinosaurs evolved, flourished and

Sea urchin cases.

were wiped out by the climatic changes that ushered in the next era.

THE CAENOZOIC

This period began about 70 million

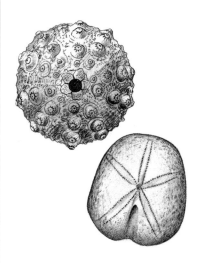

Sea shell fossils.

years ago. Typical rocks of the Caenozoic are clays and loose, shelly sands. The cliffs at *Alum Bay* (Isle of Wight) are just one notable site. Parts of the British Isles were variously dry land, under water, and under the sea, with the climate swinging from warm enough to encourage the hippopotamus to cold enough to encourage the mammoth. The Ice Age with its intervening interglacials or warmer periods is of this era.

Soil

Soil is formed from the breakdown of rock layers and carries fascinating evidence of distant epochs as well as of human activity of more recent times.

THE DISINTEGRATION OF ROCK

Where the layers of rock which underpin the landscape are exposed or close to the surface, they weather to form soil. The fact that the hardest rock does disintegrate can be deduced from any cliff face or crag: it will have at its foot a skirt of debris, or 'scree'. Sometimes more surprising evidence can be seen.

In the grounds of *Ashdown House* (Oxon) misshapen boulders litter the chalk valley. Known by the old word 'sarsens'—perhaps originally 'saracens' meaning 'foreigners'—they are all that remains of a layer of hard sandstone which once overlaid the chalk. Sarsens were once scattered across many parts of these downs— the *Ridgeway* (Oxon) still passes near some—and they were handy for the prehistoric builders of tombs and stone circles.Largely cleared from fields, they may still be seen by streams.

How did this hard rock become weathered, while the soft chalk below did not? Part of the reason must be that the chalk is porous and soaks up the rain, whereas it presumably ran in streamlets across the sandstone. A

similar example, with different rocks, is at the Devil's Jumps, Churt Common, *Frensham* (Surrey).

THE COMPOSITION OF SOIL

A child's experiment, but effective, is to shake up a jar of garden soil with water and allow it to settle. A depth of sand sinks to the bottom along with the small stones, with clay on top and above that a spongy mass of dead plant material (and some highly annoyed small animals). The fine 'seashore' sand echoes the origins of all soil. If we take the example of granite, of the three different minerals making it up (see pp. 16–17), the feldspar crystals weather to a clay, and the quartz becomes sand. In the long history of the planet, new rocks have been created from these and again weathered away and the sand in the soil reminds us of these cycles.

But in fact it often makes sense to see soil as just two main constituents: a geological fabric of rock and rock particles, including stones, sand and clay; and a biological component in the shape of countless living things: bacteria, slimes, fungi, single-celled organisms, small insects and worms and other invertebrates, together with a humus of decaying leaves and other plant matter.

Fields on the southern downlands and other chalk areas are often whitish with broken pieces of chalk.

PLOUGHMAN'S SOIL

Soils in Britain differ enormously, even within the same parish or farm. Every farm will have fields that have traditionally been ploughland, and others that in the past were left unploughed as pasture or as meadow. It is quite likely that today's best plough fields were picked out as such in Saxon times, although the pattern of hedges and the field names are of much later date. Certainly, unploughed hay meadows may be hundreds of years old, such as that at Yarnton Mead near *Oxford* (see pp. 76–77). Today's mechanized farming, with rapid drainage and deep ploughing has smudged this old pattern, but enough survives.

The farming value of the soil reflects its texture, its minerals and its nutrients, the latter created in nature by the intense activity of soil organisms. Traditionally its texture would be judged by feel—a soil heavy with clay could be fingered into a ball, for example—and its richness by its smell.

SOIL WATER

The rate at which the rain (or flood) water percolates down through the

Red soils are the result of the disintegration of a dusky bedrock, usually of desert origin.

soil is also important to the farmer. Clay soils allow less water through than sandy soils, which is why puddles form more easily on them. The humus of dead and living organic matter is important in retaining water, and on Britain's most fertile soils—that is, lowland soils darkened by humus— evaporation crystallizes the nutrients out as quickly as they are dissolved after rain, and loss by leaching is minimal. The process of leaching can produce very sterile soils.

SOIL PROFILES

Soil profiles are revealed in road and other cuttings, sometimes along the sides of holloways and sunken lanes. They show that much of the soil derives from the bedrock lying un- weathered below the surface. Many soils are to some extent a legacy of the Ice Age; boulder clay and gravels deposited by the glaciers and ice sheets are bedrock in many areas (geologi- cally, clay and gravel count as rock), while that ice also scraped rock sur- faces bare in others. Pennine moor- land soil profiles, for example, can show a skimpy topsoil on top of rock

rubble, with solid rock not far below the latter.

In some areas of the Pennines, how- ever, thick beds of dark bog peat overlie the bedrock; this peat can be seen on well-worn paths. Chalk soils also rest thinly on top of the rock. A heath has a particular kind of soil profile, the leaching creating a hard iron 'pan' below ground (see pp. 154–155).

THE COLOUR OF THE FIELDS

The colour of the ploughed field often reflects the types of rock lying below, which create the patchwork of 'coloured counties'. Many Devon fields are red, as are those at the foot of *Charnwood Forest* (Leics)—the burnt red of desert-laid sandstone. Down- land fields are often whitish with broken pieces of chalk.

SOIL MARKS

Past diggings which are now filled in can sometimes be noticed in the newly ploughed field, in the form of soil marks. A ditch infill is usually darker because of its richer humus, and this is particularly so on whitish chalk soils. Dark lines or circles mark the lines of old ditches and pits and can sometimes be seen from nearby roads. After ploughing, many old barrow circles

can be seen on the downland slopes to the west of *Dorchester* (Dorset) for example, and in many places in Ox- fordshire, Berkshire and Wiltshire.

CROP MARKS

Once soil has been disturbed by digg- ing, it never regains its original tex- ture. Modern farming aims at gaining an even crop, a whole field ripening for the harvest at the same time. Unexpec- tedly, these two facts unite to provide archaeology with an important tool.

A ditch or pit dug centuries ago and long since filled contains slightly looser soil, which holds water longer. Hence the crop above it ripens marginally later, remaining green when the har- vest all around is turning yellow. The line of the ditch or site of the pit shows up from the air as a dark 'crop mark'. The sites of Neolithic causewayed camps, Bronze Age huts, Iron Age farms, Roman forts, and the holloways and ditches of lost medieval villages have all been spotted from the air by the crop marks that remain.

Conversely, if the rubble of an old wall base lies below the surface, the soil above dries faster and the crop ripens earlier. A pale line is created in the green crop. Pale lines caused by buried rubble can also be seen on grass pasture fields in times of drought.

Walking the fields

Slight features now barely noticeable in the fields may be all that remains of once considerable timber and masonry structures of the past.

THE DESTRUCTION OF WOODEN FEATURES

Time very soon puts paid to even the most massive wooden structure. No matter how well seasoned it is, if timber is left in contact with soil it becomes invaded by agents of decay. Soil is a powerhouse of destructive, recycling bacteria, slimes and other simple plant and animal life.

The only exception is if the soil is waterlogged, when oxygen levels are low, usually too low to enable this hidden world to remain active. 'Bog oaks' or parts of them, the relic of ancient woodlands, are frequently found in fenland peat (see pp. 138–139). In the Somerset levels, wooden causeways built more than 5000 years ago have been discovered (see pp. 116–117), while there are occasional finds of preserved corpses of Bronze Age and Iron Age folk—the 'bog people' as they are called, 'Pete Marsh' being the nickname of one now on view at Manchester Museum.

THE LEVELLING OF DUG FEATURES

Even deep ditches fill up and ramparts slip. The process can be remarkably quick, as an experiment on Overton Down near *Avebury* (Wilts) showed. Here in 1960 a straight ditch was dug into the chalk, with sides 5 ft deep and cleanly cut, as would have been done by the builders of West Kennet barrow nearby. By 1964 the bottom was already buried with slip from the sides, which were by then slumped at 45 degrees. Turf and topsoil fell in, and the slopes were colonized by plants. Today only a shallow hollow remains. Excavation has shown that the slight ditches of West Kennet were 12 ft deep. The unexcavated shafts of the prehistoric flint mines at *Grimes Graves* (Norfolk) and *Cissbury Ring* (W. Sussex) remain only as shallow hollows, usually tangled with scrub.

The true might and complexity of the ramparts of Iron Age forts which drape the hill tops at *Cadbury Castle* (Som) and other places have only been revealed by excavation. Many had timber or boulder facings which have either decayed or been covered by soil slips. The slippage on these steep rampart slopes can in fact be judged by the parallel 'steps' of turf created. This natural 'soil creep' is often and wrongly called 'sheep tracks', but it might be aided by grazing sheep and cattle of course.

THE DISAPPEARANCE OF MASONRY

In time even the stubs of walls tend to become covered with soil. Factors here are the height of the stub, of course, but also the depth of the soil round about, because earthworms are largely the cause. In areas with thin, poor acid soil (which supports few worms) tumbled stone walls tend to remain—they are often found on moors and heaths, for example.

Earthworms eat soil, digesting the plant matter and expelling the rest, sometimes as a wormcast. It was Charles Darwin who realized their effect, calculating that they recycle 10 tons of soil per acre per year—that is, more than 30 stone—the weight of two plump people—of soil per square yard per century. This is not additional soil, of course, but a proportion of it is, and depth accumulates quickly once a feature is covered with drift and the decaying leaves of plantains and other pioneer plants and the worms can become active.

TURF MOUNDS

Earthen features built of loose soil tend to weather away in time. The dolmens or 'stone tables' are one example, standing now bare of their mound (see pp. 36–7). Turf is somewhat more resistant. Some Neolithic long barrows were partly built with turf, as was the Roman *Antonine Wall* (Central).

BUMPS IN THE FIELDS

Many prehistoric and historic features remain as an irregularity—bumps or hollows or both—in the surface of the field or common. In recent years the deep ploughing of old arable and of grasslands which had hitherto escaped has wiped many sites off the map and diminished many more. Evidence of these might remain only as soil or crop marks (see pp. 28–29).

The first step is to try to decide the true shape of the feature. Any pattern suggested by the fragments is important, for a pattern has rhyme or reason; it is important to decide if there are corners—not all may remain.

Simple mounds can be round or elongated, solitary or accompanied by the ditch dug for them. A prominent mound may lie close by others which have survived less well. The feature may be linked with something

This Roman camp is protected, but ploughing has all too easily wiped away other surface features nearby.

overlooked: a meaningless depression, for example, could in the adjoining field reveal itself as part of the worn holloway of a long-lost medieval village (see pp. 56–57).

A circular feature is easy to recognize. Its diameter could be a crucial clue, suggesting whether the circular ditch marks a hut site or a larger animal paddock. One important point is that a single feature can incorporate the activities of a long period of time. Hilltop fortifications sturdy enough to be certainly Iron Age in date sometimes overlie or are built around earlier and slighter camps. The earliest visible traces of a village in England, a Neolithic settlement, occupy a corner of the Iron Age fort at *Carn Brea* (Cornwall) for example. (A complete village of the same date is found in Scotland—see pp. 152–153).

SHADOW AND SHINE

Slight features are strengthened by low light at dusk or dawn, when hollows fill with shadow and even slight bumps not only cast long shadows but also catch the light and 'shine'. A thin scatter of wind-blown snow can also fill hollows and expose a feature: this is often noticed with the widespread 'ridge and furrow' of medieval ploughland in the shire counties.

DROUGHT

Drought can sometimes heighten the visual clues, the bumps scorching yellow while the hollows remain damp and the grass growing in them remains a fresher green.

IDENTIFYING OLD PASTURE

Prehistoric features are more likely to remain in fields which have been grazed (to prevent shrubs invading) and never ploughed. But many pastures are recently ploughed and sown grass 'leys', so that indicators of old unploughed pasture should be sought. An abundance of many different wild grasses and flowers is a good clue to long-unploughed grassland, the variety creating a field or hillside with a general tawny colour rather than the bright green of recently sown grass. Anthills are also a good clue to old grassland, as are the slight steps of 'soil creep' on a slope.

Beachcombing the fields

Fragments of worked stone or broken pottery found on the surface of the ground may be the only clue to forgotten farms and settlements.

FRAGMENTS OF POTTERY AND WORKED FLINTS

Deep ploughing destroys the ditches and mounds of archaeological sites. But it can unearth scatters of pottery and (in the case of an early site) worked flints and chippings, and even locate previously unknown sites in this way. In unploughed pastures, rabbits may also help. It is always worth inspecting rabbit burrows.

Potsherds—fragments of broken pottery—and worked pieces of flint are best sought after heavy rain has washed them free of soil. With experience the size and shape and even the decoration of the original pot can be conjectured; reconstructed pots can always be seen in local museums. Potsherds are useful clues to the type and date of a site.

MOSAICS, OYSTER SHELLS, COINS AND GLASS

Fragments of mosaic pavements and oyster shells, often with all colour leached to leave them a clear white, are similar clues. They signpost a Roman site. Mosaic was frequently used for the flooring of the grander rooms of a villa, while oysters seem to have been a favourite titbit, and consumed in vast numbers. But they were also popular in later times and have pinpointed at least one lost medieval village.

Coins are a study of their own (the earliest are Iron Age). Although there is Roman glassware, glass fragments cannot really be expected before a Tudor date. Soil acids attack glass, creating a 'rainbow' surface sheen after a couple of centuries or more.

RECOGNIZING WORKED FLINT

Flint breaks with a sharp fracture. A single man-made fracture is often easily recognized: there is a bulb at the percussion point and the surface breaks in 'waves' away from it. Natural percussion in a stream (not usually frost) might perhaps produce a similar fracture. Two such fractures, however, lessen the likelihood of a natural origin, while a flint core chipped or 'napped' away to leave a useful shape is usually much neater in line than a naturally chipped core. Sometimes the flint core became the tool, but often the chippings were worked up. Axes were sometimes smoothed and polished with sand. (The stone tools of the Lake District and other axe 'factories' were made in much the same way.)

Sophisticated chipping may have been used to curve or sharpen the lines of the tool to the exact shape required. The depth and angle of fracture can be controlled by varying the angle of the blow, by using steady pressure instead of a hammer blow to force the fracture, or by using wood, bone or antler instead of stone as the hammer. Overall appearance can be a clue to date: soil acids dull the blue-black of freshly mined flint with a white or yellowed (tinted with iron) skin; the deeper this skin, the older the piece.

So, part of the art is recognizing the kinds of flint tool used in prehistoric times, and some patterns did not change. To our eyes, Neolithic arrowheads and axeheads are easiest to recognize, and expertly made, and similar patterns continued well into the Bronze Age. However, more modest tools such as scrapers for cleaning skins for leather and burins for boring holes in leather were as important in the economy. It is interesting that similar tools had been made and as expertly in the distant Palaeolithic (Old Stone Age) period. The Mesolithic which followed was rather different, however: axes tended to be coarse in shape, but these people excelled at fine chipping, barbing their harpoons with

Clues to look for in the field.

worked flints (above), oyster shells and Iron Age coin

Roman ware

Neolithic potsherds

Roman Samian ware

Dark Ages pottery

Bronze Age (Beaker) potsherd

Pottery clues to settlements.

very small flint pieces. Scatters of these led to the discovery of a hut site at *Abinger* (Surrey).

POTTERY

Although clay can be easily moulded and modelled when wet, when fired its chemical composition changes and it becomes hard and serviceable.

Neolithic people were the first to take advantage of this. Pottery is indispensable evidence for the archaeologist, partly because of the mentality of *Homo sapiens*. As with the flint tool, pottery is characteristic of its culture, and often identifies that culture and its place and time.

NEOLITHIC WARE

Some early Neolithic ware, such as was found in the ditches of the causewayed camp on Windmill Hill near *Avebury* (Wilts) was perhaps made by sticking thin slabs of clay together and stroking them up into shape. It was fired in an open fire, and smooth clay with little grit was chosen so that it could the better be smeared with grease to make it waterproof.

Other, rather more elaborate ware

was decorated with rows of holes, perhaps imitating the stitching of a leather vessel. The shapes of other containers were probably copied by these early potters: 'Peterborough' ware has cross-hatching, and it was made by building up a long snake of clay, suggesting that it was modelled on a straw basket.

THE EARLY BRONZE AGE BEAKER

This is a classic pot in fine clay which turned reddish when fired. It was flat-bottomed and finely decorated. These 'beakers' are found in round barrows alongside the skeleton, and were probably ritual drinking vessels. It is interesting that the barrow mound was often scattered with potsherds, perhaps at the final farewell ceremony. Later in the Bronze Age, when burial customs changed, sturdier pots with a heavy rim were made to hold cremation ashes.

IRON AGE POTTERY

By comparison with the preceding Bronze Age, the cooking pots of the first Iron Age peoples in Britain were roughly made, sometimes rather resembling a leather bucket. On the other hand, a late Iron Age (Belgic)

cremation urn was well made and both turned on a wheel and fired in a closed kiln for the first time.

ROMAN AND LATER POTTERY

With the Romans, pottery became an industry, always wheel-made and sometimes glazed. Found at villa sites (but also some lesser farmsteads) are pieces of Samian ware, imported from Gaul, glazed a reddish brown and with finely moulded decoration. A villa should yield a whole variety of sherds, but pieces of a mortarium or mortar are typical. This was a flattish unglazed open bowl, with fragments of sharp grit protruding from the clay. It was used for crushing and grinding the pastes popular in Roman menus. Pieces of amphorae, tall storage jars for wine or oil, might be found.

Of Saxon pottery, unglazed cremation urns are the best known, distinctly different from Roman pottery. Unglazed, they are decorated with bosses pushed out from the inside which are enlivened with cuts and stabs in the clay. In medieval times glazed pottery was again made, and glazes were now often green. The 'face jug'—a jug with a handle and decorated with a face—was typical.

Man's first marks on the landscape

The earliest remaining man-made features in the landscape date from Neolithic times, an era lasting from about 4700 to 2000 BC.

PALAEOLITHIC AND MESOLITHIC HUNTERS

Wookey Hole in the *Mendips* (Avon/Som) has yielded bones and chipped flint scrapers and cutting edges that are 30,000 years old, dating from Palaeolithic, or 'Old Stone Age', times when Britain was gripped by ice. Gough's Cave, *Cheddar* (Som) has similar finds from the late Palaeolithic, from 10,000 BC. By then the Ice Age was drawing to a close, the ground unfreezing, and trees beginning to create a wildwood. Through this forest were to wander Mesolithic or 'Middle Stone Age' hunting bands, often setting up camps on open ground by lakes and marshes, or on gravelly, dry, lightly wooded knolls.

Mesolithic men used small chipped flints to tip and barb arrows and fish spears and their camp-sites are recognized by scatters of waste flint chippings often a fraction of an inch long. It is always worth looking for these in beds of gravel accidentally opened up by the roots of fallen trees or exposed by rabbits, on knolls which could have been dry places in those days. Even when whitened by long contact with the soil, these worked flints are often easily recognizable.

One known site worth a detour is at *Abinger* (Surrey) where a Mesolithic pit dwelling has been excavated—the best example in Europe. A simple hollow is scooped from the ground, but when banked around with soil and roofed with turf it would have been cosy.

NEOLITHIC CLEARANCES

The steady improvement in climate continued to melt the northern ice and the sea level rose. By about 6500 BC the Channel was permanently cut, but before 4000 BC the straits were already being crossed, probably in coracle-type boats. These Neolithic, or 'New Stone Age', arrivals had a very different culture; they brought with them seeds of wheat and barley to sow, and cattle, sheep, goats and dogs. They made the

first pottery to be seen in Britain.

They too relied on stone and flint weapons and tools, and with them set about clearing the wildwood. Choosing the more lightly wooded areas, they burnt and cleared fields for their corn, moving on when the soil was exhausted. Without proper care and leached by the rains, it was quickly impoverished. In addition, their livestock grazed everywhere, devouring any fresh shoots, keeping that open ground largely bare of trees.

This was the origin of the open heaths and chalk downs of the south. Large areas of Dartmoor and of the Pennine moorlands were cleared in the same way and the impoverishment of already poor soil and grazing, aided by climatic changes, has kept them open ever since. The gravel reaches of the Thames and other lowland areas were also settled, but here the memory is only kept in crop marks (see pp. 28–29).

THE FIRST EARTH BANKS: CAUSEWAYED CAMPS

The Neolithic farmers and pastoralists were the first to create features which actually marked the landscape. They laboriously constructed what are known, for want of a better name, as causewayed camps. Four acres or more of open ground were ringed by one or more circular ditches, the dug soil being piled up into a ring *outside* the ditch. But the ditches were never complete—short lengths were dug, broken by undug 'causeways', and so they were hardly defensive; nor is an outside bank. Windmill Hill near *Avebury* (Wilts) is a famous example, and though little remains it is worth a visit for its ghosts: the outer of its three ditches was 400 yards across, the causeways 4 yards wide. The pottery found here helps identify these early 'Windmill Hill' people elsewhere.

Livestock bones have been found in some ditches, and perhaps these 'camps' were seasonal markets. Most of them are on high ground (and sometimes later engulfed by Iron Age forts) but crop marks show that they were also dug out in some low-lying riverside areas.

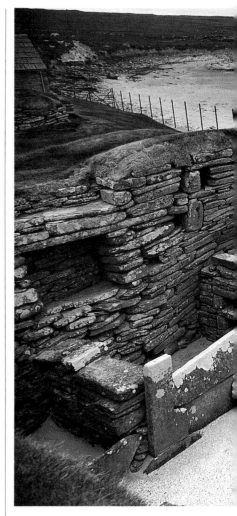

HENGES

Henges too were dug in many different areas in Neolithic times and are as enigmatic. The name 'henge' is adopted from Stonehenge, whose stones stand inside an early low-banked henge. Henges are roughly circular, banked enclosures and although many small, early ones are known from crop marks, some later ones were 300 yards or more across: the bank and ditch are enormous at *Avebury* (Wilts).

The bank is usually outside the ditch (and so not defensive), and is broken by one entrance on the smaller, and sometimes two or more on the larger henges. Finds of human bones and painted animal bones suggest a ritual

use as does the fact that many, such as *Arbor Low* (Derbyshire) and *Stonehenge* (Wilts), were later to be developed as stone circles. Sometimes henges were in pairs or trios, as at *Eamont Bridge* (Cumbria) and at *Knowlton* (Dorset).

SILBURY HILL

This must be added to the list of Neolithic mysteries. It lies near *Avebury* (Wilts), part of the ritual complex of the area. A vast cone rearing to 130 ft, its grassy slopes hide a complicated stepped chalk construction (see pp. 44–45). Its function is unknown.

THE CURSUS

The mystery of the beliefs of these people deepens with the cursus. A cursus is an avenue marked by banks on each side. One ran to the north of Stonehenge. The Dorset cursus had banks 100 yards apart, and stretched for 6 miles. It is all but wiped out by ploughing but parts can be seen near *Oakley Down* (Dorset).

SETTLEMENTS

There is equal mystery about Neolithic settlements. They are rarely found as surface features, although there are exceptions: there are Neolithic fragments of wall at *Carn Brea* (Cornwall), making it the oldest village in England. *Skara Brae* (Orkneys) is a complete village exposed to view. The waterlogged peatlands of the Somerset levels were settled, as timbered causeways found near *Glastonbury* (Som) show. But there was clearly tribal organiz-

Skara Brae (Orkneys) is unique in Europe, a complete stone Neolithic village preserved by drifting sand.

ation; the evidence is the fact that a causewayed camp needed 100,000 man-hours of labour.

WOODHENGES

Towards the end of the Neolithic, stone circles began to be raised inside some of the henges, but crop marks also reveal early timber circles, or woodhenges, long since decayed. One, known as Woodhenge, not far from Stonehenge, is marked out with concrete posts. They may have been precursors of the stone circles, but rubbish found at some suggests they may have been huge communal dwellings.

Long mounds and stone tables

The Neolithic peoples left us a legacy of magnificent and complex communal tombs which are still to be seen in many areas of Britain.

THE SPREAD OF NEOLITHIC CULTURE

Although there is no doubt that early farmers and herders did cross from European mainland to Britain, no obvious homeland is known. The oldest causewayed camps and burial mounds are not clustered near short Channel crossings and in fact are quite widespread. Perhaps the Neolithic culture that developed here was largely native, for the tombs certainly provide evidence of the growth of strongly different local traditions. How one kind of tomb relates to another is not yet certain; the sequence sketched out below is one of several interpretations.

Neolithic people in the countries surrounding the Mediterranean carved square cave tombs in limestone cliffs. This kind of tomb is not found in Britain, but to compound the mystery the Orkneys have the unique *Dwarfie Stane*, a Neolithic burial chamber laboriously hollowed out of a large block of sandstone.

The development of Wayland's Smithy.

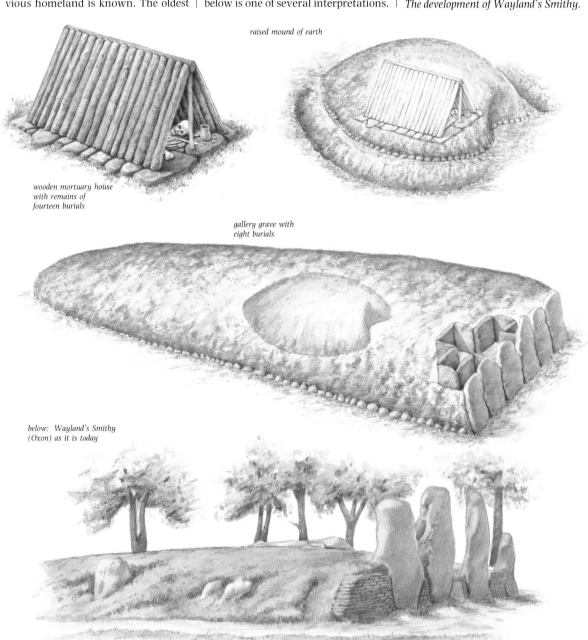

raised mound of earth

wooden mortuary house with remains of fourteen burials

gallery grave with eight burials

below: Wayland's Smithy (Oxon) as it is today

Unlike their settlements and cause-wayed camps, the tombs of Neolithic peoples are not difficult to find and visit.

BARROWS AND CAIRNS

A 'barrow' is a burial mound, in most cases of earth, turf and subsoil dug nearby, but sometimes of surface stones. In the latter case it is normally called a 'cairn'.

LONG BARROWS

Long barrows are early Neolithic tombs. The oldest might date back to 4000 BC. A couple of hundred remain, mainly on the downlands of Wessex, with fewer in such places as east Yorkshire. They are from 20 to 100 yards long, up to 20 yards across, usually straight-sided, and sometimes wedge-shaped with the broad end to the east, facing the dawn. They were often raised with material dug from long side ditches, and shallow hollows might remain. In parts of Scotland similar long cairns are found.

Excavation has shown that long barrows were piled up over wooden or turf 'mortuaries' where (judging by the scattered bones) generations of dead were exposed to kites and other scavenging birds, although the corpses were sometimes burnt. Later burials were sometimes dug into the sides of a long barrow.

In one or two places very long but low and thin banks perhaps only 3–4 yards across and maybe with a Neolithic burial or two along them, can still be seen. One at Maiden Castle near *Dorchester* (Dorset) was over 500 yards long. They may have been linked with the origins of the mysterious cursus avenues (see pp. 34–35).

CHAMBERED TOMBS

The chambered tomb was perhaps an evolution from the long barrow, providing security for the body while keeping the chamber of the dead open for later burials. There are around 250 in England and Wales, 350 in Scotland. Giant boulders or 'megaliths' (from the Greek for 'large stones') came into use as well as drystone walling, sometimes constructed to fill

in the gaps between the standing stones. Dolmens, passage graves and gallery graves are found.

DOLMENS

These are the famous 'stone tables' to be seen in the west, in Cornwall and Wales. They consist of a massive flat capstone typically held aloft by three upright slabs. In some cases they make a kind of box, closed by a fourth upright. Lanyon Quoit near *Madron* is a Cornish example and *Dyffryn Ardudwy* (Gwynedd) and *Pentre-Ifan* (Dyfed) Welsh ones (in Wales they are known as 'cromlechs'). It is thought that they were once heaped up with earth, perhaps as a long barrow, but with the capstone and doorstone left uncovered.

In Cornwall other tombs are also found which are really only a small stone cupboard or 'cist' let into a round mound.

PASSAGE GRAVES

Anglesey and the north Scottish Highlands and Islands have 'passage graves'. The mound is rounded, perhaps indicating different rituals from those of the other tombs, and covers a central stone chamber reached by a passage. *Bryn Celli Ddu* (Anglesey) is a famous example; its mound is 30 yards across and skirted by a low wall of small boulders. It stands in a henge, now disappeared. At the exact centre of the mound was a puzzling decorated stone. To increase the number of bodies, the burial chamber was in northern Scotland sometimes divided up into 'stalls' and round burial cairns at *Camster* (Caithness) have a series of narrow chambers. *Maes Howe* (Orkneys) is spectacular: here a cairn covers a beautifully built chamber with a sloping corbelled ceiling, looted by Vikings who left runic markings behind. The main chamber has small side chambers.

GALLERY GRAVES

Before Maes Howe was built, in an area stretching from both sides of the River Severn into the Cotswolds, the two traditions of long barrow and passage grave seem to have fused to

create the 'gallery grave'. In fact Wayland's Smithy on the *Ridgeway* (Oxon) was a long barrow later made into a gallery grave. It is now typical of the latter: a long wedge-shaped mound neatly edged with stone, with at one end an entrance façade of giant standing stones. The passage is short, really just a corridor giving access to side chambers in which the bodies were laid. The West Kennet barrow near *Avebury* (Wilts) is another example. At *Belas Knap* (Glos) the massive entrance with curved sides of drystone walling is in fact false, and presumably for rituals in years after the burial. The burial chambers here are placed in the sides of the mound.

Perhaps this well-developed type of tomb was spread by seafarers. It is interesting that rather similar tombs with a curving forecourt are found in the Clyde area and another similar type in the Medway area of Kent, at *Trottiscliffe*, for example.

ANCIENT RITUAL

Sometimes you will notice a small hole gouged in one of the stones of a dolmen. The Men an Tol near *Madron* (Cornwall) is in fact a giant stone doughnut set between two standing stones. There is a glimpse of ancient ritual here, but one long forgotten.

TOMBS AND TERRITORY

We today take for granted the fact that whatever other buildings there are, a village is usually marked by a church and its churchyard. In distant Neolithic days, the long barrows may also have been territory markers of a rather different kind. If on high ground, they are often not on the summit of the ridge but below it, on the skyline as seen from the valley below. West Kennet near *Avebury* (Wilts) is one example. When newly dug these downland tombs would have been gleaming white, and some elsewhere have been found scattered with pieces of white quartz or other stone.

In Dorset clusters of long barrows are often associated with causewayed camps, presumably marking tribal centres. Similar clusters are found near the ritual centre of Stonehenge.

The round-barrow people

The Bronze Age spanned the years from about 2000 to 700 BC. Round barrows are a common feature of the early part of this period.

ROUND BARROWS

A round mound, perhaps reaching head height, might be a medieval windmill mound (see pp. 108–109), a very decayed Norman defensive motte (see pp. 62–63), or a Roman or Dark Age burial (see pp. 52–53). But it is more likely to be much older, a Bronze Age barrow or burial mound, dating from 2000–1200 BC. Although some Neolithic barrows are rounded, the round barrow is the signature of the Bronze Age. There are still many left on chalk downland and on moorland. In spite of centuries of ploughing, some remain in farmland, in unploughed field corners, and crop marks reveal the circular ditches of many more ploughed out barrows scattered across today's fields. Standing barrows are often marked on Ordnance Survey maps as barrow or tumulus (plural tumuli) if of earth, cairn if raised with stones.

THE BEAKER PEOPLE AND THE BRONZE AGE

The Bronze Age had its beginnings before 2000 BC, with waves of immigrants crossing from Europe, bringing with them a knowledge of metal-working. Their warrior graves sometimes contain a copper knife, even gold ornament. They also contain flint arrowheads and archers' stone wrist guards, and a wide-mouthed drinking pot or 'beaker', from which their culture is named.

Copper was in time replaced by bronze, an alloy of copper and tin with a hard cutting edge (brass is a modern alloy of copper and zinc). Finely wrought bronze swords and other weapons were the kit of heroes, underlined by the fact that warriors were buried singly under their barrows. Dynastic heroes too, for some barrows covered women and even children. This 'golden age' of early Bronze Age culture flowered especially in Wessex—Wiltshire and Dorset—from 2000 to around 1400 BC. There had been some raising of stones late in the Neolithic, but the Bronze Age is also marked by many magnificent stone circles and standing stones found (see pp. 40–45) throughout Britain.

Burial customs tended to change as the Bronze Age continued and when barrow building ceased in the south, around 1200 BC, the ashes of the dead

were sometimes then buried in an urn in a hole in the side of an earlier barrow. Metalworking improved, but bronze remained in use until it began to be replaced by iron around 700 BC.

BOWL BARROWS

Round barrows vary in size, from 5 to 30 yards across, the largest reaching 20 ft high. The commonest are 'bowl' barrows, a simple steep mound of chalk or subsoil. They are now grassed over but, like the earlier long barrows, the southern chalk barrows must have gleamed white when newly dug (and some northern barrows were scattered with white quartz). This mound was dug from an encircling ditch which

A typical Bronze Age round barrow: mysterious, haunted — and a popular vantage point for sheep.

was often also ringed outside by a slight bank. Very often the barrow is dented on top, where Georgian and Victorian antiquarians have dug.

BARROW CEMETERIES

'Cemeteries' of barrows usually date from the golden age of Wessex. Near Priddy on the *Mendips* (Avon/Som) bowl barrows stand in lines. Other cemeteries were more scattered: they can be seen at *Oakley Down* (Dorset), *Seven Barrows, Lambourn* (Berks) (actually 30 in all) and many other places. As well as bowl barrows, such places often contain other kinds of barrow: bell barrows with a flat shelf between the mound and its ditch, saucer barrows with a flatter mound, and ring-like disc barrows with the central mound reduced to a small tump inside a circular ditch and bank and which may mark the burial of a woman.

CAIRNS AND CAIRNFIELDS

In areas where soil was difficult to dig, the mound may be a cairn of stones, usually gathered from the surface of the ground or from nearby streams and so smoothed and weathered. Many have been raided for stone walls (but the smoothed surface stones may be a clue in a wall). During Bronze Age times, much ground was also being cleared for the plough, and the resulting cairnfields may resemble a barrow cemetery, although clearance cairns are often smaller than burial cairns, only 3 yards or so across.

SETTLEMENT IN THE BRONZE AGE

It is in the uplands, swathed with mists and bitter winds, that the ghosts of the Bronze Age can be met face to face, for in some places even the stone huts survive.

One settlement which most probably dates from the late Bronze Age is Grimspound, on *Dartmoor* (Devon). Although not a defensive site, a 10 ft-wide stone wall with a massive entrance enclosed about 4 acres, in which were 16 round living huts. These are up to 15 ft across with thick stone walls and were originally roofed with turf laid on branches or maybe

with conical thatched or heather roofs. There was no chimney and smoke from the fire—there are traces of cook pits as well as benches—oozed itself out. There are other storage huts and stock pens outside the wall.

Rather similar huts can be found elsewhere on Dartmoor and *Bodmin Moor* (Cornwall), and among the northern hills. We must remember however that these areas were always remote and perhaps backward—and people may have continued in the old 'Bronze Age' way, even into the Iron Age.

'CELTIC' FIELDS

Alongside these early settlements, traces of 'fields', perhaps marked out by cleared boulders, can often be seen. These small, rather squarish or rectangular enclosures may be Bronze Age, or Iron Age. They are often called 'Celtic fields', although 'Celtic' properly describes a family of ancient languages. On some moorlands, such as the North York Moors, they are accompanied by clearance 'cairnfields'. At Grassington near *Malham* (N. Yorks) the limestone terraces preserve ancient ribs of stone walling, which are at least Iron Age and possibly earlier.

Celtic fields can also be seen on unploughed chalk downland, marked out by trackways and slight banks, such as on the slopes of Fyfield Down near the *Ridgeway* (Oxon) and below Barbury Castle, a hillfort nearby.

DEATH AND TERRITORY

As in the preceding Neolithic, some Bronze Age barrows seem to have marked family or tribal territory. On the *North York Moors*, for example, it seems that the Bronze Age settlements were placed down in the stream hollows surrounded by livestock paddocks, while paths led to higher cairnfields, cleared to give areas for ploughland. Above these were open moorland grazings, while on the highest ridges, the watersheds of the streams, the round barrows stand as territory markers. Similar patterns of communal landholdings would also have existed in the lowlands.

Standing and marked stones

Standing stones and decorated stones are evocative landscape features. They are usually early, often Bronze Age, although later examples are found.

STANDING STONES

A solitary standing stone is known as a monolith ('single stone'), or menhir from the Welsh or Cornish for 'long stone'. Solitary standing stones can be found in many parts of Britain, but they are commoner in the remoter, atmospheric countrysides of hills and moors: and few of man's symbols are as evocative as a stone standing wreathed in mist. There are some to be found in the lowlands, however.

Only excavation can show whether the monolith originally stood alone. It is often the survivor of a group, perhaps in the form of a circle, which has been plundered for local building. In fact a few are surviving Neolithic tombstones weathered free of the covering mound, their neighbours removed to be broken up for stone for walling and building.

A RITUAL COMPLEX

Tall, separate standing stones are sometimes found as part of a ritual complex, as at *Callanish* (Lewis, Western Isles). A solitary stone, called the King Stone, stands separate (across today's road) from the *Rollright Stones* (Oxon), and a solitary stone (now fallen) marks the end of one of the alignments of *Stanton Drew* (Avon). The tallest standing stone in Britain rears up in the churchyard at *Rudston* (Humberside). It is 25 ft high, and 6 by 3 ft at its base. Of gritstone, it must have come from at least 10 miles away. It appears solitary, but from the top of the church tower, in some lights, traces of Neolithic cursus avenues can be seen, seeming to lead to this great monolith.

'DEVIL'S ARROWS'

At *Boroughbridge* (N. Yorks) three massive 'Devil's Arrows' stand in a line about 120 yards long, running north–south. The tallest of these stones is 22 ft high, and the tops are deeply grooved, perhaps intentionally, although perhaps by natural weathering; they are of gritstone, which could weather in this odd way.

BOUNDARY MARKERS

Standing stones certainly made handy boundary markers in later times, but could that have been one of their original functions? Some Neolithic and Bronze Age barrows seem also to double as territory markers, and perhaps the monoliths acted in a similar way. These deep roots perhaps explain our British frenzy about the rights of walkers across private land. What is certain is that a considerable motive lay behind moving and raising a stone weighing many tons.

It may have been that these solitary standing stones were memorials or cenotaphs of a kind familiar today. Many of today's village war memorials consist of no more than a standing stone set with a plate carrying the names of the fallen.

STONE CROSSES

Some of these old standing stones were adopted in early Christian days, giving unexpected continuity to the countryside. *Blisland* (Cornwall) is one parish with prehistoric standing stones cut with the emblem of a cross, a step towards the wayside cross so common in medieval days. Such wayside crosses—although of modern date—are still a familiar sight in France. Sometimes a prehistoric standing stone seems actually to have been carved *in situ* as a cross; one such is the famous Benett's Cross near Warren Inn on *Dartmoor* (Devon).

In the Dark Ages, intricately carved 'Celtic' crosses became quite common, to judge from the many complete and fragmentary examples remaining in churchyards and stored in churches. Many older prehistoric standing stones must have been used by the masons of these later crosses.

CUP AND RING MARKS

Carving or marking stone is a very old tradition and some surprising examples can be seen throughout Britain. The Neolithic tomb of *Bryn Celli Ddu* (Anglesey) has a large stone slab decorated with zigzag designs, and a wallstone in the burial chamber has a spiral marking.

On *Ilkley Moor* (W. Yorks) and nearby sites lies a virtual National Gallery of prehistoric decorated stones, with various kinds of decoration to be seen here. Cup marks are round holes about 2 in. across, pecked into the rock. They are sometimes surrounded by rings of pecked dots. In some places these round marks seem to be tied into patterns or grids with ladders and straight lines. The swastika is also fairly common—it appears in many parts of the world as a symbol of good fortune (long before its adoption by the Nazis)—and here on Ilkley Moor it is spiralled rather than right-angled. On the famous Badger Stone a swastika is part of a design which covers one side of the boulder. Cup and ring marks are also to be found on *Doddington Moor* (Northumberland) and other places including Scotland.

These carefully made Neolithic and Bronze Age markings are not mere doodles, but there is no obvious explanation for them. One suggestion is that they imitate ornamental body tattoos; another that the act of engraving itself was of ritual meaning, a personal statement to the immutable stone—that is, to the unchanging universe. They are not 'pictures'.

POLISSOIRS

Some boulders have what are clearly rows of artificial grooves. They were used by passing warriors or traders to sharpen polished stone axes maybe, or Bronze Age axe heads or rapiers, or even medieval swords—they could have remained in use for centuries. A 'polissoir' can be found not far from the line of the Ridgeway path, on Overton Down near *Avebury* (Wilts).

THE PICTISH STONES

Marking stone with cup marks and spirals seems to have ended in Bronze Age times, but the custom of pecking designs into stone was renewed later in parts of Scotland. Here, mainly in the north-east, we find a group of 250 or so 'Pictish stones'. The Picts were among the tribes who faced the Romans, but they eventually lost mastery

to the Scots moving in from Northern Ireland. Before this, they produced these incredible stones. The earliest date from the 6th century AD and show, pecked into the surface, birds, animals and a weird 'Pictish beast' with elephant-like features, as well as emblems such as a double disc and z-shaped rod. Later stones also begin to show Christian symbols, and the latest of all carry only crosses and decoration. Some fine examples can be seen at *Aberlemno* (Tayside); a stone in the churchyard here, for example, has a highly decorated cross on one side, with a hunting scene and z rod and

The Picaldy Stone, one of the puzzling Pictish stones which may imitate tribal body tattoos.

discs on the other.

The symbols may be early heraldry. 'Picti' means 'painted men' and perhaps they portray their tattoos.

Stone circles and avenues

Stone circles became a feature of the Bronze Age, often raised within earlier earth banks. Many were linked with ritual stone avenues.

THE ORIGINS OF STONE CIRCLES

Crop marks have disclosed circles of great timber trunks, of late Neolithic or early Bronze Age date. Woodhenge, not far from *Stonehenge* (Wilts), is one example, another is marked out in the basement car park of a supermarket in *Dorchester* (Dorset). Whether these were ritual centres (and perhaps precursors of the stone circles) or large communal dwellings is not yet decided. They are of similar date to the stone circles.

Many stone circles were raised within the banks of the earlier, mysterious henges. There is perhaps nothing surprising in this, for a site once adopted as sacred has a tendency to remain so. But the addition of stone is certainly a clue that ritual had changed, perhaps a hint that stone itself had gained importance. The polished stone maces of Bronze Age date were certainly ceremonial, and the 82 'bluestones' of *Stonehenge* were brought from the Preseli Hills, 200 miles away in Dyfed, surely for ritual reasons.

RECOGNIZING A STONE CIRCLE

Stone circles vary from the diameter of a round barrow to 100 yards across. We rarely see the circle in anything like its original state, however. Very often stones have been robbed for local buildings; at some sites only a single stone remains. Many stones have fallen to lie flat (at the atmospheric site of *Arbor Low* (Derbyshire) it is thought that the 50 or more slabs were never raised). But it is sometimes safe to guess that, for example, the circle at *Keswick* (Cumbria) is complete with its 38 stones, although here too five of them have fallen.

Many stone 'circles' may have been the edging of a burial mound, now weathered away. The height of the stones is often a good clue: the 'Nine Stones' circle alongside the main road at Winterbourne Abbas west of *Dorchester* (Dorset) is only 9 yards across, the dimension of a barrow, but some of

its sarsens are man-high. On the other hand, Welsh circles tend to be made of small boulders and be of small diameter, 20–30 yards across, and Cornish stone circles are also often small.

VARIETIES OF CIRCLE

The thousand stone circles which remain in Britain have no master plan, or if they do they hide it well. Recognizing the original plan is often difficult, and often we are seeing more than one feature. *Stanton Drew* (Avon) is an example: here the original arrangement (although partly obscured by buildings today) can still be deciphered. The standing stones were arranged on two alignments. From a 'cove' of three stones (near the churchyard) a line can be drawn running north-east, which crosses the centre of a great 120-yard-diameter circle of 27 stones, most of them now fallen, and continues past this to the centre of a smaller circle. From these two circles stone avenues run eastwards towards the River Chew, meeting after a short while. The second alignment starts with a small circle more or less to the south of the great circle, crosses its centre, and then extends to a 7—ft stone (now fallen) $\frac{1}{4}$ mile away to the north.

THE ORIGINS OF THE STONE

Stone to hand is generally used, although the *Stonehenge* bluestones are from far away. As we see at *Ashdown House* (Oxon), handy sarsens lay scattered in some parts of these chalk downs, and stone was always to hand in the uplands. The circle of *Arbor Law* (Derbyshire) was quarried from limestone pavement nearby.

The stones seem sometimes roughly dressed, perhaps only on the inside face. At *Avebury* (Wilts) rather rectangular straight stones seem to alternate with kite-shaped stones. The significance of this, if any, is unknown.

THE COVE

Many stone circles have additional features. Imagination snatches at the idea of flat sacrificial altar stones, but these are often just toppled uprights. Some circles have a solitary standing

stone, perhaps central. Others have a box-like enclosure or 'cove' within but at one side of the circle. At *Keswick* (Cumbria) the cove is made up with ten standing stones.

AVENUES OF STONE

Stone avenues are as puzzling as the circles, and sometimes they are united in one monument, as at *Stanton Drew* (Avon). They are often of a single run of stones, but as often double, and clearly processional ways. However, that at Merrivale on *Dartmoor*, although 200 yards long, is far too narrow for this use. One clue may come from Corsica, where some stones of prehistoric rows are carved with an axe or other symbol, as if they represented people. Perhaps the alternate rectangular and kite-shaped stones in the avenue at *Avebury* (Wilts) represented male and female heroes or gods.

MULTIPLE USES

What is probable is that these ritual centres, like village churches, had no single use but many, and perhaps evolved with time. *Callanish* (Lewis, Western Isles) is an example. Here there is a 16 ft central slab with near its foot a small chambered tomb, with a circle of 13 slabs set around to face the centre. From this radiate a double stone avenue (northwards) and shorter single stone rows to east, south and west. The tomb is Neolithic, the rest Bronze Age.

Many apparently simple circles are not true circles, but slightly oval and this may not be accidental if (as some think) these stones were not simply aligned on sunsets and such things, but were also used for the prediction of the movements of sun, moon and stars. Many of the stone circles in north-east Scotland, for example, rise in height towards the south-west. Ritual dates are often calendar-linked, as is Easter today, and the alignments of the circles might well link sun and moon rhythms in some way.

THE MYSTERY OF THE STONES

The original use of these atmospheric places is lost, but they have attracted many legends and myths, and although much has been invented by Victorian antiquarians, slight echoes of the past might remain. The *Rollright Stones* (Oxon) consist of a 30-yard-diameter stone circle called 'The King's Men' with the solitary tall 'King Stone' (what remains of a Neolithic tomb) a few yards away. A quarter of a mile away are the 'Whispering Knights'—a Neolithic dolmen. Legend has it that the stones were a king and his men petrified by a witch, who every night carry the capstone of the dolmen down the hill to bridge a stream. The avenues at *Stanton Drew* certainly lead to a stream, as does the avenue at *Stonehenge* (and that at Avebury heads in that direction). The avenue leading to water might echo pilgrimage.

A depiction of the three circles and the two avenues at Stanton Drew (Avon) as they appear today, with most of the stones fallen.

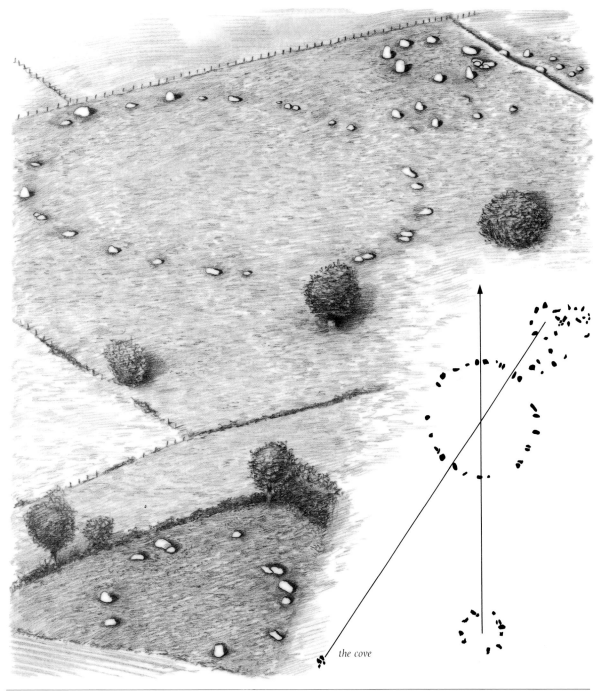

the cove

The great ritual centres

The stone circles to be found at Stonehenge and Avebury were the focus of great rituals whose significance can only be guessed at today.

THE RITUAL SETTING OF STONEHENGE

Both *Stonehenge* and *Avebury* (Wilts) are cathedrals of prehistory, magnificent in conception and in size. There is much more at those two places than the circles themselves, however. The landscape within 2 miles of Stonehenge contains more in the way of prehistoric remains than any similar area in Britain. Some are still prominent, others have been reduced by ploughing, or even gone, to remain only as crop marks. The features include Neolithic long barrows and Bronze Age round barrow cemeteries, a Neolithic causewayed camp and to the north a Neolithic cursus. Two miles to the north-east is a vast henge known as Durrington Walls with Woodhenge (see pp. 42–43) nearby — both all but destroyed — and flint mines not far off. From Stonehenge itself an earth-banked avenue loops to

Stonehenge as many remember it — dramatically lit and keeping its ancient secrets close.

the River Avon, although much of it is today ploughed out.

THE SETTING OF AVEBURY

Avebury lags not far behind Stonehenge; the site (much larger overall) is certainly as impressive, if in a different way. The countryside round about also has many barrows; and the famous causewayed camp on Windmill Hill is quite close. From the great earth banks a stone avenue leads southwards in the direction of the Sanctuary. Indicated today by concrete markers, the Sanctuary once had rings of timber and stone and may (like Woodhenge) have been a communal dwelling. The magnificent West Kennet Neolithic chambered tomb is not far off; and nearby towers the massive tump of Silbury Hill.

THE EVOLUTION OF THE MONUMENTS

Both Stonehenge and Avebury originated with henge monuments — a slight circular bank in the first case, a massive one in the second. Both went through puzzling stages, and we must remember that we see them today in part collapsed, in part destroyed, robbed for their stone.

STONEHENGE

This is usually interpreted in four stages. Phase I was a late-Neolithic henge, dated to 2200 BC, consisting of a circular bank perhaps 6 ft high (it is now only 2 ft high), and (unusually) inside its ditching. The entrance was to the north-east, facing the Heel Stone which was raised at that time. Within the bank were a circle of 56 'Aubrey holes', named after their discoverer, of unknown function. Phase II followed in 1700 BC, when Beaker — Bronze Age people built a banked avenue running to the north-east and (if theories are correct) heaved the 4-ton 'bluestones' up from the River Avon nearby. The large stones were quarried in the Preseli Hills (Dyfed) and presumably brought here by raft, by sea and via the river. Some were raised to start creating a double circle inside the henge, but the task was never finished. A circular ditch was dug around the Heel

Stone at this time, and the monument as a whole was now (and thereafter) clearly aligned on the midsummer sunrise.

STONEHENGE'S LATER PHASES

Phase III followed during the years 1600–1200 BC. The standing bluestones were uprooted and 45-ton sarsens brought from 20 miles away. Thirty sarsen uprights crafted into shape and topped with lintels made a circle, within which were five pairs of similar stones in a horseshoe. 'Station' stones were also raised inside the bank. Some of the bluestones were set up as an oval within the horseshoe, while holes were dug for a double circle of them between the sarsen circle and the bank. But this plan was also scrapped and instead these cantankerous stones were erected as a circle within the sarsen circle and as a horseshoe within the sarsen horseshoe, where some remain today. Finally, in Phase IV, the avenue was extended in a curve down to the River Avon.

One remaining mystery is the 'Altar Stone'. Although not a bluestone, it too came from Dyfed, not from Preseli but from Milford Haven on the route from the hills. It was once upright, as was the 'Slaughter Stone', which was once one of a pair at the entrance in the earth bank.

AVEBURY

The Avebury bank and ditch is more impressive than that of the Stonehenge henge, holding half a village. Although still tall, it is slumped and silted; its bank once rose 55 ft above its ditch bottom. Like most henges, the ditch is inside the bank, not defensive and perhaps rather to 'keep the devils in'. A stone circle runs by the ditch, originally of 98 massive sarsens brought from the downs nearby.

Within this circle were two smaller circles — again many stones are missing but their positions are shown by concrete markers. The north circle had 27 stones, and an inner ring of 12. At its centre three large stones made a u-shaped 'cove', of the type still seen at *Stanton Drew* (Avon). The southern

circle had 39 stones, and at its centre a monolith stood 21 ft tall. South of this circle was a 'Ring Stone' with a hole through the top.

Although the stones at Stonehenge are neatly squared, those at Avebury seem only to have been slightly smoothed on the inner facing side. What escapes the casual glance is the fact that they seem to alternate around the circles, diamond-shaped stones with straighter pillars.

DESTRUCTION OF THE STONES

William Stukeley, an 18th-century antiquarian, noted the now-lost central monolith and Ring Stone mentioned above. He and other early antiquarians waxed bitter about the destruction of these monuments, vandalism which was then in full spate. Local farmers, sometimes egged on by the church wanting to destroy these 'works of the devil', were pulling them down, and splitting them with fire.

SILBURY HILL

Silbury Hill near *Avebury* (Wilts) is a mystery of international scale. It is the largest prehistoric mound in Europe, covering over 5 acres and 130 ft high, and is the most massive monument to tribal organization in Neolithic times. It must have taken 18 million man-hours to raise: 1000 men working eight hours a day, seven days a week for at least six years. Or, as some think of these Neolithic monuments, fewer people but working generation after generation at the same task.

Excavation has found no trace of a burial, but tunnels show that it evolved in four stages, starting with a small mound at the centre of a round, fenced enclosure, dated to around 2000 BC. The third stage of enlargement produced a cone rising in steps — the top step is still just noticeable, but the others were filled in to produce smooth slopes in the final stage. Furthermore, it stands in a shallow vale to the south of Avebury and is actually out of sight of the stone circles. This means, adding to the speculation, that its top lies at about the height of the distant horizon when approached from Avebury.

Hilltop forts

The Iron Age, which lasted from about 700 BC until the Roman invasion in AD 43, left gigantic ramparted strongholds as its main legacy to the landscape.

HILLTOP CAMPS

The Iron Age, a period usually dated from around 700 BC until the Roman invasion in AD 43, was marked by more than the use of that metal. Societies underwent great change and there seem to have been forceful waves of immigration from Europe. There had been signs of territorial stress at the end of the Bronze Age when some hilltops were fortified; one was Mam Tor, the 'shivering mountain' near *Castleton* (Derbyshire). But the Iron Age has imprinted its massive hilltop fortresses—called 'camp', 'fort' or 'castle' on the maps—across the countryside, hinting at suspicious kingdoms and endless bickering. Wessex has a great many hillforts and the largest, but they are found from Carn Brea in furthest Cornwall to *Wandlebury* near Cambridge. *Old Oswestry* (Shropshire) is a fine example. They are found in Wales—*Tre'r Ceri* hillfort (Gwynedd), for example—and the north. There is even one on top of *Ingleborough* (N. Yorks). There are many hillforts in Scotland: ramparts and the hut circles lying within them on the *Eildon Hills* (Borders) are best seen from Scott's famous viewpoint. In all more than a thousand remain scattered throughout Britain.

RAMPARTS

There is no single pattern for these Iron Age forts, but they are unmistakable. The smallest are an acre or so, but most are much larger. Unlike later Roman camps (which might also have a rampart), they are often difficult to approach, usually being on hilltops or sharp spurs of higher ground, taking every advantage of the contours. Although a neck of land flanked by natural cliffs might be cut off with a bank, more usually an entire hilltop or dominant knoll is embraced. The ramparts are sometimes single, but often double or even triple, especially if the natural rise is slight, as at Maiden Castle near *Dorchester* (Dorset). We see

them slumped: originally the sides were sheer and faced with timbers or stone slabs or sometimes drystone walling. The defences of *Cissbury* (W. Sussex), which encloses 60 acres, had 35,000 cubic yards of piled chalk and 12,000 timber uprights.

THE GATEWAY

Unlike the earlier ritual henges, these hilltop forts were dug defensively with the bank *inside* and towering over its ditch. The entrance, however, was more vulnerable and it is interesting to see what special precautions have been taken with the gateways (for there is often more than one). The ramparts are often doubled up, so that the path dog-legs between them, leaving the attackers' flanks open to the defenders. These, armed with spears, bows and sling stones shot like bullets, could put up a fierce defence. Piles of beach stones for slinging were found when Maiden Castle was excavated. At *Llanaelhaearn* (Gwynedd) one gateway still has its overhead stone lintel in its original position.

THE FORTS' FINAL DAYS

They each have their own story. The Romans took some: Maiden Castle has yielded a skeleton speared by an arrow and other evidence of the last battle, but others had been deserted and become scrubbed up by then. In Roman times most of them stood deserted, although *Cadbury Castle* (Som) seems to have been the centre of a revolt for a while. Though deserted, they would have been used as cattle corals and by shepherds. A few were again brought into defensive use in the Dark Ages and Norman times. Cadbury Castle became a Dark Age stronghold, with a timber 'palace' built within it. *Old Sarum* (Wilts), the original city of Salisbury, had Norman fortifications added to the ramparts and a cathedral within.

THE PUZZLE OF THE FORTS' USE

Although their ramparts give them a family similarity, excavation has shown differences in the way hilltop forts were used. Many enclosed huts, but most seem to have been refuges for

men and cattle rather than permanent settlements—water supply would have been a problem on a hilltop. Farming intensified in Iron Age times: the Bronze Age 'Celtic' fields often still seen on the high ground of downs and moors remained in use, but farmsteads also spread across the valleys below, and grain harvests seemed to have become much more important than before. The farmsteads and many of the hilltop forts were dotted with pits, which when lined with wickerwork and capped with clay made frost- and rat-proof grain stores (the grain would have had to be roasted in a kiln first to prevent it germinating). There is also evidence of buildings raised on timber legs which may also have been granaries. Some forts were so packed with

A bird's-eye view gives a true picture of the ramparts of Maiden Castle (Dorset).

pits and granaries that they were possibly tribal tribute stores.

FORTS ON THE MAP

It is worth seeing where the camp's neighbours are. Liddington and Barbury Castle are just two of a line of forts set a few miles apart along the *Ridgeway* (Oxon). This is rather close if they were at odds with each other, but sensible if they each controlled a tract of grazing on the downs behind and farmsteads in the vale below. What is surprising is the fact that small areas of country could supply the labour to build these massive forts, and this may be the clue to a very different explanation of their purpose. Namely, rather than being refuges for local people, they were or became later in Iron Age times (when chariots came into use) a kingdom-wide network for mobile cohorts of charioteers, to be used only

at need. But maybe both explanations hold good.

FARMS AND FIELDS

Crop marks show that lowland Britain was well settled by the later Iron Age. Large, round timber huts were common, set within a stockade; one such farmstead has been reconstructed at *Butser Hill* (Hants), a fascinating place, and others can be seen at *Chalfont St Peter* (Bucks). Crop marks also show that the ploughlands and pastures were often reached by ditched trackways. In the wetlands, farmsteads or even villages were built on platforms of timber and brushwood; one has been excavated near *Glastonbury* (Som).

Remote areas were not excluded, and here we can find settlements undisturbed by later centuries. At *Chysauster (Cornwall)* an Iron Age village of round 'courtyard' houses

survives—the well-drained stone rooms opening to courtyards lack only their thatched roofs. Similar relics can be found on walks in Wales, the Lakes and Scotland (see pp. 152–153). At Carn Euny near *Madron* (Cornwall) one hut has a hidden cellar or 'fogou', a feature also of Scotland.

BURIAL

Far fewer Iron Age burials can be seen than from the previous Bronze Age, but some (both burials and cremations) were under round barrows which remain today. In the southeast, before the Roman invasion but when links with the Roman province of Gaul were strong, there were 'cemeteries' of cremations buried in urns. Nonetheless, a few princely graves have been found with iron buckets, chariots, bronze mirrors and other ornamental riches.

Hill figures

Hill figures are intriguing landscape features. Two or three may well be of Iron Age date, but others are definitely later, as is clear from what they depict.

THE UFFINGTON WHITE HORSE

High chalk downlands provide a wonderful natural sketchbook, for the shallow turf is easily stripped off to make gleaming white patterns to be seen from miles away. This must have been the thinking behind that famous hill figure, the White Horse, that races by the *Ridgeway* (Oxon). Over 100 yards long and cut in the brow of the hill, it is best seen from far beyond the village of Uffington, which gives it its name (and best of all from the air!).

UFFINGTON CASTLE

Near the Uffington horse curve the ramparts of Uffington Castle, a small Iron Age hillfort, and it is natural to assume that they are related and of the same age. Hillforts also seem to be associated with other ancient hill figures (below). The war lords of the late Iron Age were charioteers, and per-haps this Uffington horse was a tribal emblem. Its graceful lines echo decorative figures found on Iron Age shields and other metalwork. Close by is a flat-topped hill, today called Dragon Hill, separated from the horse by a dry combe called the Manger.

THE ORIGINAL SHAPE

It is said that during the scouring ceremonies cheeses were rolled and chased down the Manger as part of the fun. And yet no chalk figure could last more than a few years without scouring, for grass quickly invades. Would today's figure be anything like the original of 2000 or more years ago? Tradition says that the horse has crept uphill, as would happen with frequent scouring, for rain tends to wash fragments of soil down to provide a bed for new grass at the bottom of any bare area. Aerial photos show a darker, perhaps new area of grass below its belly. There were traces of a saddle when it was sketched in 1796, and here we have another clue. Pictures scratched on pottery of the late Iron Age, a horsey culture, have been found, showing a horse carrying a phallus on its back, a key to fertility ceremonies. In past times Oxford undergraduates were forbidden to attend the seven-yearly Whitsuntide scouring of the Uffington horse, because of the lustful fair held within the ramparts of the hillfort nearby.

THE RED HORSE

Another old horse was known as the Red Horse of Tysoe near Banbury (Oxon), so coloured by the underlying soil. There is some evidence that it was present in the 15th century, as local legend had it commemorating an Earl of Warwick's horse killed in battle.

But it could have been far older, because folk tales always tend to attach themselves to features already existing in the landscape.

OTHER HILLSIDE HORSES

Seventeen hillside horses can be seen today, of which eleven are on southern

Chalk-cut figures.

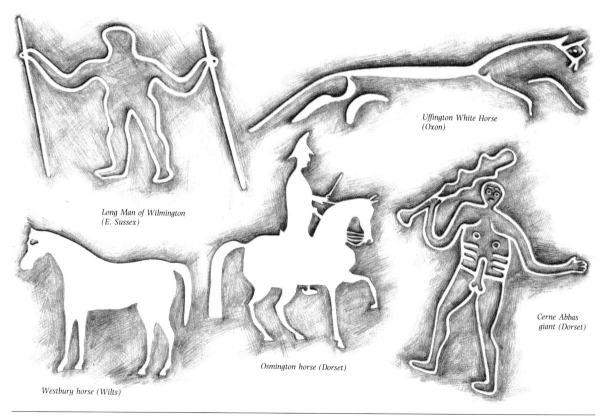

Uffington White Horse
(Oxon)

Long Man of Wilmington
(E. Sussex)

Cerne Abbas
giant (Dorset)

Osmington horse (Dorset)

Westbury horse (Wilts)

chalk downlands. One or two of those further north are whited with stone chippings. Uffington apart, they are comparatively recent however, most being of 18th or 19th century date, when it was fashionable to embellish the landscape with folly towers and other eyecatchers. They are all much more 'modern' in style than the Uffington horse. However, at *Westbury* (Wilts), diaries and other records suggest that an older horse was destroyed when today's was cut in 1778. An Iron Age hillfort, Bratton Castle, lies nearby, suggesting that this original was, like Uffington, perhaps of Iron Age date.

THE ANCIENT GIANTS

The chalk-cut 180 ft giant on a hillside at *Cerne Abbas* (Dorset) is unmistakably phallic. A small ramparted enclosure of Iron Age date, called the Trundle, lies near the head. The figure faces out from the slope (the face is marked) and holds a giant club in its right hand (the left facing the observer). Its left arm is extended but empty, and turf probing suggests an outline once hung from it. If it were a lion skin, the figure was a version of the Roman god Hercules.

Some claim that in dry winters when the grass is thin, and with a very low angle of sun to cast shadows into slight hollows, they have seen a dog to the left of the giant's right leg—that is, below the bottom of the club. The figure is now fenced in, however, and the different grass textures within and without the fence would tend to obscure such things.

As with the Uffington horse, celebrations—(originally fertility rites) —were held in the Trundle in recent centuries.

The *Long Man of Wilmington* (E. Sussex) at 230 ft is the tallest human figure in Europe. It stands astride, presumably face outwards (the face is not marked), and holding an upright staff in each hand. Some say that these are the portals to Heaven, or that the figure represents a medieval pilgrim. However, Roman coins found nearby also pictured such a figure, and it too may be of late Iron Age date. Unlike

regimental badges, Fovant (Wilts)

YMCA badge

Wye Crown (Kent)

Whiteleaf Cross (Bucks)

Some more recent hillside ornaments.

the others, this figure is often in the shadow of the hill slope, although this is possibly of no significance.

LOST FIGURES

By probing the depth of soil below the turf, one Cambridge don claimed to find forgotten figures including a club-carrying giant on the Gog Magog Hills, at *Wandlebury* (Cambs). The site is now planted with trees, but among the supporting evidence is the name Gog (which means giant), the nearby Iron Age hillfort of Wandlebury Camp, and a figure of a giant with a club scratched up on a pillar in the church at Babraham, within sight of the slopes. As at Uffington, university undergraduates were forbidden to attend merrymaking in the hillfort.

There may be many more now hidden from us.

OTHER CHALK-CUT FIGURES

A chalk-cut cross and a cone on the slopes of the Chiltern Hills at Princes Risborough (Bucks) and Watlington may perhaps be medieval, although

some argue that they could be pagan phallic symbols 'improved' in Christian times. It seems that the young Church very often adopted pagan sites (in fact many churches are built on earlier ritual centres) and pagan customs, adapting them to suit its own symbolism and beliefs.

There is endless speculation about these chalk-cut figures. Some even propose that the Uffington horse was not a tribal symbol to others across the vale but cut to send a message out to spacemen (as noted above, today's figure is most easily seen in its entirety from the air).

More seriously, part of the magnetism of these figures is the tantalizing uncertainty about their origins. However, there can be no doubt about the army badges cut into the chalk at *Fovant* (Wilts). They are firmly of this century.

However old they are, hill figures are a unique part of the British landscape.

Roman rule

The Roman occupation of AD 43–425 left a staggering variety of surface and concealed remains, many of which are marked on OS maps.

ROMAN REMAINS

Britain was invaded by Rome in AD 43, but the occupation was not a simple matter of four legions coming, seeing and conquering as Caesar had boasted on his foray in 55 BC. Britain was a medley of tribal kingdoms, all 'Iron Age' by culture but differing in wealth and power and some already familiar with Roman life through trade and contact with Roman Gaul. The invasion was accepted in some areas, bitterly fought in others and even after some years there were uprisings, of which Queen Boudicca's (Boadicea) is best known.

Rome gripped the country not to suck it dry, nor simply to fill it with its own men, retired legionaries and others (although many did settle here). The aim was to create a well-managed country yielding taxes and corn, slaves and metals for Rome. Gold was one lure and a Roman mine can be visited at *Dolaucothi* (Dyfed). But the Roman remains we see were spawned of 400 years of changing conditions, and their sheer variety is staggering. Here the Ordnance Survey maps are a great help, because most (not all) known remains appear. Most visible Roman remains consist of slumped ramparts and weathered lengths of rubble wall. Unlike those of earlier times, however, they are often wardened, and tickets have to be bought. But there is still plenty to be discovered on walks.

FORTS AND FORTRESSES

The legions, essential to the policing of the province, were established at legionary fortresses such as Caerleon, *Newport* (Gwent), where barrack blocks are traced. These were linked with other forts, some of which later became native tribal centres. *Caerwent* (Gwent) was one of these, and although small had a forum, shrines and rows of shops whose lines have been excavated. At *Wroxeter* (Shropshire) an incredible slab of wall from the baths still stands tall.

Regional forts were key sites. Some on the turbulent frontiers, such as *Hardknott* (Cumbria) make evocative visits. *Ribchester* (Lancs) was typical, a 5-acre fort, now partly removed by the river (always potentially interesting for new exposures!). Its Roman well is worth a detour, as is its packed museum.

Many forts were quite modest, their defences perhaps only of turf ramparts topped by a palisade and with a strong, timber gatehouse. One that was perhaps raised against Queen Boudicca has been partly reconstructed at *Baginton* (Warks).

At the end of Roman rule a line of strong rubble-walled forts was built along the 'Saxon shore' against the threat of these pirates. Their walls with

rounded bastions are sometimes still spectacular, as at *Portchester* (Hants) where they remain 20 ft high, *Richborough* (Kent) and *Burgh Castle* (Norfolk).

THE ROMAN WALLS

The sturdy, stone-built *Roman (Hadrian's) Wall* crossing from Carlisle to Newcastle with its serving camps and roads is almost too well known to deserve mention, but always worth a visit, especially those stretches which mount the crags of volcanic whin sill rock. Equally worth visiting is the *Antonine Wall* (Central), which marks another point in history. Running west from the Firth of Forth, it was built of turf, with defensive pits which would have been lined with sharpened stakes. It can still be well seen at Bonnybridge where a fort is built up

Hadrian's Wall still strides impressively across the empty moorlands of the North Pennines.

against it, and beacon mounds for signalling stand nearby. The defensive ditches of one of its outpost forts at *Ardoch* make one of the most spectacular of all Roman sites.

ROMAN TOWNS

In time separate market towns were established, at first walled—and the walls remain standing proud among open fields at *Silchester* (Hants). Very often the presence of those walls is only remembered as 'chester' in today's name, from the Latin *castrum* meaning fortified place. Usually today's streets engulf the site and their earlier history is buried to cellar level and only accidentally revealed. Modern streets may, however, clearly follow the neatly squared Roman grid, as they do at *Dorchester* (Dorset). But many originally Roman towns offer a slight relic of some kind, perhaps no more than a short length of wall, or the decorative pavement of a Roman town house in its original site as in *Dorchester*; the theatre is one of the prized features at *St Albans* (Herts).

THE ROMAN ROADS

The key to Roman occupation was the road system. In the frontier upland regions the roads were probably always maintained more for army than civilian use, but in the lowlands they became the key to the gradual ordering of the whole countryside. Although in the lowlands the famous roads are followed more often by mapwork than by actual traces (see pp. 120–121), in the uplands lengths of surface do remain—for example, at Wheeldale Moor on the *North York Moors* and at *Blackstone Edge* (Lancs).

THE VILLA

The sites of more than a thousand villas are known; and some are nationally famous, excavated and with colourful mosaic pavements, hypocausts (underfloor heating systems), and other features on view. Among the most impressive are *North Leigh* (Oxon), which has a splendid mosaic exposed, and its plan of wings extending around a courtyard with a bath suite in one corner clear to see, and

Lullingstone (Kent). The villa at Beadlam near *Helmsley* (N. Yorks) is one of the few in the north open to the public. *Fishbourne* (W. Sussex) was virtually a palace, and was possibly the reward for a Celtic king who accepted the Roman invasion. Among other interests, its garden has been reconstructed from the original bedding trenches.

FINDING VILLAS

Although villas were substantially built, nothing usually remains above ground; what remains of the walls is only exposed by excavation. They were looted but ignored by the incoming Saxon flood, who preferred their own timber settlements. In the lowlands they became overgrown, and in time covered by soil, now quite deep in many areas. However, the walls and plans can be detected by crop marks. They are often located by scatters of pottery and broken tiling noticed in the fields after ploughing (see pp. 32–33). Another clue is a generous scatter of oyster shells across the ploughland (or dug up by rabbits on pasture)—oysters seem to have been extremely popular with the Romans, although they were also enjoyed in medieval times. Red Roman tiling or brickwork a couple of inches thick, built into the Saxon or Norman walls of a nearby church, is another clue.

OVERLAPPING CULTURES

The villas were the centres of great farm estates, and almost the whole of the good lowland ploughland was by then being farmed and with better ploughs. The Romans also set about draining the fens and other wetlands to gain their rich soil. *Reach Lode* (Cambs) was originally a Roman dyke offering access to the Wash but also draining the land around.

The shape the farmed land took is not clear. There is scant evidence of Roman fields (see pp. 58–59), but it is likely that Iron Age patterns continued, with small fenced and ditched enclosures around the huts, and tracks now leading to the new Roman roads. Many remote Iron Age settlements such as *Chysauster* (Cornwall) continued little changed.

Dark Ages ditches and parishes

The Dark Ages, which followed the Roman withdrawal, were a time of warring kingdoms. Today's parishes had their roots in those six centuries.

CROSS-COUNTRY DITCHES

Scattered across Britain's countryside are lengths of bank accompanied by the ditch from which they were dug. Some merely cut off a bluff of hills. Others trail for miles across farmland; these are often marked on the Ordnance Survey maps, and often with the name Grim's Ditch or Grim's Dyke, even where ploughing has left little more than a shadow of a bump and hollow running across the ground. Where erosion or the plough has been at work, the slight hollow that remains of the ditch often outlives traces of the bank. But many remain massive; the bank of *Wansdyke* (Wilts) is still more than twice a man's height. A few of these banks and ditches in remote *Dartmoor* (Devon), the *North York Moors* and elsewhere are probably Bronze Age territory boundaries. Others were dug in lower country to protect Iron Age centres—the valley counterpart to the great hilltop camps—as are seen in the rolling Essex countryside near Colchester, for example.

DITCHES OF THE DARK AGES

The most impressive ditches date from the centuries-long Dark Ages which followed the withdrawal of the Roman legions in AD 425. Britain and its people were abandoned to face the threat of the 'Saxons'—Angles, Saxons and Jutes who stormed and settled the land from Northern Europe. Danes too followed in their turn. During these tumultuous years Britain broke up into warring kingdoms, and the great ditches were perhaps dug as their frontiers. They were, however, hardly defensive: although a great dyke stretching miles across country would take much labour to dig and reflects great social organization, it was difficult to defend. The Romans only managed to maintain the line of Hadrian's Wall with a disciplined, well-serviced regular army and lines of forts.

The *Wansdyke* (Wilts) strides across the open prairie fields of today's downland, as formidable a landmark as Hadrian's Wall. Far to the west, Offa's Dyke matches it in grandeur, running as a frontier between Wales and England. Offa's Dyke adapts itself to the geography; near its start in the south, a length of ditch is even cut out of solid rock. Some lengths of bank have gone, but one impressive section can be seen on an expedition from *Knighton* (Powys) running towards Clun.

THE CLUE OF THE NAMES

The name Grim's Ditch or Grim's Dyke is a clue to the origin of many of these features. Grim, from a Dark Ages word meaning disguise, was a nickname for the god Woden, who often appeared in masquerade. The Saxon dynasties traced their descent from Woden and so Wansdyke (Woden's dyke) and the many Grim's ditches more or less mean 'Royal ditch'. The common name Devil's Ditch is medieval, but also refers back to that pagan god.

Offa, however, was a mortal, a king of Mercia, a kingdom which fronted Wales. His 80-mile-long ditch faces west and the Welsh (that is, its bank is usually to the east of the ditch) but in fact it ran along only half his border. Perhaps his death in AD 796 came before his plans were completed.

DITCHES AND MAPWORK

Names yield another insight near *Reach* (Cambs) on the fenland edge. From here the massive Devil's Ditch or Dyke runs for 7 miles away from the wetlands. Not far away, shorter cousins run parallel. The words 'ley' or 'leigh' as part of a village, farm or even field name usually indicate a forest clearing, and by plotting them locally it is clear that the Devil's Ditch and its cousins ran from the impenetrable fenland to the edge of uncleared forest and were dug to block the open route of the Icknield Way, the ancient track from East Anglia (see pp. 116–117).

DARK AGES SETTLEMENTS

Less is known about Dark Age times than others. Sometimes Iron Age forts were reoccupied, as at *Cadbury* (Som).

Roman towns and villas were plundered and left to squatters, the bulk of the immigrants seeming to prefer timber dwellings of the kind reconstructed at the open-air museums at *Singleton* (W. Sussex) and *Avoncroft* (Hereford & Worcs). Kings were buried under barrows or cairns, such as that on Dunmail Raise in the Lake District. A few lesser mounds, much like Bronze Age bowl barrows, may mark the graves of individual warriors of this time. The Viking influence was strong in the *Isle of Man* and other northern areas.

THE BURGHS

Out of those troubled times the Christian English nation was forged. A key here was the success of King Alfred, who decisively defeated the Danes at *Edington* (Wilts) in AD 878, and created a network of burghs, or fortified towns, across his kingdom, each with a massive fenced rampart, and a Roman-neat grid of streets within. *Wallingford* (Oxon) was one of these; its massive banks can still be seen. But note that *burgh*, a Saxon word for any fortified site, is common in many other place-names.

THE ORIGINS OF THE PARISH

It was in these tumultuous years that parishes began to take shape. Christianity had begun to gain ground at the end of Roman times, but was then pushed back by pagan Saxons to small monastic settlements. Although renewed by St Augustine's mission, heathen Danish incursions again cut it back, and it was not until after King Alfred's victory that the Church, and church building, were put on a sound footing (see pp. 60–61).

From early minsters ('mother churches') the priests travelled to hold services at village or wayside crosses. But in time the thegns (petty lords) also built small wooden churches and it was these that evolved into parish churches. The parish originated with the Saxon lord's estate: his house with church nearby, his land and that of his tenants and serfs.

PARISH BOUNDARIES

Parish boundaries are marked on Ordnance Survey maps, and it is always worth exploring them. In the days before maps, such boundaries had to be fixed by features already existing in the landscape, natural features such as streams and the crests of high ground, and artificial features such as standing stones and burial mounds which might still remain today. The boundaries often follow lengths of a Grim's Ditch or a stretch of Roman road. All this explains why the boundary usually rambles or zigzags across country, with the lines of later fields coming up neatly on each side.

The boundary, being no man's land, is often marked by a tangled old hedge (see pp. 70–71), sometimes a double hedge. Frequently a patch of wood will be found to lie along one side of a boundary only. If so, it is probably the remaining fragment of ancient extensive woodlands which have been completely cleared from the neighbouring parish on the boundary line.

Reading the parish boundary.

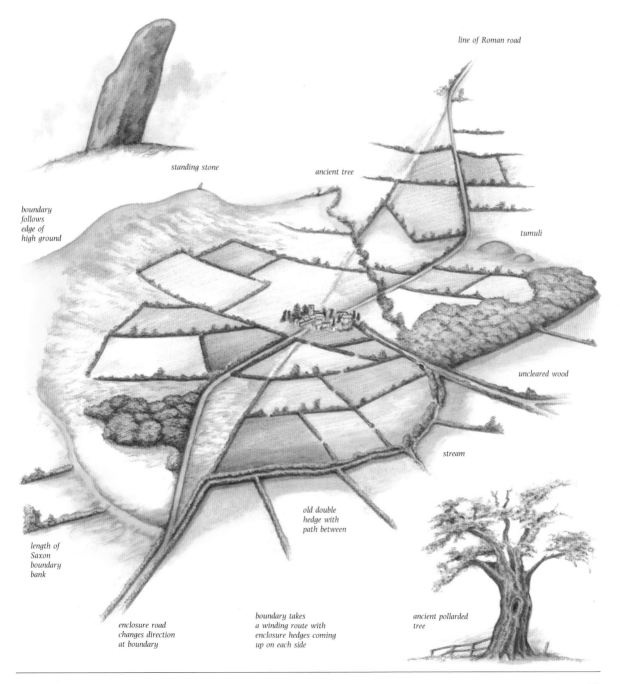

line of Roman road

standing stone

ancient tree

boundary
follows
edge of
high ground

tumuli

uncleared wood

stream

old double
hedge with
path between

length of
Saxon
boundary
bank

enclosure road
changes direction
at boundary

boundary takes
a winding route with
enclosure hedges coming
up on each side

ancient pollarded
tree

The smith's craft

Even in the Stone Age the land was being crossed by pedlars bartering stone axes and tools. In time, metal smiths followed in their footsteps.

STONE AXE FACTORIES

We cannot know about the quarrels of day-to-day life, but the absence of fortified settlements in Neolithic times suggests fairly peaceful times. The land was certainly not crowded: it is estimated that there were one million people in Britain at the start of the Bronze Age around 2000 BC. It was only towards 1000 BC, near the end of the Bronze Age, that land hunger seemed to have brought prolonged clashes, for it was now that a few hilltops were fortified for the first time with deep ditches and steep banks. However, the heroes of the previous centuries of the Bronze Age had been buried under their barrows accompanied by magnificent axes, rapiers and daggers.

Whether the land was peaceful or not, even Neolithic men had extensive webs of contact.

Stone axes are one clue. Although flint tools were popular, axes could also be made of other stone, and close-grained volcanic stone from the Langdale Pikes in the Lake District (Cumbria) and from the high crags of Graig Llwyd, *Penmaenmawr* (Gwynedd) was favoured. The axes were roughed out here (chippings are easy to find) and taken away to be smoothed and polished with sand and water. They were transported along the dry ridgeway routes that were now becoming important.

FLINT MINES

Flint rather than stone was by far the commonest material in use. And so strong were the trade links in early times that mining centres were established, where top-quality flint was mined deep from the chalk, free from frost cracks and other blemishes.

One centre was at *Grimes Graves* (Norfolk), where shafts were dug and expanded as sideways galleries to follow the flint seams. Red deer antlers were used as 'picks' which were hammered home with stones. They still carry fingerprints. The area is today pitted with collapsed shafts but one has been opened for visitors and makes an unforgettable visit. Similar flint mines are known at *Cissbury* (W. Sussex), above the Long Man of *Wilmington* (E. Sussex) and other places.

WORKED FLINT

Flint is easily fractured but a man-made fracture is usually clearly recognizable (see pp. 32–33) from one caused by accidental knocks and tumbles or frost. Hence the importance of flint flakes as signposts to camp-sites and other settlements in Stone Age and also Bronze Age times, for the use of chipped flint arrowheads and other tools continued. A scatter of worked flakes is easy enough to recognize when turned up by the plough.

GOLD

Grains and even nuggets of gold could be washed from the gravels of mountain streams and other alluvial deposits in the granite countryside of the west. Judging from the ancient legend of the Golden Fleece, the gold might have been sieved out by entangling it in wool in some way, but 'panning' must have been an early method in use. The fine shingle from a stream is swirled in a shallow bowl to separate the grains, and when stilled the heavier gold particles settle first. Gold has a low melting-point, and the metal grains were easy to fuse and hammer out into sheets and ornaments. Gold ornaments have been found in graves dating from the dawn of the Bronze Age.

British streams have now been largely 'washed out', although gold specks can still be found in some (private) streams joining the River Helmsdale in Sutherland (Highland).

By tradition, royal wedding rings are made from Welsh gold mined at Clogau. The Romans mined gold in Wales—a Roman gold mine can be visted at *Dolaucothi* (Dyfed).

COPPER

The discovery that copper could be obtained by heating its ore on a

The atmospheric galleries of the Neolithic flint mines of Grimes Graves (Norfolk).

hearth, and that a mixture of copper and tin yielded the malleable but tough alloy bronze heralded a new era. They were probably chance discoveries, although not made in Britain. But once the secret was known, copper ore could have been dug from veins which surfaced with local rock in Cornwall, Wales and the Lake District. There may have been enough in these surface exposures to meet early demand: there is no evidence of Bronze Age mining, but early workings could have been obliterated by later activity. *Parys Mountain* (Anglesey) has been mined since Roman times. There were probably also Roman copper mines in Cumbria, Cornwall and elsewhere.

Here, too, any early traces have been obliterated by later workings.

TIN

Tin was linked with Cornwall. There was at first a 'placer' supply in the stream and river gravels, weathered from the veins in the rock. Fragments of heavy ore could be panned from these streams, or gained from the hillside screes below the veins by 'streaming'—that is, floating the lighter material off with running water. Since no Bronze Age mines are known, it was possible that later on, metal dug on the Continent was imported. (Beads from Egypt have been found in Bronze Age graves.

LEAD

Lead was mined extensively in Roman times—a useful metal for water pipes (it is surmised that many Romans must have suffered from lead poisoning), coffins and other things. The pitting and trenching of Roman mining can still be seen around Priddy in the *Mendips* (Avon/Som), for example. Lead ore may sometimes have been mined by 'hushing': water was dammed up into a reservoir on higher ground, with channels leading to the cracks where the veins surfaced. The reservoir was breached, and the tumbling water broke up the vein deep into the rock. In some places shiny black lumps of lead slag can still be found.

Mendip lead ore was rich in silver, and gaining this was also a local Roman industry.

IRON

It is said that when a Roman road in the Sussex Weald was struck by light-ning, its track across the fields was scorched for all to see, for the waste slag from their nearby iron workings had been used as hardcore. Ironstone had been worked in the Weald in late Iron Age times. At first the supply came from easily collected 'kernel' stones, 2-in. globules of carbonate ore scattered over the surface of clay deposits in some places; later they mined by opencast trenching. Iron Age mining also took place in Northamptonshire, the Forest of Dean and elsewhere. There was plentiful local timber for charcoal, which was needed to reach the temperature of 2000°C which reduced the ore to metal.

It is still possible to find small fragments of ore in today's ploughed fields in these areas. The use of iron did not, however, lessen the demand for bronze.

Lost villages

Most of the villages we see today were established by medieval times, but many failed, and remain only as names or traces in the fields.

ISOLATED CHURCHES

A church standing apart from its village, or even standing solitary in the fields, can be the start of an interesting investigation.

A church that is somewhat distant usually signposts a village that has 'moved'. What has usually happened is that village growth, when the streets became sharply extended away from the church, was followed by slump, when the village core with its more ancient buildings was abandoned to become fields. *Knowlton* (Dorset) is unusual in that it was at the start built distant from its village. At Knowlton the magnet was a giant Neolithic banked ritual henge, within which the church stands. There are few placements as strange as this.

The solitary church can, however, be a clue to a lost village. The church itself might still be in good repair, although many are ruined, and others are reduced to mere fragments of wall, the rest being robbed for building stone.

DESERTED VILLAGES

Several thousand villages are known to have been wiped off the map by history. It is a fairly recent discovery, providing a startling new insight into the creation of today's countryside. We are talking here not of prehistoric, Roman or Dark Ages settlement but of medieval villages which normally evolved into the villages we see today, and which seem such a symbol of permanence.

A good many of the villages mentioned in Domesday Book are now forgotten. A good example of what might be found is *Ingarsby* (Leics); another is *Wharram Percy* (Humberside). In the latter a ruined roofless church nestles near the foot of a valley, the slopes of which are marked by a tangle of ridges. The site is interesting to visit because it is being slowly excavated to show how even modest villages grew and changed with time.

Some of its field banks are of Iron Age and Roman date, while some trackways were inherited from the Bronze Age..

FEATURES TO LOOK FOR

The features remain as bumps and hollows in the grassy field (ploughing destroys them). From the church in a medieval village ran the village streets, which in time became worn as holloways, sometimes a few feet deep. Alongside these were ranked the huts. Each stood in its own plot of land, maybe marked off with a bank or a ditch, which was perhaps a vegetable garden with a few fruit trees. Years of rubbish have often raised the actual rectangular hut sites somewhat, and sometimes collapsed walls remain as raised edges. The hut floor is likely to be level in contrast with the uneven ground round about.

In the village as a whole, a rather large, flat, unmarked area would be the village green. Part of it might have been hard-surfaced or even cobbled for the market-place. The grass grows thinly here.

Another common feature was a fishpond (or ponds), now dry most likely, but still quite deep. Elsewhere the stream may have been channelled for a simple watermill and traces of the channels, or leats, may remain. In many places the manor house was not much grander than a large hut, but separated by a wide moat and bank and palisade; traces of these with the causeway which led to the gate might also remain. Around these lost medieval villages should be the unmis-

ridge and furrow ploughland

hollow of High Street

marks of hut sites

isolated or ruined church

takable corduroy pattern of the ridge and furrow of the medieval ploughlands (see pp. 80–81).

It is rare to find a complete village; these surface traces are easily rubbed out by ploughing, and perhaps the site remains visible only in one or two unploughed pasture fields, not in the arable alongside. They are best viewed from a local high spot—maybe the church tower—and by sharp evening or dawn light, which strengthens the shine from the bumps and casts long shadows behind them (see pp. 30–31).

PLOUGHLAND CLUES

If part of the site has been ploughed, there could be an advantage in it, because the plough may have turned up pieces of pottery. The fields nearby may contain many potsherds—

manure and refuse from the huts was heaped to be taken out to manure the fields each autumn. The plough may also have scattered the cobbling or paving of the market-place and other well-used areas.

CLUES ON THE MAP

Large ponds (especially strings of ponds) which are clearly not later field ponds could be remaining fishponds. An empty area in a map that is generally dotted with villages could be another clue; clusters of converging footpaths might be another.

NATURAL CLUES

Plants can provide clues to abandoned dwellings. Stinging nettles are greedy for nutrients, and a patch of them in a pasture field often marks the site of a

hut (although perhaps only a shelter for the cattle). Elderberry is a quick colonizer of abandoned land, and rabbits do not like the taste of its bark, so that it often survives to clothe their warrens where other shrubs are nibbled down. Rabbits choose soft soil for their burrows, old banks perhaps, and so a patch of elderberry can signal something worth inspecting.

HOW VILLAGES DIED

Wharram Percy was in its prime in the early 14th century and dead by 1500, of a common cause: around 1350 the Black Death decimated the population in some areas, and with labour scarce and weak, much ploughland was turned over to sheep grazing. Any remaining villagers drifted away jobless, and the village fell into ruin.

An emotive report direct from those times remains scratched on the walls of the church at *Ashwell* (Herts).

Specialized villages such as mining villages would fail if the veins of ore ran out. Dunwich on the Suffolk coast is a famous example of a village lost to the sea; little now remains. Other coastal villages failed when changing currents brought curtains of sand to engulf the harbour.

One or two villages have more recently been sacrificed to army training, and remain in tumbledown ruin. Tyneham near *Lulworth Cove* (Dorset) is one such that can still be visited.

RELOCATED VILLAGES

Many villages found themselves intruding as a blot on the landscape when the Georgian squire improved his parklands and as a result a good many were moved. Perhaps the holloways and other clues remain in the grass in the park, with a new village built out of sight not far away. *Milton Abbas* (Dorset) is a famous example. The dispossession broke the hearts of many and Goldsmith's poem 'The Deserted Village' mirrored the fact. These transferred 'estate' villages are often easily recognizable, with neat layout and cottages all in the same style (see pp. 110–111).

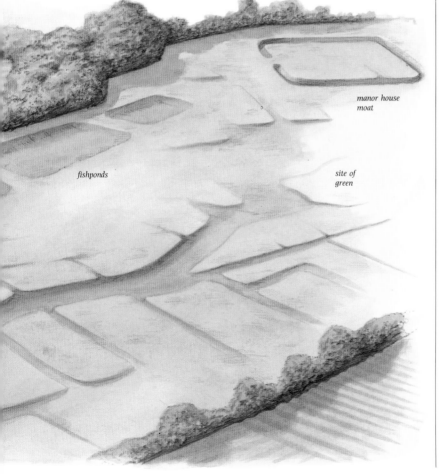

manor house moat

fishponds

site of green

Clues to a deserted village.

The history of the field

Although taken for granted, the fields themselves can be a historic part of the countryside. The oldest fields to be found are prehistoric

THE OLDEST FIELDS

Examples of our oldest fields are to be seen on *Dartmoor*, on the unploughed downlands along the *Ridgeway* (Oxon) and around *Malham* (N. Yorks). They are squarish and from $\frac{1}{2}$ to 2 acres in size, with their boundaries marked by stone or boulder walls or slight weathered banks and ditches. They are prehistoric Bronze Age and Iron Age fields, often called 'Celtic' fields (see pp. 46–47).

Less certainly prehistoric—they are quite likely to be medieval in date (or they may be both)—are the terraces, or lynchets, seen on the slopes of many valleys in the chalk downlands in the south and around *Malham* (N. Yorks) and some other places in the north. The steps can be well over head height. They were created by constant ploughing above a field boundary: the soil washed down to this boundary, it became raised, and in time a considerable step formed.

Little seems to have remained of Roman fields. We would suspect that they were regularly laid out to a neat grid. One echo might remain just inland from the coast between Holme and Brancaster, near *Hunstanton* (Norfolk), where roads and paths rightangle themselves, and some hedges are 410 yards long—twice the Roman 'stadium' used to measure land, allowing for a boundary between them. These fields are not divisible into acres (see below).

THE MEDIEVAL OPEN FIELDS

The open-field system of farming was probably introduced here in Saxon times. Although there were probably a good many small hedged or walled paddocks close by the village and also large areas of woodland and rough grazing on which the villagers had the right to graze their animals (and the extensive Royal hunting forests), vast areas of the lowlands in medieval times were dominated by giant open (hedgeless) ploughfields. Also open

were the extensive meadowlands, set aside for the vital hay crop, and which usually lay alongside the streams and rivers of the parish. Both were worked in common—that is, they were shared out between the villagers (and their lord).

There were usually three open ploughfields to a village. Although they were regularly fed with manure and rubbish from the huts, each year one was left fallow—that is, unploughed, to regain its strength.

STRIPS AND FURLONGS

Each open ploughfield was worked in long furlongs (furrow longs) by ox teams. The team had to turn at each end to retrace its direction, and the preparation for this gave the furrowing a slight, reversed-s shape. The plough threw the clods leftwards on each run, and ploughing up and down in this way threw up a distinctive corduroy of 'ridge and furrow' (see pp. 80–81). The width of a ridge-plus-furrow varied, but 4 yards could be typical. Two to five ridges were counted as a strip and a peasant was allocated strips throughout the fields by lottery, thus sharing better and poorer soils.

THE LAST OF THE OPEN FIELDS

Although traces of the great open fields might remain in other places, such as near *Ashwell* (Herts) and Braunton near *Bideford* (Devon), only at *Laxton* (Notts) is open-strip farming still practised, not only on the ground itself but also in its administration. A Manor Court acting for the Lord of the Manor (once the Ministry of Agriculture) appoints a foreman and jurors to supervise the allocation of the strips in the three great open fields. One field is fallowed each year.

THE START OF ENCLOSURE

Hedged or walled paddocks had been familiar from the start, set near the village and used for livestock at night, and for calving, lambing and such events. Gradually these smaller fields became the rule.

A great deal of enclosure of open ploughland into smaller fields followed

the Black Death, when half the 14th-century population was wiped out. The abandoned land sometimes became scrubbed and eventually wooded, but very often wealthy magnates and abbeys bought it at a bargain price, hedging it or walling it to create pasture fields for sheep.

THE AGE OF ENCLOSURES

The cross-hatching of the open ploughlands and meadowlands with hedges or stone walls increased in Tudor times, when there were three sheep alive to every one Englishman. Tudor England truly did sit on a woolsack! But the enclosure of open land reached a peak between 1750 and 1850. The motive now was no longer the profits from sheep, but the gains to be made from improved, more intensive farming in smaller fields, with better manuring and the growing of turnips and other new crops to feed the livestock in winter.

During this period—often simply called 'the Enclosures'—Acts of Parliament (at first restricted to single villages) permitted the richer and more go-ahead villagers to usurp the commons rights and annex the open ploughlands, meadowlands and common grazing for their private use. In order to avoid starvation the displaced commoners had no alternative but to hire themselves out as farm workers or move to the burgeoning towns of the time.

THE ENCLOSURE SURVEY

The common land was divided up into a neat grid of fields as specified in each Act, and planned out by the Act's surveyor. Sizes became standardized in acres (see pp. 80–81). Stone walls were prescribed where easy to quarry, or fencing planted with rows of hawthorn saplings. Straight, wide roadways ditched on each side were also laid out (and as the Acts only applied to a parish at a time, they sometimes change direction at the parish boundary). These roadways were 'green' ways, usually of a standard width between the ditches, although many became macadamized and then tarmacked to form today's roads (see

pp. 128–129).

In the church at Betchworth near *Box Hill* (Surrey) is a map of 1634 showing these new enclosure fields cutting across the open field strips. There are similar maps to be found elsewhere. In some places the later hedges or walls follow the s curves of the old packages of strips, as can be seen in the fields around *Chelmorton* (Derbyshire).

WOODLAND CLEARANCES

These neatly gridded enclosure landscapes can be seen everywhere in England and Wales and in many areas of Scotland. But there is also another, rather different kind of landscape,

The enclosure walls near Chelmorton (Derbyshire) may well follow the lines of the medieval strips.

created by assarting—that is, by the clearance of woodland in medieval times. Its main feature is an irregular patchwork of mainly pasture fields. It is described in detail on pp. 68–69.

Abbey ruins

Ruins of monastic houses are among the most romantic of antiquities. Many are hidden in superb countryside for reasons explained below.

THE BIRTH OF THE MONASTIC TRADITION

Ruined medieval abbeys and priories are familiar countryside landmarks today, and monastic roots run deep in many rural areas. In AD 313 the Emperor Constantine had legitimized Christianity for Roman citizens, and Christian symbols can be seen in villas the Romans built in Britain—at *Lullingstone* (Kent) for example. But the withdrawal of the Roman legions in AD 425 left the country open to pagan 'Saxons'—Angles, Saxons and Jutes—who pushed the young religion back to small monastic settlements in the still Celtic areas, such as at *Lindisfarne* (Northumberland), *Glastonbury* (Som), *Tintagel* (Cornwall) and *Iona* (Strathclyde). Another early example is *St Piran's Oratory* (Cornwall). Early Christianity also held up strongly in Ireland.

These monasteries were modest: grouped around a small church (of simple nave leading to a smaller flat-ended sanctuary or chancel) were the huts of the brothers, who journeyed to preach under the open sky at crosses of stone or wood set up in neighbouring settlements.

SAXON CHURCHES

Many monastic settlements were to be hard hit time and again by Scandinavian and Danish Viking raiders. Danish war bands became a scourge inland, but in time Alfred's famous victory over them in AD 878 brought relative peace and many stone-built Saxon churches were to be built between then and the Battle of Hastings (1066). Over 200 churches have substantial 'Saxon' features remaining (see pp. 106–107).

Some of these Saxon churches were 'minsters', forming part of monastic headquarters.

MEDIEVAL MONASTIC HOUSES

The Saxon monastic tradition had been strengthened by the Normans and the monasteries then grew and flourished. By the mid 13th century, England had 348 monasteries and 140 nunneries. Of these, an abbey was a monastic house with either men or women, governed by an abbot or abbess, while a priory was an offshoot (but independent) house, governed by a prior or prioress.

The Normans also strengthened the parish system. Wooden Saxon parish churches were grandly rebuilt in stone. The reason was not wholly Christian or even wholly benevolent, for the parish church was a symbol of the extra taxes, the tithes, that the settlement yielded. Under the Plantagenet kings the monastic orders were not only given grants of land to provide an income, they also bought or acquired the rectorships (the livings) and the tithes of innumerable parishes, appointing vicars as their representatives. Growing wealthy, they also grew in political power to rival the barons in their own right.

THE MONASTIC ORDERS

As with any powerful group, factions developed and various monastic orders evolved. The earliest had been the Benedictines, who had had houses here from early times—*Whitby* (N. Yorks) was founded in AD 657, although like others it suffered from Viking raids, and it was refounded in 1078. Soon after the Norman Conquest, the Cluniac order emerged, which sought tranquillity in remote places. The Cistercians too were reclusive, in an attempt to recreate the purity of the first Benedictine communities: Waverley (Surrey), Fountains and Rievaulx (Yorks) were among their foundations. But although they set themselves in sites distant from the temptations of the towns, they were anything but unworldly. They exploited to the full the grants of land made them, and increased their holdings. In the 13th century they were great wool producers in Yorkshire and other parts of Britain. Elsewhere they drained great areas of Fenland and the Somerset Levels.

The Augustinians or Austins were an offshoot of the Cistercians and were more involved in day-to-day life. They too could own gigantic estates, such as *Bolton Priory* (N. Yorks). Its estates provided the mixed grazing which produced good strong wool; it also mined coal in some places.

THE GRANGE

Like many other religious houses, Bolton Priory in time rented out some of its holdings. Like other houses, it worked distant areas through granges manned by lay brothers. Furness Abbey, situated at Barrow below the Lake District, had 18 granges, many of them far distant—one evolved into

Bolton Priory (N. Yorks) is set, like many other religious houses, in a remote fold of a river.

today's village of Ramsgill, which stands about 15 miles north-east of Bolton Priory.

THE DISSOLUTION

The religious houses sometimes overstretched themselves. Entrepreneurs of all kinds can fall flat, and they were no exception. Plagues which struck the monastery as harshly as the local peasantry, raids by Scottish and Welsh rustlers (the Scots regularly swept into Yorkshire and Lancashire) and debt repayments were common burdens. Even Bolton Priory was hard pushed and was already in reduced circumstances when Henry VIII's Dissolution of the Monasteries began in 1536. This was partly political and partly a hunger for cash to balance the nation's books. The monasteries were robbed of their valuable furnishings and fittings, their estates sold off. The ransacked buildings fell into ruin.

MELANCHOLY RUINS

Set in remote areas, often in the bend of a river with hills and woods on all sides, these monastic ruins are among the most splendid and evocative sights of our countryside. Their melancholy has long appealed to the Romantic eye—Bolton Priory (below) was painted by Turner, sketched by Ruskin. Bolton was saved in part because its nave became the parish church, and this is the story of a few other parish churches. Bolton's massive gatehouse survives because it was used as a hunting lodge for the moorlands beyond, but as with many such historic sites, the nearby mansion was built of stone plundered from the ruins.

A mansion named Abbey or Priory is clearly a good clue to a previous monastic house, maybe now completely gone, although its stone may be used in the building we see. But beware: the word 'grange' appealed to the Victorian taste for romance, and was used for many largish houses of that period for no historic reason.

THE TITHE BARN

One memorial to monastic activities might be a majestic tithe barn, considerably larger than the largest farmstead barn nearby, and built to hold a vast quantity of produce harvested by or paid to the abbey or priory. The massive barn at Great Coxwell near *Faringdon* (Oxon) is just one example, typically owned by a distant abbey.

The castle

The British countryside is studded with medieval castles. They show a rapid evolution from the simple type introduced by the Normans.

THE ORIGINS OF THE CASTLE

Some Iron Age hilltop camps are called 'castles'—Maiden Castle near *Dorchester* (Dorset) is one—but in the countryside as a whole the name is usually reserved for the kind of fortress first built here by the Norman invaders and which evolved during feudal times— that is, from the Battle of Hastings (1066) to the Battle of Bosworth (1485), which brought the Wars of the Roses to an end and saw in the Tudor dynasty.

The castle might be traceable back to the Roman marching camps and Dark Ages burghs which were frequently small enclosures defended with a rampart and palisade fence. However, the Normans were using a definite form of castle. It was very effective in the circumstances following their victory at the Battle of Hastings, when they had to quickly subdue a hostile populace. The rapidly dug, easily defended motte and bailey came into its own.

KNIGHTS

Together with this form of castle evolved the power of the knight. Although romance, feudal hierarchies and oaths of knighthood and allegiance might disguise the fact, the knight was at heart little different from a mercenary. With his mounted and armed troops he was able to make long sallies but required a well-defended base to which to retire and maybe sit out a siege. The castles became the dwellings-cum-barracks of these war bands, and when in time the barons became immensely powerful and the size and complexity of their castles reflected this, warfare remained largely unchanged: standing troops, sallies and sieges.

THE MOTTE AND BAILEY

Although it is possible that a few were constructed here in late Saxon times, the motte and bailey is the hallmark of Norman power. Many were built throughout southern Britain soon after the Conquest, but also all over the country in the years following. Fifty 'castles' are already mentioned in Domesday Book (1086).

Often a knoll was adopted as a strong point, but the motte and bailey castle could be built anywhere. The motte was a mound, its top defended

by a palisade fence, within which might be built a higher square timber tower or 'keep', offering a good stance for bowmen as well as a lookout. Alongside this motte was dug the bailey: an enclosure surrounded by a ditch and bank, also fenced, to hold horses and outbuildings, kitchen and similar. A well was necessary if sieges were envisaged.

The motte was reached from the bailey by a trestle bridge across its circling ditch, with a stairway up the slope. The entrance to the bailey (a weak point) was a well-built gateway with a raised timber walkway above it.

Although many earth and timber motte and bailey castles were solidly

Dover Castle (Kent) stands atop the famous white cliffs; at heart Norman on Roman foundations.

made, the motte being carefully constructed of layers of well-rammed soil and stone rubble, there is some evidence that the design evolved from a simple tower plus enclosure, the motte originally being a mound piled up to protect the lower timbers of the tower from attack.

Many earthen motte and baileys lie forgotten — as mysterious grassy mounds and ditches, or hidden and overgrown in woods. Many were small — the mottes vary from 10 to 100 ft in height — and after centuries of weathering can be mistaken for prehistoric burial mounds or later windmill mounds.

Within a few decades, however, important castles were being enlarged and rebuilt in stone; they began to evolve.

KEEP CASTLES

The first rubble and stone keeps were square like their wooden predecessors and with massive walls up to 15 ft thick, with the doorway for added security at the first floor and reached by an outside staircase. The windowless ground floor was used for storage — the same can be seen in many smaller later dwelling houses near the troubled northern borders. These castles were built during the first century after 1066 and examples remain at *Portchester* (Hants) — built inside Roman fortifications which act as the bailey — and *Ludlow* (Shropshire). This last is typical in that it broods over its town; the creation of well-policed market towns as local power centres was also part of the Norman system of control.

ROUND AND SHELL KEEPS

Siege was the usual form of warfare; and mining was a common means of assault. Tunnels were dug below the walls, shored up with timber to take the weight of the walls above. The timber was then set alight, and the tunnels collapsed, bringing down the walls. As the angles of a square keep can be mined from two directions at once, round keeps were built as a precaution: *Conisbrough* (N. Yorks), erected in 1180, was one of the first,

and *Flint* (Clwyd), 1277, one of the last. Other shapes were tried, such as the D-shaped keep at *Helmsley* (N. Yorks). A parallel development was that of the shell keep, which was little more than a roofless sturdy wall at the top of the motte furnished with lean-tos around an open courtyard. *Castle Acre* (Norfolk) is just one example.

KEEPLESS CASTLES

At the same time yet another approach was being devised: no keep at all. The castle had now become a strong enclosing wall (called a curtain wall) running between wall towers, which were rounded to lessen the threat of mining. With a pair of massive towers forming a gatehouse, this was the typical 13th-century castle.

Many of the Welsh castles built by Edward 1 doubled up this plan with two curtain walls, one within the other, each with towers, and with a massive gatehouse at the weakest place. *Kidwelly* (Dyfed) is just one example.

THE MOAT

With keepless castles, a moat was more often added. Although castle ditches wet with rain and seepage had been fairly normal, great trouble was now taken with channels and dams to create a topped-up moat. That at *Kenilworth* (Warks), though now dry, is still impressive.

THE END OF CASTLES

The end of the Wars of the Roses removed much of the demand for castles. Coastal forts were still built, such as the Tudor pair at *Falmouth* (Cornwall), but new domestic building often only retained a great gatehouse, and mock battlements seen in many Elizabethan mansions, although fortified pele houses — square keep-like towers — were still common in the Scottish border country.

Their end was hastened by the use of artillery. As it is, many of our castles — *Donnington Castle* (Berks) for example — stand ruined because they were pounded by guns in the Civil War of 1642–51.

Hilltop history

To the natural sculpturing of a hilltop, man has often added an edifice of his own, for many reasons and at many different periods. Some are odd indeed.

NATURAL SCULPTURES

Hilltops are stubs of rock not yet eliminated by erosion (see pp. 12–13) and often show complicated weathering. *Snowdon* (Gwynedd) is a frost-shattered remnant of a once vaster mass of rock. Chemistry plays a part, with rainwater slowly dissolving the rock minerals to weaken the rock structure, sometimes to create fantastic forms. The 170 tors of *Dartmoor* (Devon) are an example—and no two are alike. However, any prominent viewpoint is likely to be crowned with more than plain geology. Man has often added his bit.

THE HILLTOP ON THE MAP

It is part of human nature to esteem the highest point, and in the course of centuries hilltops have attracted a range of structures. Indeed, the fact that the map shows that a high point does carry something is often a clue that it is a prominence of some note—and likely to offer a view well worth the climb.

HILLTOP RAMPARTS

Earth or stone-rubble ramparts consisting of a ditch and bank (and often more than one) are usually of Iron Age date, although a few are Roman and some are from the Dark Ages. They are usually labelled on the map as 'fort', 'castle', or 'camp'—and for those of Iron Age date these names can be misleading—the first two are best used for stone-walled medieval and Tudor strongholds, while the last implies a temporary use; many Iron Age strongholds were in use for generations.

SUMMIT CAIRNS

A cairn is a pile of stones, and where it marks a summit it is usually the work of Victorian and later visitors, not earlier. That on Dunkery Beacon, *Exmoor* (Devon) is double a man's height. But some cairns on high ground are prehistoric graves. Beacon Hill on the *North York Moors* has a Bronze Age burial mound on its summit, for example.

BEACON HILLS

Certain chains of summits have been used as beacon posts, a name often found on the map. There are two on the *Malvern Hills* (Hereford & Worcs) for example. Lines of beacons to be lit at night or day (when the smoke would be visible) were possibly of prehistoric, certainly of Roman, use. The Romans built a chain of them along the north-east coast when

A Dartmoor church, one of the many hilltop churches dedicated to the archangel St Michael.

Saxon raiders were becoming troublesome. Little remains of these, but they consisted of a tall stone tower set in a stone-walled or timbered courtyard.

Belas Knap (Glos) is a massive prehistoric tomb, but its name in Dark Ages dialect means 'hilltop beacon'. Later, beacon hills were sometimes known as 'toot hills', perhaps from the word 'tote' with its meaning of carrying supplies of timber and suchlike, or alternatively from an old dialect word 'toot' meaning to stick out or be noticeable. The word is sometimes found in a place-name.

Beacon hills remained important in Tudor times and beyond. It is taken for granted that news of the Armada was spread across the nation by beacon fires, and the chain was reformed in 1988 for the 400th anniversary of that historic event. The artillery forts built by Henry VIII were backed up by a system of beacons. The pair guarding the estuary at *Falmouth* (Cornwall), for example, were speedily linked to London. The beacons were set 5–10 miles apart and would have had a metal brazier set on a post: a beacon post of this kind is reconstructed on Beacon Hill on the *North York Moors* mentioned above. Some Armada beacons were rebuilt at the time of the Napoleonic threat, and many beacon sites were used for mechanical semaphores, with a flat-roofed building carrying the posts, and a 'Semaphore Cottage' nearby which is often found on the map.

HILLTOP CHURCHES

Hilltops and other high spots have also attracted churches and chapels. It is possible, though there is no hard evidence, that these sites were already sacred in pagan times. A medieval church is perched on a volcanic stub at *Brentor* (Devon), an old defensive site surrounded with Iron Age ramparts. The tower of another (the body of the chapel has gone) perches on the Tor at *Glastonbury* (Som).

Both these churches are dedicated to St Michael. There are more than 800 churches dedicated to St Michael in Britain and many are on high spots, although this may be no more than a

knoll. Why heights should be linked with St Michael is not clear, but being an archangel, a link with heaven may be supposed. The Church, however, had the habit of adopting earlier traditions and sites. Hercules was a Roman god associated with summits. The pagan god Mercury was, like the archangel Michael, linked with the heavens and with protecting souls.

HILLTOP MEMORIALS

In Georgian and later days it became fashionable to mark hilltops with more elaborate structures, not only as eyecatchers to be admired from far afield, but also as a goal for an afternoon's walk.

One of the most dramatic is Hardy's Monument a few miles from *Dorchester* (Dorset) and well in sight of that town. The Hardy commemorated was Nelson's captain—his family lived nearby—not the novelist, who also lived in the area.

THE AGE OF FOLLIES

Imagination ran riot in Regency days and 'follies' of all kinds began to decorate hilltops. Some were towers, others imitated ruined castles; few had any

The folly atop Mow Cop (Staffs) — carefully constructed in every detail to imitate a ruined castle.

real use—hence the name.

Some hilltop follies were built to reach the magic 1000 ft: one example is the tower on Leith Hill—965 ft by itself—near *Abinger* (Surrey). A tower for a dining club with a temple decorated with busts of famous admirals was built on the Kymin near *Monmouth* (Gwent). *Broadway Tower* (Hereford & Worcs) although inhabited at one time, was built as entertainment (and, following the then romantic fashion for a dark tower, is not built of the local pale limestone!) At the castle-like folly on *Mow Cop* (Staffs) primitive Methodists held their first meeting, in 1807.

The folly builders had great panache. Awaiting discovery on a day out are the spire of a London church carted a good 30 miles away, a pile of boulders inscribed with the Ten Commandments, and a brick 'sail' setting into the sunset.

The last British folly tower was built in the 1930s at *Faringdon* (Oxon), to provide jobs during the slump.

Fields of battle

Battlefields stir the emotions, although their appearance today is likely to be markedly different from that in their hour of glory.

NAMES OF BATTLE AND BLOODSHED

Echoes of old skirmishes can linger on in the names of hills, or even individual fields—in fields called Blood Hill or Hanging. (But beware: 'gore' as a field name can mean simply a triangular field, from an old word for spearhead.) Such macabre names, although comparatively modern, could possibly commemorate a Saxon battle and its aftermath, tales of the site being handed down from grandparent to children while even the language changed. And although modern farming tends to destroy the boundaries of old fields, many fields still keep their older names.

The impressive memorial marking the site where Richard III lost his crown and his life.

NEAR THIS SPOT, ON AUGUST 22ND 1485, AT THE AGE OF 32, KING RICHARD III FELL FIGHTING GALLANTLY IN DEFENCE OF HIS REALM & HIS CROWN AGAINST THE USURPER HENRY TUDOR. THE CAIRN WAS ERECTED BY DR. SAMUEL PARR IN 1813 TO MARK THE WELL FROM WHICH THE KING IS SAID TO HAVE DRUNK DURING THE BATTLE. IT IS MAINTAINED BY THE FELLOWSHIP OF THE WHITE BOAR

Hanging Field or even Hanging Oak is in fact rather a common name, and reflects perhaps not battles but centuries of local small crime and even petty theft with Draconian penalties (sheep stealing for a starving family was a gallows offence even two centuries ago). But there were also local small-scale rebellions without number when people chafed under the yokes of both serfdom and religion. The Lollards were 14th-century heretics, and 'Lollard Pit' can commemorate the spot where they were burnt at the stake by the jealous Church.

ROMAN BATTLEFIELDS

Definite locations are unknown, but the organization of the countryside with its legionary fortresses, camps and towns makes detective work easier. It is very likely, for example, that the Saxon church of Mancetter (Warks) marks the last battle of Queen Boudicca (Boadicea) who led the rebellion against Rome in AD 60: its site has been deduced by charting various likely legionary movements along the road systems of the time. Churches often used sites already famous to the local community.

DARK AGES BATTLES

The sites of many later historical battles have also been lost and imagination runs riot in the Dark Ages. *Tintagel* (Cornwall) claims to be birthplace of King Arthur. This legendary figure almost certainly originated with a Romanized Briton fighting the Saxon hordes when Rome withdrew her army, but sagas of nearer the time suggest a northern sphere of action. Historical sources report that he was killed at the Battle of Camlann, and Birdoswald fort on the Roman Wall gained the name Camboglanna. But the Iron Age hillfort of *Cadbury Castle* (Som) housed an important leader of about the right period; it overlooks villages called Camel.

Edington (Wilts) is worth visiting. It was somewhere near here that King Alfred in AD 878 defeated the Danes, made Wessex safe, and allowed the roots of the English nation to be laid. It is quite possible that he pushed the

Danes from the downs above the church. These downland slopes and the army ranges that stretch for miles past them have never been ploughed, and dotted with bushes they may very well look today as they looked then. Most of Britain's famous battlefields look very different today.

THE CHANGED LOOK OF BATTLEFIELDS

Historical battles usually adopt the name of the place where they were waged. A battlefield is not, of course, a field in the literal sense. Indeed, in many if not most cases, the neat landscape of drained, ditched fields we see today came into being many centuries after the battle itself took place. It needs imagination to decipher the look of the countryside as it was then, to fill out its earlier features of tangled woods and swamps. Scarce any if any at all of the countryside of Saxon times remains to be conjured up at *Battle Abbey* (E. Sussex), the site of the Battle of Hastings (1066), nor of the Civil War battles of *Edge Hill* (Warks) and *Naseby* (Northants). Nonetheless, such is the evocative power of history that it is easy enough to people today's familiar landscape with the sight and sound of battles gone.

THE WARS OF THE ROSES

Bosworth (Leics) is one famous battle. Vividly commemorated in Shakespeare's *Richard III*, it was the last skirmish of the 30-year Wars of the Roses. Here, on 22 August 1485, King Richard III, a Yorkist whose followers bore the symbol of the white rose, was defeated by Henry, a Lancastrian of the red rose. The victor was the first of the Tudors.

It was a key battle in British history, and the battlefield is today well signposted and explained. Richard had taken position on Ambion (or Ambien) Hill, and visits can be made to the spring where he quenched his thirst and the site where he died under the sword cuts and where (as Shakespeare describes) the crown was found under a bush—the spot is still known as Crown Hill. But what has retreated to distant memory is the face of the

landscape then, with the main obstacle of the battlefield, an impenetrable marsh, long sinced drained. This determined the siting of the events.

CIVIL WAR BATTLEFIELDS

Battles of the time of Bosworth were confused events. But for later battles when cannon were used and the forces were organized in troops under central control, it is possible to reconstruct the actual moves. The stages of many Civil War battles can be followed on the map. We have to hazard guesses as to the detail of the terrain, for the battle often predates today's field pattern.

BATTLEFIELD MONUMENTS

Most commemorative monuments are the work of Victorian enthusiasts, but older ones remain, and sometimes chapels were built nearby. Charnel houses (bone stores) were sometimes built to hold the mortal remains of those slaughtered: not the whole skeleton but just the skull and two long bones (hence the emblem of 'skull and crossbones') believed to be the minimum necessary for Resurrection. It is said that the railway embankment at Plumpton Green (E. Sussex) incorporates the bones of those who fell at the Battle of Lewes (1264).

THE BATTLE OF BRITAIN

By far the commonest relics of recent history, and largely unnoticed or taken for granted, date from World War II. Fighter and bomber bases were common in the Midlands and East Anglia, and the concrete runways remain spread across the fields. Few of the distinctive huts and other buildings, with curved corrugated iron roofing might remain, but in their way they are as 'historic' as any Roman fortress. *Duxford* (Cambs) is a fighter station preserved, and today maintaining a museum with not only the Spitfires, Hurricanes and other warplanes of the time but also Concorde.

In addition, many river valleys were fortified with concrete machine-gun posts, thick-walled and virtually indestructible. Usually overgrown, they remain to be rediscovered.

Reading the fieldscape

The fields have various origins. The prettiest countryside is usually found where they were created directly by clearing woodland many centuries ago.

ENCLOSURE CLUES

Much of Britain, in upland as well as lowland, has a field pattern resulting from the enclosures which reached their peak in Georgian times. Its origins are described on pp. 58–59. This enclosure fieldscape is usually easy to recognize. It is neatly gridded, although the fields may not be exactly squared, with the fields divided by neat hedges or stone walls. Roadways tend to meet at right angles (and crossroads are common); they run with many straight stretches and are of standard width and ditched at each side. Bridges were frequently built to replace the old fords when they crossed streams. On unploughed pastures, the old medieval ridge and furrow that they were imposed upon can often be seen continuing from one field to the next, crossing under the later enclosure hedge.

The farms that served these new fields were built among them, often in brick (which at that time was becoming cheap). And these farms often have names which are certainly datable: for example, Waterloo Farm after the battle of 1815 in which Wellington trounced Napoleon.

In time the harsh lines of this imposed countryside have sometimes softened as the hawthorn saplings grew into hedges, breaking with blossom each spring, and the hedgerow trees which had been planted for their timber grew tall. Spinneys planted by the hunting squires grew up into small woodlands to lend their attraction to the view.

This is the common kind of British countryside, but there is another.

ANCIENT AND ORNAMENTAL COUNTRYSIDE

The term 'ancient and ornamental countryside' was coined by Professor H. G. Hoskins, who established the ground rules for the interpretation of the fieldscape. It is used to describe a countryside which has had a particular history and evolution.

Most of lowland Britain has been intensively farmed for thousands of years. No surface traces remain of the earliest fields but crop marks have shown that even by early Iron Age times much of the lowlands was already densely filled with farmsteads and their fields and tracks. It was from these ploughlands that the open-field landscape evolved.

But there were some regions, some parts of a few counties, that always remained quite well wooded, even well into medieval times. It was the creation of fields in these wooded areas that has yielded this 'ancient and ornamental countryside'. The woodland may not have been the original wildwood which covered the land at the end of the Ice Age. In the course of long centuries, many areas cleared for fields or by grazing were let go again, to become scrubbed and even wooded when the local population fell and demands lessened.

MAIN AREAS

Ancient and ornamental countryside can be found in pockets throughout Britain, but not in every county. Devon and Dorset contain some, as does Sussex. Essex has some, but there is little in Suffolk alongside. The western edges of Hereford and Worcester provide some, but Gloucestershire not so much. It is a countryside often to be met accidentally on a journey, and relished all the more for the unexpected nature of its discovery.

ASSARTING

Ornamental countryside is very likely to have been created by *assarting*—that is, creating fields by grubbing out the trees and bushes of what was woodland or 'waste' (rough grazing land, often largely scrubbed and dotted with trees). It is typically a hand-hewn countryside, and although these labours took place at least some centuries ago, it still has a frontier feel.

WEST DORSET COUNTRYSIDE

Each little pocket of ornamental countryside has its own history, but West Dorset, the countryside lying inland to the north of *Lyme Regis*,

provides a good example.

It is a sharply corrugated landscape, and the winding lanes which breast the rises provide many good viewpoints. (There are also good viewpoints at one or two well-placed Iron Age hillforts.)

In West Dorset the fields were cleared in medieval days from the Marshwood Forest and by squatters rather than by village or wide-scale organization. With fields created here or there one at a time, there is no discernible master plan. The fields are not squared off, and are generally small and of every uneven shape. They are pasture rather than arable, although today many more may be ploughed than in the past. The fields which have not been ploughed show corrugations caused by natural accidents of erosion in the past—these are best seen from a nearby hill near sunset, when the light strikes sideways. This countryside also has many footpaths. There are plenty of small copses at the corners of the fields, and even quite large woods in places, relics of the old woodland which have never been cleared.

TYPICAL LANES

The lanes in this countryside wind between the fields, taking dog-leg turns to follow their erratic edges. There are many fords, and although most of Britain's remaining fords have been bridged this century to suit car traffic, this is the countryside in which to find those that remain. These lanes are also often sunken, and usually lined with thick hedges.

THE CLUE OF THE FIELD HEDGE

The 'assart' hedges between the fields are descended from relic strips of woodland left standing when the ground was cleared. These are now tidied up and pruned back, and although the original trees and shrubs will have died out long ago, their direct successors make up the hedge we see today.

A count of the numbers of different woody bushes and trees will usually classify it as an old hedge (see pp. 70–71). But the make-up of this

Ancient and ornamental countryside is frequently to be found in the West Country, in Devon and Dorset.

assart hedge is usually also quite distinctive. There is some hawthorn, which was frequently planted to create hedges in the past, and many recent enclosure hedges contain nothing but hawthorn. In the hedges of this assart countryside, however, there are often only a few hawthorn shrubs—its frequency reflects that with which it grew in the original woodland.

THE CLUE OF THE NAME

The names of the farms in West Dorset often link a medieval personal name with 'hay', meaning a clearing in woodland: Bluntshay, Sminhay and Manshay are examples. In other parts of Britain, the clue may be 'ley', 'ly', 'lee' or 'leigh', which also mean a clearing in woodland. 'Thwaite' in northern areas might have the same meaning.

Another clue could be 'stock' or 'stocking', or 'stubbings'—all of which refer to tree stumps. 'Assart' or a name clearly derived from it and 'brake' and 'breach' can also be clues—the latter from a word meaning cleared land.

Along the hedge itself, remembering its origins, bluebells, white wood anemones, dog's mercury and other woodland wild flowers might be found.

The hedge

Hedges are a key element in the countryside. Many hedges are historic, and a good number of these are as old as the church in the village nearby.

THE ORIGIN OF THE HEDGE

The history of hedges is as old as the need for protection. The earliest would have been 'dead' hedges consisting of cut branches of prickly shrubs and resembling African *bomas*, which would have deterred inquisitive forest prowlers from entering a camp-site or cave-mouth shelter. The first written reference to hedges, which is found in Julius Caesar's *Gallic Wars*, describes hedges used by the Gauls. They too were defensive and thickened up in the way that hedges are 'laid' today (see pp. 72–73).

BOUNDARY HEDGES

At some time—when is not clear—hedges took on another function, serving as field boundaries. Boundary banks remain around Bronze and Iron Age fields in many different parts of Britain (see pp. 38–39) and possibly they were once capped with hawthorn and blackthorn bushes. Both are native species of shrub, prickly and easily planted. The word 'hedge' comes from a Saxon word *gehaeg*, which also yielded 'haw' (thorn). One or two Anglo-Saxon land documents mention thorn rows' and they may have been dead hedges, but it is probable that by now hedges were familiar, being planted around livestock paddocks, using shrubs collected from woodlands.

Any strip of land left ungrazed or unploughed might in time grow a hedge, from seeds carried in by birds or animals. Hawthorn is a pioneer in this way. Hedges would have seeded themselves on to the Saxon estate boundary banks some of which remain today as lengths of parish boundaries. Many hedges also came into existence from assarting—that is, from the strips of woodland left between fields cleared from woodland (see pp. 68–69). However, although old hedges of these origins can be found, most hedges we see today are the young hedges which were planted around the enclosures

laid out two or three hundred years ago (see pp. 58–59).

CORNISH HEDGES

In Cornwall the name distinction between defensive and field hedges remained blurred. More than one defensive rampart is called Giant's Hedge, and to this day Cornish field boundaries of boulders and stones topped by turf (on which shrubs may indeed grow), as seen inland near *Roche*, for example, are known as hedges.

HAWTHORN

There are two species of hawthorn or 'may' native to Britain. The common or field hawthorn has deeply lobed leaves and its haws (fruit) have one pip. The Midland hawthorn (not restricted to the Midlands) has blunter-lobed leaves and its haws have two

Hedgerow trees were an important source of timber and of 'smallwood' for specialized uses.

pips. It flowers earlier than its cousin by a week or more.

Both are found in woodland, although the Midland hawthorn is more restricted to it, and is a useful signpost to an old wood (see pp. 88–89). The common hawthorn is the hedgerow shrub. From early times it would have been a simple job to plant a hedge from woodland saplings, which quickly grow to create a dense, thorny barrier. It can even be 'quickset'—that is, young twigs will root given the right soil.

OTHER HEDGEROW SPECIES

Blackthorn (sloe) is the second common hedgerow shrub and once established suckers itself down the line of the hedge. Although hawthorn was often stipulated in the Enclosure Acts, other shrubs and trees were also planted or invaded the hedge. Hazel, for example, can quickly colonize light soil. Sometimes these other species are common within an area, giving a regional look to the hedgerows. In Staffordshire there are many holly hedges, the leaves being fed to the livestock as iron rations in winter. Ash-tree hedges were popular in some northern counties, as the leaves are easily stripped to feed the farm animals.

HEDGEROW TREES

Trees of many kinds grow in hedgerows, and they have been a useful source of timber for centuries. (Lines of trees across large fields usually mark hedges which have been grubbed up.) Indeed, 'field' trees were as important as New Forest trees to the Hampshire boatyards where the navy's men-of-war were built. Field trees were also a source of specialized timber, of small wood for wheelwrights and cartwrights, for example. This would have been gained by pollarding—that is, by cutting crops of branches from the tops of the trunks (in the way of riverside willows). Old hedgerow pollards, with a heavy head of massive branches all spreading from the same point at the top of the trunk, are still a common sight.

Local fashions in planting are still noticeable. Most of the hedgerow trees in Norfolk are oaks; but many miles of hedgerow have been planted with Scots pine. Hedgerows are also the place to look for ornamental trees such as horse chestnut, which is not planted as a timber tree in woodland.

But the typical hedgerow tree of lowland Britain was the elm. Although rarely setting good seed, it suckered down the hedgerow to give rows of trees of noble proportions. It was largely wiped out in the 1970s by Dutch elm disease, and the cut stumps remain along many hedgerows. In some areas, however, young elms are growing from the old root systems.

RECOGNIZING OLD HEDGES

A blowzy hedge is not necessarily an old one: its appearance will reflect when it was last trimmed or 'laid' (see pp. 72–73). On the other hand, its variety of plant life is often a good clue. Assart hedges originating from strips of woodland often contain woodland flowers such as bluebells, white wood anemones and dog's mercury with inconspicuous green flowers. The presence of Midland hawthorn might also indicate a hedge of this origin.

The variety of woody shrubs and trees can be a clue to the age of the hedge. A Georgian enclosure hedge, for example, might contain nothing but the hawthorn it was planted with. In time seeds of other species will arrive, and a Saxon hedge that has been growing untouched along a parish boundary bank for a thousand years will contain a good many. One fact to remember is that hedges growing alongside ploughland are likely to be on good soil.

DATING HEDGES

A system researched on hedges in the shires gives good results in many lowland areas. Pace out lengths of 30 strides along one side of the hedge and count how many different woody species (trees and shrubs) there are in each length. Names are not needed—they can be told apart by their leaves. Disregard ivy, brambles and climbers, and count all wild rose species as one. Find the average per 30-stride length and multiply by 100 to give the approximate age in years. A Saxon boundary bank hedge might be expected to have ten or twelve different species, a Tudor one five or six. Unlike old woods, hedges are not normally shown on old maps.

Hedgerow craft

Being a living thing, a hedge has to be cut back to keep it in shape. Hedge 'laying' is an art that is probably of considerable age, although there is no documentary proof.

COPPICING

The treatment that a hedge receives will reflect the job it has to do. Many hedges growing on old boundary banks have no real function, and some of these were (and still are) coppiced in the woodland tradition. This means that they are cut right down to the ground every four or five years. The stumps of the shrubs quickly throw up a new head of shoots.

In one tradition, known as an 'arable hedge', the cut branches are piled along the hedge after they have been cut; the growing shoots thread themselves through them to create a barrier which is firm, although not livestock-proof.

TRIMMING

Hedges are often trimmed. The planting of a hedge is only the beginning of a battle, for left to itself it will each spring shoot ever higher and wider. The hedge can be tightened up by trimming it back, and various profiles can be seen. Many are simply square or rectangular in cross-section, but some landowners and farmers favour a triangular profile. This is often a simple result of the height of the roadside bank on which the hedge grows, and whether it is growing within easy reach of the tractor's cutters.

However, the hawthorn which grows in most hedges is a tree species, albeit of small stature, and hawthorn shrubs strive to lengthen and strengthen their trunks. In a trimmed hedge there is also a danger that the lower of the interwoven mass of branches will weaken and die as they are in almost permanent shade. In other words, there is a tendency for an old hawthorn hedge to become gappy at the bottom. If the hedge is let go, after a few decades all that will remain is a row of short hawthorn trees across a pasture—a fairly common sight nowadays in Pennine valleys and other places.

A gappy hedge still serves well enough as a boundary marker to a field, but it is useless for keeping animals in or out. There is a saying that whatever sheep can see through, they can get through. Barbed-wire fencing is widely used today, but in the days before this became general (that is before World War I, when it was widely used in trench warfare) livestock hedges were tightened up by 'laying'.

LAYING OR LAYERING

It is assumed that this is an ancient tradition, although there is no documentary proof that it is older than Georgian enclosure days, except that defensive 'hedges' described by Julius Caesar in his *Gallic Wars* could have been similar. Hedge laying was certainly widely practised in Victorian times and the early years of this century, however. Hedges which were last cut and laid decades ago are common and easy to recognize. However, recently laid hedges are also common, since the skill is being maintained in many places.

It is usually counted a job for the dead days of the winter months. Even skilfully done, the work has to be repeated every 15–20 years (or perhaps less) depending on the soil and shrubs growing.

It requires sympathetic attention and a fine eye for the health of the stems and other woody matter. Laying has the individual tempo and language of all true countryside skills. It is a slow and laborious business: a few large fields would keep the hedger busy all winter and perhaps 30 yards a day would be a good rate. The professional hedge layer also boasts a special kit of tools whose efficiency relies as much on the way they are used as on their shape or cutting edge.

CLEANING DITCH AND HEDGE

Many enclosure hedges have a ditch alongside, and part of the job is to clear this. Then to the hedge itself. It is cleaned up using a long-handled briar hook or a shorter slasher to remove the ivy and other climbers and the tangled brambles and hedgefoot vegetation.

Long lengths of stems—of hazel or willow, or even bramble—are trimmed cleaned of side shoots for later use as a 'rope' or heathering. Other straight, stronger branches might be trimmed down for use as stakes. They are all put aside. All is now ready for the crucial skill of laying.

PLEACHERS

What is left is a line of strong, vertical woody stems, or pleachers, which will be the skeleton of the hedge's future growth. The crucial skill is to take a pleacher in one hand and to cut at an angle near the base, hard enough to slice down through the rigid heart-

A well-packed, tightly meshed bullock hedge. Many recently laid hedges have a looser mesh.

wood but not hard enough to sever the stem completely. A precisely judged strip of pliable bark is left untouched. The pleacher is then bent sideways, the bark strip acting as a hinge, and then the next pleacher is treated and bent. Being untouched, the bark strip continues to carry sap and is a lifeline for the future hedge, allowing the row of bent pleachers to throw out heads of new shoots which in coming years will grow densely to create a livestock-proof hedge.

FINISHING THE HEDGE

The stakes which are hammered in along the line of the hedge give vertical support to the pleachers until their new shoots grow to interweave. The hedge is often finished by tightening it with a horizontal binding or 'heather-ing' of hazel or briar shoots—or even just string—between the top of the stakes.

REGIONAL VARIETY

Olden-time hedgers claimed to be able to tell blindfold where they were, if they could feel the hedge. In Cheshire the pleachers are woven through the line of hammered stakes. A typical Midlands bullock hedge will have the brushy ends of the pleachers all facing into the field, whereas in Wales sheep hedges are laid with the brushy ends pointing out along both sides, and the whole hedge may be packed with 'dead wood' (cut branches) to give extra density.

THE HEDGER'S TOOLS

An axe is used for the heavier growth, and the slasher used to clear the hedge is really a long-handled, curved knife. The most important tool is the bill-hook. This can be single- or double-edged, but it varies from county to county. Names also vary: in the north billhooks are called brummocks, while pleachers are known as plashers, plet-chers or plushers. The traditional hedger's glove, worn on the hand that grasped the pleachers and the brambles, was a mitten with a separate thumb.

In bygone days, the mittens were made by the village saddler, of sturdy leather. The billhooks and other tools, too, are likely to have been forged and sharpened just along the village street at the village blacksmith's. Nowadays, despite mechanization, power tools are seldom used in hedge laying.

The drystone wall

Drystone walls usually replace hedges where the stone is easily won from the ground in upland and lowland alike. Field walls show local differences.

OLD STONE BANKS AND WALLS

When clearing boulders and stones for the plough from earliest times it made sense to pile them up out of the way—as round piles or cairns of stones, or heaped as a kind of rough bank. Cairns were sometimes collected in cairnfields in the Lake District and the Pennines; some could be of Bronze Age date, and confused with cemeteries of burial cairns, except that clearance cairns are usually smaller and flatter. Banks of gathered surface stones can be quite long: some Scottish examples approach half a mile. They too can be of early date.

It often made sense to pile them up as a rough wall. Many early stone walls remain on *Dartmoor*, at Grimspound and other places, still recognizable despite the fact that their stones seem haphazardly balanced with more hope than skill. On Dartmoor many lengths of early walls are boundary markers, known as 'reaves', a fact made clear if they are carefully traced across country, for they will often be found to link up with streams, lines of crags and other natural features. In Cornwall, the stone field walls we see today (called 'hedges') are of considerable age, built of rounded boulders and large stones collected from the surface round about.

DRYSTONE WORK

In the countryside, a stone wall is usually taken to mean a drystone wall, that is, built without mortar. The Scots call them drystone dykes or dikes. There was at first no need to quarry stone if there was plenty to hand on the surface. On the other hand, one advantage of quarried stone is that a much tighter wall can be made. Unlike hedge laying, we can be certain that drystone walling has been a countryside craft for thousands of years: the evidence survives.

The Broch of Mousa (*Shetlands*) which dates to AD 100–400, is a beautiful construction with a careful slope or 'batter', and made with pieces of local, thinly bedded sandstone rock. But older by far is the drystone work of the Neolithic settlement of *Skara Brae* (Orkneys), which dates to before 2500 BC. Here too the early masons took advantage of the fact that the local rock split into slabs. Far to the south, Neolithic drystone work is often found filling the gaps between the larger sarsens of the entrances and chambers of burial mounds. Sometimes low walling hems the mound, as at Wayland's Smithy on the *Ridgeway* (Oxon) and at *Belas Knap* (Glos).

Centuries of expertise lie behind drystone walling, in other words, and 'rough' walls around the fields have often been built with more skill than is apparent. A more recent masterpiece is a hole-in-the wall gateway to be found at the country park on *Portland* (Dorset).

FIELD WALLS

In countryside where stone is to hand,

In the Lake District, the neat enclosures of the fellsides surround older haphazard fields of the valley bottom.

or easily quarried nearby from crags and bluffs, drystone walls are the counterpart of hedges. Hedges are, however, still found in stone wall countryside.

Stone walls are more of an upland feature, although not absent from the lowlands. The majority were built to parcel up the land at the time of the Georgian enclosures, but they are often older in areas where earlier, Tudor enclosure Acts had more effect. Large areas of Northumberland and the Lake District were walled in the 16th century, for example, as were areas of Wales.

As with hedges, the older walls could well be those of the paddocks near the settlements. The open common lands further away were the last to be enclosed.

THE GEORGIAN ENCLOSURES

The main period of the enclosures was 1750–1850. Walling gangs were employed, often out-of-work miners. Very often several gangs would collaborate, and their work between the 'wall ends' which mark their lengths can differ

A typical wall end.

markedly, not only in skill but in what the client ordered.

THE WALL'S DESIGN

Lake District walls are classic examples of walls built for the purpose of enclosure. It is probable that a length of 5 ft. 4–6 ft high, could be

The make of a stone wall.

finished per day per man.

The first job was to firm up the foundation, and very often a trench was dug even on rocky ground and tightly packed with stone. On this were raised the two outside surfaces of drystone walling, built up with a batter—that is, they sloped in slightly as they rose. A wooden batter frame was used to help gauge this.

The inside of the wall between these faces was filled with 'hearting' of rubble or small stones with every now and then a 'through stone' passing from one side to the other to bind the two faces together. The tall walls of the Pennines usually have three rows of through stones. Great skill was used when breasting steep hillsides without disturbing the even running of the stone. It is always worth a diversion to have a close look at the way a Lake District wall meets and surmounts a rocky crag.

A good many of those crags may be the surfaces left by quarrying the stone. On the other hand a length of rounded surface stones in a wall of sharp-edged quarried stones often indicates that an old burial or clearance cairn nearby has been raided. This is very obvious in hard-rock areas such

as the Lake District, the Pennines and parks of *Dartmoor* (Devon).

THE TOPPING

The top of the wall may be finished with a row of slanted 'coping' stones. Sometimes, however, the top has simply been left with a staggered row of loose stones, easy to replace but a deterrent to ambitious sheep. In some counties tall 'cock ups' alternating with short give a battlemented effect

A Lake District hogg hole.

HOGG HOLES

For the passage of sheep, 'hogg holes' are left at the bottom of Lake District walls, closed with a boulder ('hogg' is a dialect word for a sheep). Sometimes the through stones project well out from the wall at each side to give a foothold for a man, and sometimes three or four are arranged as a convenient staircase. But stone walls have stiles and gates, as do hedges. Stone squeezer stiles are not uncommon (see pp. 126–127).

REGIONAL WALLING

There are many separate and distinct regional styles which reflect the character of the stone used. In some parts of Scotland and Yorkshire 'single dyke' walls are seen, of a single stacking of rounded stones. The rock layers of Caithness allow walls of vertical slabs to be made, and similar can be seen around Hawkshead in the Lake District. In the Cotswolds the 'cock ups' set shoulder to shoulder are like books on a shelf, no two alike.

Grass fields and meadows

Grass management has changed drastically in recent years, but the flowery hay meadows of old-fashioned farming can still be found.

THE GRASS FIELD

By Tudor times, when enclosed fields were becoming reasonably common, which fields were grass was in the main decided by the needs of the plough. The poorer soil became pasture. But 'up and down' husbandry was sometimes practised; here the field was ploughed and sown with grain until the soil was exhausted, and it was then left to grass over and be grazed, the animal dung enriching it again. 'Taking the plough around the farm' in this way was a forerunner of the crop rotations later made popular in the new 'scientific' farming.

Today many grass fields are treated in the same way as any other crop field, being 'leys' or temporary grassland. The field is ploughed and sown with lush hybrid grasses; then after a number of years (2 and 5 years are common leys) it is reploughed. If grazed, it is usually rationed out with electric fences which are moved each day to allow the animals on to a fresh strip. But grass is often cut for silage.

THE SILAGE CUT

This is a relatively recent harvest but has largely replaced hay. Silage is cut in late spring (often in May), with a second cut when the grass has grown again later in the year. Unlike hay, the grass is cut lush and green, and is stored in a darkened 'clamp' to pickle and keep for winter cattle feed. The clamp may be no more than a concrete-walled compound covered with black plastic sheeting weighted down with old tyres—a familiar sight in the modern countryside. Sometimes it is now baled out in the fields in black plastic.

THE HAY MEADOW

Hay can be cut from planted ley fields. June is the usual month. Traditionally, however, soil which grew the best grass was laid aside for permanent hay meadows. Never ploughed, these fields carried a variety of wild grasses and became colourful with wild flowers. The timing of the cutting regime gave them a chance to set seed, and also a chance for lapwings to nest. The wild flowers attracted many butterflies, so that hay meadows were busy with wildlife in early summer. Their mixture of flowers and wild grasses gave them a tawny colour quite unlike the vivid green of a sown ley. A few old hay meadows can still be picked out by their colour in the hills, in Derbyshire near *Dovedale*, for example, and in the Yorkshire Dales.

By and large, however, those that remain on lower ground usually only survive as protected nature reserves. Hay meadows often occupied the damp soil alongside streams, and in recent years this land has largely been drained and ploughed for corn.

LOT FIELDS

Yarnton and Oxey Meads just outside *Oxford* are Thames-side meadows which remain unchanged, and until very recently Yarnton Mead was managed in the traditional way. Stones set in it marked out strips which were allocated by lot among the 'commoners', local farmers who had grazing rights to the land. In early spring each year the 'meadsman' assembled them for the lottery, to pick small cherrywood balls from a closed bag. These balls carried names of past commoners (Walter of Begbroke, for example, Begbroke being a nearby

Old hay meadows can be a paradise of wild flowers, as is this one in Swaledale (N. Yorks), at its best in June.

village) and carried the rights to certain strips of the meadow. The farmers used to bargain among themselves to amalgamate the lots they had picked into workable holdings. After the hay cut they could graze cattle on the land from Lammas (1 August) to All Saints (1 November), as each hay lot also carried the right to graze a certain number of beasts.

HAYMAKING TRADITIONS

Even in these mechanized days, with tractor-drawn cutters and rakers, haymaking follows traditional lines. The word really means hay drying as the stalks (cut just before energy is diverted from leaf to seed) contain excess moisture: this can allow the hay to ferment and heat up so much that the stack may (surprisingly) catch fire. Traditionally, a mower scythed the hay, over an acre of it each long, thirsty day. After him came the haymakers, who raked it into long swathes, which were tossed in the sunshine at need, finally being piled into loose 'cocks'. Three or four fine days after the cut, these were heaved onto a wide-bodied hay wagon and carted off to be made into a stack. All the able-bodied down to the youngest were involved.

HAYSTACKS

Today's hay is usually mechanically bundled in the fields, and stored in a covered barn. Haystacks are very rarely seen, although some farms may make one for old time's sake. They were erected on a platform of timber or stone to allow air to the centre, and were as tall as could be easily thrown up with a pitchfork. They were thatched against rain (in some areas traditionally with green rushes). English haystacks were usually rectangular, those in Wales and Scotland round. In Scotland the hay was traditionally gathered by night into 'handcocks' which were sledged to the barnyard, where they were made into a row of round stacks. Round stacks

The sluice-gate of a watermeadow. Watermeadows were devised to give sheep an early bite.

can still be seen in mainland Europe, in the Alps for example.

THE WATERMEADOW

This was a completely different tradition. Some riversides today are still corrugated with a herringbone pattern of slight ridges and deeper hollows, quite unlike the ridge and furrow of ploughland. Often the central shallowly banked ditch has a sluice-gate and wooden hatches to close it off.

They are what remains of 'wetshod waterworks', usually 17th or 18th-century in date, once operated by skilled 'drowners' from the village. By damming a stream and gently flooding (or 'floating') the field with a shallow wash, the frost was kept off the grass, which thus grew to give an early bite for the sheep (and their new lambs). At

the back end of the year the process could be repeated to extend the growing season of the grass, for better grazing or even another crop of hay.

Floodwater carrying silt could also be led to these meadows, to enrich the soil, although these 'watermeadows' are more common in chalk countryside, where the river flow is more even and less prone to heavy flood. Many remain in the *Itchen Valley* (Hants) for example.

THE HAYMARKET

We have quickly forgotten how vital hay was, although horse-drawn transport was common well into this century. From early times, hay was an important market crop, and many market towns retain the street name 'Haymarket'.

Sheep pastures

Fields of grazing sheep are still a common sight in the countryside, but gone are the days when their wool was a main source of Britain's wealth.

SHEEP

Sheep merit their own chapter in any history of the countryside, and after lambing there are now more alive in Britain than at any time since records began: the total has passed 40 million in recent years. But not only are they numerous, they have also had (and continue to have) a strong influence on the landscape.

BREEDS OF SHEEP

The sheep herded in Neolithic times were probably something like the spindly Soay sheep to be seen at St Kilda and other islands. The Romans brought heavier, longwool breeds, and these were the ancestors of the old Cotswold breed and today's Leicesters. Lowland breeds include both long-wools and shortwools such as the Southdown. Mountain sheep such as the Scottish Blackface, the Swaledale and the Herdwick of the Lake District are sturdy enough to winter outdoors on the fells. In the case of the latter they are partly helped in this by a strong 'hefting' instinct, which keeps them to their own 'home' hillside. The Mule is a popular crossbreed, of Swaledale ewe and Leicester ram.

WOOL PROFITS

At certain times in history, sheep could be relied on to give good dividends. *Bolton Priory* (N. Yorks) for example (see pp. 60–61) had 3000 sheep, and in Tudor England there were three sheep alive for every man. The trade was at first in their wool, which was exported to Europe, but the European wars destroyed this market and finished cloth became more profitable. There were three main centres: in East Anglia, the Cotswolds (whose sheep gave their name to the area) and the West Country, in each of which areas the profits built fine houses for the yeomen wool and cloth dealers. Many of the churches in these areas were also rebuilt or enlarged as glorious 'wool churches' in Perpendicular Gothic style, with hammerbeam roofs and tall western towers.

THE DOWNS

These areas of chalk high ground spread as an ungainly octopus across southern England, its body centred on Salisbury Plain, with arms stretching out as the Dorset and Hampshire Downs, the North and South Downs, and another extending past the Chilterns to East Anglia to end as the Wolds of Lincolnshire and Yorkshire. The soil is thin and light and was cleared of trees in Neolithic times. Sheep grazing has kept it open since, and this grazing, together with the poverty of the soil (which has discouraged rampant weeds), has created a fine turf alight with wild flowers: as many as 30 different species (including wild grasses) might be counted in a single square yard. Wild orchids are indicators of this ancient turf.

Sheep grazing continued here well past Victorian days. Some was ploughed in Napoleonic times, but in the main, ploughing was deferred until this century, when two world wars demanded home-grown corn and (latterly) arable subsidies have made corn very profitable. The open vistas are now broken with barbed-wire fencing. Some remaining grassland areas are protected as nature reserves, and some may remain on slopes too steep for the tractor, but as they would feed too few sheep to bother, these are usually becoming scrubbed. Oddly, quite large areas of this ancient turf still remain unploughed, though becoming dotted with hawthorn scrub, as army ranges, on Salisbury Plain in particular, as can be seen above *Edington* (Wilts).

THE HILL GRAZINGS

Equally ancient grazing land is found in the uplands. The open Pennine and Lake District slopes were, like the Downs, largely cleared in early times, and grazing and climate changes have since kept them open. Wetter weather has created a good deal of bogland here. Their grazing value was jealously recognized at the time of the enclosures, when much of the ground was divided up by drystone walling.

Above this, the open character prevails and in some areas there is much high, open common grazing.

There are some cattle, but sheep reign here, even among the crags. Up here they cause considerable damage to the wild flowers; indeed these mountain flowers are usually only seen growing on rock faces, waterfalls and such places out of reach of the hungry animals. In high valleys here and in Scotland and Wales there is always likely to be a rowan, juniper or birch growing out of an inaccessible crack into which a seed lodged— another proof of sheeps' influence.

ANCIENT TRADITIONS

Where they remain unploughed, the sheep-grazed Downs and hill pastures preserve the distant past. Neolithic, Bronze Age and Iron Age remains

abound. In the north there are often echoes of the Viking tradition of shieling, of wintering livestock in the sheltered valleys and moving up with them to spend the summer on the upper slopes. Stone-walled summer corrals and the remains of rectangular summer huts can be found. In some areas linhays remain from the heyday of the enclosures; these are field barns, often perched to make use of the sloping hillside to create an animal shed below and a hay store above. Many of them stand derelict today.

THE SHEPHERD

Wide-scale sheep grazing on the boundless expanses of the chalk Downs ended within living memory, and photographs can be found of Downland shepherds and their dogs, and the vast sheep markets of some

areas. The small sleepy village of East Ilsley near the *Ridgeway* (Oxon) once held the largest sheep fair in Britain. Pub names such as The Woolpack, The Shears—and of course The Lamb—recall those days. The shepherd's crooks (possibly of prehistoric origin) were of different patterns, knowingly designed to catch either neck or leg, or (in modern times) for pushing the head under the sheep-dip.

CROSS BREEDING

Sheep are now bred for meat rather than wool, and in a unique way they play a part in uniting the uplands and lowlands of Britain. The hardiness of the hill-bred 'tups' (rams) is often bred into the more prolific qualities of the lowland breeds. At great October sales, cross-bred lambs reared in the hills are sold off as 'stores' to be fattened on

Downland lambing pens at the turn of the century. The hurdles are 'thatched' to give good shelter.

lowland pastures.

As a result, the shepherd—and the crook—are still familiar on farms throughout Britain. Although a Lake District farmer might act as his own shepherd, full-time shepherds are usually employed to handle the large Scottish flocks. They often use the traditional counting slang: yan, tan, tethera, pattera, pimp. Contract shepherds might also be called in to help with the larger lowland flocks at lambing time, and also to help with the shearing in early summer, always a labour-intensive business. Always they are accompanied by the traditional collie; the name is said to be from a Celtic word for a small dog.

Ploughland

Over the long centuries the plough field has witnessed many changes: today's ploughing by tractor is only the latest chapter in a long story.

THE FIRST PLOUGHS

The plough turns the compact soil, loosens it, and uproots and buries weeds. A crop can then be sown and gathered to yield a bountiful harvest. On this discovery is civilization based. And from the start the plough has helped to change the landscape.

Neolithic tribes were the first to sow crops. At first they very probably used antler picks or weighted digging sticks to break the ground after burning off the vegetation. Later an 'ard', a narrow, angled spade, was used, drawn by oxen to scratch shallow furrows. To turn the soil thoroughly, however, criss-cross furrowing (cross-ploughing) was necessary and shallow scratchings of this kind have been found on old land surfaces under the piled soil of Neolithic and Bronze Age burial mounds.

THE SMALL SQUARE FIELD

Cross-ploughing is easier in square plots, and so squarish fields evolved. Squarish 'Celtic' fields, marked by boundary banks (now slighted by time) are often earlier than the Iron Age (one meaning of 'Celtic'), although continuing in use throughout that period. They can be seen throughout Britain—below Barbury Iron Age fort near the *Ridgeway* (Oxon), near *Malham* (N. Yorks) and elsewhere. They are up to 2 acres.

A much heavier wheeled plough was introduced from Europe in the late Iron Age, around 100 BC. It was really a new kind of machine, with a 'coulter' to cut the furrow, a 'share' to lift it, and a 'mouldboard' to overturn it.

Cross-ploughing was no longer necessary, but the Roman love of regularity would almost certainly have introduced a grid of large square ploughfields, of which traces may remain in Norfolk (see pp. 58–59).

THE OPEN PLOUGHFIELDS

During the Dark Ages and after, the open-field system evolved, the ground being ploughed in long, narrow lines which cut down the time wasted turning the ox team at the 'headlands'. This up-and-down ploughing, always turning the sods inwards, in time created a corduroy ploughland of 'ridge and furrow', the furrows acting as drains. An advantage of this was that wheat and barley, being by origin Mediterranean crops, prefer a dry soil. (Oats and rye may have been native to northern Europe.)

The terracing of hillsides with lynchets is a puzzling feature. They were created by constant ploughing along a line above a field boundary. They may be medieval, but are equally likely to be prehistoric. Whatever their origin, they are a distinct part of the scenery where they occur (see pp. 58–59).

THE ORIGIN OF THE ACRE

In early medieval times, ploughland was estimated not by its actual area, but by the work of a yoke of oxen. In Domesday Book of 1086, the estates were assessed in 'hides'—the area an ox team could plough each year—which could never be a standard quantity as it varied from village to village because of the change in soil, the strength of the beasts and other things. In time, however, a furlong—the furrow length of the strips in the open fields—became fixed at 220 yards. A square with furlong sides has an area of 10 acres.

The word 'acre' had been in use for some time before this, to denote the area a yoke of oxen could plough in a day. Eventually a system of measurement using 'chains' was adopted, and applied to all land, pasture as well as arable. At first there were actual measurement chains 22 yards long, composed of 100 iron links. Twenty-two yards was a convenient length as it can be multiplied to give areas in terms of acres, and many enclosure hedges will be found to be measured out in units of 2 chains, or 44 yards.

It might be expected that the names of hedged fields might echo their size. However, many fields called '10 acre' are not! Why this should be can only be discovered on the spot: likely reasons are that part of the field was planted as a copse, or extra land was later taken into it.

THE PLOUGH TEAMS

Oxen were the earliest engine, and were used even until Victorian times, when great ox teams with their characteristic yokes were still seen pulling the latest all-iron ploughs. Although oxen could only do half as much as horses, not all could afford the heavyweight plough horses such as the Shire, Suffolk Punch and similar breeds. There are many farm museums with the ploughs (and the animals) to be seen: the *Acton Scott Farm Museum* near Church Stretton

(Shropshire) for example.

The traditional plough year remained. It began in early January, as most crops were spring-sown. On the first Monday after Twelfth Night, the ploughmen went the rounds of the village for contributions for their Plough Monday festival. The plough year ended before the Harvest, for the horses were needed for that.

LANDS

One result of the enclosures was that the new fields were often dug with buried 'mole' drains, pipes to dry the soil. The drained ridging produced by the up-and-down ploughing of medieval fields became unnecessary. But ridging results anyway if the field is simply ploughed up and down. To avoid this, ploughfields were divided into 'lands', which were ploughed in sequence. The problem is avoided by the modern reversible ploughs which reverse the angle of throw when they turn at the hedge at each side.

STEAM PLOUGHING

In an attempt to increase efficiency, steam engines (still seen at rallies) became common in Victorian times. Stationed in pairs, they winched the plough across the field between them. The ploughing of 10 or more acres a day was claimed, even when the ground was sticky.

TRACTORS

Today's tractor, however, will plough more than 20 acres a day with ease. To facilitate its use (and the use of the larger combine harvester which follows it) the fieldscape has again been changed, with the hedges grubbed up to create prairie fields in many areas.

The use of the tractor and artificial fertilizers means that the land is now ploughed immediately after harvest for 'winter' sowing in the autumn.

Lynchets are a puzzling feature.

The farmstead

The farmstead is the hub of the countryside. It may occupy a site of great age, and the buildings can be many hundreds of years old.

THE POWERHOUSE OF THE COUNTRYSIDE

Over three quarters of Britain is in farming use of one kind or another, and the farmstead is the powerhouse of this countryside. From it stem the activities which not only take place in the fields around, but which also to a large extent shape those fields.

The farm or farmstead is traditionally the home of a farmer. The word 'farm' itself comes from a Latin word meaning rent, and the word 'farmer' in the sense of a man renting land to cultivate has in recent centuries replaced a whole rag-bag of descriptions such as husbandman and yeoman, which evolved from the land-holding systems of feudal times.

THE OLDEST FARMHOUSES

Old farmsteads are typical of 'ancient and ornamental countryside' (see pp. 68–69). The house itself may be of considerable age, although usually added to and changed, expecially during the Great Rebuilding of the 16th century and later. At this time the introduction of brick or stone chimneys meant that the open hall of medieval days could be divided into separate rooms, and an upper floor also created (see pp. 104–105). Glass also came into use, with more and larger windows. The oldest farmhouses are at core of 13th- and 14th-century date, but adapted in this way.

There were regional and county variants (and some can be visited in 'farm museums'). Townend in *Trout-beck*, (Cumbria), is a sturdy northern version, whose family for 300 years carved their own furniture, which remains today.

THE OLDEST FARMSTEADS

The site of the farmstead may be far older than the buildings which stand there today. There is evidence that farmsteads in Devon stand on sites inhabited since the Bronze Age. These prehistoric farmsteads were typically girdled by a circular fence of stone or timber, within which were one or two stone- or timber-walled round huts, one of which was the dwelling 'farmhouse', the others perhaps used for pottery or weaving or other special

tasks. There were also grain stores (sometimes an above-ground granary, sometimes a steep-sided pit lined with wickerwork), and maybe a drying kiln to roast the grain to prevent germination. Animals may also have been penned here within the fence, for night-time safety from wolves and bears and human rustlers. These farmsteads have been excavated in many parts of Britain, and an Iron Age version has been reconstructed and can be visited at *Butser Hill* (Hants).

THE MEDIEVAL FARM

In the open-field countryside of medieval times, all buildings bar a few

A farmyard in a late Victorian photo: much has changed although many features remain familiar.

squatter farms perhaps were usually within the village, and were the ancestors of today's 'cottages' (see pp. 104–105). Some have been reconstructed at the Weald and Downland Museum, *Singleton* (W. Sussex) and the *Avoncroft Museum* (Hereford & Worcs) and elsewhere.

THE MODEL FARMSTEAD

By Georgian times, when the enclosures were in full swing, the courtyard farmstead was widespread. It reached the peak of its evolution in the 'model' enclosure farms built among their newly hedged and ditched fields. It is still typical, although Scotland is rather different (see pp. 152–153). In Victorian days these farmsteads were often built of brick, which the railways were making the universal building material. They often have commemorative names such as Waterloo Farm or even jokey names such as Turnip Farm as a clue to their date.

They were mixed farms. As well as innovations such as turnips and kale to feed the livestock wintered in the farmyard, they relied on FYM—farm yard muck, the well-trodden manure and bedding straw—to nourish the ploughlands.

This farmyard itself reflected its different uses, which changed by the season. It is typically an enclosed yard, surrounded by open sheds and roofed buildings. One, often facing south, is the farmhouse itself, while on the north side giving shelter from the winter weather is the great barn used for storing the cut sheaves and for threshing them. To one side lie the cattle sheds in which they spent the winter. Part of this range might have been adapted as a milking parlour. Alongside or opposite lay the stables for the horses with lean-tos to shelter the ploughs, wagons and other carriages. One corner of the yard was occupied by the muck heap, waiting to be ploughed into the fields. Another corner was usually occupied by a pigsty or two, while the poultry were free-range, scrabbling where they wished.

Originally the hay to feed horses and winter cattle was protected in thatched haystacks raised nearby, but a couple of centuries ago the high-roofed open-sided Dutch barn became popular for storing the hay and straw. With space tight in the farmyard proper this is usually to be found alongside. Also alongside was the granary, typically raised off the ground on mushroom-headed staddle stones to deter rats. Many 'farm museums' maintain such farmsteads: the *Acton Scott* near Church Stretton (Shropshire) is one example, and it also has traditional breeds of livestock.

TODAY'S FARMSTEAD

Farming has changed in recent years, and very often those farmyard buildings are used only for storing the tractors and other machinery. Fertilizers have made FYM obsolete (except for organic farmers) and a good many farms are wholly arable. Those that maintain cattle feed them from a silage clamp, often a concrete box built alongside the winter sheds. These sheds are now vast utilitarian buildings of concrete-slab walls and sheet roofs which have appeared alongside, sometimes instead of, the older farmyard. These sheds may also house wintering sheep, for Britain today has more sheep than ever before.

Few farms have their own pigs; pig production has become specialized in enclosed 'factory farming' units, as has egg and chicken production.

THE ORCHARD

An orchard used also to be typical of the old-fashioned farm, set alongside the farmhouse in a sheltered spot to counter the frosts and encourage the early bees to pollinate. Pigs (and sometimes geese, although they foul the grass) were often allowed to graze the windfalls.

RARE BREEDS

Many farm museums keep a few traditional breeds of cattle, sheep and pigs. There was great variety in the past—the Gloucester Old Spot, for example, was a distinct breed fattened on the windfalls in the cider orchards of the West Country and was just one breed among many.

The barn

The ancient barn is among the most handsome of traditional buildings, the cathedral of the countryside. Its design reflects the job it did.

THE ORIGIN OF THE BARN

The word 'barn' comes from words meaning barley store. Barley was the favoured grain of the Saxons and they probably had barns although the first written record of a barn is from some years after the Norman Conquest.

THE OLDEST BARNS

Some remaining barns are of medieval date, and open-air buildings museums (see pp. 82–83) have some early barns. Very often the early barns are called tithe barns—storage for the tenth of the parish produce due to the church. Many massive older barns were built by the monastic landlord: for example, the 13th–century barn at Great Coxwell near *Faringdon* (Oxon) was built for Beaulieu Abbey (Hants) and the tithe barn at *Frocester* (Glos) was once part of a monastic estate. But by the time of the Georgian enclosures, most farmsteads were likely to number a barn among the other farmyard buildings, for it was an essential workplace as well as secure storage on any farm which had ploughland.

THE WORKING BARN

In the heyday of the barn, the corn was cut by hand with sickles, and bound into loose sheaves which were propped up as 'stooks' or stacks to dry in the sun. They were then carted to the barn, to be piled deep on one side. Often it seems that one of the workhorses, ridden by a young son of the family (everyone else was out in the fields) trod the sheaves down tightly, to save space and deter rats. The central space, stretching between the facing pairs of doorways, was the threshing floor. (If the doors were set in porches, the porch floor was known as the threshold.) Threshing, using flails of wood and leather, was a hard, dusty winter job hated by the farmhands. After threshing, the spent straw was brushed aside to be stored in the opposite side of the barn, and the remaining pile of loose grain and chaff was winnowed—tossed into the air— the chaff being separated by the breeze whistling through the wide doorways, opened for the task. The free grain was then often stored in 'cornholes' or bays next to the spent straw before being taken to the granary.

LOCAL VARIETIES OF BARN

Although barns remain simple in plan,

The barn was a workplace.

weatherboarding

threshold

they incorporate many fascinating details. Past centuries were hand-made times, and utility buildings such as this were made of whatever was easiest to hand. They were often built by the family themselves, and skills and custom were unquestioningly handed down. The result is that details of the barn can change from parish to parish.

Stone and timber are common wall materials (brick only became cheap enough in Victorian times). The timbering (sometimes set on a plinth of stone to prevent the ends rotting) might be infilled with wattle and daub, or covered with weatherboarding planks (quite common in the south). The floors could be of stone—now polished by centuries of threshing—or simply of hard trodden clay.

The vertical timbers supporting the barn roof marked out compartments, or 'bays'. The oldest barns are likely to be cruck-built: a tree trunk cut in half lengthwise provided a matched pair of curving crucks, which rose up and in from their setting against the wall, sloping towards the ridge of the roof and taking the weight of the roof directly. Many northern barns on small farms with little arable have crucks. But gigantic trees were needed if the barn was to be of any size and so in large barns the roof is supported by elaborate timbering, as might also be seen in the village church. Post and truss was typical of the 17th and 18th

Examples of skilled timbering.

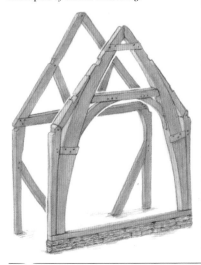

centuries. To obtain even more storage area, the barn might have aisles, the walls being set further out to create a true cathedral of the working countryside.

The roof itself might be of thatch ('hipped' roofs of thatch are typical of the Vale of Aylesbury and the Chilterns adjacent), or stone slabs (stone 'slates') or tiles. Thin Welsh slates, like brick, owed their widespread use to the Victorian railways; but a Welsh slate roof might have been added later to a much older barn.

A distinctive arrangement is seen in the former West Riding and the Dales of the North Riding of Yorkshire, where 'laithes' are buildings which combine barn and animal shed, or byre, under the same roof as the farmhouse. They are usually set along the roadside. Most of them date from the late 18th century, but sometimes the whole building is now relegated to use for livestock, with a newer farmhouse for the family built alongside.

OLD-TIME DETAILS

Fascinating details can escape the casual glance. The word 'threshold' had its origin in the porch of the barn doors as we have seen. Many stone barns had a pattern of ventilation slits in the walls, allowing air to reach the stored sheaves. These 'windeyes' or 'loopholes' often resemble the arrow slits of castle walls, widening inside. The reason is aerodynamic, for this allowed air to seep in but prevented sharp gusts entering. A circular hole high up on the end wall was the owl hole, to encourage in the barn owl, the unpaid 'rodent operative', to deal with the rats. These end walls might also have pitching doors through which sheaves could be heaved to top up the pile inside.

MACHINERY IN THE BARN

By the start of Victorian times go-ahead farmers were replacing the hand flail with threshing machines, wooden contraptions worked by a horse plodding in a circle; and some barns had round sheds called gin gangs built for the horse. These were replaced by steam threshers.

Barn features.

THE DEMISE OF THE BARN

The barn began to lose its importance as a workplace with the mechanization described above. At first stationary, steam engines were later given wheels and took to the fields, to help with ploughing (see pp. 80–81). They also operated threshing machines out in the open, and the barn became relegated to storage alone, its vast roofs and timbering costly to maintain for just this one job. Some barns became used as livestock sheds, and today many simply hold the tractor and the fertilizer bags. Many are delapidated.

FIELD BARNS

Storage barns for hay were also built in the fields in pasture areas. Most of these date from the enclosures of 1750–1850, and are linked with the new apportioning of the fields (which also affected the uplands). Typical of their regions are the linhays of the Pennines and West Country. They usually take advantage of the slope, being set into a hillside, with a hay loft above and an animal shed below opening out into a foldyard, with the manure pile to one side.

The sporting countryside

Field sports have played a role in creating today's countryside. Woods often double as game coverts, and many were planted for this reason.

THE HUNT

Hunting deer and wild boar on foot or on horseback, aided by dogs, has been a countryside passion since early times, and has played its part in creating the character of the countryside. The Norman and Plantagenet kings put aside vast hunting estates, the Royal Forests, in which farming, grazing and woodmanship and other normal village rights were suspended for the sake of the wild red deer (see pp. 156–157). The greater barons set aside 'chases' in much the same fashion. At the same time the majority of more important landholders en-

closed deer parks; these were populated with fallow as much as with red deer, to be hunted within the park pale or loosed into the surrounding countryside for the sport. These deer parks evolved into the country-house estates we admire today (see pp. 112–113).

THE SPORTING COVERT

'Covert' (or 'cover') was a word first coined in the 18th century for a small wood or thicket giving cover to game birds and foxes, and it is this sporting and hunting interest which maintains them. For without it there would be pressure to fell the coverts and take the land into neighbouring fields. Indeed in the shire counties, sporting interests may have even planted them in the first place. Shelter belts of trees often doubled as sporting coverts.

Hunting with sporting pink— scarlet coat and black velvet cap—and other ceremony evolved at the time of the Georgian enclosures, the grid of fencing and young hedges being ideal hunting country with plenty of jumps. Sporting prints of the time show this newly enclosed countryside. In prime hunting areas such as the Vale of Belvoir around *Bottesford* (Leics) the hedges are still kept neatly trimmed for hunting, and barbed wire (which would rip the horses) is conspicuous by its absence. Although a fox might have its den or 'earth' below a hedge as happily as in a wood, it will run for woodland shelter when hunted. Hence in prime hunting countryside, the coverts have been planted to lead the fox from one to the other, giving a good run for the followers. The even-

ing before the hunt it was usual for the 'earthstopper' to block up badger dens and rabbit warrens in these woods, to prevent the hunted fox finding safety.

SHOOTING

When the first muzzle-loading shotguns brought some degree of safety to the user, shooting became a pastime of the gentry. Pheasants (an exotic bird but first reported here in 1059) were always favoured, because their startling flight tested the skill of the gun. The guns usually hunted in pairs, walking through the covert with dogs ahead to flush the birds. Towards the middle of the last century, however,

Old prints offer landscape clues — this one shows a gun and his dogs and also the fencing of 200 years ago.

key inventions transformed the sport. Rapid-firing breech-loading guns came into use and the pheasant shoot, which became a bloodthirsty passion among the newly rich Victorian industrial magnates, took on a new form. The guns now stationed themselves outside the edge of the wood, while beaters moved slowly through it, flushing out the birds towards the guns.

THE SHOOTING COVERT

The shooting covert was designed, planted and managed to carry the birds high over the guns. Within the wood the open flushing areas were accompanied by a belt of high undergrowth before the edge of tall trees. Disturbed by the beaters, the birds took wing in the open area, rose over the undergrowth but then had to fly high to clear the trees—to find themselves high above the guns. These woods were often planted with rhododendron to give the pheasants good ground cover when they were feeding.

On many sporting estates (and renting out the shooting yields a considerable income) fields or corners of kale or sweet corn may also be planted to harbour the pheasants outside the wood. These too are flushed on shooting days.

THE GAMEKEEPER

Although pheasants have been wild in the countryside for centuries and would maintain themselves, they would not by themselves provide the numbers demanded by a breech-laden shoot. They are thus reared from the egg in pens roofed with wire netting to secure them against foxes and other predators. These are encountered on many countryside walks. And it is against rats, crows, jays and grey squirrels that the gamekeeper wages war, for the carnage they wreak on pheasants nesting in the wild out of the safety of the pens. While they are legally killed, owls, buzzards and kites are not. The means of doom are also now more controlled. Poisoned baits are illegal, as is the barbaric toothed gin trap. However, the macabre gamekeeper's gibbet, with rows of

small corpses strung along a fence and swaying in the breeze, is still a familiar sight. The presumption is that it is a deterrent to potential predators.

THE BAD OLD DAYS

For the villagers, the good old days were usually the reverse. The increase of interest in sport brought in laws as Draconian as the Forest Laws of the Plantagenet kings. In those days mutilation and death were common penalties for poaching deer. But 600 years later the Game Act of 1770 laid on the lash, bringing the threat of transportation to those caught even with rabbits to feed their hungry families. Many poachers were simply hung. This tangle of game legislation brutalized the countryside, filling the villages with spies. Reminders of those days are seen in the toothed man traps and other devices in local museums.

SPORT ON THE MOORS

Fox coverts and shooting coverts are more typical of the lowland countryside than the hills. Fox hunting does take place in the uplands: indeed the Lake District packs which hunt the open fells are followed on foot. It was here that John Peel hunted, in his coat of grey (that is, of unbleached local wool). Deer are stalked in the Scottish Highlands. Neither has much effect on the landscape, but the reverse is true of the grouse.

THE GROUSE MOOR

Although moorlands are often grazed by sheep, grouse moors are maintained for that grazing bird. They feed on the young green shoots of heather but need older, tussocky heather for cover. To provide both, the grouse moors are regularly burnt, usually in patches of about an acre, every eight to twelve years. This swaling (it is called 'muirburn' in Scotland) takes place after the shooting season, which runs from 12 August (the 'Glorious Twelfth') to 10 December. Young heather grows vigorously from the rootstocks unaffected by the flash fire. The mosaic of this burning patterns the shooting moors, often giving them a rather chequered appearance.

Working woodlands

In the countryside of yesterday, woodlands were second in importance only to the open fields. Some are maintained in the traditional way.

SEMINATURAL WOODLANDS

Down the ages many areas of wildwood have been cleared, and then again invaded with trees when the local population dwindled from plague or strife and the ploughlands and grazings were abandoned. This might have happened centuries ago and the wood is by now long established. Other woodland has never been anything but woodland since the days of the wildwood. However, few woods have escaped the hand of man: only Wistman's Wood remote on *Dartmoor* and parts of the relic Scottish pine wildwood such as the *Black Wood of Rannoch* (Tayside) might make the claim (see pp. 156–157). But old woodlands, especially those shown on 17th-century maps and so at least 300 years old are the nearest to natural we can find. They are known as semi-natural woods.

NATURAL INDICATORS

After the passage of centuries they harbour a range of slowly colonizing plants which signpost them. What grows where depends on the soil, but indicators of old woodland include sheets of bluebells (on heavy soils) especially when accompanied by wood anemone and early purple orchid; lily of the valley; herb Paris, and a few woody shrubs and trees such as the small-leaved lime and the Midland hawthorn (which has blunter-lobed leaves than its hedgerow cousin).

COPPICED WOODLANDS

The wild flowers of the woodland floor were in fact encouraged by man's management of the wood. This was for centuries the same everywhere in Britain (and can still be seen in French woodlands). The village woodland was a vital resource to local people and it was cropped as carefully as the open fields alongside.

The method used was 'coppice with standards'. The coppice was the underwood, cut down to the ground every seven to twelve years (and sunlight then flooded in to nourish the flowers). The cut stumps or 'stools' sprouted strongly to yield a bunch of straight shoots which thickened to poles before being cut again. This 'smallwood' had many uses, including providing charcoal, the universal cooking fuel (the tents of the charcoal-burners and their round turf-covered hearths were a common woodland sight until this century). Smallwood was used in housebuilding, for making hurdles and other fencing, and clothes pegs, and much besides.

once cut with billhook or axe, the coppice is now cut with a chainsaw

Certain trees in the coppice were chosen to be allowed to grow tall. The common oak was favoured, for when given space to spread over the coppice, its branches yielded a supply of ready-curved timbers suitable for roof- and ship-building. These timber 'standards' were felled when mature, from 70 to 100 years old. *Bradfield Woods* (Suffolk) are still worked in this way and can be visited.

READING THE DITCHES

To keep out wild deer and grazing livestock which would destroy the young coppice, these village woodlands were enclosed by a massive, meandering bank, dug up *inside* its ditch, and which was originally topped with fencing. (By contrast, the bank surrounding a deer park (see pp. 112–113), which was to keep the animals in, was outside the ditch.) Within the coppice wood, different

The cut coppice 'stools' quickly grow a head of fresh shoots, which are shoulder-high in a year or two.

compartments were marked out, usually with slighter, straighter banks and ditches than those of the wood boundary. These compartments would be cut in turn, so that the wood as a whole yielded a never-ending supply of small-wood and timber.

Much woodland has been let go, and the old coppice may now have grown into sturdy 'many-trunked' trees. Only traces of the boundary bank may remain but it is sometimes possible to follow it on as the hedgebank of the field alongside, which was at some time cleared from the wood.

WOOD PASTURES

This was rough grazing, usually scrubbed in places and dotted with trees, and open to the villagers under their common rights. To be able at the same time to continue to gain a crop of poles, the trees of the wood pastures were pollarded—that is, cut at head height, as are riverside willows, to grow a high head of shoots. In trees that have not been pollarded for many decades, there are now massive branches rising from the truncated trunk. Trees in the forests and chases designated for hunting by the Norman and Plantagenet kings were also often pollarded as this did not disturb the deer. *Epping Forest* (Essex) has many examples. It is interesting that old trees growing along the boundary bank of a coppice woodland are also likely to have been pollarded in the past.

THE OLDEST TREES

The result of centuries of such management has an unexpected result: that the oldest trees in Britain are usually old pollards—their timber value destroyed, they were not worth felling. The Major Oak in *Sherwood Forest* (Notts) is possibly an old pollard, while the Knightwood Oak in the *New Forest* (Hants) certainly is. The oldest living things in Britain might be the ancient ash coppice stools to be seen in some Suffolk woods; they may be 18 ft across. If they survive disease and

other hazards, trees do not have a fixed lifespan.

DATING WOODLAND TREES

Old woods can be recognized by their banks, plants, and from old maps. The ages of individual trees can be estimated. If the tree is close set with others in a coppice wood, each $\frac{1}{2}$ in. of girth measured at head height equals one year of age. Standing isolated with widely spread branches, 1 in. equals one year of age.

MODERN FORESTRY

Unlike the older management regimes, modern forestry is dedicated to timber production alone. The wood is cleared and felled at one go and replanted with bought-in stock. It thus grows same-aged, same-height trees. From time to time the weaker trees may be thinned, to yield a cash crop dividend of timber, and to allow space for the remainder to grow more fully. At their prime, the wood is again clear-felled.

The first of these timber plantations were on open ground, the very first being an oak plantation in Windsor Great Park in 1580. By Victorian times much old wood pasture and many coppice woods had been converted to forestry regimes, and many plantations in the *New Forest* (Hants) have not been felled and look much like seminatural woodland today.

The modern conifer plantation, which is typical of the present century, is the climax of this evolution. Most date since the creation of the Forestry Commission in 1919, although many have been privately planted. Foreign conifers such as sitka spruce are favoured, planted in regimented rows. They are thinned when about 20 ft tall, and the side branches 'brashed' away to allow the growth of knot-free timber. Unlike native woodlands, they deter wildlife, and are empty of flowers and few birds sing in their gloomy corridors. They are in a way an industrialization of the countryside. It has been recent policy, however, to try to lessen their impact on the countryside—for example, by leaving a skirt of original woodland and by planting with an eye to the contours.

The common

The term 'common' is nowadays used loosely, but in law and custom such land has a definite and particular meaning of vital importance to villagers of old.

COMMONS OF MANY KINDS

Epping Forest, Bodmin Moor, Clapham Common in London, many of the open Lake District fells—they are all commons. In Norfolk many commons are ribbons of green (as they are in parts of North Dorset). *Hindhead Common* (Surrey) is a heathy wilderness today. The village green was a common of a kind, once used for lesser grazing (see pp. 100–101). They are all the relic of customs of land use which certainly date back to medieval times and possibly much earlier.

Approximately 1½ million acres of England and Wales is common land, an area 15 times that of the Isle of Wight. The common does not exist as such in Scotland; the rough grazing on which the Scottish crofters rely is held in common but this is not quite the same thing (see pp. 152–153).

COMMONS RIGHTS

Contrary to popular belief, commons are not generally in public ownership, although the public often have free access. Nor are they simply grassy open spaces.

Although some are now held by a council or other public or quasi-public body, most commons are basically privately owned land, today's landowner being the legal descendant of the feudal lord of the manor. The land is subject to the ancient and varied rights of the 'commoners'. These were originally the people of the manor, but as village settlements grew and evolved in medieval and later times, commons rights usually became linked with the cottages rather than the people. The rights which remain today may depend on where the house is situated.

These rights are rooted in feudal times, when the manor lands were jointly worked by the villagers. The lord of the manor owned its land, and exacted taxes and services. The villagers survived because their rights guaranteed their use of the plough-lands and the hay meadow. Their commons rights also unlocked use of the unfarmed village waste lands.

Exactly which rights the commoners held depended on the terrain and on local custom, but the right of pasture was general. Agistment was the right to summer grazing. As *Bodmin Moor* (Cornwall), *Dartmoor* (Devon) and the *New Forest* (Hants) illustrate, even 'wasteland' can still give good enough grazing. Two main kinds of commons grazing were and are recognized. 'Stinted' grazing is reserved for 'gate holders', who have rights to put a certain number of animals on at certain times of year. This controlled grazing usually means the land remains in good heart. It can suffer, however, if the grazing is unstinted. Much of the high Pennines is unstinted, but the canny farmers only keep as many sheep as can survive.

Estover rights (from a Norman French word meaning essentials) allowed the commoners to cut heather and bracken for fuel or bedding. Often they could also collect fallen branches in woodland, and sometimes cut timber for house building (husbote) or cut poles for fencing (heybote). Pannage was the right to graze livestock, especially pigs, on the acorns and beechmast of the autumn woods. Turbary was the right to cut peat for fuel, and fishing (piscary) was sometimes an option, and in some areas the quarrying of gravel or stone, or of marl to lime the fields, was allowed.

OLD CUSTOMS

The lottery of Yarnton Mead (*Oxford*) was maintained until very recently (see pp. 76–77). Oak Apple Day in *Great Wishford* (Wilts) was celebrated by youngsters waking up the village shouting 'Grovely, grovely and all grovely'; later the rector read out a charter reaffirming rights to collect firewood in Grovely Wood. There are other examples.

COMMONS AND ENCLOSURES

Enclosure by fencing or hedging is usually legally prohibited on a common. Although it could give good grazing, the common land was usually

the poorest in the neighbourhood—one reason why it was not ploughland in the first place. But the new-fangled 'scientific' farming brought in by the enclosure movement could profitably take in such poor land, and as a result the Enclosure Acts stripped the commons rights from vast areas, and made farmed fields of it. Four and a half million acres of open commons had been lost by the middle of last century. The commoners robbed of livelihood were faced with the desperate options of starvation or of leaving to join the ranks of workers in the booming industrial towns.

THE BRAKE ON LOSS

By the 1870s, however, Victorian social concern was being shown in many ways. A Commons Act halted the loss of livelihood, while at the same time many scraps of remaining commons within or near the towns were

adopted for public recreation—often to become the town parks we see today. Early in this century commons lying within urban boroughs were made freely available to everyone for 'air and exercise'. The last chapter in the story was the registration of commons by 1970, establishing the identity of the owners and those claiming commons rights, for by then there was often considerable confusion. The reverse of the coin was that if the claims were not registered, the landowner could do as he wished, and many commons were developed as a result.

RECOGNIZING COMMON LAND

One clue is, of course, the name on the map. But whether or not it is high-lighted in this way or signposted on the spot (with the by-laws in force posted up), the land is likely to have an old-fashioned look to it. Never ploughed, it carries the scars of cen-

turies. Some of these may be the diggings of medieval and later times, but others are likely to be of prehistoric origin in the shape of field banks, hut circles, and burial mounds. Commons are often landscape textbooks.

Other indicators are natural. Grazing may have eased, in which case the open land may be scrubbing up. As commons are unploughed, anthills remain and a wide variety of wild flowers and the butterflies and other insects these attract.

WARRENS

Some commons carry warrens, or what remains of them. Rabbits were brought to Britain in Plantagenet times to be bred for meat and fur for the Lord of the Manor. Needing soft soil, they were kept in fenced warrens which either utilized an existing mound, such as a prehistoric earth-work, or enclosed a special 'pillow' of

A gypsy encampment in Victorian days. The making of wooden clothes pegs was an old tradition.

soil of about 30 by 10 yards. There were vast warrens in some suitable areas: Lakenheath Warren in *Breckland* (Norfolk) circled 2000 acres with a 10-mile bank and ditch, some of which remains.

SQUATTERS

Commons attracted gypsies, and there is a National Gypsy Museum at *Pembroke* (Dyfed). Being wild and remote, common land was ever open to squatters—landless refugees who took root, and unless evicted, became established. Many squatter cottages built in the 17th and 18th centuries remain along the rim of commons or along the broad verges of roads. 'End' or 'Bottom' as part of a name is often connected with them.

Market gardens and orchards

The countryside has long been the bounteous provider of fruit and vegetables, each with its own traditional means of cultivation and harvesting.

MARKET GARDENING

The market garden has a long pedigree. Around the towns of even medieval England spread acres of smallholdings, often owned by the townsfolk themselves, which provided vegetables and fruit for the town markets. Later, when the settlements mushroomed in size, market gardening to provide fresh greens, onions and other crops became a specialized industry. Visitors to old London noted the market gardens that swathed the city and the care with which they were tended. Manured with the horse droppings from the streets and the 'night soil' from bedroom slop pans, they had prodigious output. The spread of the city forced the enterprises further out, and maps of Georgian times show market gardens covering the plain from Chelsea to Brentford—a belt of river-rich, fast-draining soil, quick to warm in spring and easy to dig. Those London boroughs of today in fact occupy some of the best garden soil in the country.

The pattern was similar elsewhere, especially when the industrial conurbations accelerated into growth in early Victorian times. The Vale of Evesham fed vegetables to Birmingham, the Ormskirk plain supplied Liverpool, and Bristol was supplied by gardens east of Bath.

TRANSPORT

The service was made easier with the improved turnpike roads, giving only a day's delay in delivery. Transport again improved when the railways came into their own, guaranteeing daily delivery from a hundred or more miles distant. As a result areas of suitable soil and local climate concentrated on large-scale vegetable growing. They have to compete today not only with foreign produce flown in by air—carrots from Texas and beans from Kenya are commonly on sale—but have to match the purchasing muscle of supermarkets, which demand large quantities of prime-quality produce.

GREENHOUSES

Although the benefits of growing under glass were clear, the cost of glass in Georgian times restricted greenhouses to the kitchen gardens of grand houses, where they often grew grapes, peaches and other delicacies. Hampton Court's Great Vine, grown from a cutting in 1768, still produces. But the Victorian age witnessed an explosion of glasshouse production: London's Lea Valley was one centre.

THE EFFECT ON THE COUNTRYSIDE

These changes in turn affect the look of the countryside. Market-garden techniques are often applied on a grand scale in suitable areas, with plastic cloches for example (or often just flat plastic sheeting) lined across the fields to force the seedlings. Many farms in the Fenland, for example, may grow only peas, machine-sown and harvested; and today's economics also mean that their entire crop may be bought in advance for canning or freezing. But fluctuating markets also mean, in some places, acres of abandoned derelict greenhousing.

THE SMALL MARKET GARDEN

In spite of these changes the small market garden remains an integral

An orchard traditionally set on a sheltered, south-facing slope.

A Kentish oasthouse, for drying hops. Most of these structures have now been converted into homes.

costard, a cooker, sold by costard mongers (hence costermongers). Over 2000 different varieties are known, although today only a handful are grown on any scale. Cox's orange pippin, first ripened by Richard Cox in the 1930s, is one popular variety.

As with vegetables, the new national town markets encouraged the use of suitable areas for large-scale apple growing. Apples fruit best on well-drained soil, as do cherries and plums, and light soil quick to warm in spring is sought. The flowers are sensitive to late frosts, so orchards are often sited on a gentle, south-facing slope safely above any frost pocket. Protection against bleak north winds is given by hedges or rows of poplars, but any hedging is usually set with gaps to prevent the capture of pools of cold air. Beehives are often moved into the orchard in early spring, where they may be sheltered with bales of straw. Changes of practice have also relegated the gnarled bushy apple tree to the farm orchard. Today's commercial stock is usually grafted on to dwarf rootstocks, to rise no higher than head height, which makes picking and spraying easier.

HOP FIELDS

Hop fields are typical of Kent, around *Horsmonden*, for example, and the oast or drying house with its distinctive hood is one of the most characteristic of countryside buildings (although most have by now been converted into homes). The hop fields are equally distinctive, with their rows of wiring to support the straggling stems. Picking, once a traditional cockney holiday, is now carried out by machine.

VINEYARDS

There were medieval vineyards even in Yorkshire, but in the 14th century the climate deteriorated and growing was abandoned. In the 1950s the first modern commercial vineyard was started at Hambledon (Hants) and today there are more than 300, recognized by their low rows of vivid green foliage strung to grow along wires.

To encourage rooting, vines are planted in poor rather than rich soil.

part of the countryside. Indeed, faced with milk production quotas and overproduction of grain, many farms have taken up the production of vegetables and soft fruit as a way of diversifying. Fields turned over to 'pick your own' strawberries and raspberries are now commonplace.

ORCHARDS

Although matching market gardening in many ways, large-scale orchards are more demanding of their location. Ever since the first cultivated apples were brought here by the Romans, small orchards must have been familiar. They were certainly part of every Georgian farmstead, if consisting of only a few old gnarled trees, and such charming orchards remain in Devon and other counties. The Norman monasteries often had orchards (as well as market gardens) and it is in their estate documents that the names of distinct apple varieties first appear, such as pearmain, a pear-shaped eater, and

Village roots

Centuries of change and evolution lie behind the village we see today, yet its original form is often easy enough to interpret from the clues.

THE ORIGIN OF THE VILLAGE

The village we see today has usually grown from a medieval village. In feudal times society was sharply divided into those who fought, those who prayed, and those who laboured. The village united the manor house of the first, the church of the second, and the cottages of the third. But this medieval village evolved from an older and rather different pattern of settlement.

It seems that outside the towns and other specialized settlements the legacy of prehistoric and Roman times was a countryside scattered with farmstead-hamlets of various sizes, each working its own fields and making up the estates of lords and magnates. But slowly, in the Dark Ages and Anglo-Saxon times, a new kind of communal farming with vast shared fields became adopted—the open fields of the medieval manor—and the separated hamlets tended to coalesce into villages at the centre of the lord's estate, the better to work their joint land. The hamlets were by then often known as 'tons' or 'towns', and the still-used name of *Ruyton-XI-towns* (Shropshire)—that is, 'Ruyton-eleven-towns'—is one that clearly betrays this origin.

THE PARISH

Christianity was gaining a grip when these villages were evolving, and it was common for the Saxon thegn, or petty lord, to build a wooden church alongside his hall. In time this was to be rebuilt in stone, and become today's village church. The parish was the area yielding the tithes to maintain it, and it often matched that original Saxon estate, with similar boundaries.

BEATING THE BOUNDS

In the days before maps, estate boundaries were described verbally. Saxon charters may mention prehistoric burial mounds, standing stones and other waymarkers still to be found along today's parish bounds (see pp. 52–53).

The horn dance at Abbots Bromley (Staffs), perhaps originally a parish boundary ritual.

The church adopted the custom of 'beating the bounds' of the parish, processing the boundary on Rogation days, with stops at suitable 'gospel oaks'. Some think that the horn dance held at *Abbots Bromley* (Staffs), when dancers in Tudor dress cavort with antlers, is an odd version of these old boundary ceremonies.

VILLAGES AND HAMLETS

A typical village has a church. It may have a separate recognizable hub or centre of some kind at which you would expect to find the pub and the post-office-cum-stores, both of which underpin local life. For example, *Finchingfield* (Essex) is a classic assemblage of pond, bridge and green.

If there is no church, the village might well be by origin a 'township', a hamlet of a larger parish. *Ickwell Green* (Beds), although it has many villagey things such as a maypole and a smithy, is one of the many without a church. But no two villages are alike; and on appearance alone it is difficult to define exactly what a village is. Some large villages have features of a small town; indeed, some villages are towns that have died (see pp. 114–115).

THE VILLAGE PLAN

It has been customary to recognize two main kinds of village: the 'nucleated' village clustered around a focus such as a green or a crossroads and the 'linear' village strung along a highway. This can be misleading, however, for today's plan is usually a scrapbook of changes, of growth and

up along the village street, running down to a 'back lane'. Hence the original medieval village, rather than being confused, might occupy a neat rectangular plan, except perhaps when it broadened out to take in a green. *Laxton* (Notts), which maintains its original open fields, also has a fossilized medieval plan, with the farmhouses end-on to the roadway in narrow strips of garden.

PLANNED VILLAGES

Although encroachment on the green, the death of parts of the village and other changes may hide the fact, a good many medieval villages were planned out in the neat way noted above. This seems to have happened in late Norman times, often in the north, where rebellion had so irked the Norman William that he had devastated the land in the terrible 'harrowing'. The destroyed villages had to be rebuilt. *Castleton* (Derbyshire) is one example: its regular plan can clearly be seen from the castle on the hill above. The cottages have been rebuilt many times, but their frontages and gardens maintain the old lines.

REGIONAL VARIATIONS

Many villages in the north within reach of Scottish cattle raiders have a rectangular green, tightly pressed by cottages on all four sides which could well have served as a defensible wall. *Elsdon* (Northumberland) is one example. The vast greens of some villages must have been an important pasture, perhaps for livestock dealing. It is surprising how little can remain of such things: East Ilsley near the *Ridgeway* (Oxon) once hosted the largest sheep markets in Britain, but all that remains is a memorial plaque. In parts of the country, such as Devon but also in the Pennines, scattered settlement is the pattern, rather than the village. This is also true of Kent, perhaps because the Jutes who settled there in the Dark Ages had inheritance customs which divided estates among families rather than keeping them to one single heir — a good illustration of the possible complexity of village history.

(very often) decay in parts—in many cases a good deal of the original village has disappeared. As a result some villages seem a haphazard jumble of walls and roofs of all ages set along dog-leg lanes. Others are more orderly in plan, although even they have their own unexpected vistas.

We take it for granted that not only the church but the churchyard also lies within the village; this is worth pondering (see pp. 106–107). But some villages have a church set apart. A possible reason is that the original (late-Saxon) village was sited around the church; in medieval times the village grew, at the same time taking in a green for markets and entertainment. Plagues then took their toll, the older site was abandoned, and only the later development around the green survived. *Horsmonden* (Kent) is just one example. *Bunbury* (Cheshire) clearly resolves itself into three separate parts: a medieval village around the church, a Tudor extension around a small common and later buildings on the common itself. Other villages seem to spread untidy tentacles into the surrounding countryside; perhaps built by squatters. The names of these dead-end lanes often include 'End' or 'Bottom'. In another case, today's packed village centre with a network of narrow lanes might be squatter building on a broad open green, reducing it to the small triangle we see today.

TOFTS AND CLOSES

The feudal peasant relied on the crops from his strips in the open fields, and the beasts he could graze on the common lands, but also on a smallholding or 'toft' in the village, within which his hut was set. These were usually lined

Rural place-names

The names of villages and other countryside features can in many cases be deciphered to shed direct light on their origin and early development.

THE OLDEST NAMES

Place-names remind us that in spite of its many natural features, the countryside is a human place. The interpretation of place-names is riddled with pitfalls, for between then and now spellings were many and various. However, all local public libraries contain books on the subject—it has been a strong interest since Victorian days.

The oldest names are prehistoric. From a forgotten language comes Allen, as in *Allenheads* (Northumberland) and Alnmouth, for example. The tribes defeated by the Romans spoke Old British, a Celtic tongue from which modern Welsh is descended. A few hills and rivers keep echoes of it: Dent and Penn and Breedon are villages with hills nearby, while Bovey and Avon are words for a river. There are four River Avons in England, three in Scotland and two in Wales. The Cornish tre-, pol-, pen-, porth- are of similar age. The Celtic word for sanctuary was *nemeto*, which lingers as Nymet Tracey and Nymet Rowland in Devon.

Wales and Cornwall apart—and

Name clues on the map.

-by is a Danish Viking ending

1 2 3 4 5 6 7 8 9

-ley is a clearing
in woodland

-ey is a village on
an island site

-den can signify
a valley village

Scotland where the roots are usually Gaelic—English place-names are often rooted in the Anglo-Saxon tongues which evolved into English.

ROMAN NAMES

Strangely, few Roman names are remembered in the countryside. Roman roads carry names from Saxon times—Akeman Street, for example, which ran to Bath, took its name from the Saxon name for that town, Akemannes Caester. The word 'street' comes to us from *via striatus*, meaning a paved—that is, a well-surfaced way—and when attached to a country lane can be a clue to a Roman road (see pp. 120–121).

Most Roman town names have been forgotten, to be salvaged only from written documents or the rare memorial stone. From these it is clear that Roman York was Eboracum. York is not a corruption of that word although it sounds as if it could be, but comes from the Dark Ages name Eofor-wic or 'Boar Town', whence the Viking Jorvik. 'Wich', coming from 'wic' and originally from the Latin *vicus*, implied an important trading settlement. Droitwich and Nantwich for example are Midland salt towns, the salt being mined nearby. It is sometimes combined with 'ham' (see below), to make Wickham.

Caester (from the Latin *castrum*) was the tag given by the Saxon settlers to the decaying Roman forts and walled towns that they found—hence *Portchester*, *Dorchester* and many others. Their word 'burgh', meaning a fortified settlement sometimes became attached to a Roman fort or town, as at *Richborough* (Kent) as well as to older ramparted strongholds such as *Cissbury* (W. Sussex) and *Avebury* (Wilts).

GLIMPSES OF SAXON DAYS

Place-names of Saxon origin give tantalizing insights into the past. The Saxon words 'ham' and 'tun' both means a settlement of some kind (the latter perhaps only a farmstead-'township') and there is some evidence that they were in main use at slightly different times, and that in East Anglia and the Midlands the pair could show waves of settlement spreading across country from the rivers which were the preferred routes. 'Ing', meaning 'the people of X', X being a person's name, was in time shifted from the people to the place where they lived, and often linked with 'ham' and 'ton' as in *Wilmington* (E. Sussex).

NAMES THAT REVEAL ANCIENT LANDSCAPES

Place-names can evoke the scenery of the past. 'Ley', 'ly', 'lee' or 'leigh' come from the Dark Ages word 'leah', a clearing, and a scatter of them (villages, hamlets, or even farmsteads and field names) in one area can show areas of forest remaining a thousand or more years ago. They explain the line taken by the great Cambridgeshire dykes, running between impassable swamps and impenetrable forest, now only a memory (see pp. 52–53). 'Hurst' is a similar Dark Ages word for a clearing in the Sussex Weald.

Individual features were often perpetuated in place-names. 'Law' was a Dark Ages word for a mound, which was often a burial mound from earlier times; hence also the prehistoric banked henge named *Arbor Low* (Derbyshire).

NATURAL FEATURES

Natural features are perpetuated in place-names, and many of the longer examples are merely a catalogue of local geography such as renowned Llanfairpwllgwngyllgogerychwrndrobwllllantysyliogogogoch (Gwynedd). A shortened version ending with '-gyll' is shown on the maps, but the full name translates from Welsh as: St Mary's by the white aspen over the whirlpool and St Tysilio's by the red cave.

The Saxons had names for valleys of different kinds, seen today as -combe, -den, -hope. 'Ey' was a dry island in the midst of wetlands, such as *Romney Marsh* (Kent). 'Bourne' as in *Fishbourne* (Sussex) means a stream and is from the same root as the Scottish burn. The many Winterbournes of Wiltshire and Dorset refer to streams which flowed only in winter from chalk springs. Animals and plants are also commemorated in names of all ages: Ramsbottom is the valley of wild garlic (ramsons) while Beverley was named after the beavers of its river. The Old English word for beech was 'bec', and this may have named Buckinghamshire, still notable for its beech woodlands. The corresponding word for oak was 'ac', hence Acton.

MEMORIES OF ANCIENT FARMING

Many names recall early farming. Stock or stocking, a field of stumps, recalls newly cleared woodland. One tradition in the northern hills was that of wintering livestock under cover in the farmstead and taking them up to the shielings, the high pastures, in summer. In Cumbria, 'erg' as in *Sizergh* was one of the summer pastures, 'satter' and 'seat' spring shielings. 'Scale' was an outlying building used at these times.

THE NORSEMEN

Many such words in northern areas are Norse in origin, the countryside here being settled by Viking raiders from northern Scandinavia. 'Beck', relating to a stream, is another Norse word familiar to visitors to the Lake District. 'By' was the equivalent to the Saxon 'ham' and 'wich'—*Whitby* (N. Yorks) is one example.

DOMESDAY BOOK AND BEYOND

The power of the monasteries grew in medieval times, and their influence was sometimes reflected in the names of their land holdings. Whitchurch Canonicorum near *Lyme Regis* (Dorset), for example, refers to the fact that this village's tithes were annexed by a religious house.

Domesday Book listed not villages but townships (see pp. 94–95) and some of its names linger not as villages but as farms today. Indeed in some places where the township died completely the old name of the settlement might linger on only as the name of a field or perhaps a patch of woodland on the original site.

The reshaping of the fields during the enclosures also added new names, both of fields and farms. Some are historical, for example Waterloo Farm; others, such as Turnip Farm, jokey.

Village life

The variety of traditional buildings to be seen lining a village street shows that in the past it was home to a largely self-sufficient community.

THE SELF-CONTAINED VILLAGE

The village of the past was self-contained. Its surrounding fields gave jobs. Its cottages not only provided homes but also goods and services—bread, beer, a new wicker cradle, a repair to a leather boot were all obtained down the village street. But they were also harsh days: there were no hospitals for the sick nor much hope for the destitute. Petty punishment was meted out in the parish; and even the dovecot, now a quaint feature, can recall a harsher world (see below). The change to modern times was accelerated by an unexpected cause: World War I. Men went away in large numbers and for those who returned the old ties were loosened, mobility much greater. The village street remembers these changes.

THE PUB

Certainly by enclosure times, farmsteads usually did their own brewing, especially for 'small beer', a weak beer drunk at breakfast in the days when tea and coffee were luxuries for the gentry. But there was often a village ale house, the predecessor of the pub, which was often the livelihood of a village widow. These ale houses appear in paintings of village life, cottages like any others, with no need to be distinguished as they were known by all. The only exceptions might be travelling gypsies and drovers. For the former, a brush set above the door meant a welcome.

Inns—larger establishments offering beds—were only likely on main routes, and were more to be expected in towns, at the stops for the regular coach relays that the turnpike roads made possible. But there had always been considerable travel and the medieval pilgrim routes which predated the coach roads spawned their own hostels. These probably had names to help recognition by strangers. Signs serve the same purpose, and it is possible that village pub signs (especially the heraldic sort) started in this way.

Some pub signs reflect the life of the fields. Many pubs lying below the *Ridgeway* (Oxon) recall the bygone traffic in sheep: The Leg of Mutton, The Lamb, The Shears. The Engine, a fairly common village pub name, commemorates not railways, but the steam traction engines which dragged the plough across the fields in Victorian times.

Heraldry is favoured, often the local squire's. There could be some odd links; some claim that The Chequers commemorates not a chessboard but the speckled fruit of the wild service tree found growing in woods nearby, once used by the Romans to flavour beer (*cerevisia* in Latin).

WAR MEMORIALS

There are only 32 'thankful' villages, which lost no dead in World War I. World War II was less wasteful of lives. The memorials speak for themselves. Many are simply a commemorative cross, a direct heir of the medieval wayside and preaching crosses. Some are more unusual; that at *Ruyton* (Shropshire) is a man-made cliff cave.

PUNISHMENT

Old-time village justice, like its humour, was often raw and painful. The stocks which remain in many villages usually date from between 1750 and 1830 (when legislation changed). Many places had a pillory to hold the standing miscreant. Whipping posts are sometimes found, such as at *Bottesford* (Leics) and *Berkswell* (West Midlands); this last village has stocks with five leg holes—presumably the timber has rotted at one end. In Scotland 'jougs'—a chained iron collar—remain in one or two kirkyards.

A cucking stool was rather like movable stocks and said to be used for scolds and fraudulent stallholders in the village market. Rather nastier is the ducking stool set on one end of a swinging plank, in which they (and suspected witches) were ducked in the village pond until wellnigh drowned. Many such mementoes are kept inside the church today and without question, so easily do we allow 'history' to override any natural repugnance.

Many villages keep a 'lock-up'. Many are round ('round house' was their common name). That of *Bradford on Avon* (Wilts) was originally the medieval chapel on the bridge.

THE BAKEHOUSE

Here the villagers could have their bread baked, but also (and this reflected the general poverty of the cottagers) their Sunday joint roasted—a

The village pub was often in existence by Victorian times, and was frequently distinguished by a sign.

custom which remained in Lancashire mill towns until recently. At *Carew* (Dyfed) the round oven chimney remains.

ALMSHOUSES

These were often literally a matter of life and death. They were usually built and endowed by a local benefactor, and named in his or her memory. They brought security and peace of mind to the last years of many.

THE VILLAGE WORKHOUSE

The alternative to the almshouse was the dreaded workhouse. An Act of 1601 had made churchwardens responsible for the parish poor. In High Victorian days, the workhouse was supervised by the parish Guardians of the Poor, taking in the old and infirm and indeed all those who could no longer support themselves. The able-bodied were set to work. Families were split up, husband callously parted from wife in old age after years of happy marriage. The well-known music-hall song 'My Old Dutch' refers to this heartless separation.

THE PLAGUE HOUSE

Many villages had a plague or pest house set some way away. Few if any remain; as an example, that of Bloxham (Oxon) is now reduced to a stony mound in a marshy nature reserve. It was a small cottage where those with contagious diseases isolated themselves, surrounded by a narrow moat.

THE DOVECOT

Quaint though this is as a building, often with an elaborate revolving ladder, or 'potence' to reach the nesting niches, it commemorates harsh days. In feudal times the doves were the sacrosanct property of the lord of the manor. They provided fresh meat for the lord's table, especially young 'squabs' in winter (pigeons breed all year round if food is plentiful).

Many dovecots were sited near the church; at *Skenfrith* (Gwent) the dovecot caps the church tower.

The village green

The green was a major feature of many early villages. Some retain their full size, but streets and cottages have encroached on a good many.

WHERE GREENS ARE FOUND

Village greens can be found in every English and Welsh county, but they are more typical of the south-east and the flatter, lowland eastern areas. These were the heartlands of Saxon settlement, from which the open-field system with common grazing and other customs evolved. Village greens are in some ways like small commons.

As well as providing an area of common grazing, they provided night-time security for the village animals in the days before farmyard stables and sheds. In some places along the north-ern borders, within easy reach of Scottish raiders, the cottages tightly ringed the open green, virtually mak-ing a defensive 'wall'.

GREEN VILLAGES

In the English village of memory, the green is the focus of the village, close-set by cottages and the church, the pub, the smithy and other important buildings. Yet of the 10,000 or so villages in England and Wales, only about one in six or seven—that is, around 1500—are green villages. But building has destroyed the village green of many villages or reduced it to an unrecognizable remnant.

'GREEN' IN THE VILLAGE NAME

The use of the word 'green' to describe an area of grassy land in a village (or town) dates only from 1477, and so such a place-name is probably quite late. It perhaps marks small hamlets or dead-ends separate from the main focus. *Ickwell Green* (Beds), which lacks a church, is one example.

THE GEOGRAPHY OF THE GREEN

Greens range from small to 20 acres; larger than this and they are usually known as 'the common'—though *Great Bentley* (Essex) is an exception. Very few greens are round. Many are triangular, a shape which originated at the intersection of roads at an angle, the 'short cut' forming one side of the green. But large, rectangular greens are also quite usual (although perhaps cut across or cornered by new roads).

Greens are usually on flattish land which provided reasonable grazing: some are smooth enough for good cricket. Others, although smooth, have a definite tilt which drains them to one end, perhaps to the stream and village pond. A duck pond is often a feature of the green, more vital in the past, when it watered livestock, than today. It is quite often round, suggest-ing that it was artificially created. Some of these ponds may have doubled as fishponds in days when multiple use of all assets was normal.

As we have seen on pp. 94–95, it is convenient if misleading to recognize two main types of village, the linear and the nucleated or clustered village. These last are more likely to have greens on to which at least some of the cottages look. But the definitely linear village of *Long Crendon* (Bucks) has a green, not as a focus to the village, however, but at one end. Other linear villages have ballooned at one point to take in a green. This underlines the fact that the green was more than a pleasant outlook for the surrounding buldings, but had a definite job to do.

ENCROACHMENT

Although the green was a common of a kind, it differed in one important respect. Normally, if a squatter gained a toehold on a common and kept it for a dozen or score of years, he gained the normal commons rights of the other villagers. This did not apply to the greens, and it seems that in Victorian days squatters' hovels were cleared from many.

Nevertheless, considerable en-croachment has occurred. Strips of building have sometimes divided the green into two, or taken out a block of it, a fact which might be more obvious from the village map than from wan-dering the back lanes. One clue here could be that the cottages within the old green boundary lack gardens. In more recent times the surrounding cottages may also have encroached by grabbing land for front gardens. (In medieval and Tudor days the cottages stood flush to the road.) This theft was easier than it might seem, for it is only recently that hard-surfaced roads have given the green a definite bound-ary. Even at the start of this century it would have been bounded simply by braided tracks, with no clear line.

THE GREEN AS COMMON

The green was basically a kind of common, and it was often included in the layout of villages when they were being expanded or rebuilt in medieval times (see pp. 94–95). Like a common, a green has an owner, and the com-moners have grazing rights. These are not often exercised today. The green being of limited size, commons rights were often stinted—that is, carrying stints or restrictions on the number or kind of animals pastured. The 'brin-kers' living in the cottages overlooking the green often had the duty of main-taining it, but frequently handed this task over to the blacksmith, say, whose smithy was close by, in return for payment of some kind. For the blacksmith, this could become a valued right, handed down from father to son.

But some greens are not commons, and in fact the ownership and rights are often so complex that the legal tangle has in many cases helped to keep the green open and undeveloped.

THE POUND

The link between green and livestock was underlined by the walled pound or pinfold where the 'pinder' kept stray animals. This was especially import-ant in the days before enclosed fields, when untended animals roaming loose could create havoc in the open harvest fields. One pound remains in good order at *Elsdon* (Northumber-land); walls remain in the garden of 'Pound Cottage' at *Abinger* (Surrey), and the name is a familiar cottage name in many counties.

THE HIRING FAIR

Villages held markets, perhaps even weekly, although these were but a shadow of the large markets in the local town. They often gave space to regular visits of pedlars, their wares

manor house

Tudor housing around edge

pollarded trees

transect road

war memorial

pond

Victorian encroachment

carried in the panniers of packhorses. But the greens of many larger villages also saw the yearly hiring fairs, which were maintained until this century. In September, after the harvest, the labourers gathered on the green to offer themselves for hire for the coming year, distinguishing their skills with tokens—and for this reason these were often called mop fairs. Shepherds often wore a hank of wool, while grooms carried a piece of sponge and carters

would wear a length of whipcord tied around their hat or through the buttonhole of their coat. The thatcher would wear a wisp of straw.

When the farmer or agent of the big house had made his choice, he would seal the bargain with a shilling piece, to be spent 'on the fun of the fair'—on the shows and stalls which were often a busy part of the proceedings.

Little remains of the spirit of these ancient fairs. The farmers' stock fairs

Features of the green. There has often been some encroachment into the open space by later building.

still deal seriously in cattle but it is largely the funfair—the least important part of the traditional fair—that keeps the old spirit alive.

In some places great regional fairs survive which certainly date back to medieval times. The June horse fair at Appleby (Cumbria) is an example.

Village sports and festivities

Today's village cricket is one of the latest of a long calendar of sports, festivities and pastimes which took place on the green.

THE HUB OF VILLAGE LIFE

The green might be used for cricket, and by children playing of a summer's evening, but these are pale echoes of the activity the green has seen down the years. It was ever a busy place, the hub of village life. By the week, or year, the village market or fair, if there was one, settled itself into a corner of the green. The crucial hiring fairs were held here (see pp. 100–101), always attracting pedlars and tinkers of all kinds. The green was also the place for relaxation and pleasure, in the days when few crossed the parish boundary except for an occasional visit to a market town a few miles away. An alternative name for the green, or part of it, was the plaistow or plestow, the 'play space'.

THE MAYPOLE

The festival celebrating spring and the miraculous growth of the planted grain must be one of the oldest of all. A few villages—*Ickwell Green* (Beds) is one—retain a maypole; not an original one because the custom was to raise a fresh 'sacrificial' tree each year. At *Cerne Abbas* (Dorset) the maypole was raised in the ramparted enclosure above the giant, a clue to the age of the custom. The pole was a phallic symbol, the dance of young girls around it a fertility rite, but it was only one part of 'may day' festivities. The night before, young men and girls used to spend the night on watch away from the village, to return laden with fresh green may (hawthorn) branches to decorate cottage doors. Jack the Green, a villager adorned in foliage, went the rounds demanding food—a token sacrifice.

FESTIVITIES

These ranged from religious mystery plays to Hallowe'en parties, from morris dancing (perhaps not as ancient as

The village green has always been the place for fun and leisure as well as more serious matters.

it might seem; first recorded in the 15th century, it was revived by Victorian enthusiasts) to the olden-time midsummer fire, and the fireworks and the giant village fire of Bonfire Night today.

ANCIENT MAZES

In *A Midsummer Night's Dream*, Shakespeare wrote these puzzling lines:

> . . . and the quaint mazes in the wanton green
> for lack of tread are
> undistinguishable.

The explanation can be seen at *Alkborough* (Humberside), *Hilton* (Cambs), *Wing* (Leics) and a few other villages. Each of these is noteworthy in that it retains an old turf maze.

At Hilton, centuries of feet have worn down a circular area of the green by a good yard. Within this bowl is a wheel-like labyrinth pattern cut through the turf to the soil below. There is nothing in the way of a hedge to mask the route, which anyway has no splits in its path to fool you.

The pattern of the maze is that found on Cretan coins of the 4th century BC. In the ancient Greek myth, the hero Theseus followed the thread laid by Ariadne to escape the Cretan labyrinth after slaying the Minotaur, the bull demon. The mystery multiplies when the Roman poet Virgil describes how the legendary Aeneas fled Troy with his son Julius to found the city of Rome; the Alkborough maze is known as Julian's Bower. Julius played a game

of follow-my-leader called City of Troy, and a game with the same name was played on horseback through the street of medieval London. Some of the remaining turf mazes are called Troy Town. And the Celtic word 'troi' means to twist or turn.

The antiquarian John Aubrey, writing in 1680, mentions that the village mazes 'are much frequented on fair afternoons, and much used by young people on Holydaies and by ye School boies'. Some of the mazes seem to have been Christianized by being repatterned in quadrant form, to incorporate a cross.

During the Commonwealth and the Civil War, the Puritans put a stop to such merriment, but the village of Hilton has a memorial commemorating the fact that the maze was recut soon after the restoration of Charles II to the throne.

WAR GAMES

The open green was also a suitable site for the practice of arms—a legal requirement under 14th-century laws, which obliged every man to engage in archery practice on Sundays. Boys over the age of seven had to be trained in the use of the bow, a law which was strictly enforced by Henry VIII and only lapsed when firearms became general. A few greens carry high bumps which might be what remains of the butts; the name 'Butts Green' is also a clue.

One intriguing medieval survivor is the quintain at Offham (Kent), between Sevenoaks and Maidstone. Swivelling at the top of a post is a wooden arm with a domino at one end, a weighted chain at the other. A mounted rider had to gallop and tilt at the domino with his lance, and if successful had to duck nimbly to avoid the chain, which of course swung round. It is still used on May Days, the bruising chain replaced by a plastic bucket of water.

BULL BAITING AND COCK FIGHTING

Cock Pit Cottage and similar cottage names might recall the days when these were also village pastimes. Up to Victorian days a bull was usually baited with dogs before slaughter—it was thought to improve the flavour of the meat.

VILLAGE CRICKET

Today no true green is complete without cricket. *Hambledon* (Hants) claims to be the home of the game, where the Hambledon Club was formed by local gentry in 1760 to play on Broadhalfpenny Down (so named from the rent the drovers had to pay for the use of the grazing). But the game was already long established by then. The pub opposite the down is called the Bat and Ball Inn, of course.

TREES ON THE GREEN

The green has also been a place of relaxation for the village greybeards. There are often commemorative seats, and perhaps the war memorial also overlooks it. The green might also be home to fine trees. On grazing greens they are likely to be old pollards (see pp. 88–89), but last cut so long ago that the branches are now massive. Trees were often planted here for ornament rather than use—the horse chestnut, the conker tree, is often seen on the green. Native to the Balkans, it was introduced three or four centuries ago, but it yields poor timber, and is rarely seen planted out as a hedgerow tree. The horse chestnut is, however, sometimes self-sown.

Rather unexpectedly, the plane tree, which is common in London's squares, is unusual in the countryside.

The cottage

Even when modernized, many cottages furnish examples of the ingenious crafts-manship that can be seen in the village of bygone days.

THE MEDIEVAL COTTAGE

Arnol Blackhouse (Lewis, Western Isles) is aptly named: with no chimney the smoke had to ooze its way out, coating everything in soot. Equally primitive dwellings (though not as smoke stained) have been reconstructed in the open-air museums at *St Fagans* (S. Glamorgan), *Avoncroft* (Hereford & Worcs), and *Singleton* (Hants). Here we see simple medieval dwellings of the kinds which lined the village street. But it appears that some villages also contained rather grander houses in the shape of 'hall houses'.

THE HALL HOUSE

The hall house was derived from the open thegn's or lord's hall of Saxon and medieval days, of which a massive example can be seen at *Stokesay* (Shropshire) (see pp. 112–113). The open hall, much smaller than Stokesay, of course, became divided by cross walls to create separate rooms at the ends—a buttery and a parlour, for example. Or extra rooms were gained by adding them on at the ends, creating an H plan in some cases. The open hall might later become divided by a floor, and two stories were usual in any end extensions added to an older single hall.

THE GREAT REBUILDING

The Black Death, which struck in the 1340s, wiped out a third of the people and emptied many villages. It also shook the social fabric: men could demand wages and even set them-selves up as independent farmers, mer-chants or traders, and the Wars of the Roses, which followed, loosened feudal ties still further. Thus was a new 'yeoman' class born, who in time were to build more grandly to mark their status in the village. They often built hall houses and many remain, if altered later. Many of this pattern date from 1550–1660—a century of strong Protestant and Puritan in-fluence, lasting until the Restoration

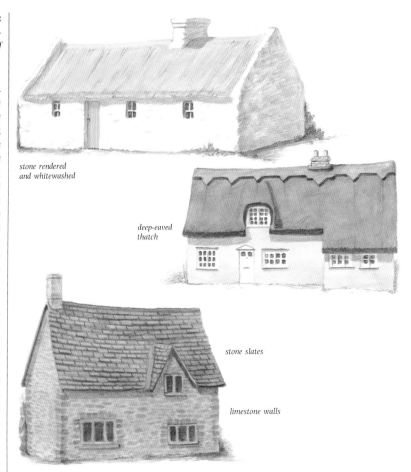

stone rendered and whitewashed

deep-eaved thatch

stone slates

limestone walls

of Charles II after the Puritan Commonwealth—a period often called the 'Golden Age' of the cottage, or the 'Great Rebuilding'.

Rebuilding started in the south-east and spread to the uplands of the north and west only later, as late as the 18th century in places. Here in the hills, where the cattle needed good winter shelter, a longhouse farmhouse had been popular, with family accommod-ation under the same roof as the byres alongside, and not separated by much of a wall as the warmth of the animals was welcome in the winter cold. The Great Rebuilding often demoted these longhouses to animal barns, with a separate new farmhouse being erected nearby.

The development was aided by the increasing use of brick: chimneys were easier to build, replacing the open fires of the older halls. Chimneys meant

Regional cottage styles.

that the new farmhouses could be two rooms deep; and if so, larger windows were possible without gales of draughts. Comfort multiplied.

QUAINT TIMBERING

Timbering was crucial even in stone houses, for supporting floors and roofs. Crucks were common, especially in the north and west. These were tree trunks split lengthwise to provide a pair of matching timbers which were inclined inwards to support the roof-ing, with the walls being built along-side. But the width of the house was limited by the lengths of trunk avail-able. A box-like timber 'frame' solved this problem and it was also self-supporting so that no stress was put on doorways and windows. There were regional dialects—'black and white' around *Congleton* (Cheshire) for example. In East Anglia, the main timber uprights were 'close studded' (set close together), while to the west the timbers formed more of a square pattern visible on the outside walls. Another early sign of status in the Great Rebuilding was extending the upper floor so that it overhung the wall below in a 'jetty'. Some villages such as *Lavenham* (Suffolk) have a wealth of such timbering.

Quaintly curving cottage beams are, however, only indirectly a sign of age: the timbers were often used green, and warped as they dried while the building was still young. Oak timbers weather to a grey silver, as still seen in the Guildhall at *Thaxted* (Essex). Most have been blackened with creosote as preservative; it came into use last century.

At first the timber frame was usually infilled with wattle (hazel hurdling) daubed with puddled clay and straw. This 'wattle and daub' was lime-washed to weatherproof it. Later it was often replaced with brick or stonework.

COLOURED COTTAGES

Lime-washed walls might be left white, but they were often coloured pink with ox blood and herbs, green or blue with berry and other juices. There are many examples in Suffolk.

BRICK

It was not until quite recent times that bricks became cheap enough for mere cottagers. They were at first gained from village brickfields worked by travelling gangs of brickmakers. Long before brick walls were built locally, old wattle and daub infill might be replaced by herringboned brickwork.

The size of bricks is a clue to their date. Those made between 1500 and 1600 were $9 \times 4\frac{1}{2} \times 2\frac{1}{4}$ in. By 1725 they were usually a standard $2\frac{1}{2}$ in. thick, but in 1784 a brick tax was levied per 1000 bricks, and to lessen it the thickness was increased to $3\frac{1}{4}$ in. The bonding, or arrangement, can also be a clue to the date: the English bond of rows alternately of lengthwise and endwise bricks is older than Flemish bond, where each row contains both lengthwise and endwise bricks.

Bricked-up windows were a response to a window tax levied from 1696 to 1851 on the number of windows in a dwelling.

LOCAL DIALECTS IN BUILDING

Early times were the days of make and mend, and what was locally available and cheap was used, lending delightful variety to cottages and villages. Of note are the chalk-walled cottages of southern downlands, footed and cornered in stone or brick and with wide eaves (often still of thatch) above to protect the soft stone from the weather. In the south-east many cottage walls are of tile hung on timbering, often imitating a more expensive brick wall. Devon has its own idiom of cottages of 'cob', or clay walls, as seen in villages near *Honiton*. Richer villages in the south might have ornate plasterwork, as seen in Suffolk and at *Ashwell* (Herts). The Victorian railway brought cheap brick and tile roofing, largely ending regional variety.

THE COTTAGE GARDEN

This is really a Victorian legacy. To be sure, cottagers from early times would have grown a few flowers along with the vegetables, and over the centuries monks and botanists had introduced many exotic plants. But the 'traditional' English cottage garden with its summer-long display of jumbled colour was largely the invention of Victorian gardeners.

Cottage details.

elaborate timber with infill

white weatherboard

pantiles

Welsh slate roof

squared sandstone blocks

The village church

The role of the church in village life spread far beyond Christian belief, and its position at the hub of the village reflected its dominant role.

THE SITING OF THE CHURCH

The young Christian Church survived the Dark Ages largely in the Celtic strongholds of the west and north. It was in monastic form, with the priests leaving to preach at crosses under the open sky. Sometimes a standing pagan stone would be cut with the cross and brought into use as a Christian marker, as can be seen in the parish of *Blisland* (Cornwall). During the Dark Ages some remote churches were built, such as that at *Bradwell* (Essex), and then key 'minsters', and eventually a host of simpler wooden 'field' churches for the households of the thegns and later the lords of the manor, as remains at *Greensted* (Essex). These humble field churches

The church at Maxey (Cambs) is sited on a slight mound which was perhaps a Bronze Age burial.

became the village churches we see today (see pp. 94–95).

Thus the parish church was often sited alongside the manor house, at the hub of the village. This suited its dual role, for the Christian church was unique in one way: it served not only as a sacred temple but also an important meeting place. But if pagan stones could be adapted as crosses, so sometimes sacred pagan sites were also adopted. *Rudston* (Humberside) has a gigantic ritual standing stone in its churchyard at what was the nexus of Neolithic ritual ways. Many churches stand on mounds which may be Bronze Age barrows, while *Knowlton* (Dorset) actually stands within a Neolithic ritual henge. Note, however, that on some soils the level of the churchyard might have been raised by 2–3 ft or more after centuries of burials within a small area. Sometimes the path to the door, or the doorway itself, is now sunken.

Many village churches were placed on the highest knoll that local geography provided: these are often dedi-

cated to St Michael and one assumption is that these sites were sacred to the Celts, and St Michael replaced their deity, perhaps via the Roman god Hercules (see pp. 64–65).

SAXON CHURCHES

Wherever a Saxon church was placed, it was usually enlarged and rebuilt in stone in Norman times. Only 200 churches keep substantial evidence of earlier, Saxon work and these are very often the original grander minsters which failed to become cathedrals in later days. *Brixworth* (Northants) makes use of Roman bricks secondhand. *Repton* (Derbyshire), *Deerhurst* (Glos) and *Bradford on Avon* (Wilts) have Saxon features worth a long detour.

GOD'S ACRE

The churchyard offers a green sanctuary amid the cottages. Indeed, we take it for granted that the dead lie at rest at the centre of the village, among the living. Although belief in the Resurrection permits this (all those saved

The churchyard could look almost industrial, as here at Haworth (W. Yorks), home of the Brontë family.

from Hell will meet together at the Last Trump) it is unusual; in France, Italy and other European countries the burial ground is outside the village, as it was in Roman days when the ghosts of the dead were feared.

There is evidence that churchyards which are oval or round were originally ancient Celtic Christian burial grounds, while they became roughly rectangular in Saxon times, when it became usual to consecrate one acre.

CHURCHYARD MEMORIALS

Many churchyards have a lych-gate at the entrance, where the coffin was rested to await the priest (the name comes from a Saxon word for corpse). The memorial stones we see today are relatively recent in date, and the 'box tombs' (the body lies buried below them, however) are usually Georgian or later. Medieval peasant graves had a wooden post or cross, long since decayed, and medieval gentry would have been buried within the church. Many churchyards also contained a medieval preaching or teaching cross, an echo of the old monastic tradition, but most were destroyed by the Puritans. In some cases the base remains.

YEW TREES

The origin of the custom of planting yew trees is not clear. They were not planted for bows (they could never have supplied the demand). They are evergreen, and so could symbolize eternal life. However, they may echo older pagan Celtic beliefs, for the Celts worshipped at natural things such as groves and springs, which were used for divination (see pp. 132–133).

CHURCH AND CHURCHYARD IN VILLAGE USE

In olden days the church and churchyard were a meeting place as well as a religious place. The churchyard as the threshold to the church itself was used in more ways than one. Part of the marriage service, for example, took place outside the church door. Church ales, which were fund-raising feasts, and merrymaking also sometimes took place here. Parish meetings took place at the church door (today's local notices in the porch echo this) and the churchyard often served as a pound while disputes over livestock were settled.

SANCTUARY

From early times the church offered not only spiritual sanctuary. It also gave physical sanctuary, immunity from arrest for any fugitive from justice or debtor who could gain entrance. Many churches boast a 'sanctuary knocker' on the main door. For centuries the church might have been the only solidly built structure in the village, offering a temporary home when the cottages were devastated by fire, tempest or flood (until this century's river engineering, winter flooding was a fact of life in many areas). This use is often commemorated by graffiti, emblems or crude line drawings scratched on walls or pillars by the refugees whiling away the hours. Limestone was easy to mark in this way, and medieval ships, knights, and animals and birds can all be found. *Ashwell* (Herts) has inscriptions describing the Great Plague.

The church could also offer sanctuary against marauders. Some churches within reach of Welsh or Scottish raiders have a 'pele tower', a massive square or rectangular tower which could be defended against assault. *Astbury* (Cheshire) and *Leintwardine* (Hereford & Worcs) are examples.

THE CHAPELS

One of the later developments of the Reformation and the Puritan revolution was the birth of many Nonconformist sects, which held that the reformed Anglican Church of England did not go far enough. They built their own chapels, commonest in areas where the Anglican establishment (with its hunting parson in league with the squire) was weakest. Chapels are thus more typical of 'squatter' and marginal countryside. In Wales chapel and trade union came to act as one.

The mill

Both water and wind power were vital sources of energy in days gone by. Water and windmills served both villages and early industry.

THE OLDEST MILLS

Five thousand mills were listed in Domesday Book of 1086. Medieval 'soke' (local) laws could make the mill a profitable monopoly with both lord and miller each taking a cut, as much as a sixteenth of the ground flour in the case of the latter. These early mills were very probably water-mills of the Norse 'click' type. One of these can be seen working near Dounby, Mainland (*Orkneys*). With a horizontal wheel which turns an upright shaft turning the millstones, it is clearly second cousin to the prehistoric hand-turned querns, which had a pair of matched stones, the upper being rotated against the lower. But many early mills may well have been turned by animals, an ox or donkey (or even a slave in Roman and Dark Ages times).

WATER POWER FOR MANY PURPOSES

Water power was not only used for corn mills. In Staffordshire mills were built (and some corn mills converted) to grind flint, which was added to clay to give fine pottery. Later the power of the streams was captured to run machinery which spun the imported cotton in the valley mills.

Watermills can also be rigged with trip systems to operate hammers. In the Pennines many mills drove fulling machinery to beat and compact the new-woven cloth. There were also 'beetling mills' for a final stage of linen making, when it was pounded by 'beetles' to give a close weave and sheen for umbrellas, bookbinding and other uses.

In the Weald there were many water-powered hammers for pounding the red-hot iron in the forges, and water power would also pump the bellows of the forge. (It was only the use of coke for smelting and the development of such places as *Ironbridge* (Shropshire) which took the iron industry north.) In Surrey and Sussex the head of water was gained by damming streams, and local topography gives these millponds a characteristic triangular shape. There are many near *Abinger* (Surrey), where the local industries were fulling, wire making and grinding down the constituents for gunpowder, as well as iron forging. Water power also operated crushing hammers at the mine-heads in Cornwall and elsewhere. At *Sticklepath* (Devon) the museum of rural industry has water-powered tilt hammers. *Haxted* (Surrey) is one of the many museums with a working mill.

In some places, such as *Carew* (Dyfed), a mill was run from the tidal flow in a narrow estuary.

THE MILLPOND

The advantage of the upright wheel is that it enables the energy of changing flows of water to be harnessed in an efficient way. Regulating the flow of water irrespective of the season was a major problem, and the solutions have often left their mark on the landscape, even when the mill building is out of use, or even gone.

In chalk country, where the streams and rivers run evenly all year round from springs and flooding is rare, the stream itself may suffice, and even an 'undershot' water-wheel might be used—one driven by the current alone.

However, it was usual to try to strengthen as well as guarantee the flow with a reservoir or millpond. This pond not only held water which could be released on demand through an adjustable sluice-gate but also raised it to give a good head. A mill was designed to suit its own river con-

Watermill features.

weir

leat

sluice-gate

undershot wheel

overshot wheel

ditions. With overshot wheels, the water meets the wheel's floats at the top and its weight helps turn the wheel. A breastshot wheel receives its water halfway up, and turns in reverse direction. Sometimes, rather than with a millpond, the water could be captured upstream above a weir which raised the level, channelled through a 'leat' to the wheel.

POST MILLS

It is thought that the Crusaders brought back the idea of the windmill from the Middle East. Primitive, cloth-sailed mills can still be seen in Greece.

The first windmills were post mills. The chamber on which the sails spun and which contained the gears and millstones was set atop a sturdy post, itself firmly bedded in a mound. A second post, the 'tailgate', extended down from this chamber at an angle, and this was used to swing the apparatus round so that the sails could catch the wind.

The oldest remaining post mill (1636) is at *Bourn* (Cambs) and the mill at *Saxtead Green* (Suffolk) is in good repair. But many older post mounds remain, perhaps mistakenly identified as a prehistoric or Roman burial mound.

CAP MILLS

Later, in the 17th century, cap millls were devised, the sails being set into a rotating cap which alone needed turning to bring the sails to the wind. They were of two kinds. Smock mills had a tapering timber tower, in profile the shape of a peasant smock, which could be turned on a round or octagonal brick base. Tower mills had a much smaller rotating cap on top of a tall brick tower. One 18th-century example with machinery complete remains at *Barnack* (Cambs). Many of these round windmill towers remain derelict on knolls and high spots; or if gone, the name Windmill Hill or simply Mill Hill on the map can be a clue.

THE SKILL OF THE MILLER

The first sails were probably of cloth tied to the wooden frame. The later,

derelict tower mill

wind pump

smock mill with brick base

post mill

familiar, thinner sails with movable slats gave easier adjustment; and fine adjustment was the heart of the problem. The miller of legend, standing belligerently with arms akimbo, was in fact keeping an anxious eye on the wind. The sails had to be angled to it, but that was only the start. If the grinding stones were too far apart, a coarse flour resulted, the hoppers were quickly emptied and, free of the 'brake' of unground corn, the spinning would accelerate. If the brake was then applied, the spinning millstone would shoot off sparks. If the stones were too close, a fine flour resulted, but if the wind was strong friction heated them. If the weather turned gusty, closing the mill required feeding grain to slow the wheels before applying the brakes. Not surprisingly, windmills on fire, their sails revolving like Catherine

Windmill features.

wheel fireworks, were not an uncommon sight in previous centuries.

MILLSTONES

Millstones were often carved from millstone grit (hence its name), a sharp-grained sandstone from the Pennines. It is convenient to quarry here, because its bedding planes fracture to give slabs of correct thickness. Half-finished stones can sometimes be found below Pennine crags.

WINDPOWER FOR OTHER USES

Like watermills, windmills could diversify from merely grinding corn. Some were put to grinding flint for pottery making. In the 18th century there were 2000 windmill-like drainage pumps in the wetlands.

Village crafts

Local circumstances meant that some villages became workshops for skills other than agriculture. The planned village was one such development.

THE SMITHY

The smith was paramount among the villagers. His smithy was often literally under the spreading chestnut tree at the village centre, near the pond for a ready supply of water for his 'bosh', a trough for quenching the red-hot metal. The smithy was a one-man factory, for with the help only of a boy to pump the bellows he turned out ploughshares and billhooks, cooking pots and frying pans, knives, nails and harness buckles, wrought-iron door hinges for the church maybe, and shepherds' crooks. He would repair armour at need. Well-preserved smithies with their array of tools can be seen at *Ickwell Green* (Beds), *Cenarth* (Dyfed) and other places, as well as in the many museums of craft skills, such as that at *Ashley* (Devon).

Ever busy, the smithy was also the hub of village gossip, with bystanders collecting around the eager forge, helping judge the temperature by the colour of the metal, cracking quips between the aching hammer clangs on the anvil. His unofficial leadership was recognized in other ways, for the smith often supervised the use of the green and perhaps, brawny as he was, acted as unofficial constable.

The old-time farrier or farrying smith had the special role of shoeing the horses, and other livestock too. Even cloven-hoofed cattle were shod with double 'cues' before they went off on the long drove to market or when they were used to pull the plough, as oxen were until this century.

OTHER CRAFTS

Other vital village skills were not in such daily demand nor so central. The woodmen worked far away, coppicing and felling trees in the village woodlands. Thatchers took their skills to villages round about, as they still do today. Brickmaking, which entailed digging the clay from the village brick-field and firing it, was undertaken by hired gangs. But many tasks were

The objects assembled for repair show just how important the smithy was, even in late-Victorian days.

undertaken by the cottagers themselves without a second thought—from constructing wickerwork 'putchers' for catching salmon on the Severn to making cheese and ale. Bread was often leavened at home to be baked once a week in the village bread oven (see pp. 98–99). They were days of make and mend, and in this respect every cottage was a craftsman's cottage.

Certain villages became centres of larger-scale 'cottage industries', producing goods for sale beyond the parish. Weaving was one of these, as it still is in the Shetland Isles today. There was an international trade in wool and also in finished cloth in medieval and later times. Early weaving houses remain in Pennine villages such as *Heptonstall* (W. Yorks), with a row of windows in the top floor to light the workshops (and there is often an extra third floor for these); and also in *Bibury* (Glos). East Anglia and the Cotswolds were also important and the profit from this trade has left a legacy of fine 15th-century 'wool' churches and impressive villages such as *Lavenham* (Suffolk), with craft symbols modelled in the plasterwork of the houses.

INDUSTRIAL VILLAGES

It was but a short step from weaving villages such as *Heptonstall* to industrial villages which housed the workers of a specialized factory. The turbulent streams of the Pennines ran

spinning and fulling machinery for treating the young cloth. It was concentration of this kind which led to the vast urban sprawls of the Industrial Revolution. Even in the villages, the demands for mass housing for the factory workers, many of them dispossessed from the countryside by the enclosures (see pp. 58–59) led to the adoption of terraced housing, with rows of families sharing water pumps and other facilities.

Even in the south, industrial villages were common: several villages and hamlets around *Abinger* (Surrey), including Abinger Hammer and Friday Street, are part of a chain of settlements which exploited water power for ironworking, fulling cloth, and making brass, wire and even gunpowder. The Guildhall at *Thaxted* (Essex) was built in 1400 by cutlers, an industry scarce fitting today's quiet image.

SCOTLAND

In the aftermath of the Highland clearances of the first half of the 19th century, industrial villages were established in Scotland, to benefit from the desperately cheap labour offered by the dispossessed. *Gatehouse of Fleet* (Dumfries and Galloway) was one, laid out with a typical grid plan and aligned on a military road.

CLASSIC INDUSTRY

Some areas or even single villages have assumed an important place in the story of industrialization. One is *Ironbridge* (Shropshire) where iron was first smelted easily and cheaply with coke, to revolutionize production.

Another is *Blaenau Ffestiniog* (Gwynedd), the centre of the slate-mining industry which once roofed much of Britain. Cornish mining villages are also distinctive.

ARTY-CRAFTY COTTAGES

Industry was not always run with disregard for the workers. Many northern mill owners had a humanitarian conscience, as did some local countryside squires, and the village may reflect it. A benevolent squire might provide more generous housing than the squalid cottage which was the norm. (In Dorset villages in 1850 there were families sleeping in relays to share the few beds, and sewage running freely in the street.)

Old Warden (Beds) is the epitome of the 'squire village', with cottages rebuilt with a rag-bag of decorative ideas from home and abroad: there is even a fake gallows over the well.

ESTATE VILLAGES

Most often, however, the village was rebuilt as a consequence of the squire's wish to 'improve' and landscape his estates. If a village impinged on the new views from his window, he razed it to build a new one out of sight, perhaps leaving only the church. *Edensor* (Derbyshire) was moved for the sake of *Chatsworth*, and then rebuilt in 1839 in a riot of architectural echoes ranging from Swiss chalet roofs to Jacobean gables. 'New' Victorian villages of this kind often have arched windows and other 'Gothic' features fashionable at the time. When the rebuilding is restrained, the similarity of the houses might be the clue. *Milton Abbas* (Dorset) was rebuilt in the 1770s, wholly with thatched white cob cottages. Such estate villages usually have doors and window-frames painted all the same colour.

A UNIQUE PASTICHE

Portmeirion (Gwynedd) is unique, and worthy of its own mention. Built this century by Clough Williams-Ellis, the bizarre assemblage includes a 17th-century town hall saved from demolition and pastel-coloured Italianate features.

The big house

Memories of the very different social order of the past are evoked by village manor houses and the grander mansions of the countryside.

THE ORIGINS OF THE COUNTRY HOUSE

History, power, wealth and convenience are woven into the story of the country house. Many had their origins in the castles of the Norman barons, which evolved from mere barracks to give some comfort (see pp. 62–63). Their last echo lay with a massive gatehouse which accompanied some grand new Tudor mansions; and even abbeys adopted gatehouses of fortified style, as seen at *Bolton Priory* (N. Yorks). As well as castles, these gatehouses were often to test their strength in the Civil War in the 17th century. Still medieval in design, however, many were battered into ruin by the cannon of that later age.

THE GREAT MANOR HOUSE

Other 'big' houses had their roots in the manor house of the normal medieval village. This was usually centred on a great hall, a Saxon tradition. Its walls were of rubble and stone, but timbering played an important part. One superb example remains at *Stokesay* (Shropshire). Here a moat circles a complex of buildings joined by walls. It presents a defensible face to the world outside, but the overall military design of the castle is lacking.

Entrance at Stokesay is by a timber-framed gatehouse into a walled courtyard, on one side of which stands the massive great hall dating to 1285. Vast timbering supports the smoke-stained roof—there was no chimney for the central fireplace. It was lit by windows closed with wooden shutters, for glass was a luxury until at least Tudor days. Here owners, guests, hired soldiery and retainers all lived and ate together as one feudal 'family'. The only privacy for the owners here at Stokesay was a 'solar', an upper chamber reached by a door behind the high table. At the opposite end of the hall, and masked by a wooden screen, were doorways to the food-storage areas such as the buttery.

The kitchen was built separately out in the yard and some distance from the hall, to reduce the risk of fire.

LESSER MANOR HOUSES

The lesser medieval gentry and richer traders emulated their betters. A few early Norman examples remain, such as the manor house at *Boothby Pagnell* (Lincs). For security, its open living hall was raised to the first floor as it is in a castle keep, and was reached by a defensible outside staircase; its ground floor was a closed storeroom. Such buildings would have been enclosed in a compound with wooden huts for retainers and animals, often surrounded with a moat and palisade.

For whatever reason, this kind of stone manor house fell out of favour, but in later centuries in the turbulent borderlands of the north, even the farmsteads were built with defensible upper floors of the same kind.

Otherwise, lesser manor houses were later built to a ground-floor open-

Stokesay Castle (Shropshire) is one of Britain's most impressive medieval dwelling houses.

Temples in classical style are among the eyecatchers which dot the park at Stourhead (Wilts).

hall plan, although often on a small scale. This was adapted in the 'Hall houses' of the new yeomanry (see pp. 104–105). In grander houses the original open hall is sometimes found at the core of later extensions.

THE MOAT

On suitable ground, even the smaller and earliest of manor houses might have a moat and a timber fence of some kind. It was scarcely real defence, more of a deterrent against stray dogs, and perhaps more a status symbol. The dry hollows of moats are often to be seen alongside later manor houses.

THE TUDOR PERIOD

Although some coastal castles such as those at *Falmouth* (Cornwall) were built in Tudor days, many mansions had only an ornamental gatehouse of the kind mentioned above, while the house itself might also carry ornamental battlements. The building was often by now costly, for the Reformation and the Dissolution of the Monasteries had released money and a host of masons and other specialists for private work. Brick was in widespread use, if still expensive.

CLASSICAL HOUSES

The wealth of the great political families continued to grow in later centuries, and their mansions remained like the castle of old, an outward sign of the true power in the land. By Georgian times, instead of battlements and gatehouse, the mansion adopted a new code derived from the buildings of Greece and Rome.

Most obvious were the 'classical' columns that framed the entrance and the main windows, within which lay the rooms where national politics might be decided. As in earlier days, such houses were serviced by an army of retainers, but unlike at Stokesay, they were no longer 'family', but kept out of sight 'below stairs'. *Hatch Court*, Hatch Beauchamp (Som) is typical.

The houses of lesser gentry also adopted many of these new classical architectural features.

THE PARK

These big houses frequently stood (and stand) in a park. This often had its origin in the Norman and medieval deer park. Apart from the Royal Forests and the chases of the grander barons, in which forest law ruled for the sake of the hunt of red and fallow deer, most baronial residences also had a deer park. This was up to 200 acres in area, and stocked with fallow deer. The deer might be released into the countryside for the hunt, but these parks were more in the nature of deer farms, guaranteeing winter supplies of fresh meat. By 1300 around 2 per cent of England was deer park. They were surrounded by a fence or 'pale' running along a massive bank, which unlike that of the coppice woodlands lay outside its ditch, to make it harder for the animals to leap out.

The deer park developed a distinctive appearance of tightly grazed grass scattered with trees, and in Georgian days this 'natural' look was strengthened with informal plantings by English landscape architects such as Capability Brown and Humphry Repton (European landscapers tended toward regimented straight lines). Even the land surface itself could be shaped into hillocks and dug for lakes.

Formal gardens of low topiary could lie as a belt between house and park, but rather than wall it, a 'ha-ha' was used, a ditch with a steep inner side to keep out deer and cattle. *Chillingham Park* (Northumberland) is noted for its wild cattle.

FOLLIES AND EYECATCHERS

Together with trees, mock buildings were often added to the estate as eyecatchers and to form goals for afternoon walks; the Greek temples of *Stourhead* (Wilts) for example. Many eyecatchers were placed on the distant skyline from the house—where they remain as 'follies' in isolation today.

The market town

Although many towns have a long ancestry, they usually gained their status from their market charters rather than their age or size.

ORIGINS OF THE MARKET TOWN

Towns equal trade and there were certainly large trading settlements alongside major rivers as early as Bronze Age times. During the Iron Age, when some of the hilltop forts were occupied for long periods (see pp. 46–47), there were also tribal capitals on lower ground, less well defended and presumably busier with trade. These lie under today's streets, at Winchester and Canterbury and elsewhere.

ROMAN TOWNS

Towns were part and parcel of the regimented society of southern Roman Britain, and fragments of Roman town wall remain at *Dorchester* (Dorset) and many places. Although stripped of facing stone, long lengths remain at *Silchester* (Berks), in deep countryside and empty but for a church and farm, an atmospheric place. At *St Albans* (Herts) lengths of the town wall, buildings and a theatre are on view. But the north and Wales remained more or less a military zone, served by legionary fortresses at York and Caerleon and Chester, although these were accompanied by considerable settlements.

TOWNS IN THE DARK AGES AND MEDIEVAL TIMES

Many (certainly not all) Roman towns seem to have been left to squatters in the Dark Ages, and in consequence their walls and buildings decayed. Alfred the Great, for example, largely ignored them when he set up his chain of fortified towns of 'burhs' (burghs) such as *Wallingford* (Oxon) to contain the Danish threat.

With the wider integration of medieval times, towns assumed a more formal place in the countryside. Some occupied the site of an earlier Roman town, but many were now developed from village-scale settlements. Their special status came from market rights, which were carefully awarded and jealously guarded, for the beneficiary—local lords or often monasteries—could wax fat on the market tolls and rents. The market charters usually placed rival markets at least 6 miles apart.

Trade meant that many towns naturally became specialists of one kind or another. The fishing and commercial ports are one example; *Lavenham* (Suffolk) is one of the many that flourished on cloth making, and tax assessments show that by 1524 it was the fourteenth richest town in England. Like many others, the collapse of its trade has left it today hovering in atmosphere between town and village. Many of today's larger villages are in fact towns that have failed.

In other places, towns grew in the shadow of important castles. *Old Sarum* (Wilts) is interesting: originally an Iron Age hillfort, the breezy site became a town in Norman times with castle, cathedral and bishop's palace. But in the 13th century, water shortage forced a move to lower ground and today's town of Salisbury came into being beside the river. *Lewes* (E. Sussex) is one of the many 'gap' towns built on a river which has cut its way through chalk downs to the sea.

Many towns flourished as a result of pilgrim traffic, providing chapels for prayer, and food and hostels, or even simply new pairs of shoes for the footsore travellers. The medieval church certainly promoted pilgrimages, in part because of the extra trade and the tolls that resulted from it, a bonus on top of the direct gifts and donations of the pilgrims.

EARLY TOWN PLANNING

Modern towns on a Roman site often keep a neat grid of streets which has clearly survived through the centuries; *Dorchester* (Dorset) is one example. The granting of a new medieval market charter usually meant that a village was expanded and if so, the expansion was quite likely to be neatly laid out, quite unlike the popular image of medieval muddle. (Even Alfred's *Wallingford* has a neat plan.) Winchelsea near the edge of *Romney Marsh* (Kent) is an example of medieval town planning: its prosperity waned in the 14th century and it stands unfinished, with only some of its regular square 'quarters' built on.

MARKET-PLACES

Towns which flank major routes might keep a broad High Street which doubled as a market-place, although the market-place was generally a distinct open space to which the High Street led. The High Street was lined with shops which backed up the weekly market, in time to become permanent, selling goods every weekday. Before glass became cheap enough in the 18th century, their ground floors would have been more like the open stalls still to be seen in some small Italian towns. In larger towns separate markets might have been held—'Haymarket' as a street name would be a clue, for example.

MARKET CROSSES

The market-places were marked with a cross, of which maybe only the base remains. The cross was frequently a highly decorated, stepped pillar rather than a true cross. Some 'crosses' were in fact elaborate arcaded, roofed shelters, such as the six-sided timbered buttercross at *Abbots Bromley* (Staffs). Crosses of this kind might be found in villages that are towns that died.

MARKET AND OTHER HALLS

Market halls remain in many towns, the older ones typically with an open, arcaded ground floor offering shelter to some of the market. The splendid 17th-century timbered market hall at *Leominster* (Hereford & Worcs) was originally open in this way. Very often these structures are known as 'town halls'—the upper rooms might be used for general town as well as market administration. The name is also synonymous with guildhall. In many towns the merchant guild of wool or other dealers ruled the roost in the days before votes and the town councils we take for granted today. The famous Guildhall at *Thaxted* (Essex) was built by the once powerful cutlers' guild, for example.

A corn exchange is also a feature of

many lowland towns, built during the Georgian enclosures to cope with the boom in crops that the new scientific farming made possible. Many remain, although they are perhaps put to other use today.

TOWN VISTAS

Rebuilding has made a shambles of many a regular town plan (the word 'shambles' originated with the narrow butchers' street so called in York), but with the benefit that towns offer as many quaint vistas as a village. The

character of the town is in one sense the sum of its now very varied streets. It has its own language: the 'snob' parts of any town are always recognizable, for example. Originally they were some distance from the High Street and the market bustle. These may no longer be 'snob', however, for the money has moved further out (rarely further in). The life of towns changes by the generation in this way.

Recent redevelopment apart, the original street plan is often confused by 'Act of Parliament' streets, usually of

A Victorian town market of a kind still familiar today, with the market hall standing behind.

18th-century date. These were made to cut through an earlier maze by a local 'Improvement Trust', to make way for larger shops and houses but also maybe to create a wide street leading to a new bridge which was also rebuilt at the time. The shops lining such streets will usually be of one age and style; the buildings may include pillars and other classical features.

Ancient tracks

The routes of ancient tracks are among the oldest features of the landscape. In a few places their original line can be followed, although their appearance has changed.

TRACKS ON THE MAP

Understanding Britain's ancient tracks is helped by an eye both for the lie of the land and its history. They keep to the high, dry line with the sky wide above (which is largely why they provide majestic walking). In the south they run along legs of high chalk ground which have Salisbury Plain as their centre and which extend north-east towards Norfolk, down towards Dorset, and eastwards as the North

The ancient Ridgeway (Oxon) runs today between ploughed fields, but still offers exhilarating walking.

and South Downs. The North Downs Way is also known as the Hoar or Harrow (Holy) Way and also the Pilgrim's Way for much of its length. The *Ridgeway* (Oxon) kept along the northern downland ridge, then crossed the Thames at *Goring Gap* (Oxon) and continued as what we now refer to as the Icknield Way up towards Norfolk.

In addition, there would certainly have been a well-used cross-country track running between the Cotswolds and East Yorkshire, on high ground which would have provided a lightly wooded line between the dense forests of the plains in prehistoric times. This belt was 20 miles across in Northamptonshire but reduced to 4 miles in Lincolnshire. This 'Jurassic Way' as it is called, ended near *Rudston* (Humber-

side) after traversing the Yorkshire wolds. The *Peddars Way*, seen at Snettisham, crossed Norfolk. There would have been similar, less obvious tracks across the Pennines. In tight-knit areas such as *Dartmoor* (Devon), which are in many ways a world of their own, many shorter prehistoric tracks survive.

Good sense dictated the actual details of the line. The Pilgrim's Way at *Box Hill* (Surrey) does not run along the summit ridge, which is capped with muddy clay, but across the drier slopes below. There are many similar examples.

THE NAMES OF THE TRACKS

Our names for the old tracks are misleading. What they were called is long forgotten: even the languages

spoken by Stone Age and Bronze Age peoples are unknown. But we know that the name Icknield Way derives from the Iceni, the Iron Age tribe based in Norfolk when the Romans arrived. Oxfordshire's *Ridgeway* is simply descriptive of the lie of the land, while the Pilgrim's Way forming the major part of the North Downs is certainly far older than the medieval pilgrims who trod it.

THE LOOK OF THE TRACK

The appearance of the track is no clue to age. Many ancient tracks are now narrow footpaths in some places, a modern dual carriageway in others. Vice versa, an appearance of age can be deceptive. A green track running between tall hedges, looking for all the world as if it was rooted in the distant

past, may be no older than the grid of Georgian enclosure fields it crosses.

THE BRAIDED ROUTE

For much of its length, the *Ridgeway* (Oxon) is now simply a track alongside barley fields, hedged off or barricaded by wire and scored with tractor ruts. But here and there the tight fields fall away. On Fyfield Down, the old line of the London to Bath road is seen, a cat's cradle of tracks mounting the unploughed slopes. The original Ridgeway would have had this appearance, each traveller choosing the best route for that day or year.

RIVER CROSSINGS

Some think that *Duxford* (Cambs), Shelford and the other 'ford' villages nearby reflect the wide braiding of the Icknield Way when it sought the best crossings of the River Cam. The crossing of the Thames by the Ridgeway at the narrow *Goring Gap* (Oxon) is a tighter affair, however.

EARLY TRAFFIC

If these open tracks were not the narrow footpaths we see today, neither were they lonely and abandoned to occasional tractors and weekend walkers. For long centuries they were dotted with the camps of drovers and their herds and busy with the packhorses of the tinkers, the original commercial travellers. In later prehistoric times, the merchandise was perhaps loaded on to sledges dragged by horses, as in Scotland and Wales until recent times.

Finds of flint axes, and the siting of Neolithic tombs such as Wayland's Smithy along the Ridgeway, prove its early use. The Ridgeway is also accompanied by later Bronze Age barrow cemeteries, Iron Age hillforts, and Danish burial mounds. Other tracks have similar.

MARSHLAND TRACKS

Although no surface traces remain, wetland and riverside settlements were also common in prehistoric times. There were plentiful fish and game, and the open water provided routes for dug-out canoes or boats of

coracle type (See pp. 140–141). Marsh or lake villages raised on artificial islands have been found from *Glastonbury* (Som) to Scotland. At Meare, near the former, early Neolithic timber trackways lie buried deep in the peat: and what is interesting is that much of the wood used was coppiced—even in 4000 BC, woodland was being managed in a productive way.

THE IRON AGE

Timber trackways of Iron Age date have also been found across what was marshy ground in those days. Clearly the tracks which feed the gateways of the massive Iron Age hillforts are of the same age as the ramparts, and in climbing the slope many have become holloways. Some show evidence of wheel ruts (below). There was also, by this date, a network of lanes, some neatly ditched on each side, serving the farmsteads of the vales. These have long since disappeared under the plough, and remain only as crop marks (pp. 28–29). These farmsteads and tracks continued in use after the Roman arrival.

Presumably, as well as the ridgeways, there were important long-distance routes across the lowlands by Iron Age times. In the later Iron Age the warlords were charioteers. Julius Caesar wrote that they threw 'the enemy's ranks into confusion by the mere terror inspired by their horses and the clatter of their wheels'. These chariot wheels had iron tyres to crash against the ruts and stones, but the twisting side scythes were added later, by Victorian imagination! There was probably regular intertribal skirmishing, and perhaps 'war paths' were recognized. Their chariots were light, with low wickerwork sides, the strategy being to use them to move in quickly, jump down to fight on foot, and if necessary retreat as quickly.

Wheel ruts found at the entrances to Maiden Castle near *Dorchester* (Dorset) and other camps suggest that they also had heavy transport. Roman writers refer to 'wagons'—presumably four-wheeled carts—which does suggest that there was a network of 'main roads' in the vales in those days.

Country lanes and paths

Old lanes and footpaths take the visitor to the secret places of the countryside. Public rights of way are to be valued and must be defended.

ROADS, LANES AND PATHS

Confusingly, these words are used in different ways, depending on who is using them. In modern law and on today's maps, a road is a route which can carry wheeled traffic and is usually (but not always) tarmacked (metalled). A lane is a day-to-day name for a quieter country road, but the word is also used for a 'green' track (see pp. 122–123). Legally a path (as in footpath and bridle path) has restricted use: it may be narrow and often is, but many wide green lanes are footpaths. A track is a day-to-day word for any kind of unmetalled path.

WINDING LANES

Many lanes and paths seem almost a natural part of the countryside. Some claim they could indeed be, arguing that in areas which were densely wooded, these twisting ways might be as old as the first badger and deer tracks which can be permanent features of woodland. However, our countryside has been fashioned more by man than nature (and in places more than once), and winding picturesque ways are largely part of the pattern of farming, although they can be of considerable age.

THE ORIGINS OF WINDING LANES

Although some Bronze Age trackways may remain to the present day undisturbed by later farming in the recesses of *Dartmoor*, the *North York Moors* and other remote areas, it is likely that our oldest lowland lanes first took their path in Roman times and the Dark Ages. The straight Roman roads were served by networks of tributary tracks running from the nearby villas and farmsteads. Crop marks show that some of these tracks were ditched, and many must have survived to become the ancestors of today's winding lanes.

SAXON WAYS

Many of the Roman roads were still in use in Saxon days. The Saxons de-scribed them with the word 'straet' meaning hard-surfaced or paved, which became today's 'street'. ('Straet' is originally from the Latin *'striatus'*.) Their surface must have been poor by then, but could be hard travelled.

Saxon sagas and documents refer to three categories of route. They talked of 'ways'—their word was 'weg'—which seem often to have been the lesser paths, but they could also have been boundary tracks, and maybe a path or winding lane which today's parish boundary follows might be one of these old ways. Parishes largely took shape in Saxon times, and many Saxon parish boundaries survive.

Longer routes were also recognized; some also took the name 'way', but this is perhaps an example of the name of one stretch becoming in time the name of the whole. The Saxons also recognized the 'here-paeth' or 'war-path' for troop movements. They were perhaps routes of more ancient ritual significance. The *Ridgeway* (Oxon) was sometimes called a warpath, and a path leading from it to *Avebury* (Wilts) is still known as the Herepath on the Ordnance Survey maps. Even if surfaces were poor, there was a national concern for main routes in Saxon times: one law bade travellers carry horns and sound them as a signal of lawful business. By implication outlaws must have been numerous.

THE KING'S HIGHWAY

In medieval times, lesser roads were not regarded as fixtures, but more as strips belonging to the community, which no one could plough or obstruct. Maintenance was poor, and as a result paths tended to wander as travellers avoided areas of mud.

One slight exception were the roads known as the King's Highway, a network serving the market towns. Their width was legally set at 50 ft—two wagon teams or 16 knights riding abreast—and to prevent ambush, a statute of 1285 obliged woodland owners to clear back 200 ft on each side. Wayside landowners or their tenants were obliged to maintain the surface, but as the fines levied in the manor courts showed, they often fell down on the job. Roadsides were often 'stolen' to add on to fields alongside.

HOLLOWAYS

Many old lanes are sunken where they rise to breast a hill, simply the result of the wear of centuries of traffic of hoofed beasts and carts. Holloways (or hollow ways) are more likely in 'ancient and ornamental' countryside where the field pattern has been in existence for several centuries. They are not so common in enclosure countryside, where the fields and the lanes which accompany them are often fairly recent.

They are usually found where the bedrock is sandstone, which is firm enough to maintain steep sides but soft enough to wear away under traffic, and so the layering exposed is often of geological interest, with seams of ironstone perhaps. Exposed tree roots exposed by slips or falls can indicate the extent of recent weathering of the sides.

TODAY'S FOOTPATHS

Footpaths (which are shown on Ordnance Survey maps) are green (unmetalled) lanes or paths on which the public have right of way. In some ways a footpath is rather like a common in that the land has a private owner and both he and the public (represented legally by the county council as the highway authority) have legal rights and obligations. These rights like those of commons originated when the use of the countryside was essential for the livelihood of most of the population.

The council, for example, should mark the path with a sign where it leaves a road and fine those leaving litter. The landowner or tenant farmer should keep gates and stiles in good repair and the path free of obstructions such as barbed wire, 'KEEP OUT' notices, and piles of muck. A farmer can plough up the line of the path, but by the strict letter of the law should make good the surface of the path afterwards. Few bother. Cars and motorbikes can be used only with the permission of the landowner, otherwise they are restricted to parking within 15 yards of the road (and the land-

owner can still order them off).

As a result of the long history of the countryside, footpaths include many stretches of prehistoric track, Roman roads, Saxon warpaths as well as many medieval salt roads and drove roads. The lines of the field hedges come up to these ancient routes on each side. But many footpaths were established when the countryside was being divided up during the Georgian Enclosures, and these will follow the new field pattern, taking turns around the field corners.

Long-distance footpaths such as the *Pennine Way* (Derbyshire northwards) are relatively modern. They are put together from green lanes and foot-paths, but also include lengths of previously private track now open to the public as a result of negotiation between the Countryside Commission, county councils and landowners. They provide access to scenically

The holloway has been worn to its present concavity by centuries of plodding traffic of man and beast.

beautiful areas such as the Pennine heights and the undeveloped coast. Footpath rules apply.

BRIDLE PATHS

Horses (and cycles) are legally allowed on bridle paths. Otherwise footpath rules apply.

The Roman road

Investigation of an old straight track or any straight cross-country alignment usually reveals that it follows the course of a Roman road.

'LEY LINES'

Earlier this century books were written (and widely read) proposing that prehistoric folk had surveyed the whole countryside with a network of rigidly straight 'ley lines' which linked sites of mystical or historic importance. The lines linked stone circles, tombs and Iron Age hillforts, and it was claimed that they were often followed by ancient prehistoric 'old straight tracks'. It was claimed that when the original marker had gone, the memory often lingered on, with village churches joining the chain, for example. Or, as one wit put it, telephone boxes and pubs too.

It is all nonsense of course. It is very difficult to draw a line for a few miles across country and (with the leeway given by a line 'through' the breadth of such things as Iron Age camps) fail to find two or three historic sites along it—so long and full is the countryside story.

The ley line controversy is an example of how not to read the countryside. A straight track is usually either a recent enclosure path or a path following the line of a Roman road. The line of a Roman road can often be followed for miles across country as lengths of road or path, sometimes as a visible ridge, or as name and other clues (opposite page). Many later straight roads were laid out at the time of the Georgian enclosures between the grid of fields, but as an Enclosure Act only applied to one parish, these tend to change direction at the parish boundary. The line of the Roman road, being older than parishes, is often followed by the parish boundary (see pp. 52–53).

ROMAN ROADS

These were at first wholly military in intention. They were for the fast traffic of messengers and troops to and from the hot spots. Although the finished network by and large radiates from the hub of London, the provincial capital,

the town had to win this honour. Perhaps the first roads ignored it. The Fosse Way, which eventually became an important road linking at least 15 Roman towns between Exeter and Lincoln, ran parallel to the turbulent frontier with the Britons of Wales. Lying behind the actual frontier, it was both a line of communication and the boundary between the civilian and military domains.

Rather similarly, *Hadrian's Wall* (Cumbria/Northumberland) is backed by a road—Stanegate linked a line of forts at Carlisle, Chesterholm, Corbridge and other places (a short section is preserved beside the modern road at High Crosby, 5 miles north-east of Carlisle). Hadrian's Wall itself was fed by a service road, laboriously cut through rocky bluffs in some places.

Sometimes the border roads, being well defined, might actually have attracted rebellion; excavations at *Cadbury Castle* (Som) show that it was forcibly taken in AD 70, many years after the invasion of Claudius' troops in AD 43. One suggestion is that the last survivors of the uprising of Queen Boudicca (Boadicea), by then outlaws, may have used it as a base to raid along the Fosse Way.

THE ROMAN LINE

Curves are rare, changes in alignment being made with a series of slight shifts of direction. Their routes suggest that they were aligned from one survey point to another on the horizon. By and large they were aligned to avoid steep slopes and other obstacles which would entail time-consuming zigzags. Exactly how the road was constructed depended on the terrain, but in general drainage ditches ran along each side of a broad bank, the agger, on top of which the road ran. The agger might be deeply packed with stone, with a final top surface of hard-packed fine gravel, with that maybe again surfaced with cobbles or paving slabs.

REMAINING FRAGMENTS

In a few places the original construction can be seen. The road on *Blackstone Edge* (Lancs) is 16 ft wide, and stone-paved. Some slabs have been

channelled with a deep groove, in which to run a pole used to brake the carts on the slope. The Roman road on Wheeldale Moor (*North York Moors*), partly paved but showing its rubble foundations, has drainage ditches on each side. There is a good paved length at *Doctor's Gate* (Derbyshire). Very often the agger remains as a raised feature across today's pastureland. The agger of the Roman road known as Ackling Dyke, which passes *Oakley Down* (Dorset), is tall enough to be mistaken for a single-track railway embankment. Just why it was built so high is puzzling, for it crosses dry chalk countryside and deep drainage was unnecessary. Some think it was built to be a status symbol forced on the newly cowed natives.

UNKNOWN NAMES

Their Roman names (or maybe road numbers) are unknown. Today's names are usually a legacy of Saxon times when English as a language was being forged. Akeman street is named from Akemannes Caester (Akeman's fort) the Saxon name for Bath, *caester* referring to the still-standing Roman walls. Street, given to more than one length of Roman road, is also Saxon in source, more or less meaning 'hard-surfaced'. 'Fosse' in Fosse Way is an old English word for a ditch ('way' comes from the Saxon 'weg', a path). Some lengths on the map appear as Stone Street or (in the north) Stanegate. 'Gate' here is a Norse word for a path or road.

Oddly, some Roman roads which did penetrate Wales became known as Sarn Helen, maybe after the wife of the 4th-century emperor Magnus Maximus—one such runs to the gold mines at *Dolaucothi* (Dyfed) and was apparently still in use in the 1930s.

TRACING ROMAN ROADS

The Roman roads remained in use long after the legions forsook Britain. Many remained in use as main roads well into medieval times, although by then in poor state. Others would have remained in use as local paths.

As a result they can be followed as footpaths and roads today. Known

Roman roads are marked on the Ordnance Survey maps, where it can be seen that parish boundaries might follow their line. The name 'Street' given to a country lane is a clue (look for a Roman villa nearby) and it is always worth stopping where today's tarmac swings away from the line of a Roman road: the agger might still be seen as a faint bank stretching across a pasture field, for example, or raising the footpath above the fields on either side.

CROSSING THE RIVERS

Fords were common, but bridges were built. Excavation has revealed bridge-work in some places, but no surface signs are still visible.

ROMAN MILESTONES

A short, round pillar, no longer in-scribed, stands by the line of a Roman road a mile to the east of *Dorchester* (Dorset)—like many it has been moved in recent road schemes. A couple are in original positions near Vindolanda fort on *Hadrian's Wall*. Others can be found in gardens, museums—and sometimes the local church, as at *Tintagel* (Cornwall).

Tracing a Roman road.

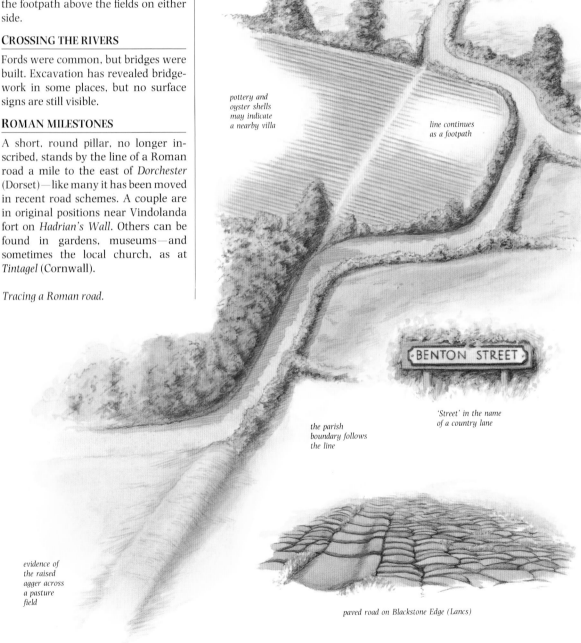

village street
on the line

pottery and
oyster shells
may indicate
a nearby villa

line continues
as a footpath

BENTON STREET

'Street' in the name
of a country lane

the parish
boundary follows
the line

evidence of
the raised
agger across
a pasture
field

paved road on Blackstone Edge (Lancs)

Green lanes and drove roads

In the days before railways and tarmac, many cross-country routes became dedicated to particular local or national traffic of men and packhorses.

GREEN LANES

'Green lane' is a general name for reasonably wide routes which have not been tarmacked (metalled). If legally recognized as 'roads' they can carry traffic and certainly tractors (with the landowner's permission, vehicles are allowed anywhere, even on footpaths). Thus the green *Ridgeway* (Oxon), in places little wider than

Until quite recent times it remained normal for animals to be walked to nearby markets.

a footpath, is classified as a road and as a result can be used by cars and motorbikes without restriction.

Some green lanes are of recent date, part of the new countryside map created during the enclosures. These are likely to be reasonably straight, and with ditches on each side. Their width will reflect the stipulations of the actual Enclosure Act, but 10–12 yards is usual. As this Act only applied to one parish, they might (as might those that have been tarmacked) change direction at a parish boundary. Sometimes, however, the enclosure lane adopts an older line, improving by ditching and surfacing what was there before. The line of a Roman road was sometimes followed. Others have equally deep

roots, in the ancient trades of salt and other things.

SALTWAYS

No community in the past was ever totally isolated. Trade was part of society, trade in food, metals, even in luxury items. Although it was not then realized, lack of sea salt with traces of iodine caused goitre. Salt was also needed to preserve bacon and other meat with which to survive the winter. Thus the saltways were among the oldest and most enduring of tracks. Some ran from the coast, from places where sea water was evaporated. Salthouse near *Cromer* (Norfolk) was one such centre, but further south, along some of the inlets near *Bradwell* (Es-

sex), are curious low 'red hills', probably the weathered debris of earthenware drying pans. Salt was also dug from geological 'dead sea' deposits in the Midlands. Curiously, many '-wich' towns such as Droitwich were linked with this trade; 'wich' originates from the Latin *vicus*, meaning market.

DROVE ROADS

Drove, or 'drift' roads as they are called in some areas, are another network of tracks, taking animals to market. The traffic peaked in the early 19th century, to be killed off by the cheap long-distance transport offered by the railways. But it had started much earlier. As medieval trade grew so did the towns, and their hunger (especially

London's) for meat created a new national traffic in livestock. The accession of the Tudors in 1485 and the closer integration of Wales and the later Union with Scotland in 1707 saw Welsh and Scottish cattle walking to London in herds 200 strong or more, and sheep in flocks of thousands under the care of drovers and their dogs. *Tregaron* (Dyfed) was one starting point, for a spectacular climb to 1600 ft en route to the Wye valley. East Ilsley near the *Ridgeway* (Oxon) was a drover's village, with the biggest sheep market in Britain.

THE USE OF ANCIENT TRACKS

Ancient prehistoric tracks such as the ridgeways were often followed, as they kept to the high, dry and firm ground and often ran far from the later villages. This last was important, for those villages nestled among enticing fields; the hungry beasts grazed as they travelled. In the Yorkshire Dales many drove roads such as Mastiles Lane near *Malham* were walled at each side from an early date to protect the Cistercian sheep grazings alongside. The lowing mass, with dogs barking at its fringes, might be advertisement enough, but the kilted drovers from Scotland also played their bagpipes to warn farmers to gather in their own beasts, for if these mixed with the drove herd there was little chance of recognition.

Close to their goal, the animals might be sold off to be fattened up again before the last leg of the journey to London's Smithfield market. Scottish cattle were often taken to Norfolk for fattening, and even fattened geese were walked down from Norfolk.

DROVERS' RESTS

On the misty moors and other wilderness areas, signposts of one kind or another would have been essential, and many wayside crosses must have acted as waymarkers. But there were other waymarkers. Both pubs and farmhouses offered night stops for the drovers with 'stances' or overnight grazing in 'halfpenny fields' (the standard charge for the beasts). They were usually remote from other dwellings. Sometimes the name remains, as at

Broadhalfpenny Down, *Hambledon* (Hants), which is said to be the original home of cricket. It is said that the stands of yew seen on chalk downlands, and stands of pine on the Welsh borders, were planted by farms offering a bed. Remote pubs with names such as The Drovers' Arms or The Ox also remember those days.

CORPSE ROADS

Some paths which cross from one valley to another in the Pennines and Lake District are still known as corpse roads. Death in a hamlet without a church and churchyard for Christian burial meant a last journey wrapped in sacking and strapped unceremoniously to the back of a packhorse. The Saxon word 'lych', meaning corpse, explains the name of Lyke Wake Walk, a track on the *North York Moors*.

PACKHORSE TRACKS

This was the beast of burden for centuries, endlessly on the move, laden panniers slung on each side. In the north the traders were called 'jaggers', and there are one or two 'Jaggers Lane' names to be found. They might use green lanes, but width was not crucial, and many important routes were only narrow paths, such as those that criss-cross the Pennines, and which served the wool and cloth trades. So important was the traffic that special bridges, with low parapets to avoid dislodging the panniers, were found everywhere in the north and in the south too. The Georgian turnpike roads with their tolls ended their profitability, and it was often difficult to find alternative routes to the town markets. Later the railways and the canals would provide cheaper transport.

SMUGGLERS' ROADS

High taxes on brandy and tea in the 18th century created a smugglers' market. There are a good many smugglers' caves, coves and paths so named around the coast. One of the most famous sites is the rendezvous of Jamaica Inn, in the tiny hamlet of Bolventor near Altarnun on *Bodmin Moor* (Cornwall) and reached by many moorland tracks.

Pilgrims and tourists

Many tracks became recognized as pilgrim routes. Pilgrimage has all but ended, although today's tourist is in a way a modern pilgrim.

PILGRIMS

For many, a pilgrimage must have been the event of a lifetime, a journey beyond the confines of the village. Some were to remote places such as *Bardsey Island* (Gwynedd). The church profited from the gifts of alms and the fees from licensing the trinkets and the many markets held in towns and villages along the main pilgrim routes, and from investing in the hostels for night stays. Toll revenue also lured the monasteries to build many bridges on pilgrim routes, bridges which are still in use today.

The pilgrimage was to the shrine of a saint at which prayers were said for health cures and requests made for intercessions for a shorter spell in purgatory. Although the Reformation ended pilgrimage, it was because of this last that the Puritans with their belief in personal responsibility eventually destroyed the shrines. One, stripped of its colour, remains in the church of Whitchurch Canonicorum near *Lyme Regis* (Dorset). They were extremely gaudy: one has been restored to its medieval glory in Dorchester Abbey near *Wallingford* (Oxon). A modest modern shrine attracts modern pilgrims at Little Walsingham, near *Cromer* (Norfolk).

So profitable was the pilgrim traffic that the medieval Church was not above invention. The cult of King Arthur at *Glastonbury* (Som) was an example: around AD 1200 his grave was supposedly found, a hollowed tree-trunk coffin below a stone slab, and he has been linked with the place ever since.

PROCESSIONAL AVENUES

For nomads such as the Golden Horde of Mongolia, movement itself had religious significance. The Neolithic people, who were also in part wandering pastoralists, might have been close in feeling. Their religious centres not only attracted people from afar, but were also accompanied by lengthy

Crosses carved by devout pilgrims on a door jamb. They are also frequently found on windows.

avenues—there is one leading from *Avebury* (Wilts) lined by standing stones, one with earth banks from *Stonehenge* (Wilts). The 6-mile Neolithic cursus seen in fragments near *Oakley Down* (Dorset) was almost certainly a processional way (See pp. 34–35).

THE PILGRIM'S WAY

The famous Pilgrim's Way along the North Downs was also known in past centuries as the Hoar or Harrow (Holy) Way. Originally a prehistoric track leading like the *Ridgeway* (Oxon) to the great ritual centres of Avebury and Stonehenge, in medieval days it became identified with the pilgrim traffic to St Thomas à Becket's shrine

in Canterbury Cathedral. Chaucer's pilgrims in the *Canterbury Tales* travelled only the final leg of this route.

PILGRIMS' CROSSES

Symbolic crosses cut by medieval pilgrims can be found on the inside stonework of windows, doorways and pillars of churches on or near pilgrim routes. They are easily recognizable, deeply incised, and in many cases with arms 2-in. long which often end in deeply pecked holes.

PILGRIM CHAPELS AND HOSPICES

The main pilgrim routes had chapels set along them for prayer and rest. Some remain, along the line of the Pilgrim's Way, for example. Hospices were usually attached to monasteries, and destroyed along with them at the Dissolution (1536–40). The hospice often had a wall marked with a cross, maybe in brick. One remains at *Castle Acre* (Norfolk) on the way to Little Walsingham (see above).

LATTER-DAY PILGRIMS

The Reformation put an end to pilgrimages, although some were later renewed by the Catholic Church. Few pilgrimages are made for religious reasons today, but strange though it may seem, the spirit to journey to a destination for its own sake, and not because of trade, barter or a better job, is in a way still very much alive—in the tourist. Tourism shows many of the aspects of pilgrimage. Like pilgrimage, tourism involves the whole of society, irrespective of wealth and rank.

It was a Renaissance man, Petrarch, who is on record as being the first to bother to climb a hill simply to admire the view from the top. The Renaissance spelt the end of medieval days and spawned a new interest in the world for its own sake. It eventually became the fashion for the lesser gentry to travel the countryside, to view the houses and estates of the great

The shrine in the village church at Whitchurch Canonicorum (Dorset) which still holds its saint's bones.

lords and natural features. The improved turnpike roads with their regular (horse-drawn) coaches were to help this traffic.

From this grew the tourist industry, with its preserved and protected views, and the teashops and postcards that we take for granted today. Tourism is big business, with theme parks often taking the place of genuine history. But invention is not new, as we saw in the case of King Arthur's grave above. A more recent invention was the tale of *Beddgelert* (Gwynedd). The master returned home to find the child dead and the hound with bloody mouth. He slew it in anger, but later found beyond the hut a savaged wolf, obviously the real criminal killed by the dog. Grief-stricken, he had the dog buried with full mourning and his grave remains. The tale was invented in the 18th century by the local innkeeper to pep up his custom, and still draws crowds.

THE FIRST GUIDEBOOKS

Guidebooks had their origins in the diaries kept with ever-increasing frequency by travellers. One early on to the roads was Celia Fiennes, who journeyed between 1682 and 1712, her voyages being the easier for that

she was well connected, never short of a relation to stay with. Her diary (still in print today) is full of her eye for details. Daniel Defoe, better known as the author of *Robinson Crusoe*, was well known for his *Tour through the Whole Island of Great Britain* (1724–7). Another was William Cobbett with his *Rural Rides* of 1830.

One early guide book was to the Lake District, by William Wordsworth in 1810—and because of his reputation as a poet, it not only flooded the area with tourists, but also spelled out why they came. Later guide books would begin to carry pictures which made it that much easier to understand the history and the view!

TOURIST MAPS

The earliest British road map was the Gough map of the 14th century; it was in fact a pilgrims' map, showing the routes between religious houses, but omitting other important trading roads. Among the earliest general maps were those by Christopher Saxton and John Speed, compiled in the 16th century.

Answering the needs of travellers of the time, they named settlements and symbolized them by a church or row of houses. Rivers and bridges, vital information, were shown—but hills (which nobody would bother to climb unnecessarily) are childishly drawn hummocks. It was only in the 1750s that the first maps showing high ground shaded with hachures were printed. The first Ordnance Survey maps were printed in the mid 19th century, commissioned as the name suggests for military rather than public use. Most of the maps that we take for granted today are simplified versions of the modern Ordnance Survey maps.

One kind of map once in widespread use but rarely seen today is the strip gazetteer, which showed the distances along a road together with details of the towns, villages and other features encountered. One version, fairly popular in the 1920s when car ownership was becoming general, showed the inclines of all the hills to be met on the journey.

Gates and stiles

Gates and stiles provide a host of neglected details, reflecting local and often ancient traditions that varied from county to county across Britain.

FIELD GATES

The paddocks of medieval and Tudor times—and perhaps even some of the prehistoric 'Celtic' fields which can still occasionally be seen—had gates. But the oldest of today's field gates mostly date from the Georgian enclosures. At this time the open common lands were being divided up into fields, each of which needed its own entrance which

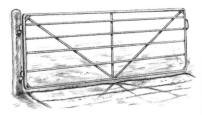

A modern metalwork gate made in a factory but to a traditional design for wooden field gates.

(because of the rotation of arable with pasture around the farm) had to be livestock-proof.

Most of these enclosure gates have already been lost. The wood has decayed, or the hedges which held them have been pulled up to create larger fields. Others have been replaced by modern gates of tubular steel or deal, to take the wider farm machinery of today. But older gates do remain, adding interest to the countryside.

Their patterns are quite varied, although their makers certainly respected any local traditions and for structural reasons the gates all have much in common. The village carpenter called on to provide gates would have responded to local needs, and although a good design might be copied locally it was unlikely to spread much past the local market town, then the centre of countryside business.

THE EARLIEST GATES

These were not swing gates, but simple barriers of wooden bars slotted into uprights. These crossbars were lifted

An old pattern of gate, opened by simply lifting it from its supports.

out when the cattle had to pass. On *Dartmoor* (Devon) and other upland areas, some stone upright posts remain, although put to other uses today. Some have L-shaped sockets for the crossbars, a device to prevent cattle nudging the bars out.

One of the most primitive gates likely to be found, the Sussex heave-bar gate, is a development of this type. It consists of a rough timber fence held between uprights. It could be made of sawn wood or of split timbers.

EARLY SWING GATES

The Romans had a primitive type of swing gate for their forts along *Hadrian's Wall*, and remains of something similar can be found on the early upland settlements. It is known as a 'wood and stone' gate. The vertical beam at the 'hinge' end of the gate is extended to fit into holes in two stones which project from the top and bottom of the wall. These pierced wall fittings can still be found near Widecombe on

An early pattern of swing gate, still sometimes to be found on Dartmoor and the northern hills.

Dartmoor and elsewhere. Many stones found lying loose with holes bored for no obvious reason might well have the same explanation.

THE HINGE GATE

Although iron was in common use by Roman times, and the actual pivots of the Roman hinge gates of Hadrian's Wall were of iron, it was to be many centuries before gates with iron fittings were to become at all common in the countryside—simply because the iron from the local smithy was too valuable to use in this way. Once it did

Details of fittings and fastenings can vary by the county. These are various latches to be seen.

come into use, however, it allowed a great deal of novelty. The iron fastenings made by the local smith could show great ingenuity and ranged from a simple loop to ingenious lockings. Some iron hinges can tighten up a gate that has begun to sag, others allow it to swing only one way. Latches also became more varied: some share the weight of the gate with the hinge while other gates rely on well-balanced woodwork and in hunting countryside some are even designed to be lifted from the saddle with the hook of a riding crop. In shepherd villages it might be found that the smith, used to making crooks, has made the latches in the same shape.

THE MASTER PLAN

The weight of the hinge gate was taken by a sturdy upright 'harr' post at

The five-bar gate is one of the commonest of all patterns, and can be seen in all counties.

the hinge end, while the 'head' upright at the latch end was thinner. Between the horizontal top and bottom rails ran other 'spanes', all of which might be tapered to save weight. The 'five-bar' gate with a total of five horizontal members was commonest. Sagging was prevented with a 'brace' or 'sword' usually rising diagonally from the bottom of the harr, while the rails were linked with vertical 'straps'.

LOCAL VARIETY

In Somerset and West Wiltshire the

The double gate's design makes it useful for counting out a few head of livestock at a time.

harr was very broad, and stepped at the top to take the top rail. In Dorset the top and bottom rails often projected past the harr and were pierced with holes to take the hinge pins. Wealden gates had a single brace with three upright straps, the nearest to the harr crossing the brace. In Oxfordshire and Buckinghamshire, however, this strap only runs from the bottom as far as the brace. In Oxfordshire's Vale of the White Horse, double gates were common, overlapping and fastening at the centre.

In general, whereas in the North of England the brace stretches from corner to corner of the gate, in the south it meets the top rail halfway along; and the gates of the sheep country of the north often have six or even more horizontal bars (there is a saying that whatever sheep can see through, they can get through). The diamond pattern of braces was originally from East Anglia but has proved itself so strong that it is now found everywhere.

Diamond bracing such as this originated in East Anglia but is now found in many other counties.

WICKET GATES

Where people rather than livestock or wagons pass, narrow 'wicket gates' could be used. The cage wicket gate creates a dog-leg passage to deter animals; the gate within the U- or V-

The wicket gate is often found in churchyard walls which overlook the village green.

shaped enclosure can be either hinged or fixed. This kind of gate is often called a kissing gate for obvious reasons. It is a design which was sometimes imitated with stone slabs in stone-wall

country, in what is often known as a 'stone stile'.

STILES

Stiles, which are designed to allow people on foot to cross a hedge or wall, are to be met with on the footpaths which were also being planned out during the time of the Georgian enclosures. Perhaps the most complex of the many varieties of stile is the 'clapper', in which there are balanced rows of horizontal wooden bars which can be pushed down at one end. The wooden step-up-and-over stile is common, especially in the south. In the north and

The widespread 'step-up-and-over' stile is found in many areas and is perhaps the commonest of all patterns.

other areas where there is stone readily to hand, stone stairs of various kinds may be encountered. Some rise straight, others provide a line of rising stepping stones up the side of the wall. Another version is the stone squeezer stile, which has two slabs or boulders placed close enough to prevent cattle squeezing through.

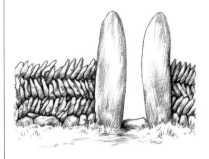

The stone squeezer stile sometimes takes advantage of existing ancient standing stones.

The birth of the modern road

The modern tarmac road had its origins in the days of the stagecoach. But even the busy roadside of today can carry a gruesome souvenir.

THE STATE OF THE ROADS

In the 17th century a new discovery of Britain was in progress. For the first time the gentry, those with money and leisure, were beginning to enjoy travel for its own sake. Stonehenge was visited, and poems written on 'The Wonders of the Peak'. Early 'field guides' describing antiquities and curiosities were widely read.

Travel diaries were kept and published and from them we gain glimpses of the state of the roads. Celia Fiennes, who journeyed between 1682 and 1712, wrote of 'sad roads' and of times when her 'horses feete could scarce stand'. She met highwaymen. It was a time when 'even so much as two wheelbarrows' could not pass each other on parts of the London to Canterbury road, and Sussex men were said to have grown long-legged from pulling their feet from the sticky Sussex clay. Main roads braided themselves past muddy patches, as can be seen on the old London to Bath road on Fyfield Down, just off the *Ridgeway* (Oxon).

Often the regulation 200 ft clear on each side of the King's Highway (see pp. 118–119) was taken into the fields alongside, leaving a narrow track. Those with coaches had need of footmen armed with axes to clear a path. Daniel Defoe, writing in the 1720s, described gentry driving to church in a coach drawn by oxen, for their horses could not cope with the mud. Indeed, it seems that even the line of the famous Great North Road was often lost in a tangle of narrow, twisting lanes. Packhorses were widely used for merchandise, because as Celia Fiennes wrote, 'The reason is plaine, from the narrowness of the lanes where there is good lands . . . and where it is hilly and stoney no other carriages can pass.'

THE LENGTHMAN

The Highways Act of the Tudors made parishes responsible for their roads, and able to use 'statute labour' for repair—'every parishioner for every ploughland and every person keeping a team of horses or a plough' had to supply a cart and two labourers for four days a year. Everyone else had to put in four days' unpaid work themselves. This system ended in 1835 when a parish rate for roads replaced the system. In Victorian days a 'lengthman' was often employed, and much of his time must have been spent keeping the ditches of the enclosure roads clear or supervising the grazing of the passing drove herds on their way to market. The baskets filled by the stone-pickers in the fields—a back-breaking job for children and the old, paid at a halfpenny for a two-gallon basket—were dumped for him to use.

TURNPIKE ROADS

Such had been the state of main roads, that the Cecil family of Hatfield House near St Albans built their own private road to Bath. Nicknamed the 'Goat Track', it skirted the London to Bath road heaving with wagons hauled by eight or more horses, packhorses and other travellers.

But a 'privatization' of roads began

Many tollbooths remain, but few keep their original 'turnpike' — a bar lowered to close the road.

when in 1663 Justices supervising the southern stretches of the Great North Road were allowed to levy tolls on the traffic, the money to be spent on repairs. From this came the Turnpike Acts, which leased our roads to 'Turnpike Trusts' for improvement, in return for which they could charge tolls and make a profit. A good one too: the Hatfield to Reading Turnpike Trust made a profit of £2000 a year in the 1820s. The Trusts could also close slip roads with gates or chains to prevent travellers avoiding the toll booth. By the end of the 18th century fifty or more new Turnpike Acts were being passed each year. The imposition was hated by lesser travellers and led to disturbances such as the Rebecca Riots of 1839 against the new tollgates in South Wales. The tolls in fact deterred much traffic and indeed encouraged the canals and railways.

THE TOLLBOOTH

The name 'turnpike' comes from a movable bar lowered to block the road; it was later replaced with gates. Though few gates remain—there are some at *Honiton* (Devon)—their accompanying toll houses are common. They are single-storey, often with pointed 'Gothic' windows and other decoration of the time, and a pair of protruding windows to enable the toll keeper to sit inside and keep an eye on the road. Some still carry a list of the tolls on their wall, including those for animals. Huge bottlenecks were caused when drove herds were counted one by one.

THE ORIGIN OF TARMAC

Improved surfaces were eventually used for the turnpikes. Thomas Telford, who died in 1834, led the way with carefully stabilized roads, similar to those made by the Romans. His contemporary James Macadam went further, creating a hard 'macadamized' surface by watering and rolling. In 1907 tar was added, to create tarmac. By then the last Turnpike Trust had been wound up, the County Councils taking responsibility for main roads, District Councils the others, as is the pattern today. Roads are now

publically funded, though a few 'private' toll bridges remain.

MILESTONES AND SIGNPOSTS

The Turnpike Acts stipulated milestones, and by 1766 they were required for all main roads, in stone or perhaps cast iron. By then the mile (which had varied) had become standardized at 1760 yards. Many milestones have been lost through road widening in recent years. Some are bizarre, donated by local gentry: one at Craven Arms near *Stokesay* (Shropshire) is 18ft high, and lists the mileages to 36 places.

Signposts too were part of this new countryside, although most have been replaced by today's signs. Older signposts in parts of Dorset are of cast iron, painted red. The wayboards often ended with a pointing 'finger', as at the corner of the Chipping Campden road near *Broadway Tower* (Hereford & Worcs); this is a 10-ft signpost.

In deeply forested areas a brazier

The day of milestones is past, but many remain, albeit often overgrown and forgotten by today's travellers.

was commonly set atop the church tower, to be lit if the night fell before expected travellers had arrived.

IN MEMORIAM

From the time of the first ridgeways with their prehistoric burial mounds, roads have been accompanied by memorials. In later days it was a gibbet, raised near the scene of the crime which caught the traveller's eye; here the body of the executed criminal swung in an iron cage. A replica gibbet stands near *Elsdon* (Northumberland) and at Caxton near *Bourn* (Cambs).

SUICIDES

Forbidden the churchyard, suicides were buried on public open ground— sometimes on waysides and at crossroads, and in one or two places the graves are marked.

The Railway Age

In full use and busy only a few decades ago, many railway lines now lie abandoned, bequeathed to walkers and wildlife.

EARLY TRACKS

An early 'tramway' with granite tracks served the quarry at Haytor on *Dartmoor*, and the railways had their origin in mining. Carts pulled by horses along tracks underground were seen in Tudor mines, and the first overground metal tracks were laid 300 years ago, on the Tanfield Line near Newcastle, for horse-drawn coal wagons. 'Plateways' appeared fairly early, being a metal track turned up along each edge to contain the wheel. Cast-iron rails were used at *Ironbridge* (Shropshire) in 1750, and 50 years later patents were being taken out for cast-iron rails mounted on sleepers and plans being laid for cross-country horse-drawn railways!

Then the mining engineers came up trumps. Steam engines had already been in use for some time to pump out flooded shafts when the engineer Richard Trevithick ran his 'tram engine'. For a bet, puffing tremendously as it released the spent steam, it hauled 10 tons of iron for 10 miles after some preliminary jousts with garden walls and trees—taking four hours. George Stephenson's historic Stockton and Darlington Railway, was opened in 1825, and in 1830 the Liverpool and Manchester railway. Soon every go-ahead industrial town and city was demanding its own railway, with the new managing class eager to invest. Advertisements appeared in local newspapers, challenging coach travel. The days of the horse-drawn coach were numbered, but early railway wagons rather resembled stage-coaches in appearance.

THE NAVVIES

It is ironic that in those days of mechanical mania, the muscle power was human. Under the direction of famous engineers such as Isambard Kingdom Brunel, armies of labourers or 'navvies' came to work on the new lines. The name came from 'navigators', for they had earlier dug out the canals (see pp. 136–137). Living rough in shanty towns, they terrorized the local populace. A normal quota per man (armed only with a shovel) was 20 tons of soil and rock each day. Specialists were also employed: when Brunel was laying out the London to Bristol railway, he recruited his stone-masons in Scotland, for there were not enough in the south for his needs.

THE RAILWAY AGE

By 1850, 5000 miles, of railway had been built; by 1900, 20,000 miles, of which less than a quarter survive. In the early days timetabling was a problem, for each town kept its own time until Greenwich Mean Time (GMT) was universally adopted. Christ Church (*Oxford*) clock still keeps old time, five minutes behind London.

Vast numbers of people travelled: in 1850 there were 73 million railway journeys for a population of less than 20 million. Over five million people travelled to London in 1851 to see the Great Exhibition. In time railways were to become the key to days out in the countryside, holidays by the sea—and eventually the popular, leafy new towns. Posters advertising all this became works of art in their own right.

CHANGING THE COUNTRYSIDE

Not only did the railways figuratively shrink the map of Britain, bringing even remotest Scotland within a couple of days of London, they also changed its face. To provide slight gradients that the engines could master, the navvies cut through hillsides or flattened their flanks, using the spoil to create serpentine embankments. Even when the rails themselves have been torn up, these usually remain. Some lines have become recognized footpaths, such as lengths of line that used to serve the slate mines at *Blaenau Ffestiniog* (Gwynedd). The Tissington Trail is 13 miles of old track extending from *Tissington* (Derbyshire). A few lines, such as the *Watercress Line* (Hants), run steam trains for holidaymakers.

ELEGANT VIADUCTS

Viaducts were built only where unavoidable, perhaps where distances

were too great for embankments. Many of the early viaducts were of timber-spar construction, but for durability brick and stone were preferred. One of the most famous is the elegant Ribblehead viaduct on the Settle to Carlisle line in the shadow of Whernside near *Ingleborough* (N. Yorks), a masterpiece of engineering. Opened in 1876, its 24 stone arches stride across the bogland of Batty Moss. Six thousand men spent six years building it.

BRIDGES

Bridges also feature strongly in the railway record. When lines are closed, bridges crossing roads are usually destroyed, but those carrying a road

across a disused line often remain, being expensive to fill in. Especially elegant are the skew bridges, which take the crossing at an angle. As can be seen from below, the bonding lines between the bricks or cut stone pieces may curve across the curve of the arch like a 3D mathematical figure. It is truly remarkable craftsmanship—and craftsmanship that can sometimes be found on the humblest bridge on a quiet lane.

Other rail bridges are of national importance—the Forth Bridge near Edinburgh, for example. Brunel's work is often interesting—such as his *Saltash Bridge* near Plymouth (Devon) and his bridge spanning the Thames at *Goring Gap* (Oxon); further up the line,

his bridge near Maidenhead, built in 1837, is that shown in Turner's painting *Rain, Steam and Speed*.

STATIONS

The mainline stations were cathedrals to the new god of travel, designed by leading architects. There were fabulous examples in London: Euston is now demolished but St Pancras remains. Whatever their state of repair (and many are now converted into homes) country stations are unmistakable, often with the popular pointed 'Gothic' windows. The platforms of deserted stations sometimes remain, and the goods yards, with sloping ramps to load the cattle into the wagons (the railways killed off the old

The stone arches of Ribblehead Viaduct stride across the boglands overlooked by limestone heights.

droving life). Occasionally in a siding a derelict guard's van might be seen, with protruding windows on each side. Many deserted lines still keep their ballast (the metal rails have gone, some sold to Third World countries).

NARROW-TRACK RAILWAYS

A few railway curiosities still entertain visitors and enthusiasts. There are a fair number of narrow-track lines, built for local purposes. One is 'Ratty', the Romney, Hythe and Dymchurch Railway running from *Romney* (Kent).

Springs and wells

Water is an essential feature of the landscape. Despite much modern manicure, natural springs can still be found, especially in chalk countryside.

SPRINGS AND WELLS

Springs have a geological explanation, which is discussed in detail below. The word 'well' is sometimes used of a spring, especially if the emerging water fills a pool, but is also used to describe a shaft sunk to reach water underground. This might be a subterranean stream, but more often the water level at the foot of the well is maintained by seepage from the rock or gravel round about.

NATURAL SPRINGS

When rain falls, some soaks down to the bedrock beneath the soil, and some is carried off in surface streams. In hard-rock and clay countryside, the latter is the main result, winter flooding is quite normal, and flash floods can even follow rainstorms.

In limestone and especially in chalk countryside, however, most of the rain quickly soaks down into the rock. Gravity pulls it down until it meets waterlogged rock or perhaps a less absorbent rock layer: the water seepage is diverted sideways and emerges from a cut-away flank as a spring. (An artesian well taps into the pressure of the water held in these subterranean layers to give a fountain-like flow.)

At the foot of the chalk downs below the *Ridgeway* (Oxon) a line of springs emerging at about the same level is marked by a line of 'spring line' villages, their sites chosen because of this reliable water supply. Such springs fed from a natural rock sponge of this kind flow fairly steadily all year round, irrespective of the recent weather. In some parts of the chalk downlands, however, the streams flow only after the rock is sodden with the autumn rains. Reflecting this fact, there are a number of villages which have 'Winterbourne' (winter-brook) as part of their name; there is a cluster of these near *Dorchester* (Dorset).

The water from chalk springs also issues at a fairly even temperature. It feels cold in summer, but warm in

This sparkling beck emerges from the foot of the natural amphitheatre of Malham Cove (N. Yorks).

winter and on winter days wisps of mist may deck its surface, where warm vapours condense in the cooler air. Hot springs such as at Bath and in places in the Peak District are heated by transmission from the inner core of the earth.

Springs can also be found in hard-rock hills, some rainfall finding its way down joints and cracks in the rock. The 'statesmen's' houses of the village of *Troutbeck* in the Lake District (Cumbria) are spaced along the valley, each at a spring. The many roadside springs of the *Malvern Hills* (Hereford & Worcs) are another example. Unlike chalk springs, which yield 'hard' water because of the lime dissolved on its passage through the chalk, these hard-rock springs can yield very pure soft water.

UNDERGROUND RIVERS

Water flow creates caverns, especially in limestone (see pp. 24–25). In these, subterranean streams might flow, to issue as a spring of a kind; one issues as a beck at the foot of *Malham Cove* (N. Yorks).

SPRING LORE

The apparent magic of springs was venerated from early times and adopted by the early Christian Church—

The 'Dropping Well' at Knaresborough (N. Yorks), one of the best known of all petrifying springs.

many Welsh chapels are built above springs or wells, for example. A three-headed goddess, Elen or Annis, was linked with springs in Iron Age days: many springs are known as St Agnes' Spring, or St Anne's spring or well, or perhaps simply 'Holy well'. The 'well dressing' practised at *Tissington* (Derbyshire) perhaps derives from pagan ceremonies. On Ascension Day the five wells in the village are framed with biblical scenes made by pressing flower petals into clay.

Healing springs were believed capable of effecting miraculous cures: the spring of St Wita, who gave her name to Whitchurch Canonicorum near *Lyme Regis* (Dorset) was thought to cure eye ailments.

Many springs, however (such as those at Bath and in the Peak District) have a high content of mineral salts, which could be curative, and could certainly have a recuperative effect on jaded livers. It was these springs that became popular spas in Regency and later times.

WISHING-WELLS

The beliefs which lie behind the origin of wishing-wells date back at least to the Iron Age. Springs were used for divination, the future being foretold from the swirls in the water, especially those seen after tossing in a gift for the god or goddess. There is a wishing-well at *Madron* (Cornwall), an area of ancient settlement. One at Carrawbrough near *Hadrian's Wall* contained 16,000 Roman coins.

CHALYBEATE WATERS

These are springs which issue or issued red, the water tinted with iron salts. Iron compounds brought to the surface are oxidized by a very ancient form of bacteria which derives its energy from the conversion. Seepages in fields can also be tinted in this way. The link with blood (and hence menstruation and hence fertility) might have given them significance.

PETRIFYING SPRINGS

Limestone springs with a high mineral content deposit calcite: hats, shoes and toys are hung in the waters at *Knaresborough* (N. Yorks) to be coated and 'turn to stone' in a matter of a year or two. Originally, perhaps, these items were substituted for the limbs or bandages of the maimed or sick, as the Romans had lead tokens cast in the shape of arms or legs to be consigned to healing or wishing-wells.

VILLAGE PUMPS

Magnates' homes might have donkey wheels to raise water, as at *Carisbrooke* (Isle of Wight), but pumps for village wells did not come into general use until the beginning of the 19th century, replacing the old open well reached by bucket and windlass. Some pumps survive, with a wooden or cast-iron case, and sometimes mounted on a ramp so that horse-drawn water carts could be filled. It was quite usual for one well and pump to serve the whole village (piped water was not universally available until after World War II). The water was collected in two buckets balanced on a yoke across the shoulders.

Solitary farms in recent decades often used wind pumps to take water from wells, maybe to fill a cattle trough in the fields. These were of distinctive design, with a circle of flat, broad sails; they have usually been replaced by electric pumps today.

Bridging the waters

Some of the oldest structures built for crossing rivers may still survive in the form of clapper bridges. Medieval bridges are still in use carrying today's traffic.

FORDS AND STEPPING STONES

The first regular river crossings were fords, but tracing the original crossing of early trackways can be tricky. At *Goring Gap* (Oxon) where today's line of the Ridgeway descends steeply to the river, the Thames cascades over a step (there are a weir and bridge here today). Although a tangle of tree trunks trapped in these rapids might

Crossing the waters.

have provided a temporary bridge from time to time, it would always have been turbulent. But 2 miles upstream is the riverside village of Moulsford, a good enough clue to an original crossing point.

In London, to prove rumours that the river once had a Roman ford, one Member of Parliament walked across the Thames at Westminster, doing so at low tide, of course. Throughout the countryside as a whole, river and stream crossings and '-ford' towns and villages are not uncommon.

Stepping stones provide an effective solution to the problem of staying dry-shod when crossing a stream. A line of

unknown age remains at *Ashwell* (Herts) for example.

CLAPPER BRIDGES

The first bridges are likely to have been wooden, maybe simply timbers roped together. Stone 'clapper' bridges might also be very old, although there is no real evidence either way. They consist of stone slabs resting on rough stone columns set into the bed of the stream. They can be found in the Lake District, on *Dartmoor* (Devon)(the largest is at Postbridge) and other places. That at Tarr Steps, *Exmoor* (Som) has 17 spans, the slabs weighing as much as 5 tons. They were a response to regular traffic, above all to regular animal traffic—cattle and sheep and packhorse—allowing it to pass what could be a swirling treacherous obstacle for many winter months.

Roman stone bridges are seen abroad, but none have been found in Britain, so presumably their bridges were of wood.

MEDIEVAL BRIDGES

Arched stone bridges became common in medieval times; that at *Bideford* (Devon) has 24 unequal arches. Some, such as the oldest at *Devil's Bridge*, near Aberystwyth (Dyfed), are early. Many were built by the monasteries, an investment which boosted not only the pilgrim traffic but also the profits to be gained from the bridge tolls. A few have a small chapel halfway across, as at *St Ives* (Cambs). The chapel at *Wakefield* (W. Yorks) was built in 1350, eight years after the toll rights were granted. Its use changed after the Reformation, and it was at various times also a library and a clothes shop. The chapel on the bridge at *Bradford on Avon* (Wilts) became the lock-up.

The monasteries would grant absolution for lesser sins in return for money (or labour) for bridge maintenance—and odd as it may seem, there are hints that sometimes hermits were given the supervision of this. The name Armitage is the clue. The bridge at *Monmouth* (Gwent) is fortified, the only example in Britain, although they are quite common abroad. Only rarely did the bridge

stepping stones

a well-shod ford

clapper bridge

medieval bridge

carry shops, as did Old London Bridge, or Pulteney Bridge in Bath.

Using the structurally strong pointed arch that first appeared in church architecture, so well made were these medieval bridges that many remain in use today. They were often built with recesses so that those on foot could avoid being jostled by the bellowing herds which regularly used them. As well as carefully masoned arches, many were also built with carefully designed cut-waters to neatly divide the powerful current to lessen its impact. Long arched 'bridges', which were really simply causeways, were also built, to cross marshy ground. Some could be a mile or more long.

CLAY VERSUS CHALK BRIDGES

Canny tradition also went into the building of bridges. In clay and hard-rock countryside, where the rivers take the run-off from the ground and often flood in spate, the arches are high. In chalk countryside, where much of the rain soaks into the ground and the flooding is less common, they need only be low.

DECORATIVE BRIDGES

The famous 'bridge house' in Ambleside at the head of Windermere near *Troutbeck* (Cumbria) was in fact a summer house, an ornamental 'folly'. Bridges were often built or rebuilt as an eyecatcher for a squire's estate in the 18th century. A 'medieval' bridge was built at *Stourhead* (Wilts), for example, when the grounds were laid out at that time.

PACKHORSE BRIDGES

Although there was wagon and cart traffic in medieval times, the bulk of goods travelled in caravans of pack-horses. Many of the older bridges which remain were packhorse bridges, especially in the uplands, where the rugged and steep tracks made the use of carts difficult. They are usually narrower than cart bridges, often high-humped, as this was structurally stronger but did not deter the animals. The surface was often deeply cobbled to give them a good foothold. The

parapets on each side were low, or even absent, so that the heavy panniers slung on each side of the animal could swing free—the bridge at Altarnun on *Bodmin Moor* (Cornwall) is one example.

TURNPIKE BRIDGES

Rebuilt bridges were part of the improved Georgian turnpike-road network and many bridges date from this time, the 18th century. Some used the then new material of cast iron. The crucial importance of bridges is underlined by notices of the time, which still remain in place on a few Dorset bridges, threatening with transport-

ation for life anyone caught damaging the bridge.

Toll bridges still remain, with dues still charged, on the 1792 Pangbourne to Whitchurch road at *Goring Gap* (Oxon), and a few other places.

THE FERRYMAN

The ferryman also needed paying; and for the Romans this took on symbolic importance: the Roman dead were buried with a coin to pay the ferryman to carry them over the River Styx to Hades. Ferries pulled across by chain were common in medieval days.

Bridges add interest.

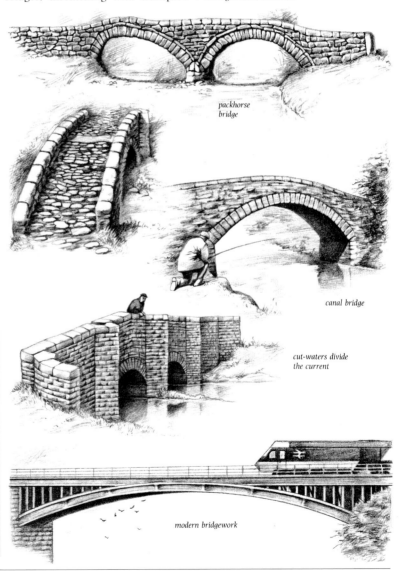

packhorse bridge

canal bridge

cut-waters divide the current

modern bridgework

Along the towpath

Canals had nearly as marked an effect on the landscape as the railways which supplanted them. Many canals are still open for holiday traffic.

THE BIRTH OF THE CANAL AGE

A problem of the early Industrial Revolution was that the rivers which would give cheap transport were far from the new inland coalfields.

The solution was to dig canals. There had been canals in Europe since the 1550s and lined with a variety of materials, but in Britain the engineer James Brindley solved the problem with puddled clay—that is, clay trodden with water to form an impermeable mass. With that achievement under his belt he could, in 1759, start to build a 13-mile canal running directly from the Duke of Bridgewater's coal mines at Worsley to the centre of Manchester, a canal which not only provided cheap transport but also made use of the water drained from the mines.

Canals were then to be dug to create a network of short cuts linking the major rivers—Brindley's 'Grand Cross' joined four main rivers; others joined towns such as *Tiverton* (Devon) to the sea. By 1830 there were 4000 miles of canals but by then their brief ascendancy was almost over, for competition from the railways was already beginning to bite.

SCULPTING THE LANDSCAPE

The hard labour of canal building was done by gangs of 'navvies'—short for navigators—armed only with picks, shovels and wheelbarrows. (The 'navvy' also became the name of the muscle that built the railways.)

James Brindley's canals compromised with the landscape by taking a serpentine course across country to follow the contour line and to avoid the need for locks. Where locks were unavoidable, he usually placed them in groups.

The second generation of canal engineers such as Thomas Telford attacked the countryside more vigorously, creating 'cut and fill' canals—that is, cutting the passage through high ground and using the rock and soil to build up embankments in lower places, as railways and today's bypasses do. It meant that more direct canals could be built, and by then cast iron was often replacing stone for bridges and (more importantly) aqueducts. Tunnels also became a feature of many canals. In some tunnels the towpath continued, in others the horse had to be led over the hill, while the bargee and his family propelled the barge themselves, lying down flat and 'legging' it by 'walking' along the tunnel roof.

RESERVOIRS

The canals were fed with water from a river system, but as lock systems lose water to the lower levels, most canals needed back-up reservoirs to maintain the water levels. The few that remain are usually notable local nature reserves, for undisturbed open water has become something of a rarity in the countryside.

AQUEDUCTS

Aqueducts to carry the canal across intervening valleys were crucial to straight-line canal systems. At first they were dumpy constructions, massively built to bear the weight of the water. Improved designs required less bulky lines without losing strength and cast and wrought iron allowed lighter constructions, sometimes made with standard prefabricated sections. The *Pontcysyllte Aqueduct* (Clwyd) which crosses the Dee Valley is one of Britain's best-known examples.

LOCKS

A lock is a device for raising and lowering the water level. Brindley's locks were of a standard size, 17 by 7 ft, which was kept in later years, and this of course restricted the size of the barges and also, as queues built up at the locks, the traffic that each canal could carry. (The competing railways were more flexible, not least because it was clearly relatively easy to construct sidings to accommodate waiting trains. Gravity locks the gates—one of the two pairs of gates will always be closed by the pressure of the higher level. When both pairs of gates are shut, sluices are opened to lower or raise the water level within the lock. With equal depth of water on each side the gates can easily be swung open.

Series of locks might be arranged in a 'staircase' as they are at the Fourteen Lock Canal Centre at *Newport* (Gwent). In one or two places the goods were loaded into small 'tub boats' which could be dragged out of water up an 'inclined plane' to reach a higher level.

The locks were supervised by lock-keepers, who also collected the tolls, and their cottages (many remain) have a great deal of charm. They were made of local materials, but some have roofs and other features fashioned from spars and timber formers used by the lock diggers.

The lock-keeper's job was usually a day job, if of long hours, for the tow horses needed nightly rest. But Pickfords, an early transport firm, in addition to the daytime 'stage' boats, started express 'fly' boats travelling round the clock with double crews and horses changed at regular intervals—and undercutting the railways in cost although (at an average of 2 miles an hour) still greedy on time.

BASINS

At key points side basins were built, with wharves, warehouses, maintenance sheds, stables and pubs. There is one at *Bunbury* (Cheshire). The stables are now workshops. The locks are unusual in being 14 ft wide—double the normal width.

THE BARGEE AND HIS HORSE

The family lived on board the 'narrow boats' still used for holidays today; typical decoration included paintings of mountains, lakes and sailing boats in traditional colours of red, yellow and green. The narrow boat may have pulled other barges behind. The motive power until well into this century was the horse trudging the towpath, slowly but surely, an even pace, the miles marked by mileposts, often of distinctive design.

THE TOWPATH

This usually ran on one side only, which created a problem when the lie of the land called for a swap from one bank to the other. A simple bridge, with the horse walking up a ramp (with treads to stop it slipping), over the water and down the other side meant that the horse needed to be unroped beforehand and reroped after the barge had passed under the arch. This could be avoided with a 'snake bridge', where the ramp curled round and under itself and under the arch on the opposite side. Several remain. Another solution, made easier with cast iron, was the split bridge, in two halves cantilevered in from each side, the rope travelling through the narrow gap between them.

Where footpaths crossed the canal, they often did so by means of a quaint little drawbridge.

Today, many stretches of canal which are still open are as busy as ever – at least in summer, when they are full of holiday craft. But others lie abandoned and derelict. This is not a complete loss, because they form important nature reserves for frogs, water beetles, dragonflies and other wetland wildlife of all kinds.

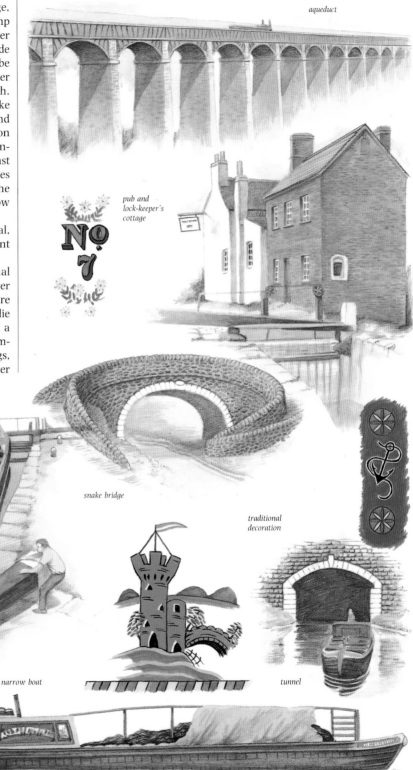

aqueduct

pub and lock-keeper's cottage

N°. 7

lock

snake bridge

traditional decoration

narrow boat

tunnel

Wetlands

The draining of wetlands has been continuing for many centuries. Their original vast extent can still be traced on maps.

WETLANDS IN THE PAST

We keep few memories of the miserable wetness of life in earlier centuries. Winter flooding was a regular fact, even in enclosure times, when the land was criss-crossed by drainage ditches. Villages would be cut off for weeks at a time, with washed-out cottagers taking refuge in the church.

Large-scale movement often became impossible in the winter months, as in warfare. Of England's 50 major battles, from the Dark Ages through the Wars of the Roses to the Civil War, only six took place after September and of those five were in October. Skirmishing began again in March at the earliest.

THE FENS

The name 'The Fens' is reserved for a vast area of drained land south and west of the Wash, recognized on the map from its grids of drainage dykes and their accompanying straight roads and tracks.

RELIC FENLANDS

But 'fen' is also the name given to a particular kind of wetland, with some open water surrounded with reed beds but largely of marshy, waterlogged soil with sedge tussocks and tangled patches of alders and other wet-loving trees and shrubs. The fen is often bedded on peat, a mass of compressed vegetation which remains only partly decayed in the airless, waterlogged conditions. Only a few relic areas remain undrained, and in anything like their original state. The *Broads* (Norfolk) with their reedy lagoons have much the same look, although they are flooded medieval peat diggings in origin. Wicken Fen (Cambs) is an authentic relic well worth a detour.

THE DRAINING OF THE FENLANDS

The drainage of the fenlands started in Roman days when Car Dyke, dug from Cambridge to Lincoln to take grain barges to the northern troops, also helped drain the land alongside. Some of the 'lodes' which connect the fens to the sea are possibly Roman. *Reach Lode* (Cambs) is one; although far inland, Reach was a small port even dealing with coal in Victorian days. These lodes also drained the wetlands.

The advantages were soon clear, for the peaty soil that was gained was light and rich. In Saxon days the attack on the wetlands continued; it was probably now that *Romney Marsh* (Kent) was first dyked to gain the rich pasture 'innings'. Low-lying Holderness in Yorkshire, parts of Sedgemoor in Somerset and extensions of the areas in the Lincolnshire Fens drained by the Romans were also tamed. In medieval times, the abbeys accelerated the process; before it set to in the 10th–14th centuries coastal shipping could reach *Glastonbury Abbey* (Som). Further attack came in the 17th century, when Dutch engineers were appointed to drain and transform 400,000 acres of East Anglia's Fens with ditches and dykes. Otmoor near Oxford became a neat chequerboard of fields, which sowed the seed for the Red Queen and the other chess imagery in *Alice Through the Looking Glass*.

THE SHRINKING PEAT

The peat began to shrink as soon as it was drained. Eventually the level of the fields fell below the level of the water in the drainage ditches, to pose a serious problem three centuries ago. Wind pumps—looking like smock-mills—were built, and there were over 2000 of them in the Fens at one time, though only a few remain today. Today electric pumps do the job, although—ironically—at Wicken Fen (see above) an old wind pump keeps the fen topped up to the old level.

As the peat dried out, the trunks of trees which had grown there long since were exposed: parts of these 'bog oaks' can sometimes be seen in roadside ditches; although once dry, the iron-hard wood disintegrates.

The 'roddens' are one oddity of the East Anglian Fens. Unlike the peat alongside, the actual river beds in the area were gravel-bottomed, and when the land around shrank, they remained standing proud, in time to become tracks and road. The river courses were serpentine, and today the roads of these roddens wind on these old courses, several feet higher than the fields alongside.

THE MOSSES OF THE NORTH

In the wet British climate thick beds of peat could also be created by bogs (sometimes known as mires). Bog moss is the agent here; it can thrive on poor acid ground, its massed floppy stems soaking up water like a sponge. The dead stems remain undecayed to form a bed of peat below the living surface of the bog, and endlessly added to from above, this can dome itself up above the land around. *Tregaron Bog* (Dyfed), on the plain of the River Teifi,

is one example of a raised bog. The bogs of *Dartmoor* (Devon) and the *Flow Country* of north-east Highland blanket vast distances.

Although the bog may no longer be 'alive', the legacy of the peat it laid down remains. These peaty areas appear on the maps as 'mosses' in northern England. *Thorne Moss* (*Thorne Waste*) (S. Yorks), is an example. Often, however, most of the peat has been extracted.

PEAT DIGGING

Peat or 'turf' has long been valued as a fuel. It burns slowly, but without acrid smoke. It was dug widely in Roman times, not only for domestic fires, but for 'winning' salt by evaporating it from sea water. One commons right

was turbary—the digging of peat for fuel. The Norfolk *Broads* are flooded medieval peat diggings which once provided Norwich with 200,000 turves a year; in some places the shape of the lagoons and the remaining strips of undug land betray their origin. Similar abandoned, but dry, turbaries can be found in the Scottish Highlands.

The peat was originally dug by hand, usually in late spring when the winter floods had abated. A long-bladed sharp spade was used to cut the peat into blocks (called mumps in Somerset) about 12 by 6 in. These were sliced into narrow turves (or 'peats' in Scotland) and loosely stacked in beehive-shaped piles to dry.

Peat is still dug, but for nursery and

garden use (although it still fuels a power station in Ireland).

THE FENLANDS TODAY

Much of the old drained fenland has in recent decades been even deeper drained. The Somerset levels and some other original fenland areas had traditionally been grazed, with the drainage ditches, or 'rhynes', offering a haven for wetland flowers, frogs, dragonflies, birds and other wildlife which matched the interest of the original fen. They have now been deep-drained and ploughed for corn; little of this wildlife remains.

Like many other old countryside activities, peat digging had its own tools and traditions.

Riverside crafts

The river and the river bank were vital to the rural economy of days gone by, and some echoes remain of their traditional importance in country people's lives.

RIVERBANK RESOURCES

Bygone days, when traditional skills were practised unchanged for centuries, were days of surprisingly intensive use: 'waste little, want not' was an old motto. This was clearly demonstrated along a river bank. The willows lining a stream would be pollarded, as they still are today, while cattle grazed to within an inch of the water below. A few yards downstream a withy bed waited to be cut for basket making. From the bank, below the rippling water, stretched unseen a woven eel hive, a wickerwork trap in which a couple of the hapless fish shuddered. The reeds growing in a placid backwater were harvested dead and dry for a quick repair to the thatched roof, while the green rushes made soft wickerwork cradles. Even the humblest field rushes that dot the pasture could be woven into a toy, a green box containing two pebbles, rattled to call the birds to the limed traps.

POLLARDED WILLOWS

The growing of pollarded willows on river banks is recorded in 13th-century documents. It was especially important in fenlands, where trees were few and firewood (or indeed any wood) was scarce.

A pollard is a tree cut at or above head height, to grow a head of branches which are regularly cut again. In time the trunk or bolling (rhyming with 'rolling') becomes gnarled. Pollarded willows grow quickly, and if pollarding is discontinued, the branches grow too heavy for the soft wood of the trunk and eventually fall, ripping the trunk.

REED BEDS

Although wheat straw was and still is used for thatching in southern counties (fields of long-stemmed wheat grown for the job are piled up in the old-fashioned 'stooks' after cutting), reed lasts up to 80 years—four times longer. Reed beds grow in shallow, still or slightly moving water. Thin beds can be found along many lake margins, but notable beds remain in the *Broads* (Norfolk). Even here they are now restricted to the quieter waters, and it is thought that the churning of the mud by the holiday craft has led to their disappearance elsewhere. The reeds are cut when dead, in winter, and can often be seen piled along the watersides at that time. Transport costs once restricted the use of Norfolk reed to East Anglia (where even many churches are thatched).

RUSHES

The true bulrush was once as popular a harvest as the reed. (The reedmace with its brown sausage-shaped seed head has commonly been known as the bulrush since the Victorian artist Alma-Tadema used it for his popular picture of Moses among the rushes!) The true bulrush was traditionally cut with a short sickle, at midsummer when the tapering stems, still green and pliable, rose a yard or two out of the water, carrying a brown tuft of grasslike flowers. Dried to a soft brown colour, the rush had many and varied uses. It was often used for thatching—of haystacks, for example. Lengthwise strips could be peeled off the stalk to reveal the pith, and when dipped in tallow this made a simple rushlight, a cheap candle which could shed a dim light for a few hours (wax candles were a luxury even two centuries ago). The pith was also used for sealing the joints in wooden barrels. The stems, wetted to regain their pliability, were woven into soft plaiting for such things as cradles for the newborn and light basketwork. Rush table mats can still be bought today.

OSIER BEDS

Weaving with soft rushes was counted as woman's work; but osiers needed a man's muscle. There was a thriving medieval trade in osiers, and they are still grown in beds in some areas of the

The reed harvest is traditionally cut in winter, when the stalks are dead and ready for thatching.

Somerset levels. A relative of the willow, the osier can be rooted from cut branches and grows very quickly to provide a continuous crop of thin rods.

It was a most necessary crop in earlier times, being used for strong basketwork—which included basket chairs (as pictured in medieval manuscripts) and the hoods of carts and wagons. Scaffolding incorporating plaited willow was often used by the masons of the great cathedrals and churches—rickety-looking to be sure, but much the same is seen in use in Japan today. Packhorse panniers were also made from it.

The harvested 'rods' were boiled, dried and then stripped of their bark. But green willow, still alive and hence somewhat rot proof, was used for crab pots and eel and fish traps.

TRADITIONAL FISHING

In these days of factory-made thin-filament nets and line, we forget countless centuries when fish were caught by different means, and never as a hobby.

Kiddles were basketwork fish traps, a deep basket with a narrow neck. They were used from early times as part of a fish weir, a wickerwork fence which blocked the river, making the fish nose sideways until they entered a kiddle. Fish weir stakes dating back to 800 BC have been found on the Trent. Kiddles were often placed where a weir was built to divert water to a mill.

EEL TRAPS

A wickerwork weir across a stream was most likely to give good catches when migratory fish were running: and eel-catching developed its own special kit. Eels spawn deep in the Sargasso Sea, in the western Atlantic, but come to Britain when small elvers to enter the rivers, swimming far upstream. They feed for about 10 years, and then these 'yellow' eels turn silver and return to the sea. Elaborate wickerwork baskets on wooden frames and able to be lowered at need were used where rivers narrowed, such as on the Thames near *Goring* (Oxon), to catch the fish on their journeys.

Dense beds of reeds are a feature of wetland areas.

SALMON AND CORACLES

The 'king of fish' was caught in similar fashion to the eels on the main rivers. Some 'scutchers' or basketwork salmon traps are still licensed on the Severn. The fish swim to the gravel headwaters to breed, and on salmon rivers national laws required a gap—the King's Gap—to be left open to give some fish a chance to slip past, breed and maintain stocks. The name is still used for the open salmon runs built to one side of modern weirs and dams.

Wickerwork coracles are still used to net a certain licensed number of salmon on the Welsh rivers Towy and Teifi—near *Cenarth* (Dyfed) for example. Made of split, pliable willow laths covered with waterproofed cloth (originally a single cow or pony hide), with edging tightened with a plait of thin hazel, the coracle dates back to Neolithic times.

The pond

Unless regularly cleared, a pond is likely to dry up. Its presence is often a clue to some past use. Many mark embryonic industrial sites.

THE FUNCTIONAL POND

In the mind's eye a pond is a small but permanent feature of the countryside. In fact a pond is usually dying. With no current to sweep them away, leaves and bankside vegetation and other debris fall to the bottom to rot into mud. As a result the pond will in time become a marshy hollow and then slowly dry out.

Dry hollows now filled with a tangled patch of scrub may recall a forgotten wetter landscape, and today's pond may be all that remains of a much larger water system. A pond may be the last reminder of a shrivelled lake.

Very often, however, a pond in the countryside is a story marker. It was usually dug for a particular purpose

Ponds are taken for granted, but often have a particular and detailed history, such as this hammer pond which lies near Albury (Surrey).

and regularly cleared out. In some valleys such as those in the vicinity of *Abinger* (Surrey) chains of useful ponds mark (or marked) the descent of a stream—village ponds, millponds, sheep dips and hammer ponds which stored water for iron working (see pp. 108–109). The latter, also called furnace ponds, are a feature of the Weald, and also to be seen at *Horsmonden* (Kent) for example.

KETTLEHOLES AND CLEAR POOLS

As exceptions, a few natural, long-lived pools can be found. One example is the kettlehole pool occurring in a few places in Cheshire. It has a particular origin: here a block of slowly melting glacial ice prevented the site infilling with silt and other debris carried by the streams round about. The ice melted, water filled the space. Another example is the deep pool which sometimes forms below a spring or is continuously fed by a hidden spring. The Silent Pool at Shere near *Abinger* (Surrey) is one example. The limpid water of such pools often appears to be a fine blue, which is the natural colour of a large mass of clear water. (Ponds are usually clouded green by algae. Peaty water has a brown colour.)

THE VILLAGE POND

The village duck pond on the green is the one most likely to have survived the centuries. Ducks are not so important to the economy—but the pond once was, providing water for livestock grazing on the green or being brought to the smithy, and also water for the smith to quench his iron. Today, maintained as a feature, it might be edged with paving to preserve its outline.

THE MOAT

The hall of a Saxon thegn, or petty lord, and its successor, the medieval manor house, usually had a moat and many remain if only as a dry hollow. In fact 5000 have been counted. They were usually rectangular in plan. A few are still whole, surrounding the old steading, but usually only a part remains wet, edging a later house built on the same site.

One mystery is that these modest moats were hardly defensive, even though they were most probably backed by a timber palisade. Even when kept topped up by a diverted stream (and so not dug simply to drain the hall site), they were usually crossed by a generous causeway. And even if this was blocked by a gateway, it would have been scant deterrence to a war band. Perhaps these village moats were more in the way of status symbols for those not important enough to merit a full-scale castle.

FISHPONDS

In the old days of make and mend, a pond was often put to many different uses, and perhaps the moat doubled as a fishpond for carp for the table. Millponds were also used as fishponds. On the other hand, the hollows of specially dug village fishponds are sometimes a feature of deserted villages (see pp. 56–57). In *Bradfield Woods* (Suffolk) some broad ditches lying among today's coppice are thought to be medieval fishponds dug by the abbey in possession at that time. The monasteries often farmed fish on a grand scale, with elaborate ladders of 'stewponds', the water falling from one to the next. The Serpentine in London's Hyde Park was originally a line of monastic stewponds.

FIELD PONDS

Although many field ponds are no more than a widening of a stream where the cattle can stand hock-deep, and impossible to date, others are definitely of recent date, dug when the fields were enclosed in Georgian days. With no piped water, they relied on a spring or stream (which may keep the area damp even when the pond itself has dried up). Such ponds (or the damp hollows) are usually in the corners of the hedged fields, and often shared by four fields, so that they may be cross-shaped with the middle acting as a 'wet fence'. These ponds fell out of use when pastureland became ploughed as arable in this century and also when piped water was laid on. This was often taken to an old bath—and

fields are the place to find old-fashioned Victorian kitchen bath tubs.

A field pond at the edge of a field alongside a footpath or green way might also recall droving days, when the modest path was in fact an important route. On the other hand, a pond or damp hollow in the centre of a field may mark an old village claypit dug for brick making or (earlier) for clay for the daub which infilled the timber walls of the cottages. It might be what remains of a marl pit, dug for limy clay to spread on the sour acid soil of surrounding fields, or old peat diggings, or a sand quarry. The nature of the rock below the soil is the clue, but some were caused by misdirected or jettisoned bombs in World War II.

WATERCRESS BEDS

These are found alongside or dammed up across chalk streams. Watercress is a wild plant, but cultivated in these broad shallow pools, often squared off and edged with stone. It is eaten green, but was usually boiled as a vegetable in Regency times (watercress soup is still popular). The cry of the watercress girl was one of the classic street cries of old London.

DEW PONDS

These are found on high dry downlands, and were an important source of water for sheep and shepherd alike. They are saucer-like depressions about 20 ft across and were being built up to World War II, when piped water replaced them. As they seem to fill magically, some link their name with 'Dieu', the (Norman) French for God. They are in part filled by rain running off the ground, in part by dew (which is another explanation of their name).

They are lined with straw with a topping of clay (or concrete in recent times). Dew falls not as rain, but by condensing from the layer of air near the ground when the ground is saturated and its surface cool. On clear nights, the clay loses the day's heat quickly and the straw insulates it from warmth rising up from the ground below. Dew condenses on to this cold surface, adding to the water already collected from run-off.

Lakes and reservoirs

In the geological timescale, lakes have a short life. They are relatively uncommon, and most lowland 'lakes' are artificial creations for use or ornament.

UPLAND LAKES AND TARNS

These often occupy high-lying valleys gouged out by glaciers, and are fed by streams tumbling with the copious rains. They back up behind a natural dam which is often a moraine, a dump of material left by the dying glacier. Like lowland ponds and lakes, they are in the process of silting up. Buttermere and Crummock Water in the Lake District were once one, but have been separated by material brought down by a side stream. In Kentmere, the lake has already been filled, to leave a dead-flat valley floor and the flat surrounds of other lakes foretell the same fate. Elsewhere water fills hollows worn in the bedrock, to create the lochans near *Suilven* (Highland) and Dozmary Pool near Altarnun on *Bodmin Moor* (Cornwall)—said to be the lake where King Arthur seized Excalibur; by legend bottomless, it is in fact shallow. One unusual lake is Malham Tarn above *Malham* (N. Yorks), trapped on an impermeable bed in a bowl in the porous limestone rock.

LOWLAND LAKES

Contours and climate make lakes rather a rarity in the lowland landscape. Even in areas covered by the ice sheet, natural lakes are not at all common. An ice sheet is not like a glacier: its effort is dispersed, and does not gouge great hollows. Some lowland lakes were formed by ice, but in a curious way. In some places, a large area of ice sheet remained unmelted; the usual melt-water debris of 'boulder' clay and gravel which was spread over the lowlands was built up around its edges. When it did melt, it thus left in the new land surface a depression which filled with water. *Loch Leven* (Tayside) with its famous island and castle in which Mary Queen of Scots was imprisoned had this origin—it is rounded in shape, unlike the long, thin lakes typical of mountain valleys.

One or two small meres of Cheshire were probably formed in rather the same way—although many pools here are the result of subsidence from salt mining below (see pp. 142–143).

Like ponds and in fact any open waters, lowland lakes also tend to dry out, becoming silted up with material brought in by their feeder streams and dead vegetation encroaching from the banks.

DUCK DECOYS

Lakes have been dug or adapted for many uses, including the little-known duck decoys: but they were once not uncommon on country estates.

A shallow lake was dug or extended, with three or four narrow, curving channels leading off it and spaced out around its rim. These 'pipes' were covered in netting stretched on looped poles, making a barely visible tunnel. Alongside was a row of overlapping woven-reed screens, tall enough to hide a man. A trained dog walks out through the gap nearest the lake and back behind cover at the next. The instinct of any wild duck on the open water is to approach, perhaps to check whether a fox has been seen. The dog appears again, but further up the pipe. The duck paddle closer, into the pipe entrance, and are thus led up it to its end, where the man lurks ready to reach over and pull the net across behind them. One decoy remains working at *Boarstall* (Bucks) but the birds are now ringed by bird watchers, not necks wrung. The name decoy remains in many places on the map, even when the open water itself has gone. *Martin Mere* (Lancs) has also been created for birds, though for a very different purpose.

ORNAMENTAL LAKES

Ornamental lakes were an important feature of the landscaped parks of Regency and Victorian gentry. Originally they had been little better than straight canals running between a vista of tree plantations, but the 'natural' look became fashionable, and serpentine banks were gained by damming a stream valley and letting the water flood to the natural shape of the contours.

The lake at *Stourhead* (Wilts), which has a prominent dam, was fed by a stream (which higher up also fed a chain of fishponds) and also by a spring, around which a grotto was built, adorned with statues of Neptune and a delicious sleeping nymph.

FLASHES

Although many natural lakes have been lost to drainage schemes in recent centuries, their number has been made good by innumerable man-made waters. Flashes are seen in coal-mining areas, above abandoned seams, where the collapse of the tiers of working tunnels creates a hollow in the surface above. The hollow floods and, being shallow, reeds and rushes take easy root, so that the area becomes a wildfowl haven. They are often called 'ings' in Yorkshire, and there are many on the map.

FLOODED GRAVEL PITS

These are now a major feature of many lowland areas alongside the great rivers such as the Thames. The beds of gravel (largely a legacy of torrential post-Ice Age floods) are dug, then fill with water and in time green up along their banks. They too are wildlife refuges.

RESERVOIRS

Artificial storage lakes can be found everywhere in Britain. The oldest are those at the Roman gold mines at *Dolaucothi* (Dyfed) supplying water for separating the metal from the crushed rock. Millponds, hammer ponds and other small-scale industrial waters can also be counted as reservoirs, but in the mind's eye the word really means the vast storage lakes of open countryside. Many were built in the uplands in Victorian times to supply the growing cities with clean water. The alert had been sounded by the cholera epidemics of the 1830s, sweeping the slums but no respecter of geography. Improved housing and sewage disposal were a result, as well as drinking-water reservoirs.

The scale of the work was impressive. Thirlmere in the Lake District was dammed and deepened to supply

water to Manchester, 80 miles away. Sheffield dammed Pennine valleys, while Birmingham drank water from *Lake Vyrnwy* (Powys). London took Thames water from upstream, storing it in great earth-banked reservoirs at Staines and elsewhere. The filtration and treatment plants can still be seen.

Rather different are the latest generation of reservoirs set not in the hills but in gently rolling lowland countryside. Filling the gentler contours, they look reasonably natural, and in fact they are usually designed for use also

The scalloped edge of an upland reservoir makes it a dramatic landscape feature in its own right.

by anglers and holidaymakers. Many have nature reserves. *Foremark* (Derbyshire) is one example.

Water fit to drink

Clean drinking water has always been one of society's main preoccupations and efforts to ensure a supply are evident in the landscape.

WATER SYSTEMS

A river today is part of a tightly controlled water system which stretches far wider and further than its natural course on the map. Magnificent water-working buildings such as those at *Hereford* (Hereford & Worcs) rose in Victorian days. Ever since those times lakes and rivers in the hills have been dammed and their water piped to cities, and that water once used has been poured into the local river. Many towns still obtain part of their drinking water from further upstream, purifying it before use. Widespread networks of water pipes lie underground with a water-storage tower perhaps the only visible reminder. These towers not only store water but also supply a head of pressure for local taps. They can be plain concrete structures, and rather elegant in shape, or in red brick. Great pumping stations were once familiar, often disguised or built in opulent architecture, and containing steam pumping engines of the kind devised for mines. More recent are modest pumping stations—small, windowless, concrete huts set in field corners, identified by their aerial, the machinery being under remote radio control.

And cleansing the waste water from homes and factories is virtually an industry in its own right.

AQUEDUCTS

Attempts to guarantee good water are quite old. The Romans were used to arched aqueducts carrying the water down from the hills to the city. There are none in Britain, but aqueduct channels cut into hillsides remain. One set supplies the gold mine at *Dolaucothi* (Dyfed); another supplied Roman *Dorchester* (Dorset) and its channel 5 ft wide and 3 ft deep can still be seen crossing the slope below Poundbury hillfort nearby.

CONDUITS

Conduits—the word could include aqueducts, but usually refers to closed channels—were familiar in medieval times. One of the first was the Great Conduit in London's Westcheap, filled from sources in Paddington, then green countryside. Another well-known one, open at its end, is Hobson's Conduit, built in 1614 and still to be seen at the western edge of Cambridge. Hobson also rented out horses and the choice he offered—the one nearest the door or nothing—led to the expression 'Hobson's choice'.

MINERAL WATERS

One particular taste was for mineral water—that is, water that has become impregnated with some of the minerals of the rocks through which it has percolated. The bitter purging qualities of the spring waters at Epsom (Surrey) are created by magnesium sulphate, known as Epsom salts. They were considered beneficial both inside and out in Roman times and perhaps earlier. The continuing taste for mineral water has in recent years led to the growth of a substantial industry.

SPAS

The word 'spa' derives from the Belgian spa town of that name. One of the best known of British spas is Bath. Here, as well as being potent with minerals, waters also emerge hot at 49°C. It was developed in Roman times: the original bath can be viewed and altars and temples were also built. Bath regained its popularity in Regency times, the waters being noted for their presumed benefit to the innards. There was also some bathing in that period.

The limestone Peak District provided rival springs. Buxton modelled itself on Bath, although its waters were cooler, at 28°C, but still warm enough to keep off the chills of the winter. It too had been discovered by the Romans, its name Aquae Arnementiae—the waters of the Goddess of the Grove—being an allusion to older Iron Age Celtic beliefs. By contrast Harrogate (N. Yorks) only came into its own in Victorian times while in the south near London, Tunbridge Wells (Kent) became (like Epsom) popular in the 17th century. *Llandrindod Wells* (Powys) was the largest of the Welsh spas in the Victorian era.

RIVER ENGINEERING

Floods are more a human concept than a natural disaster; indeed, by spreading rich silt across the land, they were beneficial. However river engineering was introduced by the Romans which not only gained new farmland but which also probably helped with flood control (see pp. 138–139). Wetlands were also drained in Saxon and medieval times, but there was nothing like the control of river systems we take for granted today.

Modern river engineering has two aims: to control water flow and flooding and to provide a well-drained soil for neighbouring farms. Wheat and barley are by origin Mediterranean crops and prefer well-drained soil; nor can grass grow well if submerged, especially the lush modern hybrids. River engineering has had a great effect on the appearance of the countryside, a fact that is little realized.

Key rivers and streams have been straightened to carry the floodwater faster. Very often the old meander has been left as a small pond alongside, or become (since ponds dry up) a mere hollow in the field. Very often the river banks have been graded, their profile steepened and curved to ease the flow while the willows and other riverside vegetation have been cleared. Early ditches have been deepened, the faster to drain the fields.

THE SEWAGE FARM

As important a part of the management of a river system is cleaning up the water once it has been contaminated in house or factory. Together with pipes supplying clean water, the Victorians also built new sewers. These could discharge into a local river, but quite often they were led to a sewage 'farm'. Here the solids were settled off in shallow pools, and the water allowed to overflow its holding tanks, and seep across a field or two to the river. With plenty of air and exposure, the sewage liquor was acted on by bacteria and the noxious sub-

stances broken down. The solids were often sold off as manure.

MODERN SEWAGE TREATMENT

Modern systems separate the solids but then actively mix the liquor with plenty of air (often by spraying it over round, raised beds of clinker). Primed by the easy oxygen, bacteria in the muck multiply to break the matter down so that at the end it can safely enter a local river. Providing it is adequately diluted, no damage is done—the process simply mirrors the natural process whereby dead plant and animal matter is broken down. But if too much is dumped in the river, or the river is seasonally low and the bacteria continue active, the latter deplete the oxygen in the river water

Old postcards found in junk shops are often a good source of information. Above, the spring at a Victorian spa.

so that fish kills occur (the fish are not directly 'poisoned').

A natural indicator of clean water in a stream or river is the sight of mayflies dancing over the surface. They are very sensitive to low oxygen levels.

Mountain heights

The haphazard shapes of mountains have a geological explanation. Many have been characteristically sculpted by ice. Ice erosion leaves many clues.

HILLS AND MOUNTAINS

In the past the word 'hill' was the general word for any height, but it is now reserved for those under 2000 ft (although the Scots still use it more loosely). Britain's mountains are low by international standards; nonetheless they exhibit a wide variety of form. The extent of the sculpturing and the times involved are vast.

THE 'SUGAR LOAF'

As recently as 50 years ago sugar was usually sold in solid conical loaves, hence the term 'sugar loaf' to describe mountains such as *Suilven* (Highland). Its domed summit rises dramatically to 2399 ft from a flat plain dotted with small lakes. Exposures show that these 'lochans' fill hollows in a hard granite-like rock. It is Lewisian gneiss (pronounced 'nice'), one of Britain's oldest rocks. The sugar loaf itself is of sandstone, which gleams plum-red on a sunny day, while its domed top is of a rock called quartzite.

Ice sheets were the chisel here. They eroded the sandstone and quartzite which lay in layers above the gneiss, leaving today's mountain as a relic stub (Suilven's remaining cap of hard quartzite gives some protection against later erosion) and scored the hollows in the gneiss. Here as elsewhere, we see that the landscape is a negative of a kind, rock masses remaining after erosion.

BEN NEVIS

Britain's highest summit (4406 ft), Ben Nevis is a plum pudding steeply eroded by ice to leave a steep face to the north-west.

THE PLATEAU

From many places along their feet, the *Cairngorms* (Highland) look like a range of peaks, the highest passing 4000 ft. At close hand from the top of the ski chair-lifts (which operate all summer) it is clear that this is a rolling granite plateau pitted with giant scoops which were the birthplaces of glaciers. This plateau is the widest tract of high ground in Britain, and at the top the climate remains sub-Arctic, freezing for seven months of the year and with some patches of permanent snow. Up here grow relic communities of fragile flowers which were widespread during the Ice Age but which are now found only in the Alps and the Arctic tundra. Such flowers would also brighten the Lake District fells, the high Pennines and Snowdon were it not for sheep grazing (see pp. 78–79).

THE ICE-SCULPTED SUMMIT

Snowdon (Gwynedd) is one of the best known and (because of the mountain railway from Llanberis) one of the most visited of summits. The rock picture is more complicated here than at Suilven and the Cairngorms, with layers which have been folded and suffered faulting or side-slipping in three-dimensional confusion at different periods in the past. Close examination of the rock exposures of the summit shows that in fact they once formed the bottom of a syncline, a 'valley' of rock layers. Vast heights of rock above today's summit have been eroded away.

There are hard volcanic rocks in the area, derived from compressed ash and lava spewed out under ancient seas. There are also thick beds of slate derived from the clays of those ocean floors (see pp. 16–17)—these have yielded grey roofing slates familiar all over Britain.

The scenery of Snowdon today has been cut from the contorted rock layers by ice action. Classic clues of ice action can be found everywhere in Snowdonia. The cauldron-like 'cwms' (called 'corries' in northern Britain) gave the glaciers birth. Snowfall compacted to form ice, plucking at the rock surfaces to create these sheer-sided bowls. Fed by endless snowfall, the ice spilled from a cwm as a tongue-like glacier, scouring a steep-walled valley. Narrow ridges were created where glaciers bit away at each side. Today, with the ice a distant memory, the rock walls have their feet hidden beneath slides of scree which are in places firm enough for rough grass to grow, and the hollow cwms usually now contain small lakes.

Closer inspection reveals other clues, such as 'erratic' boulders carried miles by a moving glacier, and rock faces scored with parallel lines by the movement of the ice. Ice melts under pressure, however, and just how the glacier files away rock is a matter for debate; embedded rock fragments possibly provide the rasping surface.

THE LAKE DISTRICT

Here too, glacier action is evident, with hard volcanic rocks yielding the dramatic scenery of Borrowdale and other central areas. The deeply trenched valleys which hold Derwentwater, Windermere and the other lakes run like spokes in a wheel from a hub near Scafell (3206 ft). The explanation begins with a raised dome of relatively young rocks lying on top of a jumble of older volcanics and others. When the Ice Age set in, this dome was beginning to be cut by rivers flowing away from its centre, and the glaciers deepened these preliminary etchings, cutting down through the dome deep into the rocks which lay below. Fragments of the old dome cap remain in only a few places today. There is a fine view of the form of this erosion from *Helvellyn* (Cumbria).

Here, as in Snowdonia, side valleys of tributary glaciers sometimes 'hang' above the main glacier valley. Here too, stream erosion has scarcely had time since the death of the glaciers to do more than cut shallow notches on the ice-worn valley slopes. Those streams are really little more than cascades of waterfalls, feeding the lakes penned behind natural dams in the valleys below. But they ceaselessly carry down grit, and in time that lake will silt up and dry out, leaving a flat bottom to the valley, as can be seen in the lower Kentmere valley.

THE PENNINES

These too were sculptured by ice. Shapely *Ingleborough* (N. Yorks) (2373 ft) is (like Suilven) a relic stub capped by a horizontal harder band of

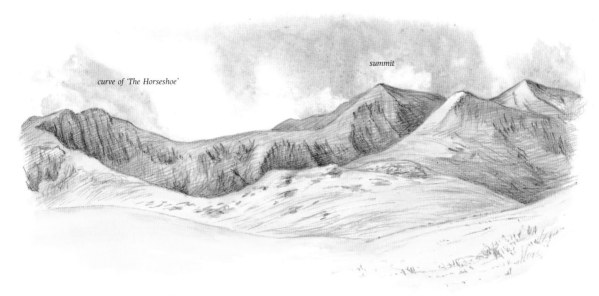

curve of 'The Horseshoe'

summit

rock, in this case millstone grit. This rock forms the scenery of the 'Dark Peak' between Manchester and Sheffield, and can be seen protruding in broken cliffs which in some places have been quarried for millstones, and half-finished they litter the ground. Elsewhere, limestone creates fine scenery, especially to the south. These southern 'White Peak' landscapes were sculptured mainly while the glaciers were dying, when the rivers were swollen with melt water. Potholes (also known as swallow holes) and caverns were also created at this time (see pp. 24–25).

THE BRECON BEACONS

Reaching 2906 ft, these too are scooped and sculptured by glaciers and some of the valleys leading south carried the ice to the sea. They are at about the southern limit of ice influence (although Dartmoor, for example, can match them for atmosphere, ice has not directly had a hand in creating its character).

The Brecon Beacons are, like Dartmoor, a National Park. where the protection of scenery overrides many (not all) other considerations. It is worth speculating why it is that only wilderness areas have been designated as National Parks and not, for example, the equally fine scenery of the chalk South Downs and other lowland areas.

Above *One of the classic views of Snowdon, magnificent scenery almost entirely sculptured by ice.*

Below *A bird's-eye view shows the cwms and other classic ice features of Snowdon more clearly.*

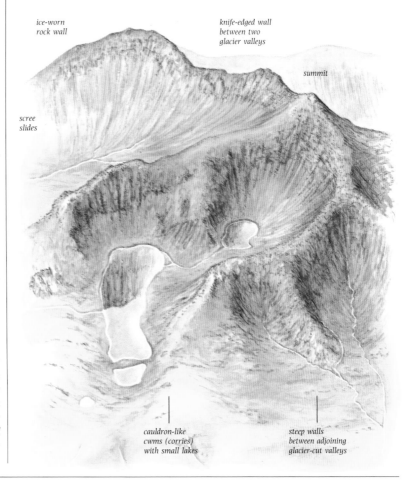

ice-worn rock wall

knife-edged wall between two glacier valleys

summit

scree slides

cauldron-like cwms (corries) with small lakes

steep walls between adjoining glacier-cut valleys

Moorland

Moorland seems as typical a wilderness as any, but in fact has had a particular and detailed history and management.

TRUE WILDERNESS

Bare of trees, with tussocks of heather and grass swaying deliriously in the wind-blown mist, and marked with patches of treacherous green bog, the moor seems true wilderness. But these hostile folds were once not only tree-covered but inhabited.

Clues can sometimes be found in the sides of a bare peat 'hag', in the shape of preserved fragments of wood or twig, or even nutshells, and even a stone tool or flakes. Another clue is a relic tree, usually a red-berried rowan growing from a cleft of the streamside rocks out of reach of the hungry sheep. In places a derelict scrap of woodland might be found in its last decades of life, its protective stone wall breached and the sheep wandering free to shave the ground of any saplings which would replace the standing trees. The modern conifer plantations which now blanket many moorland areas are proof that trees will grow here.

When the Ice Age ended, trees of one kind or another grew everywhere in England and Wales up to about 3000 ft. Their clearance on the higher slopes was well under way in Neolithic times and livestock grazing aided by changing climate has since kept them open to create today's moorlands. The veer of the climate to wetter regimes and the poor acid soils typical of many upland areas favoured the formation of bogs which created deep beds of peat (see pp. 138–139). Bog mosses still grow in some areas, but the bogs are 'dead' over much of the Pennine moorlands. The reason here may be a reversal of climate, but air pollution from the smoke of industrial Lancashire and Yorkshire is partly to blame. These dead bogs are often indicated by heavy growths of cotton grass, with dancing white heads visible from afar.

MOORLAND SETTLEMENTS

Ancient settlements often lie forgotten among the boulders and rocky bluffs. Cairnfields can be found, roughly round piles of surface stones collected when skimpy fields were cleared. These could be mistaken for burial cairns, although they are usually lower and smaller.

On some northern moorlands settlement sites can be discovered. The ragged lines of small boulders which formed the base of walls for animal corrals cannot be mistaken, nor the boulder circles forming the base of the huts. They are probably of late Bronze Age or Iron Age date. There are easily identifiable Bronze Age settlements on the *North York Moors*, which lie strung along valley streams. From these settlements worn holloways lead up to cairnfields, while past these at the far ridge is a line of barrows which are clearly boundary markers. Stone circles can also be found in some places on the northern moorlands.

DARTMOOR

Dartmoor (Devon) is very rich in prehistoric remains: standing stones, a few stone tables, barrows and cairns, ritual circles and avenues and also hut-circle settlements which seem tied to the landscape with low stone walls or 'reaves'. Grimspound is notable, probably of Bronze Age date; here the huts were enclosed by a stone wall within which the livestock were presumably kept, to be grazed on the surrounding moor. On the drier and more sheltered eastern and south-eastern flanks of Dartmoor groups of huts with small squarish 'Celtic' grain fields can also be found.

Settlement continued in the Iron Age. *Chysauster* and Carn Euny near *Madron* (Cornwall), have 'courtyard' houses with rooms opening from a central courtyard: at Chysauster these rooms are built into the thickness of the wall. Like other stone-walled huts, they probably had conical thatched roofs. Thereafter a change to a bleaker climate forced the desertion of such places to the mists.

THE MOORS IN LATER TIMES

Dartmoor may have remained virtually deserted in Roman times, but more northerly moors and those alongside Wales were busy with troops

and skirmishes. There was probably active use of the moorlands in the Dark Ages; and in the north Vikings or Norsemen have left evidence of 'shielings'—summer pastures for livestock on higher ground—with the occasional find of the tumbled walls of rectangular huts. From the Norse also come nostalgic place-names of the Lake District and elsewhere: 'fell' is a rough pasture, 'force' a waterfall, 'scale' a summer pasture of a farmstead. Later, the lower settlements grew into villages, crystallizing from scatters of farmsteads as they did in the lowlands.

FIELD WALLS

From medieval times fields became a more noticeable element in the moorland scene. The earliest were in the valleys, to control grazing or for marking out arable on the flat valley bot-

toms. These irregular older fields by the farmsteads, called 'inbye' in the north, give way to rather squarer, larger intake fields on the slopes and the hillsides above. Above this lies the open moor, the 'fell' as it is called in the Lake District. The *Haworth Moors* (W. Yorks) are typical.

The Georgian enclosures which transformed much of the lowland landscape also bit in the uplands, when the open commons grazings of the upper fells and moors were also taken in. The intake may be of this date. These enclosure fields are, like their lowland counterparts, neat and grid-like, with straight, wide tracks, or greenways. It is noticeable that while the older inbye valley fields are often made of rounded stones cleared from the surface of the fields or collected from the streams, these later walls are of sharp-edged quarried stone—except

perhaps where a nearby prehistoric burial or clearance cairn was raided.

EXMOOR

On *Exmoor* (Som) much reclamation —the fielding of the open moor—was delayed until Victorian and modern times. For example, the Knight family created 15 new farms in the 19th century, their fields being surrounded by tall earth banks set with beech trees. Heather moorland now only remains in the area's heart.

HEATHER MOORLAND

Heather grows naturally on the drier peat alongside bilberry. Grouse feed on the young green shoots and shelter among the older tussocks. To provide both, on the grouse moors which cover vast areas of the Pennines and Scotland, the heather is regularly burnt in patches of around an acre, to

Prospects from the edge of the moors across the gentler Coquet Valley (Northumberland) underline their difference.

impart a patchwork appearance. After this 'swaling' (called 'muirburn' in Scotland) young heather grows vigorously from the older rootstocks undamaged by the fire and from seeds washed down into the soil.

GROUSE SHOOTING

The income from renting out grouse shooting probably keeps many moorlands free of conifer plantations. The season begins on 12 August—the 'Glorious Twelfth'. The birds are driven over the sportsmen, who stand within shooting butts. These are round, with breast-high turf or stone walls, and at first glance resemble prehistoric hut circles.

Scotland's Highlands and Islands

The terrain of Scotland, already of a distinct and complex character, also has dramatic antiquities of a kind not seen further south.

THE HIGHLAND STORY

In few parts of Britain do history and the landscape knit together as closely as they do in Scotland, and in particular in the Scottish Highlands. The Highland frontier lies along a massive rock fault running approximately between the lower Firth of Clyde and Aberdeen. Another great fault divides the Highlands along the line of the *Great Glen*. The Highland hills—they are called 'hills', not mountains, in

Glen Coe, a Highlands scene where angry rock and history interweave (see also Gazetteer entry).

Scotland—are the highest in Britain but the land is lower and flatter towards the north-east.

There was vigorous Neolithic and Bronze Age settlement as shown by, among many examples, the village of *Skara Brae* (Orkneys); the tombs at *Camster* (Highland) and *Maes Howe* (Orkneys); and the stone circle at *Callanish* (Lewis, Western Isles).

By Roman times southern Scotland at least was held by tribes who were probably Celts (Iron Age immigrants) by blood and spoke Old British, a Celtic tongue from which modern Welsh comes. They built ramparted forts, as they did in the south. The Romans christened tribes they encountered the Picts, or painted men; it is not certain who they were but their Gaelic name is related to our word 'Briton'. More

definite are the Scots who flooded into Argyll from Northern Ireland around AD 500, speaking Gaelic, another Celtic language. Fresh blood was again given by Scandinavian Vikings but these differences in tribe, language and geography became smoothed to give a remarkable identity to 'Scotland'.

The fate of the Picts is obscure; perhaps they were assimilated by the Scots. They did leave the incredible symbolic Pictish stones to puzzle us today (see pp. 40–41).

FORTIFIED DWELLINGS

'Brochs' are found mainly in the distant north-west part of the Highlands. They are tapering circular drystone-walled towers originally quite tall (up to 40 ft) and with rooms and staircases within the width of the wall. Their makers are unknown, but they are probably of Iron Age (post-500 BC) date. The Broch of Mousa (*Shetlands*) is the best example. They seem to have been replaced by round 'wheelhouses' with rooms arranged in a ring.

In south-west Scotland brochs had an equivalent in 'duns', rounded farmhouses with massive walls, of which hundreds are known. In some places as further evidence of strife-torn days small 'crannogs' or 'lake villages' were built up on artificial islands. Little remains of these settlements apart from an occasional scrubbed-up hummock in the water.

SOUTERRAINS

Some of the Iron Age farmsteads had underground passage-rooms, often with an elaborate narrow neck which is clearly defensive in purpose. Curiously, there are also one or two examples to be seen in the west of Cornwall (where they are called fogous) at Carn Euny near *Madron* and *Chysauster*, for example.

VITRIFIED AND OTHER FORTS

From around 500 BC hillforts were built in Scotland, sometimes rather similar to the English patterns. As in the latter, their ramparts were sometimes strengthened with timberwork running internally within them. What is unusual, however, is that in some

cases (too many to be put down to accident) this timberwork has been fired, to burn so fiercely that the heat has fused the stone. It is possible that they were ritually fired after defeat. There is a line of these 'vitrified' forts down the *Great Glen*, for example.

CLANS AND CLACHANS

As was the case elsewhere in Britain, centuries of settlement saw the disappearance of the wildwood, which was here an ancient pine forest of which a few fragments remain (see pp. 156–157). It was cleared for pasturing cattle and growing a few oats, but was also being fired in the endless skirmishing between the clans.

A clan (a Gaelic word for 'family') was often centred on one or several valleys, or glens—and it is said that the tartans originated with the different plant dyes collected in their glens. The clans were rather like large families with common interests and united under the paternal protection of the chief. The people normally lived in 'clachans' or loose clusters of farmsteads with none of the order of a village. They made use of shielings, communal high-lying summer pastures, during which time the herdsmen slept in simple stone and turf bothies. Around the clachan, the 'infield' (the 'muckled land') was

ploughed for grain in massive ridges as much as 6 ft high and 30 ft wide to gain drainage. These strips were allocated among the clan 'runrig'—that is, at random.

MILITARY ROADS AND THE CLEARANCES

The pine forests were also fired to rid the country of wolves, and by coincidence the last wolf was killed at about the time that the last rebellion against English rule failed at Culloden in 1745. It was the end of a century of turmoil and the Highlands were now controlled from London. Military roads were built, often named after General Wade (a name that remains on the maps)—*Wade's Road* runs through the Great Glen. There were killings and transportations, and for those highlanders who remained, the power of the benevolent clan system was destroyed, the chiefs becoming landlords to whom the clansmen paid rent. Soon after, during the infamous Highland Clearances of the first half of the 19th century, vast areas were to be cleared of people, the land being given over to sheep for the benefit of southern investors and landlords.

Those thrown off their ancestral clachans had to compete for crofts, and even if successful there was little security: it was not until 1976 that the

A traditional thatched Highland dwelling known as a 'blackhouse'.

crofter won the right to permanent residence and the right to buy his croft outright at a fair price.

THE CROFT

This is typically a small homestead with two to eight small fields and 'stinted' (controlled) grazing rights to land common to the crofters. It is subsistence farming, and nowadays is usually supplemented by other work. Livestock are raised, oats and potatoes grown, often in raised 'lazybeds' made of piles of animal muck, seaweed and turf. *Durness* (Highland) is a typical scattered crofting village, the *Skye Croft Museum* (Highland) another.

THE BLACKHOUSE

The original dwelling of the clachans and crofters was simple, of drystone walls and a thatched roof roped down against the winds, but with no chimney, so that the peat smoke from the fire blackened everything—hence the name 'blackhouse'. Family rooms were often under the same roof as the animal quarters. *Arnol Blackhouse* (Lewis, Western Isles) is one that can be visited and there are some at the 'ferm town' museum, *Auchindrain*, near Inveraray (Argyll/Strathclyde).

Lowland barrens

In recent decades a greater proportion of heathland has been lost or degraded than of any other type of landscape to be seen in Britain. It is now quite rare.

HEATHLAND

A heath is an area of sand or gravel bedrock yielding a soil which is rather acid and poor in nutrients. As a result plants characteristic of moorland, which also has poor acid soils, grow on a heath—heather is one of the most obvious and the most typical.

Heathland is similar to moorland in many ways. The poor acid nature of the soil means that in damper patches bogs can develop to form layers of peat. However, heaths are found in lower and usually drier areas than moors, and this added to the fact that water can quickly drain down through the bedrock (a moor often has solid rock below) makes extensive bogs a rarity. Streams are also a rarity on heaths. Further features are linked with this basic difference in the rock: the sandstone or gravel bed which outcrops is often loose, and quickly weathered, and as a result the rocky crags, bluffs and loose boulders of moorland are the exception rather than the rule on heathland.

The milder conditions also mean that gorse often grows here and (unlike a moor) pine and silver birch energetically seed themselves in; nor are there sheep to pose another hazard for young trees. Although some grazing may still take place on a heath, intensive sheep grazing would be an exception.

AN ENDANGERED HABITAT

Extensive areas of heathland remain in Surrey, Hampshire and Dorset. The old Royal Forests of the south usually contain quite a bit of heathland. But although still an important feature, today's heathland is but a fragment of what was once there: 40 per cent of the heathland remaining in Britain in 1950 has been wiped off the map, cleared for ploughland or planted with conifers, built over or used for army training. What remains is often in very small, vulnerable pockets. Although taken for granted, heathland is one of

Britain's endangered habitats and easily destroyed.

THE PREHISTORY OF HEATHLAND

The origins of heathland are much the same as those of downland and moorland. It was covered, if patchily, with wildwood and the thinner scattering of trees attracted Neolithic farmers and pastoralists. Grazing and poor management have kept it open ever since. The porous soil means that without tree cover and the holding effect of their mesh of fine rootlets it is quickly leached of nutrients.

Never worth the plough, heathland can as a result carry a good many burial mounds and other prehistoric sites. The soil is likely to have been impoverished early on, and these areas had perhaps little attraction for Roman, or even Iron Age, farmers. But what remains may today be hidden within the depths of recent conifer plantations.

THE HEATHLAND 'PAN'

By exposing the soil to continuous leaching, the early clearances also changed the soil structure of a heath. The characteristic profile can be seen alongside deep-worn tracks and in cuttings. Below the plants there is often a pale band, below which is often a darker band of loose, dry peat. This peat is formed from dead plant material when conditions are unfavourable for decay—the peat acts as a kind of lid, preventing the movement of air into the soil and so slowing the activity of bacterial decay.

The rain leaches material down from these upper bands and various reactions take place in the acid surroundings and it is precipitated out as iron-containing solids. These become compacted and create a 'pan', a layer which is so hard that roots cannot penetrate it. All that can now grow are those plants with shallow root systems, of which heather is one.

BURNING HEATHS

Heaths are at risk from fierce, devastating fires today, but in the past heathland was regularly burnt in controlled fires. It did give some, if poor,

grazing—perhaps ponies may still be grazed today. The firing was undertaken to burn off the invasive pine, gorse and birch. The grass and heather quickly recovered to provide fresh grazing for the livestock.

BRECKLAND

A rather unusual heathland is found in East Anglia's *Breckland*, an area originally some 400 square miles in extent, lying around and especially to the west of Thetford. The prehistoric flint mines of *Grimes Graves* (Norfolk) lie within the area.

Chalk underlies the area, but it is patchily covered by sands and gravels carried by streams flowing from the melting ice at one stage of the Ice Age. The climate is also rather harsh in winter—in fact it is continental, with hot, dry summers and very cold winters, especially when the wind comes direct from the Urals. As a result the area carries many flowers which are unusual in Britain and, as a non-botanist might notice, because of the mosaic of soils, plants fond of lime such as might be seen on chalk downs grow quite close to acid-loving heather.

Although never densely settled (the chalk makes for few streams and the villages are confined to the river valleys) this poor area was grazed in recent centuries. It remained largely unploughed until this century, and much of what has not been ploughed carries immense conifer plantations; there is also much army land.

Archaeological evidence suggests that it is likely that more people lived here during the late Neolithic and Bronze Ages than at any time since. The Icknield Way leads south (see pp. 116–117) and flint arrowheads and worked flint pieces are to be found in today's ploughed fields.

WARRENS

Maps of Breckland carry a good scatter of 'warrens', and they are to be found on heathland elsewhere. They were originally a Plantagenet feature, set aside for the breeding of rabbits, introduced from France (see pp. 90–91). Warrens were in use until Victorian times. Oddly, although escapes must have been frequent, it was not until then that the rabbit population seems to have built up in the open countryside. There are no reports of them being frequent in earlier centuries — unless they were taken for granted.

Certainly rabbits have played an important part in the countryside story. They played two roles.

In Victorian days they were abundant, natural lawnmowers. This had direct relevance to the chalk downlands. For centuries, these had been kept short-turfed and free of scrub by diligent sheep grazing, but when changes in markets and farming

Rabbits were an important village resource in bygone days, and rabbit poaching a fact of life.

slumps led to a change in direction in agriculture, rabbits took over their job, keeping smooth and shorn those areas of chalk grasslands which had escaped the plough. The close-grazed turf was alight with wild flowers and lively with butterflies.

Then, in the 1950s, the disease myxomatosis struck the rabbit population. As a result the open turf started to scrub up, with hawthorn and blackthorn leading the way, growing from seeds voided by birds.

The second role of rabbits was as a source of free protein — if they could be caught (which often entailed a spot of poaching). Up to and past World War II it was quite normal for some villagers to keep a ferret or two. This half-tamed relative of the stoat and weasel

was used to terrify and chase the rabbits out from safety into nets placed over the exits of their burrows. The ferrets were sometimes muzzled to prevent them killing and eating their prey, and remaining below to do so.

A SPECIAL HEATH

The *Lizard* (Cornwall) carries an expert's heath. The rock which colours the cliffs and coves is serpentine, ornamental when polished. The soil is thin and poor, and a local heather, known as Cornish heath, grows here. The salt spray does the job of fires elsewhere, keeping scrub and trees at bay.

In recent years the rabbit has been making something of a comeback, and numbers will presumably continue to rise.

The forest

Like other types of wilderness, the true forest had a distinct role in the landscape story. Fragments of the original forests remain in many areas.

THE WILDWOOD

The story of our woodland begins some 12,000 years ago when the Ice Age was drawing to a close. As the land began to warm, trees and other plants could invade from the south, for Britain was still part of Europe. Birch was among the pioneers, followed by Scots pine. Oak, ash and other trees followed as the climate gradually improved, shaded out the pine and eventually grew to create a tangled wildwood covering all but the bleakest and wettest places. The pine remained strong in Scotland, where fragments of native pine woodlands remain.

At the same time the melting of the ice and frozen ground was raising the sea level until eventually the Channel was cut and Britain separated. The beech was the last tree to arrive before the divide, the last of our native trees. Clearance had possibly started earlier, when Mesolithic tribes burnt forest to drive game, but this was the wildwood tackled by our first farmer-pastoralist bands in Neolithic times (see pp. 34–35) and clearance continued unremittingly until by Norman days woodland was decidedly patchy on the open ground in both uplands and lowlands. The main concentrations of trees were in the village woodlands worked by coppicing (see pp. 88–89) and in the wastes and forests. These too were managed (see below).

RELIC WILDWOOD

As a result of long centuries of management and use, few areas of woodland remain which can claim to be untouched by man. One scrap in the south is Wistman's Wood remote on *Dartmoor* (Devon), where gnarled trees sprawl over boulder-strewn ground. Although it is woodland of a very different kind, some remoter fragments of the old Caledonian pine forest might also be virtually untouched. Our older woodland, which has been influenced in part, is described as 'seminatural' (see pp. 88–89).

SCOTLAND'S PINE FOREST

After centuries of felling and firing by the clans, the once vast Caledonian pine forest is reduced to fragments strung out in the Dee and Spey valleys, on the west coast and in a few places in the central Highlands. Typical fragments are seen below the *Cairngorms* (Highland) and in the *Black Wood of Rannoch* (Tayside). Their widely

Wistman's Wood, remote on Dartmoor, is possibly the only English wood totally untouched by man.

The statuesque hornbeam pollards which are a magnificent feature of Epping Forest (Essex).

spaced trees give them an open feel, quite unlike that of the conifer plantations which now clothe many of Scotland's hills.

EARLY FORESTS

Although in the mind's eye the word 'forest' conjures up a picture of ancient greenwood, the refuge of Robin Hood and other outlaws, the reality was different. The term has a definite meaning in landscape history. Derived from the Latin word *foris* meaning 'out of doors', it was land set aside for the royal hunt by the Norman and Plantagenet kings. Such land was not always thickly covered with trees: parts would have been farmed in Roman times and earlier, and as a result it could often contain great areas of open grazing, of heathland and moor. The patchwork of the *New Forest* (Hants) is an example. The granite hinterland of *Dartmoor* was one of the Royal Forests.

FOREST LAW

Over 80 Royal Forests were designated. In them Forest Law was applied by keepers, punishments being awarded in Forest Courts. Keepers were of various kinds and elected verderers of the New Forest are the only ancient office to survive, but keepers included foresters in charge of the 'walks' or forest areas, woodwards supervising felling, coppicing and pollarding, and agisters controlling grazing of the commoners' cattle and pigs.

The interests of the deer (both red and fallow) were paramount. Punishments were vicious: killing a deer was a gallows offence, disturbing them when breeding rewarded with blinding. Forest law took precedence over the normal peasant rights of the time, but as the above reveals, local commoners still retained some benefits and could gather wood or graze livestock at certain times of year.

POLLARD TREES

In some wooded areas of the forests, the trees were regularly pollarded, as are willows on river banks today— massive ancient pollards are a feature of *Epping Forest* (Essex) for example. The beneficiaries were either the king directly, or local commoners, who had the rights to cut branches in this way. Pollarding ruins the timber value of a tree: not worth felling, many of our ancient trees are old pollards. The Major Oak in *Sherwood Forest* (Notts) is probably an old pollard, and the Knightwood Oak in the *New Forest* (see pp. 88–89) certainly is.

THE NEW FOREST

Still retaining the feel of an ancient hunting forest, the *New Forest* (Hants) was literally William the Conqueror's new forest, decreed in 1079. It is a mosaic of heathland and woodland, with grazed grassy 'lawns' by the valley streams. There are many deer, but visitors usually remember the ponies, born and bred in the open and possibly directly descended from wild stock. Those with pure blood have plain coats; piebald or skewbald ponies are not related, but interbreeding does smudge the divisions. Semi-wild as they are, they each belong to commoners with grazing rights. The animals are herded once a year in an autumn 'drift', counted, the year's colts marked, and either sold or (grazing fees paid) released again.

PLANTATIONS

Alarm caused by the fall in the timber stocks essential for the men-of-war and trading ships on which Britain's might relied (a 74-gun wooden warship needed 4000 tons of timber— almost everything on the vessel was made of oak except for the masts), led to steps being taken to plant timber trees on a large scale. The first plantations of oak were in the Royal forests: the first was at Windsor in 1580, and here as elsewhere, many tangled and ancient-seeming woodlands are plantations that have been let go.

The modern conifer plantations which now blanket so many landscapes are largely the work of the Forestry Commission. During World War I German submarines threatened the ships carrying timber for pit props for British coal mines, coal then being vital for survival. On the 'never again' principle, the Forestry Commission was set up soon after the end of the war, in 1919, with the task of growing a reserve of timber. It bought up land, but also grant-aided private planting.

The wild coast

The geological rules which have shaped the coast are very different from those responsible for fashioning the landscapes that we find inland.

THE CHANGING COAST

Although the coastline is imprinted on maps (and the mind's eye) it is continually, if slowly, changing. In some areas it is receding. Perhaps the best-known example of this is at Dunwich on the Suffolk coast, where only a fragment remains of what was a Norman town, its streets now mere sunken lanes leading to the cliff edge. Vice versa, New Winchelsea and other places around *Romney Marsh* (Kent) are decayed ports now isolated from the sea by grazings. The once open waters became salt marsh and the natural process of silting has been assisted over many centuries by drainage schemes which were started as long ago as Saxon times.

The sea itself is erosive, cutting away at land within reach. The melting of the ice at the end of the Ice Age raised the sea level appreciably, so bringing more land within range; but at the same time the disappearance of this mass of ice from northerly areas eased the pressure on the land raft, and the land could rise to some extent. Tides and currents also vary as a result both of local and wide-scale changes. Today's coastline is therefore more in the nature of a single snapshot of a changing scene. However, by the use of dyking, breakwaters and cliff defences, human ingenuity has worked to considerable effect.

DROWNED VALLEYS

The most scenically pleasing results of these shifts in level are the drowned or sunken valleys seen in Cornwall—the Fal estuary at *Falmouth* (Cornwall) and *Salcombe* (Devon), for example—and seen as 'sea' lochs in western Scotland. At Falmouth fingers of sea seem to explore the land: here a stream and its tributaries cutting the rather steep-sided valleys typical of hard-rock areas were flooded by the sea. The Menai Straits between Snowdonia and Anglesey provide another example: two valleys once running from south-

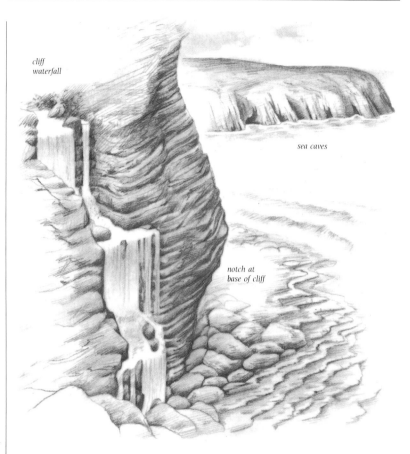

cliff
waterfall

sea caves

notch at
base of cliff

Cliff features.

east to north-west have joined up to create a single channel.

In western Scotland there are many raised beaches, now out of reach of the waves. There are many other examples of changes in level between land and sea.

THE WAVES

Waves attack by simple hammering, by scouring when laden with sand or shingle and also by implosion—that is, by trapping air pockets in rock cracks and slapping them with such pressure that there is something like a small explosion. Repeated wave after wave and tide after tide, this clearly has an effect, lines of weakness being opened.

The swash of an incoming wave is stronger than the backwash. Hence the former can move pebbles up a beach which the latter may not be able to move back, and in time a beach is sorted, with pebbles ranged in a shingle bank at the top, and the fine

sand below and running towards the low-tide mark. There is also a sideways motion. Waves rarely meet the beach head-on—tides and currents tend to give them a fairly regular direction of approach. The strong swash being at an angle, the weak backwash running directly back down to the sea, the disturbed pebbles are given a sideways nudge at each wave. This builds up the beach on one side of a groyne or other obstruction, and explains why bays often have a noticeable sweep of sand at one end, boulders and shingle at the other.

LONGSHORE DRIFT

The process also explains 'longshore drift', which can carry pebbles for miles along the coast. The build-up at groynes indicates the direction—longshore drift runs from north to south down the east coast, for example, and it runs from west to east along the south coast.

CLIFFS

As is the case inland (see pp. 12–13), the landscape features represent land remaining uneroded. A bay thus represents the erosion of weaker features, a promontory or cliff evidence of relative resistance.

Implosion attacks joints and other cracks in the rock. At wave level a flat platform will be noticed at the base of a cliff: a notch is quarried at the cliff foot until the rock above tumbles, to be worn into smoothed boulders scattered over the platform and abrading it when shifted by the waves. The softer the rock, the faster the cliff is cut back.

If the rock is very soft, chalk for example, the cliff falls frequently and is undermined all the way up: a steep cliff results. The famous Seven Sisters cliffs

Clues to coastal erosion.

near *Wilmington* (E. Sussex) are an example. Here the sea has cut across a set of valleys. They are dry here, but similar erosion along the north Devon coast near *Hartland Point* breaches stream valleys, creating coastal waterfalls. If the rock layering contains soft clays or gravel beds, the cliff may slump, to give an 'undercliff'—these platforms are a feature of the coast along from *Lyme Regis* (Dorset).

ROCK STRATA

Sea cliffs often yield magnificent displays of rock strata with folding and faults exposed and fossils easy to find. There are spectacular examples at *Hartland Point* (Devon) and at *Lulworth Cove* (Dorset). This last is a bowl-like scoop in the land with only a very narrow sea entrance. The layering here presents harder rock to the sea, with softer behind. Once a breach is made in the outer armour, the sea runs in to erode the softer rock. A

smaller example can be seen nearby at Stair Hole: here the seaward entrance is still a hole.

SEA CAVES

The nicking of the cliff foot might in time create a cave, its shape and depth reflecting the layering and jointing and other weaknesses of the rocks at that point. In some cases the cave extends through to the cliff top to create a 'blow hole' up which spray blows in stormy weather. A more common result, however, is for a narrow promontory to be attacked from two sides. When the two caves meet an arch might be formed; and when this falls the end of the promontory is left as a separated stack which will in time diminish to a small island.

ROCK POOLS

The presence, depth and shape of rock pools reflect the type of rock and its layering or jointing.

arch

island

stack

the alignment of the
rock strata
influences the
shape of the rock pool

The soft coast

Although lacking the resistance of rock, features consisting of no more than sand, mud and shingle have remarkable coherence and permanence.

THE SEA'S IMPRINT

Although seeming more fragile than the rocky cliff, mud, sand and shingle create their own distinctive and long-lasting coastal features. Damage can be done with a spade, but these features are in a way the expression of the considerable physical power of the dynamic systems of waves, currents and tides, as those involved in coastal defences know to their cost.

THE BEACH

A beach accumulates where the sea is unable to move the beach material on. Beaches are as a result typical of bays, although they can also be found on exposed coasts where wave direction and current patterns conspire. These physical factors give a beach permanence as a feature, although the material is mobile. Beaches can change their profile as the winter brings storms but these changes later reverse themselves and the picture over a year is remarkably constant.

Wave direction and longshore drift (see pp.158–159) fit the beach into its bay, coarser and pebblier (and with boulders) at one end. Although there is animal life below the sand, the movement of the shingle is normally too damaging for both plants and animals.

SAND DUNES AND GOLF LINKS

Sand-dune systems are found in many coastal areas: Braunton near *Bideford* (Devon) and *Gibraltar Point* (Lincs) are examples. Sand dunes show an intricate evolution from loose sand to firm ground. It is not an accidental progress and is similar in any sand-dune system.

The seashore sand is blown inland by strong breezes and storms, and aerodynamic laws dictate that it is not swept far but builds up behind any small projection in the way that snow drifts deeply behind a fence. As time passes, a ridge of sand develops and into this marram grass with a dense mesh of underground stems can root

to bind the sand. New layers build up, each firmed in place by layers of marram roots until in time a tall, broad sand dune is formed. Other plants can then take root when the sand is reasonably firm, and their decay builds up a thin mixture of humus with the sand. Mosses and lichens can then grow and when they cover the ground the dune (now known as a grey dune) is reasonably stable. Only the fiercest storms (or people) might rupture the surface so that the wind swiftly punches through the breach to 'blow out' an area of fresh loose sand.

The dune system is thus ever expanding out towards the sea, with the oldest dunes at the back. The hollows between the ridges are often damp, and maybe even hold pools. Trees can root on the older dunes. Rabbits thrive on the vegetated dunes, creating a fine turf.

The mosaic of turf and sand is in Scotland called a 'link'—hence golf links. They were ready made for this purpose and golf has been played on the links at Dornoch (Highland) since 1616.

THE SHINGLE BANK

Shingle too can form some distinctive features on the coast, the seaward face bare and raw, but with scatters of plants where more sheltered. The 16-mile-long Chesil Beach running up to *Portland* (Dorset) is one example. Portland Bill acts as a gigantic natural groyne blocking the eastwards movement of the shingle—and longshore drift and wave action mean that the largest pebbles, 2 in. across, are at the Portland end, double the size at the start. As with many shingle features, Portland Bill's permanence is underlined by the lagoon behind. Dungeness, alongside *Romney Marsh* (Kent), is another vast shingle feature.

Maps show that shingle banks are often found at the mouths of rivers, and are as often sculptured into curved bars—fragile in themselves but permanent features.

THE ESTUARY

The estuary, the mouth of a river, with its acres of mud exposed at low tide, is

scarcely dramatic scenery, yet fed as it is by the washings from a whole river system it is biologically immensely rich and one of the richest habitats. Hence the regular flocks of birds dining on the shellfish and worms fattened by this soup. But this biological richness also helps to create regular features in the estuary.

SALT MARSHES

Tides and river flows (no two estuaries are exactly alike in pattern) sculpture the mud into stable channels, and where the mud nudges the surface, a salt marsh can begin to develop. The process mirrors that of a sand dune. Early-colonizing plants (glasswort is one) stake a claim in the mud, and enable a succession of plants to root. The mud becomes 'fixed' and builds up until it is only doused a few times a month at the highest tides of the month. A colourful natural meadow of wild flowers then grows.

And they grow luxuriantly, because of the richness of the mud below. Because of this potential, many salt-marsh systems have been dyked to keep them dry and turned over to grazing. *Romney Marsh* (Kent) had this history—it produced its own plump breed of sheep feeding on the best natural grazing in Britain. However, these pastures have now often been 'reclaimed', being ploughed for arable.

SHELLFISH

Cockles and mussels have been harvested from estuaries for centuries. Cockles, which are mobile, are still 'dredged' with a wooden rake, or simply dug from just below the surface at low tide, back-breaking work. Shrimps too are a commercial harvest of some sandier estuaries. Mussels are immobile and it has been possible to 'farm' small mussels collected wild on ropes and frames.

OYSTERS

Unlike other shellfish, oysters are regularly farmed in purpose-built enclosures which make a mark on the estuary, although the sites are usually simply extensions of existing natural oyster beds. Young oysters are seeded

in these and kept free from smothering mud and predators.

SALMON FARMING

Salmon farming is a new industry which is making an impact on hitherto deserted Scottish sea lochs. The fish are reared in net cages supported on floating pontoons stretching out into the loch. Large areas of formerly open water are blocked in this way, and there are in addition storage sheds and

Tidal mud flats, salt marshes and sand dunes are normal features of the mouth of a river, as in this view.

access roads on these hitherto untouched coasts.

Coastal structures

Although narrow, the coastal strip displays a wealth of features, usually of distinctive form, reflecting its importance in man's affairs.

THE ROMANTIC COAST

To admire the grandeur of the coast is a relatively modern turn of mind. It is a legacy of the Romantic movement of the late 18th century, a revolution of ideas that also showed itself in literature, poetry and painting. For those born earlier, the sea meant nothing but danger and terror. Even travellers due to make the relatively safe crossing of the English Channel deferred their journey time and again. The Romantic movement could do nothing to diminish the actual danger: even in the 1870s British vessels were being lost at sea at the rate of about 2000 a year. Nonetheless it was firm and definite enough to change opinions, so that today our coastline is treasured for its own sake.

HARBOURS

Early harbours exploited natural shelter. The land form gives *Falmouth* (Cornwall) a splendid harbour. While modern eyes are schooled to vessels of oil-tanker dimensions, the demands in the past were modest. The natural shelter at Dover, a rather open coast, might have been slight; however, it was a Roman port as the clifftop lighthouse testifies. *Lyme Regis* (Dorset) is today a modest enough holiday harbour, yet it was once notable as the only important anchorage for men-of-war for a considerable distance west of the naval dockyard at Portland. These thriving little ports often had very little to do with the country inland; *Whitby* (N. Yorks), for example, is backed by the inhospitable North York Moors.

Many were within the shelter of an estuary, to their eventual cost. Winchelsea (Kent) is only one of the many that have died, their approaches silted up and now dyked and drained.

Harbours usually have a kit of parts, familiar to all, which reflect the fact that they are in a way a version of an

Man's hand on the coast.

Welsh coastal castle

lighthouse

prehistoric rampart

haven

Cornish mine-head building

industrial village devoted to a single industry. The breakwater extends the protection while the buildings (now often converted to serve the holiday trade) would include net lofts, sail-making rooms and shipyards in which damaged boats were repaired. As with many an inland village, it is possible to discern the old core and later developments. In some, museums such as that at *Wick* (Highland) show life as it was, when fishing was a crucial industry.

HEADLANDS

With sides already impregnable, a good many headlands could be made secure with merely a cross rampart. There are several Iron Age promontory forts of this kind on west and south-west coasts, such as that at *St David's Head* (Dyfed). The ramparts are typical of those used on inland forts, with the entrance facing inland at the centre point of ditch and bank.

SHORE FORTS

In Roman times 'forts of the Saxon shore' were a chain of strongholds stretching from *Portchester* (Hants) round and up the east coast, built to counter the Saxon threat. *Richborough* (Kent) is also an imposing ruin, while the early Saxon chapel at *Bradwell* (Essex) is worth a detour: it is built on the site of another Saxon shore fort, on a desolate coast.

Several medieval castles controlled important harbours (albeit small by today's standards) which are all but forgotten below the ruined walls. Bamburgh and Dunstanburgh just south of *Lindisfarne* (Northumberland) are examples. The builders of *Tintagel* (Cornwall), possibly Britain's best-known romantic ruin and said to be the birthplace of King Arthur, took advantage of a partly separated crag linked with a natural rock bridge; this has now fallen away. The first fortification here dates from AD 400, towards the end of Roman power, but the ruins we see are medieval.

Fortification continued at key coastal sites in Tudor days, when castle building had ceased inland. The pair of forts guarding the harbour at *Falmouth* (Cornwall) are typical.

Just as typical of their time are the remaining traces of gun emplacements from World War II. Recognizable concrete gun posts may remain, squat blockhouses sunken into the clifftop with openings for the gun barrels. Otherwise concrete slabs with no obvious purpose might be the clue. The bays below were also defended against landing-craft: typical were anti-tank barriers of rows of concrete pyramids about a yard high; some remain although most have been dumped at sea.

CHAPELS

Coastal chapels are found in one or two places, wedged securely between crags but with a good outlook to sea. Few early descriptions remain, but they may have been staffed by hermits, and some certainly doubled as a light-house for an anchorage nearby.

LIGHTHOUSES

These are immediately recognizable, many being tall, slim towers, a shape which could not be improved for coping with hurricane-force gusts of wind. There are notable examples at *Hartland Point* (Devon), *Portland Bill* (Dorset), at the famous Needles off the Isle of Wight, *Whitby* (N. Yorks), *Cromer* (Norfolk), Cape Wrath near *Durness* (Highland)—there are 150 principal lighthouses in all. A Roman lighthouse still stands ruined above Dover, and a dozen were built along the south coast in the 17th century, but they did not come into general use until the next century. Many of the earlier were of simple construction: even the famous Eddystone off Plymouth was at first a wooden tower; a stone version was not built until 1760.

COASTGUARDS

A terrace of coastguard cottages is typical of many harbours, and typically they are on cliffs above the harbour with a good sea view. Modern coastguards coordinate sea-rescue operations; there are some hundreds of employees, and thousands of volunteers, manning 1500 lookouts around the coast. They are linked with the 120 lifeboat stations, which have either long-distance or inshore boats, the latter being outboard inflatables.

SMUGGLERS

The coastguards originated with the 16th-century anti-smuggling Preventive Service. In the early 19th century a Naval Waterguard was formed but it was the coastal blockade set up during and after the Napoleonic Wars which spelled the end of the large-scale smuggling in which all and sundry were involved, even the parson chipping in for his tobacco. Smuggling had been given a boost in the 17th century by the introduction of fore-and-aft rig, which enabled small boats to sail both in and out of harbour on the same wind, docking and making off again under cover of darkness. Behind the harbours lay a well-established distribution network dealing in brandy, rum, tobacco and other goods.

Souvenirs of World War II.

machine-gun post

anti-tank obstacles

SOUTH-WEST ENGLAND

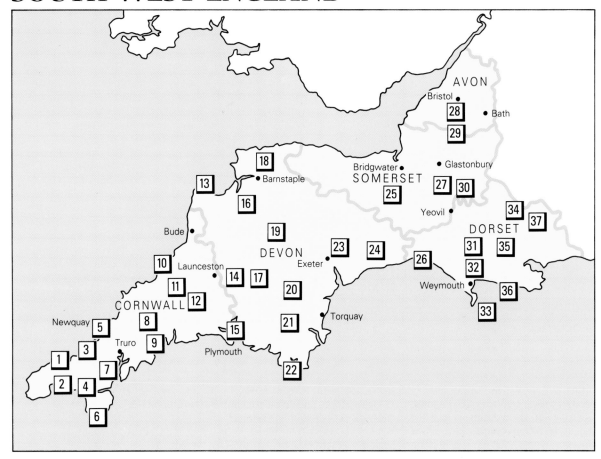

Bristol · Bath · 28 · 29 · 18 · Bridgwater · Glastonbury · 27 · 30 · 13 · Barnstaple · 25 · Yeovil · 34 · 37 · 16 · 31 · 35 · Bude · 19 · 26 · 32 · 10 · Launceston · 23 · 24 · Exeter · 36 · 11 · 14 · 17 · Weymouth · 33 · 12 · 20 · 6 · 8 · Torquay · 5 · 21 · Newquay · 3 · Truro · 9 · 15 · 1 · 7 · 22 · Plymouth · 2 · 4 · 6

1 **CHYSAUSTER** (Cornwall)
No visit to England's toe is complete without Chysauster, an Iron Age village of courtyarded huts (see pp. 46–47 and 150–151).

2 **MADRON** (Cornwall)
This dour granite village has an ancient wishing-well (see pp. 132–133). Two miles distant, on the road to Morvah is Lanyon Quoit, a typical dolmen or 'stone table' (see pp. 36–37). About ½ mile north-east of this road is the Men an Tol—a doughnut-like holed stone set between two others. It is probably Bronze Age, and in medieval times it was thought possible to cure young children of rickets by passing them through the hole.

Three miles south-east of Madron, near Sancreed, is Carn Euny, an Iron Age settlement with a puzzling hidden cellar—a 'fogou' (see pp. 46–47). CHYSAUSTER is not far off.

3 **CARN BREA** (Cornwall)
For those who like records, this modest Iron Age hillfort (see pp. 46–47) reached by track from Carnkie (between Camborne and Redruth) embraces a tumbled wall running between crags around the summit at the east end of the hill, with tumbled huts and lean-tos—very probably all of Neolithic date (around 3000 BC) and the oldest village in England (see pp. 30–31 and 34–35).

4 **HELSTON** (Cornwall)
Home to the quaint Furry Dance—an echo of a Celtic May rite welcoming the summer in by dancing. At Wedron nearby is the famous Poldark mine museum: a tin mine with beam engine and other mining relics (see pp. 22–23).

5 **ST PIRAN'S ORATORY** (Cornwall)
Hidden among the sand dunes north-east of Perranporth is the ruin of a Dark Ages oratory (a small private chapel), now encased in concrete for preservation. It matches that at Bradwell (Essex) in age. It was founded by St Piran, an Irish missionary in the 6th century (see pp. 60–61), but was buried beneath the sands until rediscovered in 1835.

6 **THE LIZARD** (Cornwall)
The Lizard cape is so unlike other stretches of the Cornish coast that it is well worth a diversion. Serpentine rock forms most of it, lending green

and purple tints to the cliffs of Kynace and other Cornish coves (see pp. 16–17). The rock and exposure to the gales together create an unusual heathland (pp. 154–155).

7 FALMOUTH (Cornwall)
Two Tudor forts (see pp. 62–63) guard the entrance to this harbour, one of the best natural havens in Britain.

Geologically and scenically the Fal is of great interest as an example of a drowned valley—a river valley flooded by slow sinking of the land. This phenomenon explains why the river snakes wide as far as Truro (see pp. 158–159). This subsidence perhaps also flooded dry land between the Scilly Isles from the mainland, echoes of which may have lingered in the myths of the lost land of Lyonesse.

8 ROCHE (Cornwall)
This is a pleasant place, with cricket pitch and ancient church. Much of the countryside around is typically Cornish, with the fields surrounded by boundary banks, which in Cornwall are known as 'hedges' (see pp. 70–71). To the south are Roche Rocks, a group of crags capped by a chapel reached by an iron ladder.

9 ST AUSTELL (Cornwall)
Some of Britain's most spectacular lunar landscapes (see pp. 22–23) are to be seen near St Austell, created by the Cornish china clay industry. The white clay, known as kaolin, is one of the end products of the breakdown of granite; it was and is used in the manufacture of porcelain, paper, paints, and medicines. There is a museum of the clay industry at Carthew, a few miles north of St Austell, with a spectacular pit-viewing area.

10 TINTAGEL (Cornwall)
The Romans were here (the church holds a Roman milestone) and it was said that King Arthur was born here (see pp. 66–67)—not impossible if he was a Dark Ages warrior, for it was an important Celtic centre in

those days (see pp. 60–61). But the famous castle strewn across the cliffs is younger, of Norman and later date (see pp. 62–63). The Old Post Office is in origin a medieval manor house.

Delabole slate quarry nearby is the biggest man-made hole in Britain, a true lunar landscape (see pp. 22–23).

11 BLISLAND (Cornwall)
Set in a dour landscape of scattered farms this is an unexpectedly attractive village, clustered around a green, which is unusual for Cornwall. It has a fine early church, but the parish is also remarkable for a number of prehistoric standing stones some of which have been adopted as wayside crosses (see pp. 40–41).

12 BODMIN MOOR (Cornwall)
Like Dartmoor, Bodmin Moor is a windy but grand place, littered with stone circles and huts (see pp. 38–39) and in places scarred by medieval tin mining (see pp. 22–23).

Altarnun makes a good goal, a village of slate and granite tumbling down a slope to a stream crossed by stepping stones and an old packhorse bridge (see pp. 134–135). Dozmary Pool of Arthurian fame is nearby (see pp. 144–145) while Jamaica Inn, romantically linked with smugglers, is 4 miles to the west (see pp. 162–163).

13 HARTLAND POINT (Devon)
Awesome seas mount when storms add fury to the tide-rips here. Recent wrecks lie below the lighthouse. Two miles south is Hartland Quay, abandoned last century, although the coastguard housing is now an inn with its back firmly set against the ocean gales. The tusks and scallops of rock that arm the bay alongside result from the erosion of contorted layers; the folds of rock are clearly seen in the cliffs (see pp. 18–19 and 158–159).

14 BRENTOR (Devon)
A medieval church perches on a volcanic plug with vast views. It is dedicated to St Michael as many hilltop churches are (see pp. 64–65).

The site was probably also a beacon post; there are traces of Iron Age ramparts around it.

15 SALTASH BRIDGE (Devon)
A triumph of Victorian engineering, the masterpiece of Isambard Kingdom Brunel, this iron bridge was opened in 1859 and to this day carries the railway across the river Tamar into Cornwall (see pp. 130–131)

16 BIDEFORD (Devon)
This is now a sleepy holiday town, no longer the bustling port it once was, although in medieval times it had enough energy to build a fine bridge, which still (though widened) remains (see pp. 134–135). Not far to the north is Appledore, with a maritime museum which relates the story of its mariners (and smugglers).

Across the estuary lies Braunton Burrows, well worth a journey—it is one of England's largest expanses of sand dunes, with hundreds of wild flowers, birds and butterflies (see pp. 160–161). Vestiges of the medieval great open fields remain at Braunton (see pp. 58–59).

17 LYDFORD (Devon)
Tin mining was so important that in medieval days the miners formed almost a race apart, ruling Dartmoor and its environs. The castle of Lydford gained ill repute for its treatment of offenders against the stannary (tin) laws (see pp. 22–23).

18 EXMOOR (Som)
Unlike Dartmoor in neighbouring Devon, much of the original open moor has been reclaimed (see pp. 150–151) but heather still crowns the high ground with hidden combes with chuckling streams below, made ever-famous by the tale of Lorna Doone. There are wild ponies and red deer. There are many attractive villages and odd corners with burial cairns and standing stones to be discovered. Allerford has a famous packhorse bridge (see pp. 122–123); there is a clapper bridge at Tarr Steps.

19 ASHLEY COUNTRYSIDE COLLECTION (Devon)
Most counties have a handful of farm museums; this is an excellent example, with rare breeds of sheep and smiths' and other workshops (see pp. 110–111).

20 STICKLEPATH (Devon)
Just to the east of Okehampton an old mill houses a museum of rural industry, with water-powered tilt hammers and other machinery shown working (see pp. 108–109).

21 DARTMOOR (Devon)
Dartmoor's tors are stubs of granite eroded into weird shapes and skirted by fractured scree (see pp. 64–65). Sometimes erosion leaves a rocking- or logan-stone.

Haytor is one of the more easily reached of the 170 tors. Between them spreads moorland grazed by hardy ponies and sheep, often bleakly cloaked in rains and mists, broken by mires of ill repute. The prison at Princeton adds a further dismal note to the bleakness of the moorland round about.

Few trees survive on the open moor: stunted Wistman's Wood near Postbridge is an unusual relic (see pp. 88–89 and 156–157), although the fringing valleys with their old farmsteads are more welcoming.

There are many oddities to be seen, including clapper bridges (see pp. 134–135) and ancient gates (see pp. 126–127), old tin workings and ancient sites of national importance. Grimspound near Widecombe, lying at 1500 ft amid heather slopes, is a late Bronze Age settlement of hut circles with a protective wall (see pp. 38–39 and 150–151).

Near Merrivale are two unusual ritual stone rows and a small stone circle. Old field systems remain in many places (see pp. 58–59).

Dartmoor is a world of its own, with many personal discoveries to be made.

22 SALCOMBE (Devon)
The Salcombe estuary is a splendid example of a drowned valley (see pp. 158–159). This drowning, although hardly rapid, was possibly recognized by our ancestors, for there is evidence that it was taking place in Neolithic times (there is a datable submerged forest at Tor Bay, for example).

There are striking cliffs near Salcombe, especially to the west past Bolt Head. Kingsbridge still keeps echoes of its old plan, a market town built around quays, from which wool from the West Country was exported six centuries ago.

23 TIVERTON (Devon)
An 11-mile stretch of restored canal and towpath starts from Tiverton Basin (see pp. 136–137). It was part of the Grand Western Canal, linking up with Taunton, Bridgwater and the Bristol Channel.

24 HONITON (Devon)
This market town on the old London to Exeter coach road has, thanks to a modern bypass, regained some of its peace. On the Axminster road at its eastern edge is a white toll house, not unusual, but it has its gates remaining (see pp. 128–129).

Five miles away, off the Cullompton road, is Broadhembury, a village hidden away along quiet lanes and with the low, heavily thatched cob cottages (see pp. 104–105) of this region. Most are buff-washed, and some have sturdy buttresses supporting walls which are little more than dried clay. It is well worth a diversion, with Hembury hillfort, the finest in Devon, set above the village.

25 HATCH COURT (Som)
This is a typically Georgian house, finely built in Bath stone in 1755, and gracefully adorned with an arcade of columns (see pp. 112–113). Also typical is its setting in a small deer park, amid rolling countryside at Hatch Beauchamp. The house was chosen as the location for filming one of Jane Austen's novels.

26 LYME REGIS (Dorset)
This is a quaint and unexpected harbour on this open coast, and in the days of men-of-war under sail the only secure haven for many leagues. 'Snakestone' and 'thunderstone' fossils are ten-a-penny in the soft grey clay cliffs (see pp. 26–27) and fool's gold can be found in places (see pp. 20–21). To the west lies the famous undercliff walk through a jungle clothing vast cliff slumps (see pp. 158–159). The scenery inland is of some interest (see pp. 68–69) and Whitchurch worth a visit (see pp. 124–125).

27 GLASTONBURY (Som)
Below the tor crowned with the tower of a ruined chapel was a powerful abbey, now in ruin, although a magnificent barn remains. Its origins were early (see pp. 60–61) but now myth mingles with history— it was held that Joseph founded the first British church here, and his staff grows as the famous thorn tree. Glastonbury was also claimed as Avalon, the lost isle where King Arthur died (see pp. 124–125); before the levels were drained this dry ground stood among marshes—a lakeside village has been found nearby and wooden trackways (see pp. 34–35 and 46–47).

Also potent in myth was a 'blood' spring on the flanks of the tor (see pp. 132–133).

28 STANTON DREW (Avon)
Worth a detour is this late Neolithic ritual site, particularly since it is less well known than Avebury (Wilts). It is complex in plan (see pp. 42–43) with stone circles, a 'cove' of three stones (next to the churchyard), stone avenues and standing stones. The stones are all arranged on two alignments, one running north-east from the cove, the other crossing the main circle north to south.

29 THE MENDIPS (Avon/Som)
Stone walls and swallow holes are evidence that the Mendips are a whaleback of limestone. Gorges cut the flanks: Cheddar Gorge with its show caves is itself a collapsed cavern

(see pp. 24–25). Burrington Combe with its famous Rock of Ages (see pp. 18–19) is also worth a visit. Both Cheddar and Wookey Hole have yielded evidence of Old Stone Age man (see pp. 24–25 and 34–35). The area around Priddy is rewarding to explore, with Bronze Age barrows and stone circles (see pp. 38–39) and also the surface pitting of Roman lead mines.

30 **CADBURY CASTLE** (Som)
Brooding over the plains below, this magnificent Iron Age hillfort has been excavated to reveal an astonishing occupation from Neolithic to Dark Ages times, when a timber palace was perhaps linked to tales of King Arthur (see pp. 52–53). Evidence of massacre at the time of Queen Boudicca (Boadicea) has been found (see pp. 46–47).

31 **CERNE ABBAS** (Dorset)
Apart from its chalk-cut phallic giant wielding a club (see pp. 48–49) this village also boasts a 'wishing-well' of some age (see pp. 132–133).

32 **DORCHESTER** (Dorset)
Dorchester is a main touring centre for the 'Wessex' countryside of chalk downs (see pp. 28–29), water meadows, quaint villages and heaths immortalized in the novels of Thomas Hardy (see pp. 154–155). The cluster of 'Winterbournes' is interesting (see pp. 132–133). It is an old countryside, peppered with barrows and other earthworks, stone circles and traces of mysterious woodhenges (see pp. 42–43). South-west of the town lie the ramparts of Maiden Castle (see pp. 46–47), and beyond them stands Hardy's Monument, which dominates the skyline for miles around (see pp. 64–65).

Dorchester's streets follow the line of the Roman town which lies beneath (see pp. 50–51)—there is a good museum of finds from here and elsewhere, including the famous excavations at Maiden Castle. Other Roman items are a simple aqueduct (see pp. 146–147) and a milestone a mile to the east where the bypass meets the old road (see pp. 120–121).

33 **ISLE OF PORTLAND** (Dorset)
Stone quarried from this famous snout was used to build St Paul's and many other London landmarks (see pp. 16–17). It is a shelly limestone with fossils. There is an unusual drystone gateway at the country park (see pp. 74–75).

The Isle (it is not in fact an island) acts as a natural groyne, and the 16-mile shingle strip of Chesil Beach has built up in its lee (see pp. 160–161).

Water of deep Mediterranean blue races past Portland Bill. Here there are lighthouses, one of which is now a bird observatory.

34 **OAKLEY DOWN** (Dorset)
Half a mile north of the intersection of the Salisbury to Blandford A354 with the A3081 lies a magnificent Bronze Age cemetery with a variety of round barrows (see pp. 38–39). Cutting across it is the massive causeway of Ackling Dyke, one of the best-preserved lengths of Roman road in Britain (see pp. 120–121). This bank can also be viewed where it crosses the A3081, and 400 yards east of this point are traces of the mysterious Dorset Cursus, a 6-mile-long banked avenue of unknown use (see pp. 34–35). Neolithic long barrows accompany the Cursus—for example at Gussage Hill 2 miles to the south.

35 **MILTON ABBAS** (Dorset)
When Regency gentry improved their estates and a village interrupted the carefully planned view, they often razed it and (if only for the sake of keeping staff) built a new one. Milton Abbas with its neat white houses is a classic of this kind (see pp. 56–57 and 110–111).

36 **LULWORTH COVE** (Dorset)
This tourist mecca with its limpid water is also a textbook example of rock pleating (see pp. 18–19). Geologically, it is a perfect cove. Hard limestone layers form a shield against the waves but are backed by softer rocks. Once a breach is made, the restless sea slowly erodes the bowl we see here. Stair Hole nearby shows the start of the process (see pp. 158–159).

Nearby in the army ranges is the deserted village of Tyneham (see pp. 56–57).

37 **KNOWLTON** (Dorset)
Three large Neolithic henges lay here, aligned NW/SE (see pp. 34–35). One remains undamaged, embracing the ruin of a Norman church. It is puzzling why this was built here, $\frac{1}{4}$ mile away from its settlement (see pp. 56–57 and 104–105).

SOUTH-EAST ENGLAND

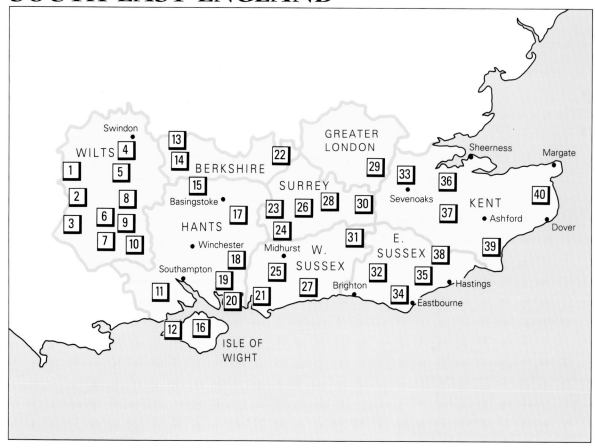

---

1 BRADFORD ON AVON (Wilts)
This charming old cloth-producing and market town has many fine stone buildings. One of special interest is the church of St Laurence. This small building dates back to the 7th century AD. It is an almost entire Saxon church, miraculously preserved through centuries of use as a cottage and barn, its real character lying forgotten until it was rediscovered in 1856 (see pp. 106–107).

The bridge here is also interesting: it is of late-medieval date, with a chapel halfway across, which was used as a lock-up in recent centuries (see pp. 134–135).

2 WESTBURY WHITE HORSE (Wilts)
A mile south-west of Bretton (see pp. 48–49) is this lively, long-tailed animal cut into the turf. It was cut in 1778 and there were contemporary reports that it replaced another, older one in this place. This may well have been cousin in style to the UFFINGTON WHITE HORSE. As with the Uffington horse, an Iron Age camp, Bratton camp, lies near this Westbury horse.

3 STOURHEAD (Wilts)
This is often cited as the epitome of landscaped estates in Britain (see pp. 112–113). At its centre lies a lake created by damming a stream to give serpentine banks which follow the contours. Around the lake eyecatchers are found, attractively set out along a walk; they include temples, memorials and a grotto.

4 WANSDYKE (Wilts)
This massive brooding rampart runs across today's prairie fields like a scar from the past—a good view of it is given where it cuts the A361 north of Devizes. Its name derives from Woden, the pagan god (see pp. 52–53). It is of Dark Ages date although there are few clues to its builders or function. Its ditch is to the north of the bank (that is, it 'faced' north), but as with many such ramparts, its length would have made it difficult to defend.

Mapwork, including the way that it relates to parish boundaries and other features suggests that it was built in two stages, the eastern half, which tracks through Savernake forest, being later.

5 AVEBURY (Wilts)
The village of Avebury is built partly within the massive encircling bank of what is arguably the most

dramatic stone-circle complex in Britain. The bank is in fact a henge of Neolithic date (see pp. 34–35), the stones (which alternate in shape in what was probably a meaningful way—see pp. 42–43) being erected later, perhaps in early Bronze Age times (see pp. 44–45).

As with Stonehenge, the stone-circle complex is part of a wider area of ritual importance. Earlier than anything is the causewayed camp on Windmill Hill nearby (see pp. 34–35). From Avebury itself a stone avenue leads south-east in the general direction of Overton Hill, a 'woodhenge' and possibly a communal dwelling of some kind. The West Kennet gallery grave (see pp. 36–37) lies to its east, well worth a short walk. Dating to before 3000 BC, it contained the remains of 46 people, one with an arrowhead in his throat. To the west of Overton Hill looms the massive tump of Silbury Hill, the largest man-made earthwork in Europe (see pp. 34–35). There are also Neolithic long barrows and Bronze Age round barrows in the area.

Today's line of the RIDGEWAY (Map 4) passes about a mile to the east of Avebury. The countryside is now intensively farmed, but a sarsen stone field of scattered boulders can be seen on Overton Down here; areas like this provided the stone. One of the sarsens on Overton Down is a polissoir, deeply scored where it has been used for sharpening weapons (see pp. 40–41).

6 EDINGTON (Wilts)
This is an atmospheric place, with to the south the mysteriously furrowed flanks of the chalk downs.

Somewhere near here was fought the crucial Battle of Edington in AD 878 (see pp. 52–53), and perhaps Alfred's army rushed down those very same downland slopes.

Alfred spent the night with his troops somewhere near Eastleigh Wood, 2 miles south of Warminster. They moved towards Edington at dawn to fall upon the entire Danish army. The direct line from Eastleigh Wood to Edington descends the

furrowed slopes we see today. It may be one of few battlefield approaches that has actually kept its appearance over the centuries (see pp. 66–67).

In general the downs south of here do recapture the past. They are now army training ranges, never ploughed, dotted with scrub. The A390 a few miles south of Edington gives a good view of this terrain—a landscape which may be much as it looked in pastoral Neolithic times.

7 FOVANT (Wilts)
On the flanks of the chalk downs are cut several regimental badges. The cutting of such tribal symbols can trace its origins back to the Iron Age at least (see pp. 48–49).

8 STONEHENGE (Wilts)
One of the best known of prehistoric monuments, the stone circle we see is the final phase of a complex evolution at the site which started in the late Neolithic (see pp. 34–35) and ended during the Bronze Age maybe around 1200 BC (see pp. 44–45). The area was clearly a ritual focus of some significance, for in spite of much ploughing-out, many Neolithic long barrows and Bronze Age round barrows still dot the plain, while a short distance to the north-east are the mysterious (although all but destroyed) sanctuaries of Durrington Walls and Woodhenge (see pp. 42–43).

9 GREAT WISHFORD (Wilts)
Scarcely can a more typical Wiltshire village be found. There is a typical almshouse (1622) and school (1722), and in the churchyard wall a stone registering the price of bread since 1800. The village is home to the unusual 'Grovely' ceremony, celebrating the villagers' commons use of local woodland (see pp. 90–91).

10 OLD SARUM (Wilts)
Two miles north of Salisbury lies its precursor—the name Old Sarum means simply 'Old Salisbury' (see pp. 114–115). The site was originally an Iron Age camp (see pp. 46–47); its ramparts were refortified by the

Normans, who also built a castle and cathedral within. Water shortage was one of the causes prompting the removal of the town to the valley below.

11 NEW FOREST (Hants)
Designated as a royal hunting forest in 1079, this (although now much smaller) retains a patchwork of woodland and open barren ground typical of the original forests (see pp. 156–157). Today's woodlands, however, are often by origin plantations started when shortage of timber was threatening the building of the navy's men-of-war. Commons grazing rights are still jealously guarded here (see pp. 90–91).

12 ALUM BAY (Isle of Wight)
The multilayered cliffs of this bay yield 12 differently coloured sands, an intriguing example of the variety created by rock layering and buckling (see pp. 18–19). Colour apart, these cliffs of shelly sand also yield many late (Caenozoic) fossils (see pp. 26–27). The Isle of Wight is of great and varied interest, its highlights ranging from a Roman villa near Brading to the medieval castle of Carisbrooke.

13 SEVEN BARROWS (Berks)
This Bronze Age cemetery lies a couple of miles north of Lambourn (take the left turn a mile up the A4001). In fact many more than seven barrows remain, and one group lies alongside the road, with bowl, disc and other types (see pp. 38–39).

14 DONNINGTON CASTLE (Berks)
Near Newbury, this is one of the ruins that 'Cromwell knocked about a bit', to quote an old music-hall song. During the Civil War it was twice beseiged by his troops and razed by his cannon. Castles built in the old way were clearly no match for the artillery of the time (see pp. 62–63).

15 SILCHESTER (Hants)
Reached only by a maze of lanes, long lengths of Roman wall (or at least the flint-rubble core) stand

empty over the fields, with only a medieval church and a farm inside. Once a Roman town (see pp. 50–51) called Calleva Atrebatum, it was somehow ignored by later development. Temples, shops and other buildings have been excavated (there is a museum with many finds). The amphitheatre outside the walls has not been dug—its terraces still tower 18 ft above the arena.

16 CARISBROOKE CASTLE (Isle of Wight)
This is a well-situated castle, with an impressive gatehouse. Of interest is the 16th-century waterwheel in a wellhouse, still worked by patient donkeys, raising the water 160 feet. The well itself was dug in 1150. Animal power of this kind was at one time common (see pp. 132–133).

17 THE WATERCRESS LINE (Hants)
During the summer, steam engines make the 10-mile journey along this line between New Alresford and Alton. Two intermediate stations have also been restored. Opened in 1865, it is a typical Victorian rail line (see pp. 130–131).

18 BUTSER HILL (Hants)
Butser Hill is the highest point of the South Downs and from it stretch fantastic views. It forms part of the Queen Elizabeth Country Park.

Within the Park, below the flanks of Butser, lies the Ancient Farm project. The focus is a reconstructed Iron Age farmstead (see pp. 46–47 and 82–83) with round, snugly thatched hut and outbuildings based on huts excavated in Dorset. The project also conducts trials of grain drying and other Iron Age customs.

It is well worth a visit.

19 HAMBLEDON (Hants)
Although it claims to be the home of cricket (see pp. 102–103), Hambledon's cricket club dating back to 1760 was not the first, but here the rules of today's game were developed. The name of the club ground, Broadhalfpenny Down, recalls droving days (see pp. 122–123).

20 PORTCHESTER (Hants)
This is one of the best preserved of all Roman forts, one of the so-called Forts of the Saxon shore built to defend the east-facing coasts against Saxon invaders (see pp. 50–51). Its defensive wall is almost entire, with many original bastions. The Normans later used it as a bailey, building their own keep inside (see pp. 62–63).

21 FISHBOURNE ROMAN PALACE (W. Sussex)
This, the largest of known British Roman villas, has one wing restored and houses a museum of life in Roman Britain. The restored garden is interesting (see pp. 50–51).

22 WINDSOR GREAT PARK (Berks)
Although of Norman origins, Windsor Castle itself is largely 19th-century. The Great Park is more of an original relic, a remnant of an extensive royal hunting forest. Although much changed with recent trees and plantations (including pines and cedars) many massive old pollard oaks remain. It was here that the first British plantation, of oaks, was placed in 1580 (see pp. 88–89).

The park has been landscaped in places, and lakes dammed.

23 FRENSHAM (Surrey)
Almost 1000 acres of heathland (see pp. 154–155) are in National Trust care here; the two famous ponds were once used as fishponds by Waverley Abbey not far off.

The Devil's Jumps on Churt Common are an intriguing example of rock stubs left after erosion (see pp. 28–29).

24 HINDHEAD COMMON (Surrey)
Wild heathlands such as this are a disappearing countryside feature, but these 1400 acres are now safe as National Trust property. The name is the clue to its former communal use (see pp. 90–91), but the names of individual features, such as (on Hindhead) Golden Valley and Stoatley Green may reflect private inroads in the past. The name Gibbet Hill needs no explanation.

25 WEALD AND DOWNLAND MUSEUM (W. Sussex)
This open-air museum at Singleton comprises a collection of 14th to 19th-century buildings, saved from demolition and re-erected here (see pp. 52–53) Medieval farmsteads are among them (see pp. 82–83 and 104–105).

26 ABINGER (Surrey)
Abinger Common has a green and stocks. Worth a detour (enquire at the Manor House for permission and a key) is a Mesolithic pit dwelling; a small museum holds the finds (see pp. 34–35).

Abinger Common and Abinger Hammer make good starting-points for exploring the many hammer ponds or the remains of them (see pp. 142–143) and other souvenirs of ironworking and other early industry in the neighbourhood (see pp. 22–23, 108–111, 142–143) often reached via holloways (see pp. 118–119).

27 CISSBURY RING (W. Sussex)
This egg-shaped Iron Age fort encloses 60 acres with entrances to east and west (see pp. 46–47). Its slumped ramparts hide the fact that 12,000 timbers were used for strengthening them. Lying empty in Roman times, the ground both inside and out was ploughed and traces of 'Celtic' fields can be seen. More interesting, however, are the slight pits and mounds within the west end, what remains of Neolithic flint mines (see pp. 22–23 and 54–55).

28 BOX HILL (Surrey)
This famous bluff is part of the chalk ridge which forms the North Downs. An ancient track, known today as the Pilgrim's Way, followed the line of the high ground, although on Box Hill itself it keeps to the drier slopes rather than the clay top (see pp. 116–117 and 124–125).

There are many quaint villages nearby; in the church at Betchworth is an interesting early field enclosure map of 1634 (see pp. 58–59). Betchworth is also worth a diversion for its watermill.

29 CHISLEHURST CAVES (Kent)
These caves were dug for chalk and are unexpectedly extensive, with 22 miles of galleries in all. There is argument about how old they actually are, but claims of an early date are not likely to be true. Fifteen thousand Londoners regularly used the caves as an air-raid shelter in World War II (see pp. 24–25).

30 HAXTED MILL (Surrey)
This is a well-restored water mill, its oldest parts dating back four centuries. Although the wheel is working, the building is now a museum showing the uses to which water power was put (see pp. 108–109) with a Cornish tin-mine wheel and a local pumping water-wheel on view, among other things.

31 WEST HOATHLY (W. Sussex)
This is a handsome village, with a mellow stone manor house, a priest's house and other features. The rivers have cut deep valleys into the sandstone bedrock in some places, and the exposed faces have sometimes been deeply weathered by rain aided by wind (see pp. 12–13), to create odd rock sculptures. At Rocks Wood, for example, one large undermined mass is aptly called 'Great Upon Little'.

32 LEWES (E. Sussex)
The southward-flowing rivers of the Weald escape to the sea through gaps they have cut in the chalk downs. The ancient dry routes along the chalk had to descend to cross the rivers, and today each is marked with an ancient town (see pp. 114–115). Lewes is an example of the many towns which had a medieval castle, but these must surely overlie much earlier settlements.

33 LULLINGSTONE ROMAN VILLA (Kent)
This Roman villa (see pp. 50–51) is noted for its fine mosaic floors, and for what is thought to be an early Christian shrine (see pp. 60–61).

34 WILMINGTON LONG MAN (E. Sussex)
Possibly of Iron Age date, this hill figure is the tallest of all—226 ft (see pp. 48–49). In places the chalk down is pitted with the slumped shafts of Neolithic flint mines (see pp. 22–23 and 54–55).
The village is attractive, with cottages of flint and brickwork set along a village street which runs from green to church (and the remains of a priory).

35 BATTLE ABBEY (E. Sussex)
It is difficult today to imagine the battlefield as it looked in 1066, but this is still an emotive place to visit (see pp. 66–67). The abbey was built in 1070 on the ridge where Harold positioned his troops, and its high altar marks the spot where he fell. There is a battlefield trail to guide visitors to the key points.

36 TROTTISCLIFFE (Kent)
Coldrum chambered tomb, which is prehistoric, is set into a flank of the North Downs, east-north-east of Trottiscliffe, above Ryarsh Wood. It is a splendid example of a 'Medway' type Neolithic gallery grave (see pp. 36–37). Four gigantic sarsens enclose the burial chamber.

37 HORSMONDEN (Kent)
This village has a square green (known as The Heath) and a church now more than a mile to the south of today's centre—it is a village which has moved, in other words (see pp. 94–95). The sheep sales which were held here every July recall an early pastoral tradition dating to long before the countryside round about became filled with hopfields (see pp. 92–93).
Also of note is the furnace pond, a hammer pond for iron and other industrial use (see pp. 142–143).

38 BODIAM CASTLE (E. Sussex)
From the outside this archetypal castle, set in a quiet moat, seems intact. It only remains as a shell, however, for like many it was besieged and partly destroyed in the Civil War, having been designed for earlier, gun-less warfare.
Interestingly, the castle stands on a slight slope; the moat is fed by a spring. On the approach path is a World War II machine-gun post—in its way as historic a relic (see pp. 62–63 and 66–67).

39 ROMNEY MARSH (Kent)
Originally salt marsh, this has long been protected with a sea wall and drained to gain rich pastures, the best natural grazing in Britain, which gave their name to their own breed of sheep (see pp. 160–161). But the tidal and other flows have been changing—and Winchelsea is a coastal harbour that died when its approaches became too difficult for navigation (see pp. 162–163). Dungeness is a notable shingle feature—a desert plain of rounded stones combed into lines and curves by a giant hand, perhaps the largest in Europe (see pp. 160–161) and the Romney-Hythe narrow-track railway is great fun (see pp. 130–131).

40 RICHBOROUGH (Kent)
It was here that the Roman legions landed in AD 43, although the coastline has changed much since those days. Short lengths of the ditches dug to defend their first beachhead have been excavated and can be seen. The Roman walls, however, are those of a later Saxon shore fort, one of a chain built as a defence against Saxon raiders—each strategically sited with a harbour nearby (see pp. 50–51).
From the west gateway the Roman road now known as Watling Street ran to London and across the Midlands to the legionary fortress at Chester (see pp. 120–121).

EASTERN ENGLAND

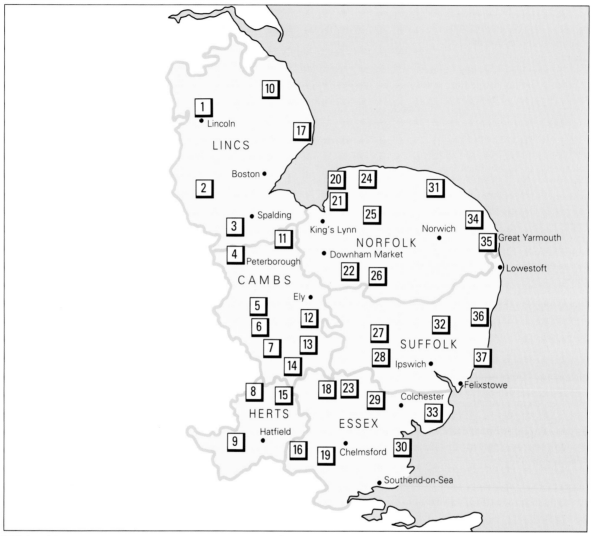

1 LINCOLN (Lincs)
Today's city occupies the site of a Roman garrison guarding the meeting of the roads now known as Ermine Street and the Fosse Way. A Roman gateway remains.

Also of interest are the 'Jews House' on The Straight and 'Aarons House' on Steep Hill—both are Norman dwelling houses little altered and similar is BOOTHBY PAGNELL (Lincs). They were some safeguard against the anti-Jewish riots of medieval times.

2 BOOTHBY PAGNELL (Lincs)
The stone manor house is a rare Norman survival dating from 1180. Its doorway, which is typically Norman in style, is set on the first floor, reached by an outside staircase in the fashion of the part-defensive farmsteads of England's northern border (see pp. 112–113).

3 DEEPING ST JAMES (Lincs)
This village boasts a lock-up. The name is a familiar linkage of Dark Ages settlement name (see pp. 96–97) and a later church dedication.

4 BARNACK (Cambs)
This is a stone village—the sweeping lines of the drystone field walls run up to farm buildings which resemble small castles in their own right. There were famous quarries here, the stone from which went to Ely and Peterborough cathedrals and a good many Cambridge colleges—all that remains of the diggings are scrubbed-up pits scattered in various fields around the village.

There is an 18th-century windmill here (see pp. 108–109).

5 ST IVES (Cambs)
Although there are many medieval bridges to be found in Britain, few keep a chapel (see pp. 134–135). The bridge chapel here

is small, two storeys. Bridge chapels were perhaps usually chantry chapels—that is, chapels in which the donor endowed services to be regularly said to ease and shorten his (or her) time spent in purgatory. In the case of a bridge, it may well have been the chantry chapel for a group of local craftsmen, a craft guild.

6 HILTON (Cambs)
This village boasts one of the clearest turf-cut mazes in Britain. Only a handful of these remain (see pp. 102–103); as the memorial here relates, Hilton maze was suppressed during the Puritan Commonwealth but recut on the restoration of Charles II.

These mazes are old—this one at Hilton has clearly been worn down a good way below the level of the surrounding ground by centuries of trampling.

7 BOURN (Cambs)
The church here has a maze pattern set in tiles below the tower; it may date from the 13th century and may have symbolized the path through life to salvation, or stood in as a symbolic pilgrimage. Its pattern rather resembles that of the village turf mazes as still seen at HILTON (see pp. 102–103).

Also of interest is the post mill just outside the village, the oldest remaining (see pp.108–109). At Caxton crossroads not far off stands a replica gibbet (see pp. 128–129).

8 ASHWELL (Herts)
This village is notable for graffiti scrawled on walls and pillars within the church—some relate to the devastations of the Great Plague, when the church acted as refuge (see pp. 56–57 and 106–107). The cottage names echo the past—Bear House and Chantry House among them (see pp. 98–99). Springs bubble up at the end of the main street, crossed by stepping stones of unknown age (see pp. 134–135). Historians have found traces of the great open fields of medieval times around the village (see pp. 58–59),

although today's farming gives it as hedgeless a look as ever it had in the past.

9 ST ALBANS (Herts)
Many remains of the important Roman town of Verulamium remain to the west of the modern town of St Albans—in the shape of lengths of town wall which once enclosed 200 acres, mosaic floors, and the semicircular terracing of a theatre (see pp. 50–51).

Today's town grew up around the shrine of Alban, martyred in AD 304. His shrine in the abbey was a popular pilgrims' goal (see pp. 126–127). In fact, so important a shrine was it that in medieval times it was independent of royal rule, being the 'liberty' of the abbot—at that time one of the most powerful men in England.

10 LINCOLNSHIRE WOLDS (Lincs)
The Lincolnshire Wolds are a high ridge of chalk extending northwards from the main finger of chalk running into East Anglia. There were settlements by Dark Ages invaders crossing the North Sea, but the large concentration of long barrows speaks to far older settlement. Many of these earlier remains have been damaged by ploughing, but one of the best-preserved of these long barrows is at Ash Hill, 10 miles north of Louth on the western edge of Swinhope Park; another lies at Hoe Hill nearby. There are also many round barrows, some of which are clustered in cemeteries (see pp. 38–39).

11 THE FENS
The Fens is a name reserved for a vast area of flat land lying south and west of the Wash—once a forbidding marshy wilderness but now drained. The peaty soil has shrunk when dried and so today's field levels are well below that of the drainage dykes. One oddity are the raised 'roddens' which snake across the countryside, the tracks of the ancient river beds which, being gravel, did not shrink as much as the land on either side (see pp. 138–139).

About the only sizeable tract left undrained is at Wicken Fen, north of Cambridge—about 3 miles west of Soham. It is National Trust land and can be visited.

12 REACH (Cambs)
This unassuming settlement has an interesting place in local history. Reach Lode was a Roman dyke (see pp. 50–51) dug partly to improve water traffic and partly to ease the pressure of the tides on the walls protecting the newly drained areas of fenland (see pp. 138–139). The massive rampart of the Devil's Dyke ends at Reach; it once blocked the Icknield Way, between these fenny lands and the uncleared forest (see pp. 52–53).

Reach, like many villages, has but a shadow of its former business—it was a bustling port and there was a great horse fair here once a year in spring.

13 WANDLEBURY (Cambs)
This is a fine Iron Age camp (see pp. 46–47) sprawled on the Gog Magog hills. The words of the name 'Gog Magog' mean giant and giantess, and may be evidence of a chalk-cut hill figure on the slopes below, of a giant wielding a club (see pp. 48–49).

14 DUXFORD (Cambs)
Duxford is now one of the necklace of villages which serve Cambridge with commuter homes. It is noticeable that the village is on a ridge of higher ground above flood level. Its relationship with the river is interesting, for it is one of a handful of 'ford' villages in the neighbourhood; these originated with crossings of the ancient track now known as the Icknield Way over the marshy land and the river itself (see pp. 116–117).

Also of interest is the flying museum at Duxford airfield—a famous fighter base in World War II (see pp. 64–65).

15 ROYSTON (Herts)
There is a puzzling bell-shaped cave hollowed out in the chalk (see pp. 24–25), almost directly below the spot where the Roman Ermine Street

crosses the even older Icknield Way. It was rediscovered in 1742, and seems to be medieval—the walls carry carvings of St Christopher and St Catherine, together with the wheel on which the latter was martyred, and other figures, as well as hearts, hands and other symbols. It may have been a storehouse for Knights Templars who held land round about; or maybe a hermit's hideaway. Access is arranged via the bank building nearby.

16 EPPING FOREST (Essex)
This is a fragment of a once extensive royal hunting forest—the Epping Forest Museum is housed in a hunting lodge of 15th-century date.

The forest still offers remoteness and is noted for its giant pollarded hornbeam trees—the fact that they have been pollarded reflects the mixed land use common in past centuries (see pp. 88–89 and 156–157).

17 GIBRALTAR POINT (Lincs)
This National Nature Reserve lies 3½ miles south of Skegness. It is a magnificent sand-dune system (see pp. 160–161), with associated salt marshes, and with clear-cut boundaries despite the lack of solid rock of any kind. Only a thin skin of plants binds the loose sand, however, and if this skin is broken disastrous blow-outs can occur. The area is notable for its bird life, offering a variety of nesting sites—for the rare terns, for example—while many migrant birds also land to rest and feed.

18 THAXTED (Essex)
This town made its wealth from (rather surprisingly) cutlery—there were around 100 cutlers and silversmiths at work here in 1381. Their trade Guild built Thaxted's splendid half-timbered Guildhall (see pp. 114–115) which became the town council offices when the cutlery trade declined. There is a windmill museum here of some interest.

19 GREENSTED (Essex)
This village harbours a unique relic, the timber walls of a Saxon church (see pp. 106–107). The nave walls are of split tree trunks, originally set into a timber sill lying along the ground. The sill rotted, however, and has been replaced by brickwork.

20 HUNSTANTON (Norfolk)
This small seaside resort is not only notable for its views across the extensive flats of the Wash, but also for the cake-like banding of its low cliffs, with chalk interleaved with light brownish sandstone (see pp. 18–19).

Some think that the pattern of roads and footpaths found inland between here and BRANCASTER, which is gridlike in some places, reflects Roman field layouts (see pp. 58–59).

21 PEDDARS WAY (Norfolk)
This ancient track can be picked up about a third of a mile south-west of the village of Fring, near Snettisham, and followed as a series of trackways and green lanes. Apart from its traffic in prehistory (see pp. 116–117), it was used by the Romans as part of their East Anglian communications system. It has also served as a medieval pilgrim route and a drove road. Its route ran north-west across Norfolk, from Coney Weston in Suffolk to Holme next the Sea.

22 GRIMES GRAVES (Norfolk)
These Neolithic flint mines lie north-west of Brandon. The ground is pitted with the collapsed shafts, but one has been opened for the public. From the bottom of the shaft galleries radiate away, following the best flint seams. The blocks of flint were levered out using deer antlers as picks—and the thumbprints remained on these and on the hammer stones when the excavators uncovered them; some are on show on site (see pp. 22–23 and 54–55).

23 FINCHINGFIELD (Essex)
This is among Britain's most familiar villages, appearing on countless calendars. It has a pleasant assemblage of pond, bridge, green and a charming array of white-fronted and gabled houses climbing to a Norman church (see pp. 94–95). Worth a detour.

24 BRANCASTER (Norfolk)
The '-caster' suggests that there was a Roman station here of some kind (see pp. 96–97). The North Norfolk coast is an interesting mixture of 'soft coast' types—with sandbanks and shingle ridges, salt marshes and sand dunes—much of it is protected as nature reserves (see pp. 160–161).

25 CASTLE ACRE (Norfolk)
The name comes from the Saxon word *aecer*, meaning field or ploughland (see pp. 80–81). There is a fine example of a shell keep on a motte (see pp. 62–63) and there was also a priory here—now equally ruinous— and a pilgrim hostel marked by a cross of red bricks set into a wall. Situated at the crossing of the River Nene by the ancient track known as the PEDDARS WAY, this must have long been important as a settlement.

26 BRECKLAND (Norfolk)
Soil and climate conspire to provide (in those areas not ploughed or coniferized) unique patchworks of plant communities (see pp. 154–155).

The area was settled in prehistoric days—from Neolithic times there are long barrows and Grimes Graves flint mines (see pp. 54–55); and Bronze Age round-barrow cemeteries remain.

Rabbit warrens were also a feature in medieval days, and the name often remains on the map (see pp. 90–91 and 154–55).

27 BRADFIELD WOODS (Suffolk)
These woodlands lie about 6 miles south-east of Bury St Edmunds. They are ancient coppiced woodlands (see pp. 88–89)—there are written records of coppicing here in 1252.

Coppicing continues, organized by the local county Conservation Trust, for the sake of the wild flowers, birds and other wildlife that it encourages.

The woods make a delightful walk, filled with flowers and butterflies. They also contain features such as fishponds (see pp. 142–143).

28 LAVENHAM (Suffolk)

Half-timbered houses often gained their bends early on (see pp. 104–105); there are plenty of old ones here, along irregular streets. The market was laid out in the 13th century, but the houses—and the church—were built with the profits of the 15th-century wool and cloth trades (see pp. 110–111). Many houses have ornate plasterwork.

Although its present population (1300) makes it a large village, Lavenham was in 1524 the fourteenth richest town in England (see pp. 114–115).

29 LITTLE MAPLESTEAD (Essex)

Although much rebuilt, the round church here is linked with the pilgrim traffic of medieval days. It was originally part of a hospice of the Knights Hospitallers, who with the Knights Templars had protected and provided for the needs of pilgrims to the Holy Land and elsewhere (see pp. 124–125). Their round churches were modelled on the church of the Holy Sepulchre in Jerusalem.

30 BRADWELL (Essex)

There are splendid salt marshes and open flats along this coast, which attract many wintering birds (see pp. 160–161). But there is something here of equal interest. On the east-facing coast, about 2 miles east of Bradwell hamlet, is what is possibly the oldest church in the country, built by the missionary St Cedd in AD 564

and restored this century. It was built on the site of a Roman fort of the Saxon shore and Roman brickwork was used in its construction.

In places along the coast of Essex south of here are mysterious deposits of red soil—these 'red hills' are maybe all that remains of pottery evaporating pans for a salt-drying industry.

31 CROMER (Norfolk)

This resort came of age with the railways, as the architecture of the town reveals. Holidaymaking apart, the coast here provides excellent fossil grounds where the sea has eroded the soft rock cliffs. There are small oysters to be found in the chalk, and mammal bones, plant seeds and other fairly late fossils at West Runton, for example. The gravels are largely Ice Age deposits (see pp. 20–21).

32 SAXTEAD GREEN (Suffolk)

In this village can be found one of Britain's finest remaining post mills, and although the superstructure we see dates from last century, the mill site is in fact much older—it is known that a medieval windmill stood here. The present mill was retired from work about 40 years ago (see pp. 108–109).

33 GREAT BENTLEY (Essex)

This is a green village par excellence (see pp. 100–101)—in Victorian times its 45 acres were surrounded by clusters of boarded and thatched houses. The immense green, because it was important for grazing and the annual calendar of village functions, united this rather scattered community.

34 THE BROADS (Norfolk)

The lagoons fill what were medieval peat diggings; shallow and reed-lined, they have over the centuries become an all but natural wetland habitat (see pp. 138–139). Recent pollution and boat traffic in this popular holiday area have destroyed much of the wildlife, but Ranworth and Hickling Broads are two enclosed Broads which retain their old variety. They and others similar have restricted access but can usually be viewed from neighbouring footpaths.

35 BURGH CASTLE (Norfolk)

Signposted from the A12 about 2 miles from Great Yarmouth, this Roman Saxon shore fort has some well-preserved lengths of wall—one block shows the footing for a ballista or catapult (see pp. 50–51).

36 DUNWICH (Suffolk)

Four miles south-east of Southwold, this was a Norman town and harbour by origin. The latter was destroyed by a storm in 1326, and the waves have since eaten their way inland. Nine churches have disappeared and not much more remains than part of the graveyard at the edge of the cliffs and narrow holloways. The cliffs are receding at 3 in. a year (see pp. 160–161).

37 ORFORD NESS (Suffolk)

This is a fine example of a permanent shingle feature, of loose material but sculptured by tides and currents into something wellnigh permanent. Apart from the shingle spit, the salt marsh attracts many breeding birds (see pp. 160–161).

SOUTH MIDLANDS

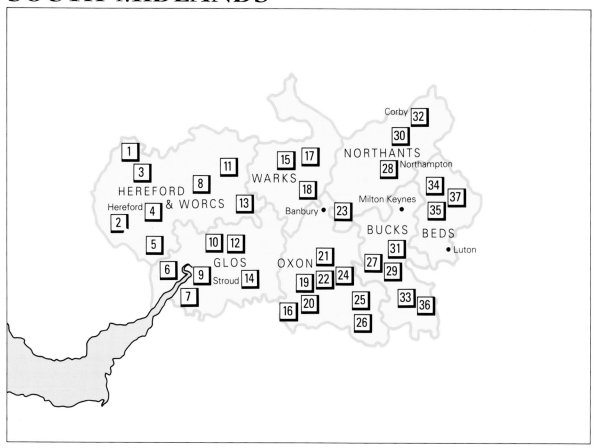

1 **LEINTWARDINE** (Hereford & Worcs)
This hillside village boasts a charming array of stone, brick and black-and-white timbered cottages.
Of special interest is the defensive battlemented tower of the church, with massive walls. Stronghold church towers such as this were built in the turbulent border regions between England and Wales and Scotland (see pp. 106–107).

2 **KILPECK** (Hereford & Worcs)
This village contains one of the best-preserved Norman churches in Britain, famous for its remarkable decoration. Of particular interest are the gargoyle-like heads which might echo the head-hunting traditions of the Iron Age Celts, who displayed the heads of their slain foes (see pp. 106–107).

3 **LEOMINSTER** (Hereford & Worcs)
This was once an important wool town, and still has some black and white gabled medieval streets, although there is also some fine Georgian building. Of note is the elaborate timbered town hall of 1630s date (see pp. 114–115). Like many such structures, its lower arcade was open and sheltered the market, the whole later becoming enclosed.

4 **HEREFORD WATERWORKS MUSEUM** (Hereford & Worcs)
A Victorian pumping station houses an unusual museum relating the development of Victorian water supply. However, the buildings far outweigh the story in interest (see pp. 146–147). Surmounted by a 70-ft chimney, the magnificent structure encloses boiler houses (in steam on

Bank Holidays) and other chambers. It is a veritable cathedral of industry, with polished brass taking the place of gold.

5 **SYMOND'S YAT** (Hereford & Worcs)
This is one of the famous viewpoints of the River Wye, with a bird's-eye view of its sinuous curves. The river here is geologically strange, however, since it leaves the upland to turn back into it almost immediately; the explanation is that it is following an older course (see pp. 14–15).

6 **FOREST OF DEAN** (Glos)
A green triangle between the Severn and the Wye, this has been a mining centre as well as forest. The timber once provided charcoal for the smelting of metal. The mining here possibly dates back to Roman times

(see pp. 22–23). A museum 2 miles south of Cinderford explains the history of the area.

7 **BERKELEY CASTLE** (Glos)
This brooding medieval castle has a splendid medieval great hall and deer park (see pp. 62–63). It overlooks the Severn estuary, an internationally important area for wintering birds: the mud flats, salt marsh and natural salt grazings are backed by open levels of reclaimed salt marsh (see pp. 160–161). Bird watching is focused on the Slimbridge Wildfowl Sanctuary.

8 **THE MALVERN HILLS** (Hereford & Worcs)
Although only stretching 6 miles, this range of hills gives outstanding views. It has two 'Beacon Hill' summits (see pp. 64–65), one of which is contoured by British Camp, an Iron Age hillfort with impressively deep-cut ramparts and a well-marked contemporary trackway to the western entrance (see pp. 116–117).

To the south of this (though reached by a roundabout route) is Gullet Quarry, one of a number which bite into the slopes of these hills. This quarry has an interesting rock exposure (see pp. 18–19).

The Malverns are also noted for their many springs of pure water; some are tapped for bottling but there are many to be seen along roadsides (see pp. 132–133).

9 **FROCESTER TITHE BARN** (Glos)
A well-preserved 13th-century tithe barn stands in the grounds of what were once administrative buildings of a monastic estate. Gigantic storage barns such as this, with its 13 great 'bays' or storage divisions, were fairly common on monastic estates (see pp. 84–85). They were built to hold the tithes—a tax of a tenth—of a vast area. Original timbers still carry the weight of the stone-tiled roof.

10 **DEERHURST** (Glos)
A village noted for its church— the first stone church was in place in

the 8th century and it was massively enlarged to become a minster—all before the Norman conquest. It is famous for its Saxon carvings (see pp. 106–107).

As interesting is a second Saxon building a couple of hundred yards to the south-west—this, Odda's chapel, now forms part of a timber-framed building.

11 **AVONCROFT MUSEUM** (Hereford & Worcs)
This open-air museum of buildings is situated 2 miles south of Bromsgrove. More than 20 are on display, having been rescued from demolition and re-erected here, including a working windmill and early cottages (see pp. 104–105).

12 **BELAS KNAP** (Glos)
This massive chambered tomb lies to the north-east of Cheltenham, on the right of the country lane which leaves the A46 for Charlton Abbots. At its north end two horns faced with fine drystone walling (see pp. 74–75) embrace a ritual forecourt, but the entrance here is false, the actual burial chambers being along the flanks of the mound (see pp. 36–37).

13 **BROADWAY TOWER** (Hereford & Worcs)
This tower is well sited on the brow of the Cotswolds, looking to Wales across the Vale of Evesham, which is a fine geological spectacle (see pp. 12–13 and 64–65). Such structures are often called folly towers, being erected for no good use. However, this was inhabited for a time.

The field walls here are oolite (see pp. 16–17). Not far way, at the corner of the Chipping Campden road, is an interesting coachman's signpost (see pp. 128–129).

14 **BIBURY** (Glos)
This charming, once important craft village (see pp. 110–111) contains Arlington Row, a terrace of weaver's cottages overlooking the mill stream. The 17th-century corn mill retains its original machinery

and now serves as a museum with olden-time farm implements and costumes, and rooms dedicated to cobblers, blacksmiths and other village craftsmen.

15 **KENILWORTH CASTLE** (Warks)
This was one of Norman Britain's chief strongholds, with one of the most notable of all keeps, built at the end of the era of great keeps in the time of King John. Later buildings were largely dismantled after the Civil War (1642–8)—the walls of the Great Hall are now fragmentary, for example, although it was clearly one of the finest built. The gatehouse and great barn and stable are still impressive.

Notable is the moat—or rather its dry bed: it was once extensive (see pp. 62–63).

16 **ASHDOWN HOUSE** (Oxon)
Ashdown House is an exceedingly elegant, though small, 17th-century mansion. Its interest here, however, lies in its grounds, which are open to the public. In front of the house, in part tree-covered, massive sarsen boulders lie scattered—the remains of a layer of sandstone which once covered the chalk rock, and an odd relic of erosion (see pp. 28–29).

The estate of Ashdown House was formerly a deer park, once quite common in the countryside (see pp. 112–113) and traces of its boundary bank can still be seen. At the back of the estate, beyond the woodlands, is Alfred's Castle, a small, ramparted stronghold of unknown date. Alfred did fight one successful battle somewhere in the area, but this small fort is likely to be earlier.

Not far from here, reached by going to Lambourn and then turning north and taking the left fork a mile or two outside the village, is the Bronze Age cemetery known as SEVEN BARROWS (Berks).

17 **BAGINTON** (Warks)
Just to the south of Coventry, hard by Coventry Airport, is a flat field become one of the most interesting

sites of Roman Britain—namely a reconstruction of a Roman fort known as The Lunt (see pp. 50–51). It is complete with earth and timber defences and fine gateway. The central HQ building has been marked out and close by it a timber granary has been reconstructed.

18 EDGE HILL (Warks)
Living up to its name, Edge Hill runs across the A41 Warwick road about 6 miles north of Banbury. Here in 1642 one of the famous battles of the Civil War took place. Charles I raised his standard on Edge Hill itself; a tower now marks the spot, from which there is a view over the area of the battlefield, although field enclosures have much changed its appearance (see pp. 66–67). There is a battle museum in a barn in the grounds of Farnborough Hall.

19 FARINGDON (Oxon)
This is a typical charming Oxfordshire town—now of village size—with an arcaded town hall at its centre. The last folly to be built in England was erected just outside this town.

Two miles to the south-west, in the village of Great Coxwell, stands the finest medieval barn in England, stone-walled and with a vast timbered roof. It was owned by a distant religious house, Beaulieu Abbey, in Hampshire. (see pp. 60–61 and 84–85).

20 THE RIDGEWAY and THE WHITE HORSE (Oxon)
The Ridgeway, one of the ancient Neolithic trackways, follows the ridge of the chalk. It was part of a longer route extending from East Anglia to Salisbury Plain; the length east of the Thames is known as the Icknield Way, named after the Celtic Iceni tribe who held East Anglia.

In Saxon days, the Ridgeway was a 'warpath' (see pp. 118–119). Today's path is classed as a road and can therefore carry cars and motorbikes without restriction. It would originally have braided itself across the land as can still be seen nearby

(see pp. 116–117).

The Ridgeway is accompanied by a number of prehistoric burials. Wayland's Smithy is a Neolithic gallery grave (see pp. 36–37) and there are many Bronze Age round barrows near the line of the track. There are also numerous Iron Age hillforts (see pp. 46–47): Barbury Castle, south of Swindon, for example, is accompanied by well-marked 'Celtic' field systems of small squarish enclosures (see pp. 58–59 and 80–81).

One of its most famous companions, however, is the Uffington White Horse nearby (see pp. 48–49). In recent centuries the Ridgeway has been an important drove route and there are many sheepy associations (see pp. 94–95 and 98–99).

21 ROLLRIGHT STONES (Oxon)
The name is given to a cluster of prehistoric monuments ½ mile north of the village of Little Rollright. The King's Men is a stone circle, the King Stone is a solitary standing stone (see pp. 40–41), while ¼ mile away are the Whispering Knights, a group of stones with a capstone at an angle. This dolmen was once at the end of a long barrow, the mound of which has been washed away (see pp. 42–43).

22 NORTH LEIGH ROMAN VILLA (Oxon)
This is one of the classic villas of middle Britain (see pp. 50–51) in the form of a range of low buildings around an irregularly shaped courtyard. Today two of the arms to west and south have their wall footings exposed. The ranges each consisted of a long corridor with rooms of various kinds off it. At the north-west corner was the main heated room (heated with underfloor hypocaust hot-air system) with a fine mosaic which is displayed under cover. The bath-house suite was at the north-east corner.

Villas such as this reached the height of their prosperity in the 4th century AD.

(To find the villa, leave the A4095

Woodstock-Witney road up the lane for East End before reaching North Leigh village itself.)

23 BRACKLEY (Northants)
This was a medieval wool town, but also known for its jousting. This was held on Bayard's Green, which is still open, although adapted as a racecourse in the 16th century (see pp. 102–103).

24 OXFORD MEADOWS (Oxon)
The Thames like any other river was accompanied on both banks by lush hay meadows. Most have been deep-drained and ploughed for barley, but one or two nationally important examples remain untouched near Oxford. One is Yarnton Mead, to the west of the city, in which the 'lot field' practice continued until recently (see pp. 28–29, 76–77 and 90–91). Within the city boundary, Iffley Meadows are well known for their fritillary flowers; the vast expanse of Port Meadow is too heavily grazed to retain much floral interest—nonetheless the 'commons' grazing itself is of interest (see pp. 90–91).

25 WALLINGFORD (Oxon)
This was one of the burghs or fortified townships established by Alfred after his victory over the Danes (see pp. 52–53). A length of earth rampart remains in the north-west corner, cut by the Didcot road. Within this, the town was laid out to a neat grid, which today's streets still echo. To the north-east, alongside the river, lie the massive earthworks of a Norman motte and bailey castle, among the most handsome of relics.

26 GORING GAP (Oxon)
The Thames has cut itself a deep, 6-mile-long gash through the chalk on its way to London and the sea. The geological implications of this are surprising (see pp. 12–13). Somewhere near Goring (maybe at Moulsford upstream) the Ridgeway would have crossed the river (see pp. 116–117)—there is still a toll bridge of old style on a side road at Goring (see pp. 134–135).

27 **BOARSTALL DUCK DECOY** (Bucks)
Hidden away in woods near Boarstall village is a duck decoy, a wildfowl trap once common in the countryside. Boarstall is unique in that birds are still caught (but legs are ringed not necks wrung) in the old way (see pp. 144–145).

28 **BRIXWORTH** (Northants)
The church here is well worth a diversion—at core it is a Saxon minster (see pp. 60–61 and 106–107). Largely 7th-century in date, it made use of bricks and tiles from nearby Roman villas.

29 **LONG CRENDON** (Bucks)
This is a typical 'long' village, but taking in a green at its end (see pp. 100–101). It also boasts a 14th-century 'courthouse'—originally perhaps a wool merchant's store, later used for the manor courts.

30 **NASEBY** (Northamptonshire)
Naseby was one of the crucial Civil War battles. It was here in 1645 that regiments of cavalry lined up and made decisive charges where barbed wire now blocks the path—like all battlefields it is much changed (see pp. 66–67). It was here that the Roundheads routed Charles I. He fled, leaving state papers proving that he was negotiating with foreign armies; it was one of the most important turning points in the history of British democracy.

31 **WING** (Bucks)
The village has an impressive Saxon church.

32 **ROCKINGHAM** (Northants)
This grand castle was Plantagenet in origin but largely converted into a Tudor mansion.

Up from the river climbs a line of stone cottages, holding many of today's population of 100; this village is certainly a town that died (see pp. 114–115), for as its castle suggests, it was an important market in medieval times, with a jousting ground—still an open meadow known as the Tilting Ground.

33 **WEST WYCOMBE PARK** (Bucks)
This estate typifies Georgian conceit and eccentricity. The approach from High Wycombe is dominated by a hilltop church on which is poised a golden dome, built as an afternoon viewpoint for friends of the owner. The church, although originally medieval, has been rebuilt so that the inside copies a 6th-century BC Greek temple. Next to this rear the high walls of a hexagonal mausoleum monument, open to the sky.

They are both the work of Sir Francis Dashwood, founder of the rousting Hellfire Club, which met in caves cut into the hill below.

34 **BROMHAM** (Beds)
There is a fine watermill here, restored and open as a museum of milling history (see pp. 108–109).

The meadow land around it is now a picnic area, but is still quite rich in wildlife, with Kingfishers being seen. Nearby is a good example of an early-medieval (12th century) bridge (see pp. 134–135) crossing the river with 26 arches.

35 **OLD WARDEN** (Beds)
This is a 19th-century estate village (see pp. 110–111) of thatched houses of ingenious and catholic decoration, the ideas collected from here, there and everywhere. The estate also houses the Shuttleworth collection of more than 50 historic aeroplanes, including Hurricanes and Spitfires from World War II.

36 **CHALFONT ST PETER** (Bucks)
Two miles north of the village lies the Chiltern Open Air Museum, with buildings of all periods, including facsimile farmsteads of Iron Age (see pp. 46–47) and Saxon style, and also later buildings, including a Victorian smithy, rescued from their original sites and re-erected here.

37 **ICKWELL GREEN** (Beds)
This is one of the maypole villages (see pp. 102–103) on May Day brought into use with sideshows on the green (which is vast). There is a smithy with a door in the shape of a horseshoe (see pp. 110–111) but no church or pub—it lies in fact in the parish of Northill. It is a settlement that did not quite make village status. (see pp. 94–95 and 100–101).

WALES

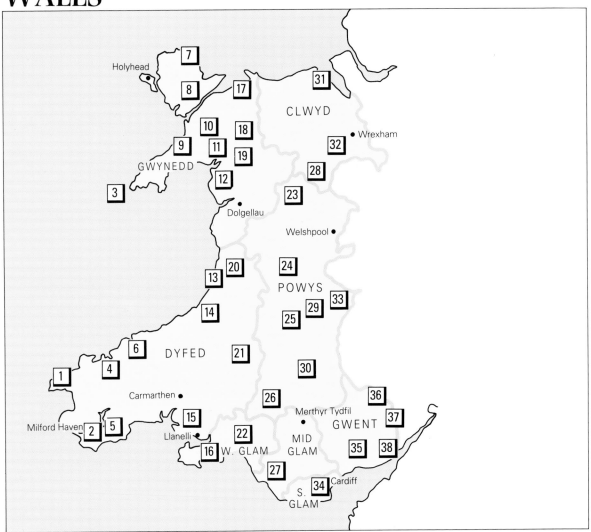

Holyhead

7

8

17

31

CLWYD

Wrexham •

10   18

9   32

11   28

GWYNEDD   19

12

23

3

Dolgellau

Welshpool •

20   24

13

POWYS   33

14   29

25

6   DYFED   21

4   30

1   36

26

Carmarthen •   Merthyr Tydfil   37

15   •   GWENT

Milford Haven   2   5

Llanelli •   22   35   38

16   W. GLAM   MID

GLAM

27   Cardiff

34

S.

GLAM

---

1 ST DAVID'S HEAD (Dyfed)
There are the ramparts of two
Iron Age hillforts here. One is ranged
around the 600-ft summit of Carn
Llidi, a little distance inland but with
marvellous views of the coast. On the
coast itself is a small promontory fort,
taking advantage of the natural
defences afforded by the cliffs (see
pp. 162–163).

2 PEMBROKE (Dyfed)
This town was once heavily
fortified, the hub being the
magnificent castle. Apart from this it
is worth a detour for its National
Gypsy Museum, containing

everything from painted caravans to
cooking utensils (see pp. 90–91).

3 BARDSEY ISLAND (Gwynedd)
This small island lying 2 miles off
the coast (and reached by boat from
Aberdaron) was an important place of
pilgrimage in medieval times, when
three pilgrimages to it were counted
the equal of one to Rome (see
pp. 124–125). The churches serving
the roads leading here are often
rather grand as a result. The ruins are
of a 13th-century monastery.

4 PENTRE-IFAN TOMB (Dyfed)
This impressive burial chamber

or 'cromlech' (see pp. 36–37) is well
worth a detour. It stands north-west
of the village of Brynberian on the
B4329 from Haverfordwest to
Eglwyswrw, just before it joins the
A487. Take the minor road north of
the village for 1½ miles.

Its covering mound has gone, but
the gigantic stones which made up
the burial chamber still stand; it is a
classic of its kind.

5 CAREW (Dyfed)
One of Britain's most stately
ruins (in course of restoration) stands
here beside the tidal creek. From
castle it evolved into Elizabethan

mansion as the windows suggest (see pp. 62–63), although the fortifications were kept. There is a 14-ft-high Celtic ornamental cross near the entrance, commemorating the death of a king's son in 1035. Reached by footpath from here is Carew tide mill, a rare survivor (see pp. 108–109). The rising water is stored in a pond and released at low tide to work the wheels. The village bakehouse is notable, with a free-standing chimney (see pp. 98–99).

A diversion to Carew Cheriton is worthwhile; the church contains old floor tiles and other details, while there is an ossuary in the churchyard. It is empty, but was quite a common feature. Only the skull and two long bones were kept—the minimum believed necessary for Resurrection—hence the skull and crossbones emblem.

6 CENARTH (Dyfed)

This village stands on a spectacular stretch of the River Teifi, with waterfalls. There is an 18th-century bridge, a mill and a smithy (see pp. 110–111) but perhaps more of note are the coracles still used here for fishing. Coracles are rounded, open boats of ancient origin, of tarred cloth (originally leather) stretched across a wooden framework (see pp. 140–141).

7 PARYS MOUNTAIN (Anglesey)

Resembling a rotted tooth with countless dead shafts, this was once the richest of all copper sources (see pp. 22–23). It may well have been mined in Roman or even Bronze Age times, but if so traces have been destroyed by later working (see pp. 54–55). Amlwch is its port, with old quays remaining.

8 BRYN CELLI DDU (Anglesey)

This stands 4 miles south-west of the Menai Bridge, off the A5. It is a fine example of a Neolithic passage grave (see pp. 36–37). A long entrance passage leads to a central burial chamber, within which are decorated stones of unknown significance (see pp. 40–41).

9 TRE'R CERI HILLFORT (Gwynedd)

Tre'r Ceri stands poised 900 ft above the road (signposted from the B4417) a mile south-west of Llanaelhaearn—it is one of Britain's most spectacular Iron Age hillforts (see pp. 46–47) with well-preserved drystone walls. The remains of stone huts (about 150 in all, of all sizes) lie within the rampart.

In Wales, unlike in southern England, life often seemed to continue unchanged after the Roman invasion—Tre'r Ceri remained in use in Roman days.

10 BEDDGELERT (Gwynedd)

This typical and compact Welsh mountain village contains the famous grave of Gelert—the name means 'Grave of Gelert'—a hound which was unwittingly killed in anger after itself killing a rampaging wolf. The legendary story was, however, dreamed up in the 18th century by the local innkeeper, to bring in the tourists—which it still does (see pp. 124–125).

11 PORTMEIRION (Gwynedd)

Flights of steps, fountains and pools, statues and nooky corners looking out across the estuary to the hills beyond, a bizarre mixture of colour-washed Italian and other styles—this unique village is an exotic fantasy created in the 1930s and 1950s (see pp. 110–111). The cottages are rented out for holidays.

12 DYFFRYN (Gwynedd)

The Neolithic tomb at Dyffryn Ardudwy has two chambers, once covered with a cairn of water-worn stones, but little remains of this. The older of the two chambers with capstone supported on upright slabs is a fairly typical dolmen or cromlech as they are often called in Wales (see pp. 36–37). There are other Neolithic tombs in the neighbourhood, at Carneddau Hengwm.

13 DEVIL'S BRIDGE (Dyfed)

Devil's Bridge is marked on the maps, about 2 miles south of the A44

between Aberystwyth and Llangurig. There are in fact three bridges here (see pp. 134–135), built one above the other. The lowest is oldest and of 11th-century date, the second was built in 1708 and the highest is a modern road bridge.

14 TREGARON BOG (Dyfed)

This bog extends over flat land beside the B4343 north of Tregaron. Two miles by one, and slightly domed, it is a fine monument to the natural world. A bog (see pp. 138–139) is neither smelly nor muddy, but a rather fragile habitat in which in the course of time beds of peat are slowly laid down. Here they rise up above the valley floor. Heather grows on the drier hummocks and it and sedges give an overall reddish colour to the site. It is a National Nature Reserve.

Tregaron town was a staging post for welsh drovers (see pp. 122–123).

15 KIDWELLY CASTLE (Dyfed)

Although ruined, this castle still dominates the village. Dating from the days of Edward I, it is of the later, keepless plan, with doubled curtain walls ('walls within walls') (see pp. 62–63). The towering gatehouse (built on the weakest stretch of the natural lie of the land) is impressive.

A mile north-west of the village is an Industrial Museum on the site of old tin-plating works.

16 GOWER FARM MUSEUM (W. Glamorgan)

This farm museum at Lake Farm near Llanddewi is unusual in having as its focus the lives of the family who lived here. As well as old-time exhibits, there is a farm trail around today's working farmstead.

17 PENMAENMAWR (Gwynedd)

The outcrops of volcanic rock on Graiglwyd Hill behind Penmaenmawr provided an easily split but tough rock, very suitable for stone axes. The rock was quarried here in Neolithic and Bronze Age times (see pp. 54–55). Although the original workfaces have been obliterated by later quarrying, fragments of the finished tools and flakings can be found here and on the moorland south towards Dinas and Llanfairfechan. The axes were roughed out on site, and probably taken to lower ground to be polished with wet sand.

There was a similar axe factory on the Langdale Pikes (Cumbria) and roughed-out axes and flakes can be found at the foot of the slopes there.

The axes from such places were traded across Britain.

18 SNOWDON (Gwynedd)

Snowdon is an aristocrat of a mountain. Although not so very high at 3560 ft, accidents of geology and the later erosion of glaciers mean that many of her approaches provide marvellous views. Indeed Snowdon is a textbook example of geology (see pp. 18–19) and glaciation (see pp. 148–149).

The summit is easily gained, via the mountain railway that runs up from Llanberis.

19 BLAENAU FFESTINIOG (Gwynedd)

The town used to be the centre of a slate industry which in Victorian times roofed much of Britain, the slate being carried by the then new railways.

Slate is a metamorphic rock with a fine cleavage yielding thin but hard sheets (see pp. 16–17). It was quarried here in vast caverns: there are two gigantic mines—Llechwedd and Gloddfa Ganol. The former has an underground cable railway, the latter provides visits by Landrover. The working conditions and cottages of the miners of a century ago have been reconstructed in a museum (see pp. 22–23).

20 LLYWERNOG lead-silver mine (Dyfed)

This site lies in what is now remote countryside about 10 miles from Aberystwyth. It was once a thriving lead-silver mine, but after a century of dereliction has now become an open-air museum, with the attraction of restored machinery and water wheels (see pp. 22–23).

21 DOLAUCOTHI Roman gold mines (Dyfed)

These lie near Pumpsaint, off the A482, and it is the only British site where it is known for certain that the Roman mined for gold (see pp. 22–23 and 50–51). The mine was in use from AD 75, and the metal was gained both by opencast digging (jagged bands of rock lie among the shrubs) and by mining. These workings were backed up by an elaborate water system with aqueducts and cisterns (see pp. 54–55 and 144–145).

22 ABERDULAIS FALLS (W. Glamorgan)

These magnificent waterfalls, which thunder through a ravine (see pp. 14–15), have been used to supply industrial power. The earliest water-wheel here, recorded in 1584, was used to drive the bellows for copper smelting. The buildings of this primitive industrial site are being restored.

23 LAKE VYRNWY (Powys)

This vast reservoir was created a hundred years ago to satisfy Liverpool's requirements, the water being carried via canal and aqueducts. It is the largest man-made lake in Wales, 5 miles long and up to ½ mile wide and containing 12 million gallons of water held back by a dam that is 1200 ft long and 120 ft high. A village was drowned but later rebuilt at the foot of the dam, and is a good example of a 'model' village (see pp. 144–145).

24 BRYN TAIL LEAD MINE (Powys)

Located 3 miles north of Llanidoes, this mine was closed in 1884, but has survived, being one of the few lead mines to have been preserved (see pp. 22–23). It has now gained a new lease of life as an open-air museum explaining all aspects of the industry.

25 BUILTH WELLS (Powys)

The town's springs were thought to possess healing qualities and it became a busy spa in Victorian days. There is a fine arched 18th-century

bridge here, and other relics of its prime include the 18th-century pump room in which the waters were drunk.

The local rocks contain trilobites and other early fossils (see pp. 26–27).

26 DAN-YR-OGOF 'show caves' (Powys)

Situated 3 miles north of Abercraf (7 miles north of Ystradgynlais) these caves open from a boulder-strewn hillside. The 'cathedral' chamber is the largest to be seen in any British show cave. There is a plentiful display of stalactites and other features (see pp. 24–25).

27 KENFIG DUNES (Mid Glamorgan)

The 1000 acres of sand dunes, 2 miles north of Porthcawl, and a spring-fed freshwater lake, make a botanist's delight—500 or more species of wild flowers have been recorded, and waterfowl both breed here and visit in winter (see pp. 160–161).

28 PISTYLL RHAEADR (Clwyd/Powys)

This waterfall (see pp. 14–15) has a spectacular drop of 240 ft, the top half nearly sheer, the water then passing through a natural arch before cascading the rest of the distance. It is situated 3 miles north-west of Llanrhaeadr-ym-Mochnant.

29 LLANDRINDOD WELLS (Powys)

This was a classic Victorian spa (see pp. 146–147) and is largely preserved. There is still a pump room where spa waters of three kinds can be tasted; they were believed to cure gout, rheumatism and other ailments.

30 BRECON BEACONS (Powys)

The Brecon Beacons form one of Britain's ten National Parks. The Beacons themselves are a range of sweeping hills, gouged out by rows of glaciers, and wide, unfenced sheep-grazed moorland (see pp. 148–149).

Brecon, a quaint old town, is a good centre. One visit is to the Brecknock Museum here, once the shire hall with a Victorian assize court preserved entire.

The archaeology displays include a prehistoric dug-out canoe found locally. The Scywd-yr-Eira waterfall (see pp. 14–15) is not far off.

31 FLINT CASTLE (Clwyd)

Now ruined, but its plan is still easy enough to make out—a square layout with rounded towers at each corner and the keep (see pp. 62–63) separate on a small island (the setting is a small promontory into the Dee estuary).

Flint was the first of Edward I's Welsh castles. Not far to the south-east is Ewloe Castle, situated halfway between Buckley and Connah's Quay. It is interesting to visit and compare because it is entirely Welsh, built before Edward conquered north Wales. It has a D-shaped tower which is typically Welsh and is well preserved although most of the rest is ruinous.

32 PONTCYSYLLTE AQUEDUCT (Clwyd)

This tremendous memorial to the canal age which carries the Shropshire Union Canal 127 ft above the River Dee was opened in 1805 (see pp. 136–137). It was a pioneer in cast iron, by Thomas Telford.

It is 4½ miles east of Llangollen (which has a Canal Exhibition Centre).

33 KNIGHTON—OFFA'S DYKE

Knighton (Powys) is home to the Offa's Dyke Heritage Centre. Offa's Dyke runs from Prestatyn (Clwyd) to Chepstow on the Gloucestershire–Powys border (here it is on the English side).

Long lengths are slighted and scarcely traceable, but a well-preserved section of the earthwork can be seen in the hills north-west of Knighton, running up towards Clun in Shropshire (see pp. 52–53).

34 ST FAGANS (S. Glamorgan)

The open-air sections of this Welsh Folk Museum have 30 rural buildings from all over Wales and of many different periods. There is a pillar-box-red farmhouse of 1630 (with furniture of that century), a village school of 1880, corn mill, saddlery, bakehouse, cockpit and smithy. Of great interest is the longhouse from Cilwent, a type of dwelling that was familiar in medieval days in many parts of Britain (see pp. 104–105).

The Welsh Folk Museum is set in the grounds of St Fagans Castle; it is no longer a fortified residence, however.

35 NEWPORT (Gwent)

The castle is Norman in origin, built in 1171 but ruined in the Civil War (1642–8). Better known is the transporter bridge across the river Usk, built in 1906. The canal centre is worth a diversion, with a staircase of locks (see pp. 136–137).

Three miles north-east at Caerleon is one of the three Roman legionary fortresses (Chester and York were the other two). Part of the bath house and the west corner of the fortifications stand, and such things as lavatories and cookhouse and the foundations of barrack blocks have been exposed (see pp. 50–51).

The outstanding relic is the amphitheatre, which has some fairly good detail such as gladiators' waiting rooms with stone benches. There is a museum of finds on the site.

The museum at Newport contains finds from sites in the area.

36 SKENFRITH (Gwent)

The castle in what is now a quiet village was once one of an important trio of Norman castles in the area. The ruins we see today with their formidable curtain wall (see pp. 62–63) date from the rebuilding in the 13th century.

The church has a sturdy tower, which could have been useful for refuge. It is unusual in being capped by a open woodwork dovecot (see pp. 98–99).

There is also an old watermill in the village.

37 MONMOUTH (Gwent)

In medieval days this town was the key to the security of the whole of south Wales. The castle is ruinous, but the medieval fortified bridge across the River Monnow remains— the only one in Britain, and one of the few left in Europe (see pp. 134–135).

Just outside the town is the Kymin, which is a wooded hill with fine views across the Wye valley and with a rather eccentric building for a dining club at the top, alongside a naval temple with a statue of Britannia and memorials to great sea battles (see pp. 64–65).

38 CAERWENT (GWENT)

This is one of the most impressive Roman sites in the whole of Britain (see pp. 50–51). It was the market town of the Silures tribe and although small had all the usual buildings, such as a forum, temples and baths, surrounded eventually by the stone wall the core of which we see today. The north and south gates are quite well preserved, although the latter is blocked off. Some house and shop foundations are exposed (in Pound Lane) and the shop has the remains of a forge.

NORTH MIDLANDS

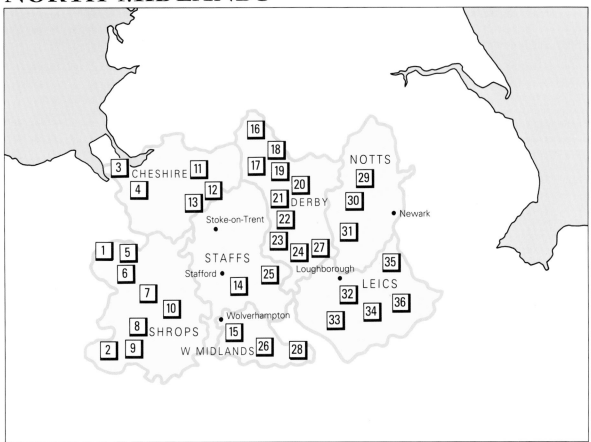

NOTTS
CHESHIRE
DERBY
Stoke-on-Trent
STAFFS
Stafford
Loughborough
LEICS
Wolverhampton
SHROPS
W MIDLANDS
Newark

1 **OLD OSWESTRY HILLFORT**
(Shropshire)
This splendidly ramparted Iron Age
hillfort (see pp. 46–47) is a mile to the
north of Oswestry, commanding the
farmlands to the east. In places there
are series of seven earthworks, some
riding the contours of the knoll. It was
used as the endpoint for a later, Dark
Ages boundary bank, which can still
be seen.

2 **CLUN** (Shropshire)
This place still has a frontier feel
of the olden Welsh Marches, the
much-fought-over no man's land
between Wales and England. The
melodramatic ruins of the Norman
castle overlook the river, the great
keep perched on the edge of its motte.
A good stretch of Offa's Dyke runs
between here and KNIGHTON
(Powys) (Map 5).

Earlier in time are the five Iron Age
ramparted camps in the area—Bury
Camps to the north is accessible—and
the museum contains even earlier
flint tools collected locally.

3 **ELLESMERE PORT BOAT
MUSEUM** (Cheshire)
Ellesmere Port was a great canal town
in its heyday, and the Boat Museum
here (off Junction 9 of the M53) is set
in canal docks, with warehouses and
workshops dating back to the
1790s—the peak of the canal age.
Forges sometimes work and the
exhibits include an early dug-out and
coracles as well as examples of canal
folk art (see pp. 136–137).

4 **BUNBURY** (Cheshire)
The buildings of this quaint
village range from timber Tudor to
Georgian brick and beyond. It is an

interesting example of village history
(see pp. 94–95) as it evolved as three
separate settlements—an original
medieval one around the church, a
later Tudor one around the common,
and the third when the common was
built on later.

It is also interesting for its lock
centre (see pp. 136–137) with
warehouses and stables (now
workshops) and double-width locks
(14 ft instead of the normal 7 ft).

5 **ELLESMERE MERES VISITOR
CENTRE** (Shropshire)
This Ellesmere is many miles from
Ellesmere Port (see 3 above), in an
area where meres and mosses dot the
map. The meres are often 'kettleholes'
formed in a peculiar fashion at the
end of the Ice Age and this exhibition
explains them and their wildlife (see
pp. 142–143).

6 RUYTON-XI-TOWNS (Shropshire)
Many villages evolved from scattered 'townships' and the name of this clearly shows that origin. The name dates from 1308, when Ruyton joined 10 other communities to form a small 'borough' (see pp. 94–95). There is a black and white timbered smithy house, and Norman church and 14th-century castle vestiges. The war memorial is a cave cut in a cliff face (see pp. 98–99).

7 WROXETER (Shropshire)
The baths were the social centre of any Roman town, and at Wroxeter—once the fourth largest town of Roman Britain—a massive range of wall from the exercise area of the baths complex still remains, some 26 ft high. Somehow it escaped medieval stone robbing and became known as the Old Work. The foundations of the rest of the baths have been laid bare and the museum here has a fine display from the site, but most of the town still lies below the fields (see pp. 50–51).

8 ACTON SCOTT FARM MUSEUM (Shropshire)
Three miles south of Church Stretton, this show farm has shire horses regularly at work as well as displays of old-time threshers and other machinery. There are also rare breeds of pigs and other livestock including longhorn cattle (see pp. 80–81)

9 STOKESAY CASTLE (Shropshire)
'Castle' is something of a misnomer since this is really a fortified manor house, with a timber-framed gatehouse, and rather low walls and a moat making a defensive enclosure. There is only one truly castle-like tower. It is outstanding, however, for its great hall, preserved much as it was in the 13th century. It has its original timber roof, stained by soot from the open fireplace at the centre.
Privacy was almost nil—at one end is a solar, an upper room for the private use of the owner, reached by a ·door behind the high table. It gives a first-hand feel of medieval life (see

pp. 104–105 and 112–113).
On the way there, at Craven Arms, you might notice an unusual signpost (see pp. 128–129).

10 IRONBRIDGE (Shropshire)
This mecca is worth a long diversion; it was the birthplace of, and is today a memorial to, the Industrial Revolution which changed the face of urban and rural Britain 200 years ago (see pp. 110–111)
Ironbridge comprises six main sites spread down a gorge of low limestone cliffs cut by the Severn. They include a recreated industrial township and (at Coalbrookdale) the furnace which in 1790 first smelted iron with coke and so was instrumental in bringing the iron industry from the Sussex Weald and elsewhere to the Midlands and the North, where coal was mined (see pp. 22–23). The gorge is spanned by the 'iron bridge' itself, the first cast-iron bridge in the world. There is also a bitumen mine of some interest (see pp. 24–25).

11 ASTBURY (Cheshire)
This village is marked by a splendidly stalwart church. The original Norman tower (with a spire added) now stands rather separate from the later church; but the tower of the latter rises massively over the west doorway. It is a pele tower, with rooms for women and children when Welsh raiders were abroad (see pp. 106–107).

12 CONGLETON (Cheshire)
The countryside around has the 'black and white' dialect (see pp. 104–105) typical of Cheshire. There is no easily gained rock, hence the older cottages tend to be built of timber and infill, now whitewashed between the black beams. The epitome of this style stands 4 miles south of Congleton in the shape of Old Moreton Hall, a magnificently timber-framed small mansion.
The black-and-white uniform of Cheshire is underscored by the fact that in this county of abundant pasture there are many black and white cattle.

13 MOW COP (Cheshire)
This hilltop on the Staffordshire border between Congleton and Kidsgrove rises to 1100 ft and has splendid views. On the rough ground at the top is set a folly in the form of a castle tower, now ruined—a typical folly (see pp. 64–65). It was here that Primitive Methodists held their inaugural meeting in 1807.

14 CANNOCK CHASE (Staffs)
This is worth a detour, a surprisingly wild area for central England, 16 square miles of heather moorland, scrub, streams and plantations. Late summer is the most spectacular time, when the heather blazes purple.
It is geologically interesting for its exposures of gravel diggings of round pebbles embedded in sand; coal was also dug here.
A Chase was originally a hunting preserve of the greater magnates (see pp. 156–157). Today the fallow deer are an attraction, still roaming the area, and there are also a few red deer.

15 BLACK COUNTRY MUSEUM, Dudley (West Midlands)
A replica early steam engine and a small colliery are among the features celebrating early industry. The canals were vitally important (see pp. 136–137) and here electric narrowboats offer trips through the canal tunnel nearby.
Dudley itself was an important medieval town, with a fine market square still extending around its fountain. A castle sits on a ridge above the town—its gatehouse, keep and parts of the curtain wall remain, but there is also a range of later Tudor buildings including the Great Hall. Today the castle is also home to a zoo.
'Dudley butterflies' were at one time well known. The rock quarried here could be stuffed with fossils, among them a trilobite with legs fanned out to rather resemble butterfly wings (see pp. 26–27).

16 DOCTOR'S GATE (Derbyshire)
There is a well-preserved length

of Roman road to be traced here (see pp. 120–121), part of one that ran from Brough to a Roman fort near Glossop. The easiest access is from the summit of the Snake Pass between Glossop and Sheffield. From here walk a quarter of a mile north-east along the Pennine Way. The Roman road crosses it, and the paved section is a short distance down the slope.

17 CHELMORTON (Derbyshire)
We are here in the heart of the White Peak — a platform of limestone which can be seen in numerous small crags and in the stone walls. Many of the crags are natural, others must have been quarries for stone — and an occasional limekiln can be found. Up here the snow can drift deep but despite today's winter rigour there are signs of early settlement (when the weather was milder). ARBOR LOW is nearby and there are chambered tombs (one at Five Wells at Taddington Moor nearby is, at 1400 ft, the highest in Britain).

The fields around Chelmorton were largely partitioned at the time of the Georgian enclosures, but in some places they follow the older medieval strips and the fields they mark out are long and narrow with a slight s shape (see pp. 58–59).

18 CASTLETON (Derbyshire)
This is the centre of a famous area. Nearby is Mam Tor with its rapidly eroding faces and slippery screes, surmounted by an impressive Iron Age fort (see pp. 46–47). There are many lead-mine buildings and shafts in the area. Treak Cliff and other caverns can be visited (see pp. 24–25). Above the village rears Peveril Castle, Norman in origin. From it the neat medieval plan of the village can be seen (see pp. 94–95).

19 SHELDON (Derbyshire)
Though ruined, a fine array of old mine buildings remains standing here, including the engine house and its chimney. There are also waste dumps, and examples such as these can often yield interesting mineral samples (see pp. 20–21).

20 CHATSWORTH (Derbyshire)
Chatsworth is one of Britain's grandest of grand houses with remarkable water engineering in the form of cascades and fountains in the grounds.

The village of Edensor was in 1839 moved to a new site so as not to impose into its views; its houses are a medley of designs with such things as Swiss chalet roofs, Italian windows and English Jacobean gables (see pp. 110–111). Baslow nearby has the smallest toll house in England and a packhorse bridge (see pp. 134–135).

21 ARBOR LOW (Derbyshire)
This mysterious Neolithic monument is well worth a detour. It is basically a henge (see pp. 34–35) with a circle of stones added later, but they lie flat, never having been raised (see pp. 42–43). There are fine open views, but pollen evidence shows that when this monument was created the area was thickly wooded.

22 DOVEDALE (Derbyshire)
Although often crowded with visitors, Dovedale retains considerable atmosphere. It is a long, narrow, wooded gorge set with rocky limestone bluffs and other features on either side of a charming stream. It was most probably created by the collapse of a series of water-worn caverns (see pp. 24–25) and various caves and caverns open into it. The stone-walled countryside round about has many flowery old meadows (see pp. 76–77).

23 TISSINGTON (Derbyshire)
On Ascension Day the five wells of this picture-book village are framed with biblical scenes created with flower petals. The origins of this 'well dressing' are obscure (see pp. 132–133). It also takes place in some other Derbyshire villages.

24 REPTON (Derbyshire)
The church here has fascinating Saxon features including a Saxon chancel with below it a Saxon crypt containing the mausoleum of Mercian kings (see pp. 106–107).

25 ABBOTS BROMLEY (Staffs)
This village of black and white cottages has a fine buttercross (see pp. 114–115), almshouses and other features. It is noted for its 'horn dance' held on the first Sunday after 4 September, when a group adorned with reindeer horns pace a 20-mile circuit of the area (see pp. 94–95). They wear Tudor dress, but the ritual may be much older — the reindeer horns (which are stored in the church) may be a thousand years old, for the animals were last recorded in Britain in the 12th century.

26 SUTTON PARK (West Midlands)
This was originally one of Britain's innumerable medieval hunting parks (see pp. 112–113) but is now virtually a museum to the countryside, surrounded on all sides by roads and development and actually lying within the City of Birmingham.

Woodland, bog, heath and grasslands give an idea of the look of the countryside three centuries ago. The Park also contains an Iron Age camp and a well-preserved stretch of Roman road (see pp. 120–121).

27 FOREMARK RESERVOIR (Derbyshire)
Victorian reservoirs were boldly placed in the upland scenery, where dramatic shorelines could result naturally from filling a steep-sided valley with water. This century's reservoirs are usually in the lowlands and have to be planned with care if they are to be visually attractive (see pp. 144–145).

Foremark, a few miles south of Derby, is handsomely landscaped. Public use is also important in modern planning (by contrast Victorian reservoirs tend to be out of bounds to the public).

28 BERKSWELL (West Midlands)
This is an interestingly varied village (see pp. 100–101) with green, well, windmill and whipping post and stocks (see pp. 98–99). These last have five leg holes — presumably an end of the wood has rotted away.

29 LAXTON (Notts)

By some chance the ancient medieval tradition of farming has been preserved here—with three great hedgeless open fields divided into one-acre strips allocated among the 'commoners' (see pp. 58–59). It still continues. As a result the entire village is registered as an ancient monument.

The village plan shows medieval origins, with farmhouses end-on to the roadways (see pp. 94–95).

30 SHERWOOD FOREST (Notts)

Around 500 acres of old oak woodland remain here. A visitor centre explains it and waymarked paths lead to various points of interest, including Major Oak, which is an ancient pollard tree maybe 500 years old (see pp. 88–89). The forest has long been associated with the legend of Robin Hood, which first made written mention in a ballad of 1377, when Major Oak was no more than a seedling.

31 PAPPLEWICK (Notts)

This is an example of how a village can throw up the unexpected. It has a fine church with an interesting squire's pew, but its main attraction is a highly decorated Victorian pumping station—a Victorian waterworks with two beam engines in an ornate engine house (see pp. 146–147).

32 CHARNWOOD FOREST (Leics)

This is a remnant of an old hunting forest, but geologically a remnant far older, for the rocks which surface here are the tips of a hidden mountain chain which have been surrounded by younger rocks (see pp. 12–13). There is moorland as well as woodland.

33 BOSWORTH (Leics)

A crucial battle took place here in 1485, when Richard III was killed and his crown passed to the first of the Tudors, bringing the Wars of the Roses—and the Middle Ages—to a close. Two miles south of Market Bosworth a visitor centre explains the course of events. Although the countryside has much changed, some features can still be discerned, such as the spring where the hapless Richard drank beforehand (see pp. 66–67).

34 INGARSBY (Leics)

Britain has many hundreds of deserted villages, very few of them named on the maps. This is not surprising, as little may remain but a scatter of bumps and hollows on the ground and perhaps a ruined church, the only building to be made of rubble and stone.

Ingarsby lies a mile north of Houghton on the Hill, which lies on the A47 east of Leicester. The site, which is crossed by footpaths, lies to the east of the road from Houghton to Hungarton. It extends as a well-marked pattern of holloways and paddocks (see pp. 56–57) across slopes running down to a stream.

The history of Ingarsby is typical: it probably became a village, like many others, towards the end of the Dark Ages—its name, meaning Ingwar's Village, suggests that it was founded by Danes. It is in Domesday Book, but by the end of the 14th century there were only a handful of families surviving the various plagues of medieval times. The village land was then bought up at a bargain price by the nearby abbey and the old open plough fields split up into smaller, hedged fields and turned over to sheep. The village then slowly disappeared.

35 BOTTESFORD (Leics)

Set in prime shire hunting countryside, (see pp. 86–87), this has an interesting church. Many churches contain memorials to the local gentry, but this has an unbroken sequence which allows changes in armour and fashion to be traced. The village also contains stocks and whipping post, remnants of a market cross and an old footbridge.

36 WING (Leics)

The Old Maze here is one of the few remaining turf-cut mazes in Britain. Their origin is an unsolved mystery (see pp. 102–103).

NORTHERN ENGLAND

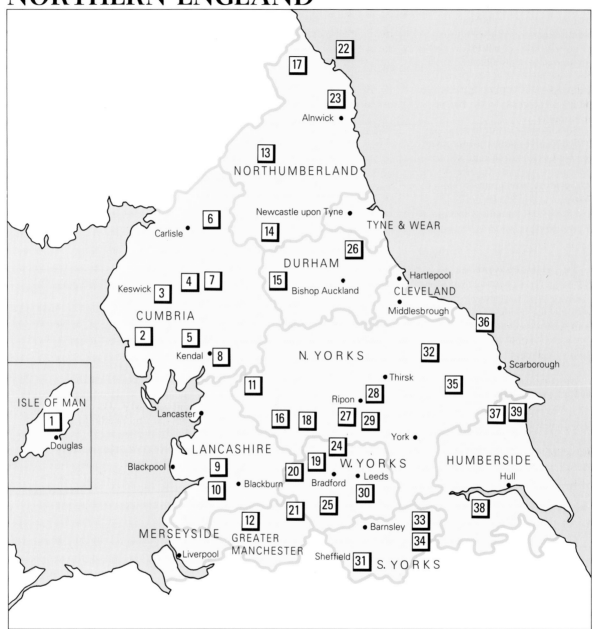

Map of Northern England showing numbered sites:

22, 17, 23, Alnwick

13 NORTHUMBERLAND

6, Carlisle, Newcastle upon Tyne, 14, TYNE & WEAR

26, DURHAM, Hartlepool

Keswick, 4, 7, 3, 15, Bishop Auckland, CLEVELAND

CUMBRIA, Middlesbrough

2, 5, Kendal, 8, N. YORKS, 32, 36, Scarborough

11, 35

Thirsk, 28, Ripon, 27, 29, York, 37, 39

ISLE OF MAN, 1, Douglas, Lancaster, 16, 18, 24, HUMBERSIDE, Hull

LANCASHIRE, 19, W. YORKS, Leeds, 30, 38

Blackpool, 9, 20, Bradford, 25

10, Blackburn, 21, 33, Barnsley, 34

12, MERSEYSIDE, GREATER MANCHESTER, Sheffield, 31, S. YORKS

Liverpool

1 ISLE OF MAN
This island is crammed with Celtic and Norse relics of the Dark Ages (see pp. 52–53). Many crosses and other carvings are stored in churches. There are several ship burials—Viking chiefs were laid out in a longship, the whole being covered with a mound. One easily accessible site is on Chapel Hill, a low hill a mile west of Castleton; the ring of supporting stones can be seen, although the mound has disappeared.

2 HARDKNOTT (Cumbria)
One of the outstanding sites of Roman Britain (see pp. 50–51): a well-preserved fort in a spectacular position on the once turbulent border. The base of the walls with their corner turrets is reasonably intact and the foundations of HQ, granaries and other buildings are plain.

Outside there is the shell of the bath house and an impressive levelled parade ground.

3 KESWICK STONE CIRCLE (Cumbria)
This stands ¾ mile north-east of

Castlerigg. It is a circle of 38 stones, many of which have fallen. At the east side, within the circle and touching it, there is a rectangular 'cove' of 10 stones. 100 yards to the south-west is an outlying stone. This combination of circle, cove and outliers is quite common (see pp. 42–43)

4 HELVELLYN (Cumbria)
This is probably the most climbed 'real' mountain in Britain (see pp. 148–149). Although Helvellyn embraces the vertiginous Striding Edge, the climb itself is not too steep. The summit gives a marvellous view of the geological form of the hills and valleys around.

5 TROUTBECK (Cumbria)
This village near Windermere is strung out with typical 'statesmen's' (yeomen's) farmsteads at convenient springs (see pp. 132–133). Townend one statesman's house open to the public; built about 1626, it contains furniture and other items from several centuries, some made by the family living here (see pp. 82–83).

6 HADRIAN'S WALL
(Cumbria/Northumberland)
Built around AD 120–30 by the Romans, the wall was 72 miles long, 10 ft wide and up to 15 ft high, set with forts and smaller milecastles and supported by a network of roads (see pp. 120–121). The forts of Housesteads and Chesters are perhaps the most interesting places to make for—both are excavated, with the foundations of the garrison buildings clear to see. The most dramatic stretches of wall cross the crags near Housesteads and Walltown (see pp. 18–19 and 50–51). There is an old 'wishing-well' at Carrawbrough (see pp. 132–133).

7 EAMONT BRIDGE (Cumbria)
Two Neolithic henges (see pp. 34–35) stand where the Eamont and Lowther rivers meet just south of Penrith. One, known as Mayburgh Henge, has a bank of stream stones with a central standing stone, the

only one left of four (and perhaps of a circle of stones within the bank). The other, known as King Arthur's Round Table, has a slighter bank of river silt.

8 SIZERGH CASTLE (Cumbria)
Not only interesting as a castle, its name like many places in the area is of historic interest. The word 'erg' is Norse (Viking) for a summer pasture (see pp. 96–97).

9 RIBCHESTER (Lancs)
A 5½-acre Roman fort (see pp. 50–51) was set in an elbow of the river here (and the river has eaten away one corner of the area). The crammed museum of finds is well worth a detour. Not far away, along today's river bank, is the Roman well *in situ*. A civilian settlement lies under today's village—the four columns of the doorway of the White Bull pub are probably Roman.

10 MARTIN MERE (Lancs)
Lying 3 miles north of Ormskirk, this lake has been largely recreated for the sake of birdlife (see pp. 144–145) —it was at one time drained and partly used as a rubbish dump. It is now notable for its flocks of winter visitors, including swans and geese. There is a visitor centre with observation windows.

11 INGLEBOROUGH (N. Yorks)
This mountain is a stub of limestone remaining after the erosion of depths of rock round about (see pp. 64–65); it has to some extent been protected by its cap of harder millstone grit. The summit carries an Iron Age fort—hut foundations have been found within it, but access to a supply of water must have been a problem.
Of extra geological interest are the Ingleborough show caves, off the A65 2 miles north of Clapham (see pp. 24–25) and just to the north of this is the entrance to Gaping Ghyll, a pothole. This is open to the public on spring and summer bank holidays— the descent to the depths is by bosun's chair. The famous Ribblehead Viaduct is in the area (see pp. 130–131).

12 HALL I'TH' WOOD (Greater Manchester)
This manor house is 2 miles north-east of Bolton. Its oldest part is half-timbered and 13th-century, but nothing has been changed since additions of 1648. A typical Lancashire kitchen of the time is one of the features to be found inside (see pp. 112–113).

13 ELSDON (Northumberland)
Features in this isolated village echo turbulent frontier times. Many of these Northumberland villages have a central green tightly hemmed by houses to form a secure livestock fold, easy to defend against Scottish raiders (see pp. 94–95). Elsdon also has a pinfold in good order (see pp. 100–101); the motte and bailey of a Norman castle; a medieval church with bellcote (an early prototype of the tower and used for sounding the alarm) with nearby to the north a vicar's pele tower, also defensible.
Two and a half miles away beside the Newcastle road stands a replica 18th-century gibbet.

14 ALLENHEADS
(Northumberland)
This village was in former times the centre of a considerable lead-mining industry. Ruined furnaces and chimneys stand scattered across the bare countryside and the spoil dumps often yield mineral samples (see pp. 20–23).

15 HIGH FORCE (Durham)
This lies just off the A6277 from Barnard Castle to Langdon Beck. It is Britain's most dramatic waterfall (see pp. 14–15), deep in the steep-sided gorge it has cut in the rock: here the 'lip' is of volcanic whin sill (see pp. 18–19) which also outcrops at the Roman Wall further north.

16 MALHAM (N. Yorks)
This village and its neighbourhood are worth a day. The village is attractive with stone cottages divided by a sparkling beck, but the main interest is in the local limestone features.

Just over a mile to the east is Gordale Scar, a monumental gorge created by the collapse of a cavern (see pp. 24–25). Nearby is Malham Cove, a natural amphitheatre with 300-ft-deep walls (and a fabulous echo) while further to the north across miles of limestone pavement lies Malham Tarn, a large natural lake lying in an impermeable bed in the porous rock (see pp. 144–145). Full directions and descriptions are to be found at the information centre in Malham itself.

17 DODDINGTON
(Northumberland)
On the moors ¾ mile south-east of Doddington (alongside the A6111) are ditched and banked enclosures containing huts. Known as Dod Law Camps, they are possibly of late Bronze Age date. There are many cup-and-ring marked stones found in the area—at OS grid references NU011312, 004318 and 005317. These are almost certainly of Neolithic date (see pp. 40–41).

18 BOLTON PRIORY (N. Yorks)
The picturesque riverside ruins lie 6 miles east of Skipton, off the A59. A formidable gatehouse remains, and part is still used as parish church (see pp. 60–61).

19 HAWORTH MOORS (W. Yorks)
These moors are not only typical in their form and vegetation, but have also played their part in giving moorland a place in British culture (see pp. 150–151), due largely to the Brontë sisters, who lived at Haworth. Emily Brontë's *Wuthering Heights* is set on these moors.

20 HEPTONSTALL (W. Yorks)
This village clinging to steep slopes below the moors was once an important hand-loom weaving centre. This was a home-based industry (and 18th-century weavers' cottages can be seen) before the work was gathered into factories in the valley bottoms, where the streams could be used for powering the machinery (see pp. 110–111).

21 BLACKSTONE EDGE (Greater Manchester)
A well-preserved section of a Roman road crosses the county boundary here, 7 miles west of Ripponden (see pp. 50–51). Its paving remains in place, with a central channel probably acting as a course for a heavy pole used as a cart brake (see pp. 120–121).

22 LINDISFARNE (HOLY ISLAND) (Northumberland)
For certain periods of the Dark Ages this was an important monastic settlement, one of the main cradles of Christianity in Britain (see pp. 60–61), even though it was harried by Vikings and other raiders and twice destroyed. The final priory, known as Lindisfarne Priory, was rebuilt in the 11th century in red stone. Monastic buildings were added in the 13th century in grey stone. They still stand, though ruined, but the carving of the hard, dark-red stone is still sharp. The island also carries a 16th-century fort converted earlier this century into a romantic 'castle'.

23 CHILLINGHAM PARK (Northumberland)
This park is 14 miles north of Alnwick and is well worth a detour. It was enclosed in medieval times (see pp. 112–113), and by chance a small herd of wild cattle which may have been directly descended from wild oxen were shut in. Their descendants have been there, wild in habit and with thick white coats and curved horns, ever since.

24 ILKLEY MOOR (W. Yorks)
Apart from the pleasure of the breezy moorland itself, there is spectacular rock-cut decoration here, of Neolithic and Bronze Age date. There are an unusual number of rock carvings (see pp. 40–41). They consist of hollows pecked into the rock, many surrounded by rings and there are also other lines and patterns. One decorated stone can be seen in the public gardens opposite St Margaret's Church, Ilkley; others are

on the moors—there are, for example, groups on Addington High Moor and Green Crag Slack. The famous Badger swastika stone has the OS reference SE094470. Casts of these decorated stones are to be seen in Leeds Museum.

There are also some notable stone circles and burial cairns in the neighbourhood of Ilkley.

25 PENNINE WAY (Derbyshire northwards)
Although some lengths are roads and footpaths with ancient rights of way, much of the route is private, with access allowed by agreement (see pp. 118–119) with landowners and others.

26 BEAMISH (Durham)
Two hundred acres of parkland house an open-air museum, which includes a colliery and an easy-access 'drift' mine (see pp. 22–23), tramways and Victorian houses brought brick by brick from elsewhere. Home Farm has working horses and a smithy.

27 BRIMHAM ROCKS (N. Yorks)
Large-scale examples of wind erosion, which can sculpture vast desert areas, cannot be found in Britain (see pp. 12–13), but where soft sandstone rock is exposed as it is here, wind and rain combine to create bizarre shapes. Brimham Rocks are about 2 miles east of Pateley Bridge, south of the B6265.

28 BOROUGHBRIDGE (N. Yorks)
An important market town in Norman days, this still has a good many inns. It is famous for the 'Devil's Arrows'—three massive standing stones aligned north-south, standing alongside the busy A1. The nearest source of the stone is 6 miles away. Their tops are fluted, but it is not certain if this is the result of natural weathering or purposeful (see pp. 40–41).

29 KNARESBOROUGH (N. Yorks)
There is a castle here and a fine church; a remarkable chapel cut into a cliff and reached by boat across the

river; and a mile or so downstream a hermit's cave dating from the early 13th century, unique in Britain.

Most visitors are lured to Mother Shipton's cave near High Bridge—she was a 16th-century prophetess. Here too is the 'Dropping Well', a spring so rich in lime that it coats items left in it for a few months. It is usually festooned with hats, shoes, toys and other oddities, which become 'petrified' (see pp. 132–133).

Not far away are the oddly shaped BRIMHAM ROCKS.

30 WAKEFIELD (W. Yorks)
A detour to this town is worthwhile to see its bridge with chantry chapel—both of 1350 date. It is one of the few bridge chapels to survive (see pp. 134–135).

31 ABBEYDALE (S. Yorks)
This early industrial hamlet lies on the south-west edge of Sheffield. It was once an important producer of scythes and other farm tools, the machinery being water-powered. It has been restored to its 19th-century appearance: a self-contained enclave, with craftsmen living alongside their workshops in terraced cottages (see pp. 110–111).

32 NORTH YORK MOORS (N. Yorks)
The rolling moorlands of the central and northern areas of the National Park are scattered with burial cairns, stone circles, ditches (see pp. 52–53) and other prehistoric remains (see pp. 38–39). Beacon Hill near Danby, for example, is topped with a burial mound (see pp. 64–65).

There are many old tracks (see pp. 122–123). A fine stretch of Roman road has been exposed on Wheeldale Moor just south-west of Goathland (see pp. 50–51 and 120–121). (Goathland lies west of the A169 between Pickering and Whitby.) It matches the famous

stretch at Blackstone Edge (Greater Manchester).

One oddity is the North Yorkshire Moors Railway, which operates steam trains on an 18-mile stretch between Pickering and Grosmont.

33 THORNE MOSS (S. Yorks)
Although mechanically dug for peat, parts of this area lying east of Doncaster echo the vast fenny wildernesses of former times (see pp. 138–139), of which only relic patches remain.

34 CONISBROUGH (S. Yorks)
A spectacular white limestone keep stands here, one of the first rounded keeps (see pp. 62–63). Although partly ruined it still imposes itself on the streets below.

This was a typical mining village although much of the back-to-back terracing has been cleared. In some of the nearby river and other cliffs, seams of poor-quality coal can be seen sandwiched with the limestone (see pp. 18–19). The productive seams are far underground.

35 HELMSLEY (N. Yorks)
There is a castle here—with a not very common D-shaped 12th-century keep and moat and a 16th-century hall (see pp. 62–63)—but more importantly a Roman villa at Beadlam, 1½ miles east of Helmsley along the A170 and 200 yards west of the turning to Pockley. It is the only Roman villa in the north of England open to the public (see pp. 50–51).

North-west of Helmsley is the romantic ruin of Rievaulx Abbey, worth a long detour in itself (see pp. 60–61).

36 WHITBY (N. Yorks)
A robust fishing town. The church is 200 steps above the town, alongside a ruined monastery—there was a Saxon foundation here, but today's ruins date from the 12th and

13th centuries (see pp. 60–61).

Soft grey rock similar to that seen at Lyme Regis in Dorset outcrops here with similar fossils (see pp. 26–27). Jet is also found in the cliffs and in places on the beaches (see pp. 20–21).

37 WHARRAM PERCY (Humberside)
The site of this deserted village is signposted from south of Wharram le Street, on the B1248 running south-east from Malton.

There was originally a Saxon settlement here, but the goal is the deserted medieval village with ruined church and hut sites, holloways and paddocks and other enclosures seen only as ridges and hollows under the grass. A mill with dammed pond and a separate manor house across the open green are two other features.

But the site is under complete excavation and is yielding a number of insights into medieval life.

The village died when its lands were given over to sheep in the late 14th century (see pp. 56–57).

38 ALKBOROUGH (Humberside)
This village contains one of the mysterious turf mazes. It is situated south of the church, in Julian's Bower, a name which compounds the puzzle (see pp. 102–103).

39 RUDSTON (Humberside)
Rudston village lies to the west of Bridlington. The churchyard houses a gigantic standing stone, 25½ ft tall, 6 ft wide and more than 2 ft thick (and with more unseen below ground)—the tallest monolith in Britain (see pp. 40–41 and 106–107). The nearest outcrop of the gritstone is 10 miles away. There is a smaller stone and a prehistoric burial on the north-east side of the churchyard.

From the church tower (and the air) traces of Neolithic cursus avenues can be seen leading towards the standing stone (see pp. 40–41).

SCOTLAND

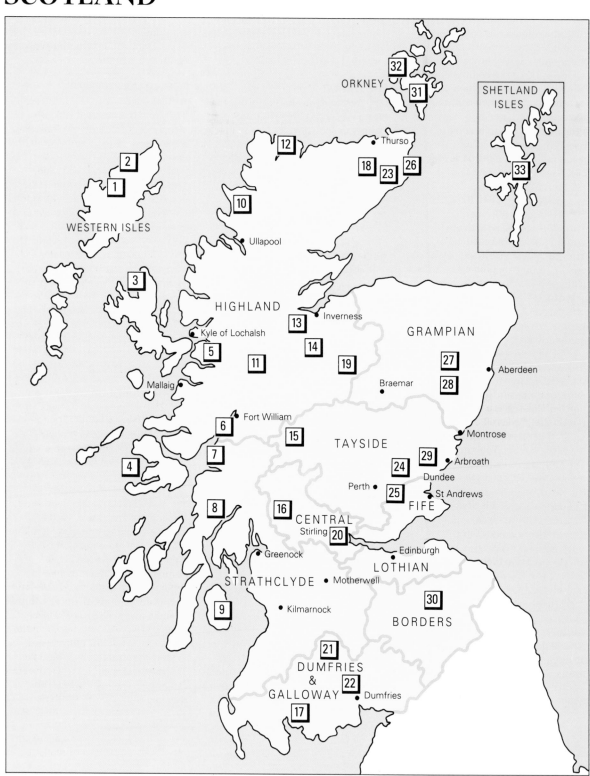

WESTERN ISLES

HIGHLAND

ORKNEY

SHETLAND ISLES

Thurso

Ullapool

Inverness

GRAMPIAN

Kyle of Lochalsh

Aberdeen

Mallaig

Braemar

Fort William

Montrose

TAYSIDE

Arbroath

Perth

Dundee

St Andrews

FIFE

CENTRAL

Stirling

Greenock

Edinburgh

LOTHIAN

STRATHCLYDE

Motherwell

Kilmarnock

BORDERS

DUMFRIES & GALLOWAY

Dumfries

1 CALLANISH (Lewis, Western Isles)

Structure and situation combine to make the stone circle here one of the most haunting of prehistoric monuments. Like many others (see pp. 42–43), it has a complex plan—a tall central monolith which also acts as headstone of a small ruined tomb chamber is encircled by 13 tall stone pillars. From this circle run three short lines of standing stones to east, south and west; while to the north-north-east runs a stone avenue.

2 ARNOL BLACKHOUSE (Lewis, Western Isles)

This traditional type of dwelling is worth an entry and excursion in its own right, being built without mortar and thatched on a timber framework without eaves. Human dwelling and cattle byre are under the same roof. A central peat fire and lack of chimney gave it the name (see pp. 104–105 and 152–153).

3 SKYE CROFT MUSEUM (Highland)

Situated at the north of Skye, 7 miles north of Uig, this is a museum of four typical thatched croft cottages (see pp. 152–153) including a smithy and a weaver's home. Tools and implements of a century ago are among the items of display.

4 FINGAL'S CAVE, Staffa (Mull/Strathclyde)

The basalt rock has set in gigantic six-sided pillars (see pp. 16–17) with a sea cave cut into them.

5 EILEAN DONAN CASTLE (Highland)

This is one of Scotland's more famous castles, in its setting of water and brooding hills. It stands on an island at the meeting of three lochs. It dates from 1220 and was possibly built against Viking raiders, but was reconstructed this century, faithfully to the original.

6 GLEN COE (Highland)

The Glen proper is about 7 miles long, with a col, or pass, at 1000 ft, but the name is often given to the whole 15-mile valley. An awesome place of angry rock, the valley is a typical ice-sculpted valley (see pp. 148–149). A main glacier cut the Glen but as was often the case it was joined by subsidiary glaciers and these scalloped out the Three Sisters.

Here landscape and history merge. In 1692 the Glen was the scene of an infamous massacre of some 38 of the MacDonald clan by Campbell soldiery in English pay. In Glencoe village (in two traditionally heather-thatched cottages) is a museum of farm tools and other souvenirs of those days.

7 BONAWE (Strathclyde)

Before the age of the railways, which offered cheap transport, metal was usually worked where raw materials and/or fuels were to be found (see pp. 22–23). Bonawe was an important iron-smelting centre, making use of charcoal from the surrounding woods. The massive furnace, dating from 1753, is well preserved. The site is north of Taynuilt, near the shore of Loch Etive.

8 AUCHINDRAIN MUSEUM (Argyll/Strathclyde)

Scatters of cottages and barns make up this unusual open-air museum. It is a working museum, with the land (originally held jointly) still being worked in the once widespread communal system, with several families sharing the rent and labour. Cottages and barns are furnished as they were in olden times (see pp. 152–153).

9 ARRAN

This island is a Scotland in miniature, an island of mountains and glens with a delightful coast of coves and sandy beaches. At the entrance to Broderick Castle is a Heritage Museum with a smithy, cottages and other traditional buildings as they were at the turn of the century.

On the west coast is King's Cave, often used as a refuge in the past, and possibly the setting for the legend of Robert the Bruce and the spider. It is worth visiting for the old carvings which decorate the walls.

10 SUILVEN (Highland)

Suilven is a distinctive sugar loaf mountain some 4 miles south-east of Lochinver. It covers only a small area but its sides rise abruptly from the surrounding moor and boggy land, and the domed summit reaches 2399 ft. The sugar loaf consists of a sandstone rock, the moorland at its feet is very ancient gneiss hollowed by glaciers. It is a good example of a mountain left as a feature after rock around it has been eroded away (see pp. 148–149).

11 THE GREAT GLEN (Highland)

The Great Glen is a deeply cut valley eroded along the line of weakness caused by a massive fault or side slip of rock (see pp. 18–19). The line is marked by long, thin lochs—Loch Linnhe, Loch Lochy and the 24-mile-long Loch Ness—and the islands at the south of Loch Linnhe maintain the line. Of historic interest is the number of vitrified forts found along the Great Glen.

12 DURNESS (Highland)

There are magnificent beaches here, but the interest lies in the settlement itself, a typically scattered crofting community created soon after the infamous Clearances (see pp. 152–153). There is also a craft community village at Balnakeil, a mile to the north-west. Ten miles to the west is Cape Wrath with its 800-ft cliffs, while in the opposite direction, a mile east of Durness, is Smoo Cave, one of the most famous of Scotland's caves. The main chamber is 67 ft high with deeper extensions reached only by fully equipped divers.

13 CALEDONIAN CANAL (Highland)

This canal, cut in the early 19th century, runs through some of Britain's most dramatic scenery, in a straight line from Inverness to Corach near Fort William. It is some 60 miles long in all, and has man-made cuttings as well as making use of natural lochs. There is a lock staircase at Bonavie (see pp. 136–137).

14 WADE'S ROAD (Highland)
Wade's Road or General Wade's Road is the name of several lengths of tracks and roads found in the Highlands, of which one runs along the Great Glen.

They are named after General Wade, and were built after the battle of Culloden (1746). This ended Scottish hopes of a separate Stuart kingdom. Wade's roads were one of the signs of imposition of 'redcoat' soldiery and rule from the south.

15 BLACK WOOD OF RANNOCH (Tayside)
This is one of the relic areas of native pine forest, a forest of a type which covered much of Britain before the advance of the oaks and other deciduous trees (see pp. 88–89 and 156–157).

The species is the Scots pine (most of today's plantations are of sitka spruce and other aliens) with perhaps heather and bilberry and shrubby junipers in lighter areas.

These are rather open woods, quite unlike the dense modern conifer plantation. In the past some trees may have been felled for timber, but woods like this are almost living museums free from man's hand. Being self-sown, the trees have a great variety of shapes and are of all ages. There is much birdlife and other wildlife.

16 POTS OF GARTNESS (Central)
These are but one of the features of interest to be seen near Loch Lomond, and worth a visit. It is on leaps such as this that the wild salmon may most easily be seen, between August and October, jumping the tumbling water on their way from the sea to their spawning grounds in the headwaters.

Loch Lomond, from which the river runs, is scenically famous.

17 GATEHOUSE OF FLEET (Dumfries and Galloway)
In some places, after the Clearances, attempts were made to provide homes and jobs for the dispossessed families, for whom the alternative was emigration (see pp. 152–153). The original mills and housing can be seen in this planned settlement (see pp. 110–111).

18 THE FLOW COUNTRY (Highland)
The name is given to the extensive tracts of bog land in north-east Scotland (see pp. 138–139) which still remain although large parts have been drained and planted with conifers. This is to the dismay of naturalists, for this seemingly empty ground attracts many nesting waders and other birds (see pp. 150–151).

Also of interest are the stone-slab walls to be seen in some areas of Caithness (see pp. 74–75).

19 CAIRNGORMS (Highland)
The Cairngorm chairlift carries visitors near to the top of this high ice-sculpted plateau, the widest tract of high ground in Britain, where the climate remains sub-Arctic (see pp. 148–149). The lifts carry skiers in winter, but operate also in summer, taking walkers to view the plants and wildlife typical of the high Alps and the Arctic tundra.

At the foot of the slopes are many areas of relic Scots pine forest (see pp. 156–157).

20 ANTONINE WALL (Central)
Bonnybridge makes a good starting-point to view lengths of the Antonine Wall (see pp. 50–51). It was much simpler than Hadrian's Wall being constructed with cut turves on a boulder foundation (see pp. 30–31) — and built a few years later than Hadrian's Wall. It ran for 37 miles from Bridgeness on the Forth to Old Kilpatrick on the Clyde.

Although the bank is now sometimes barely a feature, the ditch often survives. Rough Castle is one of its forts, well worth visiting (it is signposted from Bonnybridge). Here the wall and ditch survive and the fort itself, although small, is well preserved. There were also frequent beacon stances, raised mounds set at the back of the wall, and many of these remain.

21 WANLOCKHEAD (Dumfries & Galloway)
One of the highest settlements in Scotland — over 1300 ft above sea level. Lead mines were opened here in 1680 (although there may have been Roman mining in the area). Gold was also mined.

The museum has a working model of a 19th-century water-powered beam engine and smelters as well as some workings open (see pp. 22–23). There are also miners' cottages to visit.

22 GREY MARE'S TAIL (Dumfries and Galloway)
One of Scotland's highest waterfalls, this is seen from along the A708 north-east of Moffat. The burn plunges 200 ft in a double fall, and is one of the most picturesque of waterfalls (see pp. 14–15).

23 CAMSTER (Highland)
The Grey Cairns of Camster stand 100 yards west of the Watten-Lybster road, 6 miles north of Lybster. The group comprises two round cairns and a long cairn with four 'horns'. They are chambered tombs (see pp. 36–37) and can be entered, although the passages are narrow and gloomy. Of Neolithic date, these tombs are of national importance.

24 ARDOCH (Tayside)
This Roman fort is near Braco, Dunblane, and was a northern outpost of the ANTONINE WALL. There remain three superposed camps and lesser marching camps, which are more difficult to make out. The resolute ditchworks of the main camp are clear and make one of the most spectacular sights of Roman Britain — along the north and east sides there are no fewer than five ditches with causeways crossing them (see pp. 50–51)

25 LOCH LEVEN (Tayside)
Loch Leven was created when a glacial hollow on open ground flooded

(see pp. 144–145); its rounded shape is markedly different from the multitude of Scottish lochs, which fill elongated beds in the narrow, glaciated valleys.

From an island rises the jagged profile of Lochleven Castle, elaborated around what is still (although ruined) a fine example of a 14th-century tower house.

26 WICK HERITAGE CENTRE (Highland)

Wick grew around a good harbour (see pp. 162–163) and is still a busy port. The Heritage Centre, however, concentrates on the turn of the century, when fishing was an important way of life in many Scottish harbours—indeed a major Scottish industry. There are reconstructions of such things as fish kilns and a blacksmith's shop and the restored cottage of a fisherman and his family.

27 CRAIGIEVAR CASTLE (Grampian)

This is a typical 'Scottish baronial' castle, with a great tower with conical roofs atop projecting towerlets. It was completed, fully fortified, in 1627, when castle building had all but ceased further south (see pp. 62–63).

28 TARLAND (Grampian)

In this parish is a good example of a souterrain or hidden cellar—similar to the 'fogous' of Cornwall (see pp. 46–47)—and possibly of Iron Age date. It lies 2½ miles to the north-east of the village next to Culsh Farm on the B9119. The curving passage is roofed with vast lintels.

29 ABERLEMNO (Tayside)

The parish contains a hillfort and castle ruins, but is notable for some fine examples of figured Pictish stones (see pp. 40–41). North of the church on the Forfar-Brechin road are two: one has serpent, double-z rod and other standard (but inexplicable) motifs; the other has a hunting scene. In the churchyard is a third Pictish stone of later type with a finely carved decorated cross.

30 EILDON HILLS (Borders)

These are best seen tinged with melancholic blue from the viewpoint favoured by the Victorian novelist Sir Walter Scott, whose novels helped start mass tourism to Scotland and its mountains. A hillfort and hut circles crown the top of the Eildons (see pp. 46–47).

Scott's View lies near Redpath, a few miles from Melrose. Scott is buried in the ruins of Dryburgh Abbey further along the road.

31 THE ORKNEYS

These are a cluster of 70 or so islands, often with a good soil on low hills and gentle slopes (although there are some ferocious cliffs) and a rather mild climate tempered by the Gulf stream.

Many of the islands were inhabited in prehistoric times, and a rich legacy of monuments has survived. Among these of note are:

Maes Howe on Mainland, the largest island. This is a large burial cairn, a chambered cairn of Neolithic date with a burial chamber of surpassing craftsmanship (see pp. 36–37 and 152–153). It was robbed by Vikings, who left Runic marks on the stone surfaces.

Skara Brae, also on Mainland, is a Neolithic stone village (see pp. 74–75 and 152–153) preserved almost in entirety in sand dunes, the huts being furnished with stone-slab beds and cupboards (see pp. 34–35).

The Dwarfie Stane is on the island of Hoy and worth a journey. It is the sole example in Britain of the Neolithic Mediterranean tradition of quarrying squared tombs in cliff faces. Here, however, a giant block of sandstone has been hollowed with a passage and two side chambers. It was originally sealed with a stone slab which still lies outside the entrance (see pp. 36–37).

32 DOUNBY MILL, Mainland (Orkneys)

This settlement boasts a surviving 'click mill', a primitive type of watermill with a horizontal wheel turning an upright shaft (see pp. 108–109).

33 THE SHETLANDS

There are a hundred islands in this group, and although they lie far to the north, their climate is tempered by the Gulf Stream, which swings north in winter. The sheer number of sites shows that they were hospitable to early settlers.

The main island is (like that of the Orkneys) called Mainland. Here too are several prehistoric sites of note. One is the Broch of Mousa, which stands on a small coastal island. It is the best preserved of these Iron Age fortified towers (it is almost complete) which are found only in Scotland (see pp. 74–75 and 152–153).

It is over 40 ft tall, the circular walls enclosing a courtyard. Within the walls are a series of windowless rooms or cells and galleries, with a linking staircase spiralling up through the thickness of the walls. This formidable construction is entirely of drystone walling.

Index